Alterities in Asia

This book investigates the politics of identity in Asia and explores how different groups of people inside and outside Asia have attempted to relate to the alterity of the places and cultures in the region through various modes (literary and filmic representation, scholarly knowledge, and so on) and at different points in time. Although coming from different perspectives such as literary criticism, film studies, geography, cultural history and political science, the contributors collectively argue that Asian otherness is more than the dialectical interplay between the Western self and one of its many others, and more than just the Orientalist discourse writ large. Rather, they demonstrate the existence of multiple levels of inter-Asian and inter-cultural contact and consciousness that both subvert as much as they consolidate the dominant 'Western Core-Asian periphery' framework that structures what the mainstream assumes to be knowledge of Asia.

With chapters covering a wealth of topics from Korea and its Cold War history to Australia's Asian identity crisis, this book will be of huge interest to anyone interested in critical Asian studies, Asian ethnicity, postcolonialism and Asia cultural studies.

Leong Yew is an Assistant Professor in the University Scholars Programme, National University of Singapore. He is the author of *The Disjunctive Empire of International Relations* (2003).

Routledge Contemporary Asia Series

Alterities in Asia

Reflections on identity and regionalism

Edited by Leong Yew

Routledge
Taylor & Francis Group

LONDON AND NEW YORK

First published 2011
by Routledge
2 Park Square, Milton Park, Abingdon, Oxon OX14 5RN

Simultaneously published in the USA and Canada
by Routledge
270 Madison Ave, New York, NY10016

Routledge is an imprint of the Taylor & Francis Group, an informa business

Typeset in Times New Roman
by Pindar NZ, Auckland, New Zealand
Printed and bound in Great Britain
by CPI Antony Rowe, Chippenham, Wiltshire

British Library Cataloguing in Publication Data
A catalogue record for this book is available from the British Library

Library of Congress Cataloging-in-Publication Data
Alterities in Asia : reflections on identity and regionalism / edited by Leong
Yew.
    p. cm. — (Routledge contemporary Asia series)
    Includes bibliographical references and index.
    ISBN 978-0-415-58750-1 — ISBN 978-0-203-83936-2 (eISBN) 1. Group
identity—Asia. 2. Identity (Psychology)—Asia. 3. Social psychology—Asia.
4. Other (Philosophy)—Social aspects—Asia. 5. Regionalism—Social
aspects—Asia. 6. Asia—Social conditions. I. Yew, Leong, 1969–
    DS12.A495 2010
    302.4095—dc22   2010019646

ISBN 13: 978-0-415-58750-1 (hbk)
ISBN 13: 978-0-203-83936-2 (ebk)

Contents

Preface

As it is in many other cases, this book emerged quite fortuitously. Its origins lay in a chance meeting with a colleague in a cafeteria at the National University of Singapore towards the end of 2004. Facing an impending deadline to submit panel proposals for the Fourth International Convention of Asia Scholars (ICAS), which was to be held the following year, we were pleasantly surprised to discover the topical similarity of our panels. The result of this meeting was two back-to-back panel sessions named 'Imaginations of Southeast Asia I: Cross-national Perspectives' and 'Imaginations of Southeast Asia II: Cross-disciplinary Perspectives'. At a time when there was increasing interest in the way cultural, social and political representations among Southeast Asians and by outsiders could be seen as unsettled, problematic or mined for their various relations of power and knowledge, we felt that these panels were especially timely. We felt bold enough even to anticipate an edited volume that would nicely sum up the fruits of our conferential labour. Sadly that book did not materialize, as various logistical problems and difficulties faced in bringing panellists to Shanghai led to a particularly scaled-down experience at the conference. We had, at the most, three to four chapters – nowhere enough to fill a book.

While my colleague was no longer interested in pursuing the project, I continued to identify potential contributors who might have presented a paper on a similar topic at the conference or written it under different auspices. Three years and a number of setbacks later, the book that finally re-emerged became very different from how it was originally conceived. As I sat back and read through the initial manuscripts, I noticed a number of thematic continuities and departures. First of all, the focus was no longer on Southeast Asia anymore, but more broadly about Asia. Second, while the original plan was for the object of enquiry to be on 'representation' the manuscripts more broadly coalesced around the idea of otherness and identity. So I realized that contributors, although coming from different disciplinary backgrounds and writing about different subjects, were indeed attempting to reconstruct (and also recover) the politics of Asian alterity from the various other positions of identity. These identities could, in non-mutually exclusive ways, be framed as other 'Asians', Westerners, dominic ethnic groups, literary worlds and so on. The result, then, is this current book, and I hope that it would contribute to further developing what I identify in the first chapter as 'axial politics', or simply ways by which people within and outside Asia could communicate and think about each other outside the usual frameworks of core–periphery, Asia and the West.

Over the last six years, this project has brought me into contact with a wide variety of individuals whose inputs have been important. In particular I wish to thank my aforementioned colleague, whom I will leave anonymous for obvious reasons. My gratitude also goes to the two reviewers of this book. While I have tried to incorporate their comments or get the contributors to respond to them as much as they could, some of their requests could not be so easily met because of the specific interests of the contributors and their disciplinary backgrounds. Stephanie Rogers at Taylor & Francis whom I approached in 2005 with ideas for the post-ICAS volume has been especially patient. I thank her and her colleagues, Sonja Van Leeuwen, Leanne Hinves and Ed Needle, for all their assistance and superb editorial guidance. But the most important debt of gratitude goes to my contributors. For some this has been an extremely long wait, considering that university research committees (and the pressures that they bear) are seldom so patient and forgiving. For others they have had to endure incessant demands from me for this revision and that addition. Without their commitment, passion, and most importantly their desire for a more socially just way of thinking about Asia, this volume would not have been possible. Finally, every effort has been made to contact the copyright holders of all images and illustrations and any queries should be sent directly to the publisher (Routledge).

Leong Yew
April 2010

Contributors

Ian G. BAIRD is a Canadian who has resided in mainland Southeast Asia for most of the last 25 years. Having completed his PhD in Human Geography at the University of British Columbia in Vancouver, Canada, he is presently an Assistant Professor in the Department of Geography at the University of Wisconsin–Madison, USA. In 2007, he co-edited *Fishers' Knowledge in Fisheries Science and Management* (UNESCO), and in 2008 co-authored *People, Livelihoods and Development in the Xekong River Basin, Laos* (White Lotus). In 2009, he authored *Dipterocarpus Wood Resin Tenure, Management and Trade: Practices of the Brao in Northeast Cambodia* (Verlag Dr. Müller). He has also authored a large number of peer-reviewed journal articles and book chapters. His research interests are broad, and include identity issues in mainland Southeast Asia, various forms of colonialism and domination in the region, political ecology, and the social and spatial organization of ethnic Brao people in southern Laos and north-eastern Cambodia.

Karina Africa BOLASCO has been in the book publishing business for thirty years now – ten years at National Bookstore and twenty years at Anvil, which she founded and grew into the biggest and most prestigious publishing house in the Philippines today. Anvil has been cited Publisher of the Year nine times and close to 130 of its titles have been given the National Book Award in different categories by the Manila Critics Circle. Karina was hailed as one of the Ten Outstanding Women in the Nation's Service in 1995 for her work in book publishing and literacy development. She was the 2004 Fellow for the Asia Leadership Fellow Program of the Japan Foundation and International House of Japan. She also represented the Philippines in the US State Department International Visitor Program of 2005. She was a former chair of the National Committee on Cultural Education of the National Commission on Culture and the Arts (NCCA) from 1995 to 2001 and a former governor of the National Book Development Board (NBDB). She has delivered a paper twice at the International Publishers Association Congress, in New Delhi (1992) and in Berlin (2004), and has spoken in many other book publishing conferences on publishing issues. She holds a Bachelor of Arts degree in Literature.

Antonio P. CONTRERAS is Professor of Political Science at the De La Salle University, Manila. He is the author of *The Kingdom and the Republic: Forest Governance and Political Transformation in Thailand and the Philippines* (2003) and *Locating the Political in the Ecological: Globalization, State–Civil Society Articulations and Environmental Governance in the Philippines* (2002). He has published substantially in the area of environmental policy and governance, among others. Currently, his area of scholarly inquiries has shifted to cultural politics and the politics of everyday lives.

KIM Ye-rim is Humanities in Korea Professor in the Institute of East Asian Studies, Sungkonghoe University, Seoul. She specializes in modern Korean literature and culture, and her current research interests are the history of Asian regionalism, Cold War culture, postcolonialism and the transnational exchange of culture. She published *Literature-scape and Cultural Circumstance* (2007) and edited *War as 'Threshold'* (2010), which is a comparative study of coloniality between South Korea and Taiwan.

Sally PERCIVAL WOOD is a Research Fellow at Deakin University's School of History, Heritage and Society. Her research interest is in India and China, and their interactions with the West in international relations during the Cold War. She has published most recently on the Anglosphere's media representations of Premier Zhou Enlai at the Bandung Conference, 1955; on the history of Australia's diplomatic relationship with India; and Australia's relations with the Middle East. Her jointly authored book *Identity, Education and Belonging: Arab and Muslim Youth in Contemporary Australia* was published in 2008.

Christopher SELVARAJ is currently a graduate student of sociology at the Faculty of Arts and Social Sciences, National University of Singapore. His research interests lie broadly in historical sociology and the sociology of power. He is presently working towards his master's thesis that investigates the relationship between elite schools and social power in Singapore.

Tamara S. WAGNER is Associate Professor of English Literature in Nanyang Technological University, Singapore. She is the author of *Financial Speculation in Victorian Fiction: Plotting Money and the Novel Genre, 1815–1901* (2010), *Occidentalism in Novels of Malaysia and Singapore, 1819–2004: Colonial and Postcolonial Financial Straits and Literary Style* (2005) and *Longing: Narratives of Nostalgia in the British Novel, 1740–1890* (2004). She co-edited *Consuming Culture in the Long Nineteenth Century: Narratives of Consumption, 1700–1900* (2007) and has authored over 50 articles and essays, appearing in other edited volumes and journals like *ARIEL, the Journal of Commonwealth Literature* and *the Atlantic Literary Review*.

David WALKER is Professor of Australian Studies at Deakin University, Melbourne. He is recognized for his innovative cultural history of Australian interactions with Asia, *Anxious Nation: Australia and the Rise of Asia, 1850–1939* (1999). *Anxious Nation* won the Ernest Scott prize for History in 2001 and has been translated into Chinese and published by China Renmin University Press, Beijing, in 2009; an Indian edition published by SSS publications, New Delhi, appeared in the same year. Professor Walker co-edited and contributed to *Legacies of White Australia: Race, Culture and Nation* (2003), a comprehensive examination of immigration policies, engagement with Asia and racial anxieties generated by Australia's proximity to Asia. He is a Visiting Professor in the School of Foreign Studies, Renmin University, Beijing, and in 2010 was appointed to the Distinguished Visiting Chair of Australia Studies, University of Copenhagen, Denmark. His latest book, *Not Dark Yet* (2011), examining sight, memory and history, is published by Giramondo Publishing, Sydney.

Leong YEW is Assistant Professor in the University Scholars Programme, National University of Singapore. His research interests are cultural theory, postcolonialism, and the politics of Asian identity. He is the author of *The Disjunctive Empire of International Relations* (2003) and is working on his next monograph project, 'Asianism: The Politics of Regional Consciousness in Singapore'.

1   The Asian as other

Leong Yew

Reforming the other

In the last few decades, the dominant Western imagination of Asia has taken on increasing complexity towards the way the people, places, society and culture in that part of the world have been represented. On the one hand, this imagination appears to display greater cultural forbearance, displacing earlier depictions that might have portrayed Asians as hostile, cunning, barbaric, menacing but also naive, primitive, exotic and even alluring. In the contemporary setting, overtures of greater celebration of difference, respect and tolerance abound. For instance, in main-stream cinema and television, Asians are taking on more central and heroic roles; there is a greater consumption of Asian cuisines by non-Asians; increased interest in Asian subjects and languages in colleges and universities; and also elevated profiles of Asians making inroads into the literary and cultural scene, such as the Booker Prize shortlists. On the other hand, there are also moments in which these representations of Asia/Asians could be seen as superficial or when expressions of cultural sensitivity lapse.

Let me reflect on this by considering the highly imaginative but nonetheless hyper-orientalist cinematic text, *The Pirates of the Caribbean: At World's End* (2007).[1] In many ways, *At World's End* seems to be regressive in its apocalyptic theme and cultural insensitivity, but is also playfully disestablishmentarian. Its portrayals of the non-Western other here (as well as in its two predecessors) are immediately reminiscent of an earlier phase of Hollywood, dominated by images of the inassimilable tribal savage and the calculating and depraved Chinaman. But at the same time too, the text possesses its own mechanisms of dissociation from these stereotypes. For example, the engagement with the Chinese other takes up a sizeable proportion of the film. The highly imagined and temporally unspecified Singapore is a starkly sinicized negation of Venice. Dark, chaotic and lascivious, its architecture is matched by the Qing-era cloaked pirates who rule the place. In addition, the figure of Sao Feng, pirate lord of Singapore, is the quintessential Fu Manchu reincarnate, juxtaposed aptly by the appearance of another Chinese pirate lord – this time a woman – the Dowager-esque Mistress Ching. Arguably, unlike much earlier colonial texts, *At World's End*'s negative image of the Chinese other is matched by the equally avaricious and maniacal traits of the Western pirates.

However, what appears to redeem the absolute anti-hero status of the pirates is by force of inversion. The highly romanticized image of the pirate has now transmuted into the fetishized cosmopolitanism of the Brethren Court, while the monoracial and megalomaniacal nature of the British (East India Company) is depicted as the main obstacle to the pirate's implicit quest for (American-styled) 'freedom'. *At World's End*, therefore, has political resonance with contemporary ethical norms, particularly those that see the multicultural and the cosmopolitan as preferred societal conditions over the statically monoracial, and this in turn allows texts to playfully depict identities as fluid and mobile. Thus, the film claims that we have all become others now.

At the same time that the Western self is being recast as the other, the film also has its own methods at resolving tensions arising from characters whose subjectivity might become too unstable. Perhaps, no character demonstrates this better than Elizabeth Swann, the governor's daughter who degenerates (or regenerates) from a Victorian debutante to an androgynous pirate. While in the earlier instalments she engages in gender crossdressing, the transformation takes on a more profound shift in *At World's End*. Having witnessed the death of Sao Feng at sea, she agrees to represent him at the Brethren Court. At her arrival, she is decked out in Sao Feng's tunic, a costume that resembles (but not quite) outfits worn by the male officials at the Qing court. This transfiguration is at once highly reminiscent of earlier colonial texts. But what also makes Elizabeth's case noticeable is the film's urgency in returning viewers to a heterosexual and non-miscegenated status quo. Since Elizabeth's character is Will Turner's love interest, she needs to be returned to some earlier form where their marriage can be unproblematically consummated. Indeed, towards the end of the film, Elizabeth is seen to be ethnically and sexually reinstated, now recast as a dutiful wife and mother awaiting the return of her husband.

When these two complexities of how Asians are represented are put together – the coexistence of more inclusive and generous depictions of Asians with their apparently regressive, racist and condescending counterparts – a more deep-seated problem with the way Western texts now conceive of alterity and difference needs to be addressed. In some ways there are already many explanations. One possibility is to think of these complexities as not fundamentally novel but as demonstrating the circularity of history. In this connection, there have historically been instances when Asians were seen positively, such as the Sinomania in the US that accompanied the romanticization of Generalissimo and Madame Chiang Kai Shek in the late 1930s. Another explanation, as alluded to above, is to frame this in terms of the social and demographic changes in large Western cities. In this case, the existence of larger diasporic Asian populations in these places has given rise to societies now identifying themselves as multicultural. Yet another way of thinking about this complexity is that changes to representations of Asians are purely superficial. In this sense, these changes retain an underlying and more latent form of Orientalism.

Although these accounts of contemporary Asian representations vary to some degree, they can be collectively located in what I have termed elsewhere as 'the ambivalent economy of desire'.[2] In this context, representations of alterity are not simply rational assertions of a dominant, clearly identified (Western) self over a putative (colonial) other, but represents more disjunctive operations of colonial desire: both self and other cannot be clearly delineated but constantly intersect and interoperate, impeding and obfuscating the West's attempt to subdue its other while also ironically contributing to its own ascendancy. So earlier stereotypes of the Asian other in conjunction with more playful subversion and parody of all identities are instances of this economy of desire. At this juncture, I also wish to extend this to the cultural present, which could, to all intents and purposes, be labelled as 'postmodern'. Sifting through the panoply of meanings of the 'post-modern', there are two senses of the term that are especially instructive – social justice and the social place of difference. I raise these two issues because in spite of the anti-essentialist nature of postmodernism, postmodernity as a condition could be noted for its increased sensitivity towards various transgressions that have emerged alongside modernity: exploitation, racism, sexism, colonialism, violence in all forms (physical, structural, epistemic) and the like. One of postmodernity's attempts at addressing social injustice is, therefore, its treatment of difference, which by subverting dominant narratives seeks out spaces in which the other (in this case the identities and communities marginalized, elided or eviscerated by their dominant counterparts) is allowed to coexist. At the same time, postmodernity is anti-essentialist and it refuses to acknowledge identities as having any real or concrete form. By doing so it forestalls any identity from becoming hegemonic and transcendent.

As seen from this postmodern lens, it is possible to deduce how the complexity of representing the Asian other has come about. However, both postmodern difference and social justice give rise to as many challenges as they claim to circumvent. For in spite of its disavowal of categories, it can be said that postmodernity is embedded in its own particular historicism, which has been identified by Jameson as 'late capitalism'[3] and by Sardar as an ongoing, although changeable, project of imperialism.[4] In the first instance, postmodernity's treatment of otherness, apart from the context of social justice, must also be seen in terms of commoditization, which then reinscribes alterity as both exotic and as an object of mass consumption,[5] while in the second, postmodernity 'avoids, by glossing over, the politics of non-western marginalization in history by suddenly discovering Otherness everywhere, and arguing that everything has its own kind of Otherness by which it defines itself'.[6] The postmodern is thus in Rorty's understanding an act of 'redescription' in which the foundational and essential are eviscerated, but for the other this task becomes 'humiliating' because then there is nothing left – no identity, no categories, no culture – that it can claim to be its own.[7]

I raise this problem of the postmodernity because it demonstrates the fundamental ambivalence attending to Asian alterities. On the one hand the postmodern condition in all its sensibilities about social justice and difference have inaugurated not only projects in the popular cultural domain but also academic as well. Thus, at the height of the behaviourist movement, the social scientifically-orientated area studies that tended to hide so much Western subjectivity and hegemony under the guise of objectivity and positivism have become much more self-conscious and critical about their complicity in the production of area knowledge. In this way Harootunian and Miyoshi's call for the 'afterlife' of area studies echo these concerns of postmodernity:

> The moment that has decentered the truths, practices, and institutions that belonged to a time that could still believe in the identity of some conception of humanity and universality with a Eurocentric endowment and to the acknowledgment that its 'provinciality' must now be succeeded by what Said called 'a contrapuntal orientation in history.'[8]

But at the same time too it is difficult to dislodge area studies from their complicity with the consumption of the postcolonial exotic and/or the reduction of Asian alterities to mere social constructions.

These issues of Asian representation in the supposedly 'reformed' Western mentality also reflect other more fundamental problems, and this could be labelled as axial politics. To this point, the nature of alterity that I have discussed has to do with only one dimension, namely, how the 'West' – both as a geographical/political identity and as a set of epistemologies adopted by peoples around the world – comes to terms with Asia as other. The axis here is therefore between the 'West' and Asia, and the self-reflexive critical inquiries of area studies are inordinately focused on this. But outside this framework, there are potentially many more axes that have not received adequate attention. These axes could also be geographical, in that different communities in Asia engage, imagine and represent their counterparts in the region. These axes could also be transboundary such as sexual minorities, religious communities and internally displaced persons who are either non-national in nature or do not identify themselves with any physical location. The interactions between and among these groups within the given region, therefore, implicate other practices of alterity.

Let me return to *At World's End* and suggest how these alternative axes of alterity have taken place. While *At World's End* is undeniably a Western text invoking a particular trajectory in alterity, the film's varied reception by Asian audiences evinces other cultural dynamics that occur parallel to the dominant axes. For instance, the film's representations of the Chinese incited different responses in China and Singapore. In China, online forum participants saw fictive texts as still needing to be responsible in providing accurate fundamental depictions and characterizations of the Chinese civilization. And as such, they lambasted the film for its 'unflattering' and 'insulting depictions of the Chinese people' and chastising Chow Yun Fatt (who plays Sao Feng in the film) for being complicit in the representation.[9] However, in Singapore, the responses were more positive. Coming from a more empirical modernist position in which fiction and fact could be seen as delineated categories, Singaporean viewers were satisfied that the otherness of Singapore in the film had little correspondence with reality or could at least be overlooked due to the film's historical aspecificity.[10] The axes that are immediately brought into play here are, thus, between national communities (Singapore and China) and also different metaphysics of interpretation (responsibility in accurate civilizational portrayals as opposed to the elasticity of fiction).

In mentioning alterity as being both framed and challenged by an undeterminable number of axes, I am stressing that any critical knowledge production of Asia needs to conceptualize difference in terms of 'alterities', pluralized relationships between communities inside and outside Asia. I am not necessarily suggesting that there is a dearth in scholarly attention in this area, for as Huggan notes, there is already a substantial 'cosmopolitan alterity industry whose products are geared, in part, for educational use'.[11] In this sense, the works of Edward Said, colonial discourse analysis and its associated style of critique can be said to fall into this category. The lacuna is, therefore, a patchiness of coverage. While much has been done to inquire about the dominant axis, which arguably ends up being a self-reflexive venture on the part of a postmodern West, little has been done to interrogate alterities as they are played out in the many other axes. At best, the emergence of the Inter-Asia Cultural Studies (IACS), which I will discuss in a later section, attempts to redirect our attention to different cultural alignments in the region, but there have been few systematic assessments of this subject. In thinking about Asian alterities, it is important to also infuse what Chakrabarty terms as 'provincialization'[12] – the separate domains or provinces that cannot be reduced to each other. For instance, in Gayatri Spivak's aptly titled new book,[13] *Other Asias*, the emphasis was more to celebrate the different provincializations of Asia that existed outside dominant, hegemonic forms than to reflect on how and why we must speak about these different forms of Asia in the first place and what might be at stake in accepting these notions of radicalness.[14] These concerns collectively call for a need in re-examining the notion of otherness and alterity as the basis of critical contestations of 'Asia'. Following Spivak's lead I ask what and how does otherness – in this historical phase termed variably as postmodern or late capitalist – give rise to intellectual thought about Asia in the last decade and what relationship does it have on scholars within (and outside) Asia who are compelled into deploying representations of Asia that are more socially just?

I would like to see the above questions as the agenda-setting or framing idea of this volume, although admittedly this would be immensely ambitious. The volume does not claim to resolve this, but at best strives to move towards that direction. Specifically it is driven by the following questions. First, what does it mean to speak about alterity in the midst of increasing complexity in Asia? Second, what are the dynamics of representations of Asia as a whole or as incongruous parts by communities inside and outside the region? How profoundly do critiques of Orientalism affect the production of otherness? In academic circles, how do the heterogeneity, pluralism and politics attending to Asian studies in Asia and the West configure and reconfigure alterity? The essays in this volume address these questions in their unique ways, they gravitate around this central premise: Asian otherness is more than the dialectical interplay between the Western self and one of its many others, and more than just the Orientalist discourse writ large. Because the constituents of Asian studies are made up not just of the archetypal West, the self–other positionings have become deployed relentlessly across different communities inside and outside Asia as they attempt to shape the intellectual, cultural, epistemological and ontological relationships with each other. Consequently, they attempt to construct a picture of otherness that would hopefully be the basis of further investigation. To further introduce these essays, the rest of the chapter contextualizes the current forms of thinking about Asia and the types of conversations that appear to be taking place in different sites, particularly in the 'reformed' Western academy and within Asia. It subsequently examines the contemporary enthusiasm in the 'alterity academy' and attempts to relate it to critical Asian studies. Following this, the chapter ends with an overview of the essays in this volume.

The politics of knowing Asia

When did area studies, and by imputation Asian studies, become 'critical'?[15] The prospect of a specific date might be too elusive to call, but perhaps 1978 might be a good starting point. This was the year Edward Said's landmark text *Orientalism: Western Conceptions of the Orient* appeared, and while it in no way was the first to unravel the politics involved in the Western production of Orientalist knowledge,[16] its controversial reception marked certain fundamental changes in intellectual trajectories. As a self-defined exiled Palestinian scholar in a prestigious US university, Said received much more attention than his counterparts located in the Third World. But more notably, his book employed an unusual synthesis of Focauldian and Gramscian thought as the basis of critiquing Western knowledge practices.[17] Consequently the conjunction of these intellectual positions signal the arrival of an era that motivated critics of area studies outside the immediate concerns of the book (the Anglo-French-American imperialism and knowledge of the Middle Eastern Orient) to construct parallel arguments about area knowledge that concerns them. First, the realness and essentialism of geographic areas and regions as well as the social and cultural phenomena existing there are put in suspension or noted as problematic. Second, traditional area studies are seen to be complicit with reinforcing dominant metanarratives (the West, modernity, patriarchy, capitalism) or instrumental in rationalizing some form of intentionality (dominance, the civilizing mission). Third, because of the constitutive role of Western scholarship, the critical area studies expert has become self-reflexive in the way he or she contributes to the knowledge of regions/areas.

The point that is being asserted here is not necessarily that Said inaugurated a new critical method of examining area studies, although he continues to remain extremely influential in this regard. But more appropriately *Orientalism* is symbolic of a phase in Western academia that emerged surrounding the politics of area/regional knowledge production, in some cases borrowing, echoing, resisting and also eliding *Orientalism*. Indeed, since Said's work had very little to say about the Orient of the 'Far East' or East Asia, a number of works examining the American empire and its cultural relationship with this part of the world have been published, claiming to extend theoretical deficiencies present in *Orientalism*, while extending imperial discourse analyses to these areas. For example Yoshihara looks at the role played by white women in American Orientalism in the late nineteenth to mid-twentieth century 'inscribed gendered meanings to Asia, both complicating and replicating the dominant Orientalist discourse'.[18] Focusing on a later era (1945–61) Christina Klein also attempts to reframe US Orientalism, but in this case amidst the intersection of the Cold War, cultural texts, American sentimentality and the changing notions of race.[19]

There are a number of other expositions of American Orientalism in (East) Asia, and while they make different contributions to this subject, they do represent significant shifts in the direction taken on Asian studies by the American academy. In this regard, the Ford Foundation grants programme, 'Crossing Borders: Revitalizing Area Studies' is emblematic of the palpably mainstream recognition of required interdisciplinarity in a field now becoming informed by Transnationalism[20] and the fluidity of boundaries. In 1999, 18 universities in the US were grant recipients of this programme, each receiving from $150,000 to $350,000.[21] Outside this scheme, Critical Asian studies have been pervasive. For example the University of Washington was sponsored by the Rockefeller Foundation to embark on a two-cycled decade long 'Critical Asian Studies Project' that emphasized social and critical theory as well as political criticism. In its first phase, it focused on 'immigration ethnicity and area studies' and in the second, 'trauma in historical terms and a restlessly re-regionalizing "Asia"'.[22] One of its continuing outcomes – apart from the network of scholars it created – is the journal, *positions: east asia cultures critique*.

While these intellectual and institutional developments appear remarkable and even enabling, their arrival at this juncture needs to be contextualized and historicized. In terms of the political circumstances, the transition from the Cold War era to the post-Cold War era plays a part. Since area studies was instrumental to the deployment of US strategies in the Cold War, the latter's demise marked the change in the nature of governmental support in area studies, something noted by Harootunian and Miyoshi as a disciplinary 'afterlife'.[23] This consequently led some quarters to stress on the urgency of transforming area studies and making them relevant to the current epoch. Furthermore, it might also be important to examine critical thought about Asia from a much longer-term and more enduring historical and intellectual perspective. Oddly, the current impulse to think of Asian knowledge in subjective terms, as contingent, constantly open to (re)interpretation, and informed by hegemonic political practices is not an entirely new development. In effect, area studies have traditionally been divided between empiricist and positivist approaches on the one hand, and more hermeneutical forms of engagement, on the other. For instance, K.M. Pannikar's *Asia and Western Dominance*,[24] which Said references in *Orientalism* appears to be early forms of consciousness about the constructed nature of Asia and the Western complicity of this. Even much later texts, such as Donald Emmerson's 1984 essay on '"Southeast Asia": What's in a Name?' similarly critiques the arbitrariness and strategic utility of this concept for the Europeans and Americans during the Second World War,[25] without recourse to the familiar language of postmodernism or poststructuralism.[26] There are also many other examples of hermeneutical approaches to Asia and its subregions, as there are writings revisiting and critiquing the complicity of Asia knowledge with dominant forms of power. In the 1970s the emergence of the radical or New Left motivated criticisms of America's new imperial relationship with Asia, brought on by its debacle in Indochina.[27] *The Bulletin of Concerned Asian Scholars* was launched in the 1970s with these concerns in mind, emphasizing various topics that during the time were considered 'critical': the effect of American power on Eastern Asia. Notably its 'goals explicitly included examining the intellectual approaches by which Asia was understood in the West and the ways in which reigning theoretical frameworks in universities and professional institutions excluded Asian aspirations and experiences'.[28] In 2001, the *Bulletin* was renamed *Critical Asian Studies* largely to reflect global social and political changes of the twenty-first century as well as to accommodate the emergence of new social movements and scholars/activists in Asia. Nonetheless the revamped journal remains committed to the original objectives of the *Bulletin*.

One more aspect of the historicism of critical Asian studies needs to be broached, and this is the tension that they have generated within conservative intellectual circles in the post 9/11 era. While the terrorist attacks of 2001 renewed the interest and relevance of policy-oriented area studies, they also invoked a backlash against certain scholars and specific forms of area studies that might be construed as anti-American or going against the requirements of US national security. Claiming that area studies have become substantially influenced by, among others, postcolonial theory, and that the latter claimed the use of a scholar's expertise in support of American power as immoral, critics like Stanley Kurtz became successful in arousing US governmental interest.[29] Subsequently in 2003, the US House of Representatives passed the 'International Studies in Higher Education Act', which placed foreign language and area studies programmes under greater governmental oversight. At the centre of this was the debate about the establishment of an advisory panel to supervise these programmes, but it also incited concerns about the intrusion of the government into academic freedom. The final passage of the act in August 2008 did away with this but instead required institutions to now account for balance and impartiality in these programmes before governmental funding could be approved.

These issues of historicism and contextualization suggest that something more Manichean is afoot here. Superficially, each of these episodes – the transition from the Cold War to the post-Cold War era, the uncanny resemblance of hermeneutical modes of Asian studies to contemporary forms of critical Asian studies, and domestic debates on social and political responsibilities of area studies – indicate that critical perspectives in Asian studies appear to have the capacity and scope for displacing and decentring hegemonic narratives of the field at one level. Yet, at another level, the greater acceptance of dissent, as seen in the controversy surrounding the Higher Education Act, or the traditional existence of hermeneutical approaches alongside positivist ones, affirms and continues to reproduce the presence of a latent epistemic centre rooted in modernity and the Enlightenment. Consequently, this leads to two interrelated logics of disjuncture. First, hermeneutical approaches in Asian studies should not be thought as curiously antagonistic towards empiricist and positivist methods. In effect, both necessarily uphold a 'modernist tension', which although disjunctive requires both approaches to knowledge to be 'understood as the sum of a complex dialectical interaction involving the inexorably linked behavior of creative individuals within a broad sociocultural context'.[30] Second, and more broadly speaking, countervailing and opposing positions/frameworks in Asian studies are under the current logic of global capitalism open to disjuncture, difference and contradiction,[31] rather than being ways of thinking about Asia that are outside any prior structure. Hence, even both postmodernism[32] and postcolonialism[33] could be conceived necessarily to be products of the age of late or global capitalism.

As much as the foregoing has alluded to certain immanental continuities in critical thought, one should be careful not to label critical approaches like postmodernism, poststructuralism, feminism and postcolonialism as 'business as usual' under a new liberal intellectual disguise. Notwithstanding the ironic revalidation of the Western epistemological core, no critique of this has been sufficiently potent to dislodge the myriad of marginal and subaltern appropriations of Asian studies that came in its wake. Writing in a slightly different context, Dipesh Chakrabarty's movement both recognizing the omnipresence of Western epistemologies nonetheless intimates that knowledges and practices could indeed be 'provincialized',[34] thus arguing for parallel epistemologies that now need to be considered. In this respect, these relationships of provincialism between the dominant and alternative can be expressed as a form of axial politics, in which the axes connecting the 'observer' subject and the 'observed' object need to be premised upon a set of shifting, diffuse and unstable reference points.

Let me discuss further what is potentially at stake by considering critical Asian studies as axial politics. Particularly, it might be instructive to consider knowledges of Asia and the subjectivities that give rise to these as deployed across multiple, geographical, imaginary and cultural axes. These axes constitute relationships that represent really existing spaces, boundaries and communities, and the easiest that come to mind will be how communities outside Asia think about specific communities within. But these axes could also represent the shifting and eliding subjectivity of, say, the postcolonial intellectual. In this instance, there may only be one geographical place or one community involved, and what make up the different ends of the axis are fragments of the colonized mind – different histories, different worldviews, different traumas and anxieties. As the discussion has attempted to accentuate, the dominant axis of the Western observer and the Asian subject is still retained, notwithstanding more critical or dissenting approaches to Asian studies. In some works already mentioned, such as by Klein, Yoshihara, or the recent anthology edited by Sears entitled *Knowing Southeast Asian Subjects*,[35] the self-referentiality still remains anchored in American academic and cultural contexts, and they do reflect the transformed historical conditions that have led to their emergence. Simply stated they revolve around the need to question 'what is wrong with the way Asia is being represented in the US and by the West?' Yet, it might also be premature to acclaim this as a new form of Western triumphalism because the various subject positions that constitute the axis is much more fissiparous. Not all writers working under the auspices of the American academy can be said to be echoing Western epistemologies. Similarly, looking across to a more 'intra-Asian' axis, a Taiwanese scholar writing about Japan could, in effect adopt a subject positioning with greater affinity with traditional Western Orientalist scholarship than an observer geographically located in the West, working on the same topic.

The messiness of axial politics is not an intellectual problem in need of a solution, but should be considered as a way of thinking through the circularity and the leviathanic features of dominant epistemologies in critical Asian studies and to establish different ways of knowing Asia through alternative axes. Let me focus for awhile on critical Asian studies that are emerging purportedly outside Western intellectual centres, and in particular, a formation identified by Dirlik as the 'Asianization of Asian Studies', which is avowedly concerned with addressing the 'hegemony of Eurocentric knowledge'.[36] I contend that the particular intellectual subjectivity that stands in the midst of this alter-configuration of Asian studies is what Thongchai coins as a 'home scholar', Asianists whose objects of study are their own home locations.[37] This subjectivity is certainly open to criticism since the native-ness or indigenousness of the home scholar does not necessarily result in a more accurate representation of the subject of study, but borrowing somewhat from the language of postcoloniality, the home scholar's 'interstitiality' – between his or her influence by Western frames of reference and yet to be articulated commitment to the local – he or she possesses the 'opportunity to turn the alleged weaknesses or disadvantages, namely expertise in local matters within particular language and cultural sensitivity, into advantages for theorization'.[38] In this way, the home scholar connects Asian studies back to the dominant axis of the Western observer/subject–Asian object on the one hand, while on the other hand pointing the way to the many multiply constituted axes representing intra-Asian relationships.

Dirlik's exposition on the 'Asianization of Asian Studies' is instructive in this regard but is in need of further exegesis. He situates two large projects in this context: the Australian-based 'Asian Studies in Asia Network' and the Inter-Asia Cultural Studies collective.[39] Arguably both projects are somewhat different: the first seems to promote Asian studies within Asia by encouraging the formation of networks of scholars, brought into bearing at a time when Australia was 'Asianizing'; while the second is a more systematic research grouping with an implicit although diverse programme of study. As Kuan-Hsing Chen and Chua Beng Huat, two of the leading figures in the IACS, reminisce, the objectives of the collective are to:

> contribute to the integration of an imagined Asia at the level of knowledge production. More specifically, we set out to:
>
> (1) generate and circulate critical work in and out of Asia and beyond;
> (2) slowly link and facilitate dialogues between the disconnected critical circles within Asia and beyond; and
> (3) provide a platform on which academic and movement intellectual work can intersect.[40]

One of the most notable developments, in this regard, was the inauguration of its eponymous journal series in 2000, but this was also prefaced by the two 'Trajectories' conferences in 1992 and 1995. In a sense, the resulting edited volume to emerge out of the conferences, presented a wide variety of essays that both reacted to the dominant Western-centric axis of Asian studies while also attempting to initiate discussions constituting different axial relations as a decolonizing gesture.[41]

The Inter-Asia Cultural Studies collective is significant in a number of respects, not least they lay bare the charges that the 'Asianization of Asian Studies' might in its 'establishment version', pander to or be complicit with transnational global capitalism, but also suggest 'possibilities and actualities of a radical opposition politics'.[42] More importantly, while Dirlik might be thinking typically of the Inter-Asia Cultural Studies collective in this case, it might also be useful to think of it as broadly more symbolic and representative of parallel gestures toward Asia knowledge production that is occurring along very similar axes and inhabiting the same politics. For example, Dirlik makes no mention of the Southeast Asian Studies Regional Exchange Programme (SEASREP), quite understandably because of its subregional focus, but its somewhat non-Western exclusivity also meant that it attracted less attention outside its immediate membership circle.[43] Nonetheless, the 13-year-old organization's funding support from Japanese foundations and its promotion of intra-Southeast Asian academic collaboration demonstrates various attempts at Asianizing Southeast Asian studies. Furthermore, in Singapore, know-ledge production undoubtedly tracks the wholesale embracing of capitalism, and hence developments like the shifts in research focus and methodology in older centres like the Institute of Southeast Asian Studies, the organizing of regional conferences like 'We Asians' in 2000, or the emergence of new research centres like the East Asian Institute, Asia Research Institute and the Institute of South Asian Studies, could all be noted for their complicity with policy needs and the ways by which global capitalism is entrenched in Singapore's most recent phase of Asianization. Yet, because of the inherent pluralism in new approaches to Asian studies, different and alternative spaces become possible in the construction of Asia knowledge. In this way the 'home scholars' mentioned earlier can now transition into being scholars of a different sort: as intellectuals working across different axes, spurred on by different purposes surrounding the constitution of knowledge.

At the time the present volume is being assembled, there are way too many examples of these writings to give a considered account for. However, in order to give a sense of how Asia scholars might have benefitted from or employed 'axial politics' in the work, I shall offer a number of broad groupings. The first are the various 'landmark' or the 'state of the field' essays that have been published (and republished) either individually in journals or in larger edited volumes over the last decade.[44] In many of these cases, the mode of engagement has been heteroglossic. Some remain persistently self-referential with regard to Western discourses in Asia, while some others dialogical – being aware of the self-referentiality on the one hand but also desiring to articulate an alternative regional discourse. Two commentaries, one by Chun and Shamsul and the other by Sun Ge, are illustrative of this point. In the first article, Chun and Shamsul are aware of the differences in the dialectical interplay between local/global and are concerned about the role of the colonial and postcolonial academy in the production of Asia knowledge.[45] The authors attribute this tendency to native scholars who might have pursued graduate studies in the

West. But to be representative of the broader critical concerns in 'Asia' one also needs to be sensitized against the universality of critical theory in Asia and the culturalism it represents. Rather, as Chun and Shamsul aver, critical knowledge and social action in Asia should find as their basis the 'local and political context of institutional power that created and continues to regulate academia and academics'.[46] Appearing also in the same journal issue, Sun Ge elucidates the impact of local institutional regimes. In the context of Chinese intellectuals, the Saidian Orientalist critique becomes decontextualized, and a form of 'misunderstanding' emerges through a trans-cultural dialogue; it comes to be confusingly received as 'ethnonationalist fervour' rather than 'cultural relativism'.[47]

The second set of writings are, attempts at renarrating the perspectives and referentiality of Asia knowledge. As it has been raised constantly throughout this chapter, these perspectives have almost always been implicitly Western, with continued reference to scholars like Fairbank and Reischauer. Yet, alternative axes have seldom been discussed, which perhaps explains the importance of works like Stefan Tanaka's *Japan's Orient* in 1993.[48] While produced as a work of Western scholarship and nuanced by the Orientalist discourse, its concerns about narrating the production of Asian knowledge for Japan meant that it could not so easily adopt the same terms of reference as Western colonial discourse. Instead, it had to account for the historical and cultural specificities, such as the difficulty in culturally placing modernity and the Meiji restoration. Consequently, Japan's knowledge of its Orient was a product of a more complex relationship with the West, modernity and Japanese identity; in this sense Western modes of knowledge were not always immediately accepted and comprehensible. In any event, Tanaka's argument was authorized by the language of poststructuralism. By the time of the later writings by Sun and Wang, who also attempted to re-authorize Japanese knowledge production of 'Toyo', the terms of ambivalence and hybridity had become more pronounced as Japanese intellectuals attempted to come to terms with Westernization and their own sense of the (imperial) greatness of the Japanese civilization.[49]

While Tanaka, Sun and Wang provide some insight into how knowledge of Asia has been produced adjacent to, but not necessarily fully outside of, the Western-centric axis, other attempts at renarrating knowledge about Asia have also taken place along and *in situ* axis, which I mentioned earlier. For this we can return to Thongchai's idea of home scholarship, which appears to be a retrospective expression of his earlier and much acclaimed, *Siam Mapped: A History of the Geo-Body of a Nation*. In this example, we have a Western-trained (and currently located) native Thai scholar writing specifically about the history of the Thai consciousness of nationhood.[50] Certainly, no work of this nature omits the constitutive impact of the West, in particular, how Western techniques of cartography and the 'discourse of the geo-body' shaped the production of Thai-ness, and in this sense Western Orientalism is invoked. But the object of investigation for Thongchai is still Thailand, and the axial relationship that the work is preoccupied with is not immediately across different geographical spaces or national communities. Instead, the axis occurs within the home scholar himself, as a way of navigating, relating and circumventing the various subjectivities and politics that have come to historically and spatially demarcate the work. Cross referencing Thongchai's two writings[51] it is possible to see how the axis is one of internal negotiation; a gesture of recognizing the Western epistemologies, including the postmodern language the text adopts and the Western academic audience it seems to be partly catering for, while attempting to capture the particularity of Thai-ness that Thongchai (and not the foreign observer) is uniquely privy to.

The third group can be more appropriately termed as acts of appropriation or re-categorization. If concepts like 'modernity' and 'capitalism' were to have any critical utility, intellectuals would have to be conscious of how they are complicit with the production of material reality, and how they submerge broader structures of Western historicism and canonicity. By doing so, however, such gestures merely invoke the Western/bourgeois self-referentiality while at the same time destabilize the knowledge they are responsible for producing. This act of anti-essentialism deprives and undercut alternative applications of these categories that might prove instrumental in the recovery of (Western) modernity's other. Thus a number of writers have attempted to reconfigure the concepts by adopting a double movement: on the one hand they accept the Western-centric nature and origins of the terms, but on the other hand they invoke different strategies to enable these concepts to function disjunctively opposite to their presumed Western contexts. For example, although Dilip Gaonkar's discussions of 'alternative modernities' are made much more generally, his splitting of modernity between 'societal modernization and cultural modernity'[52] allows for the continued recognition of modernity's predication on its original Western, historical form, while allowing for a 'difference that would destabilize the universalist idioms, historicize the contexts, and pluralize the experiences of modernity'.[53] Gaonkar is clear not to commit himself to any particular definition of 'difference' here, but this also follows from the tendency to think of modernity as 'multiple', as articulated by Eisenstadt and other authors of a special issue of *Daedalus*.[54] Specifically, in William Lim's reading of Asian architectural landscapes and urbanism, the duality of even multiplicity enables Western canonicity to be made visible, while another term like 'contemporariness' expresses some material and concrete historical developments that do not instantly invoke tropes of Enlightenment progress.[55] Thus, different cultural innovations, changes and development in Asia that may have spatially occurred in different ages, before colonization and after, become conceivable in ways that are not merely reducible to absolute articulations of the Modern, the rational and progress. Likewise, Dirlik's well-known critique of postcolonialism in the age of global capitalism is also more generally a critique of Third World scholarship than about critical Asian studies *per se*. Yet, in arguing that the popularity of postcolonial theory in the First World is emblematic of the current historical conditions of capitalism, Dirlik recognizes the irony in that, under such a specific instance, one is employing a Western-centred concept to critique another, since Marxist criticism is also driven by Eurocentric teleology, incorporating the world relentlessly to the narrative of modernization-industrialization as a form of passage to socialism. Responding to this, however, Dirlik suggests that the 'separation of capitalism from Eurocentrism' is indeed possible, largely as a result of the deterritorialization and fragmentation of capital.[56]

The resulting notions of 'Asian capitalism' then become much more problematic entities, both embroiling movements of resistance while also replicating Orientalist stereotypes.

What I have attempted to do in this section was less an account of the development of critical Asian studies, and more an attempt to suggest how problems associated with the knowledge production of Asia could be understood in terms of 'axial politics'. Typically, what we know about Asia has become intricately interlinked with how we have come to know Asia and who we are in terms of such overlapping subjectivities as intellectuals, academicians, policymakers, Asians, Westerners, men, women and so on. Potentially, and under an increasingly pluralizing environment, these different knowledge productions of Asia are now enjoyed and fetishized precisely for their incommensurability, which raise serious questions of whether or not this moment marks the emergence of a decentred intellectual environment (where Western epistemologies have diminutively come to parallel others than being superordinate), or heralds a new disjunctive empire that continues to revalidate or reimpose the sovereign figure of the West in a more Manichean way. While this discussion of axial politics was not intended to authoritatively lay to rest this debate (if this can at all be resolved), it tried to provide a framework in which alternative conceptions of Asia, its provincializations and its constitutive positionalities could be more effectively broached.

The location of the other

In the postmodern, poststructural, feminist or postcolonial academe, it has become increasingly commonplace to speak about 'otherness', 'alterity' and 'difference' as radical categories. They are radical because their intrusion into the critique of knowledge suggests that there are alternative positions, epistemologies, subjectivities, worldviews and frameworks that have been evacuated by a particular dominant and self-universalizing discourse. Oddly, however, such intimations of otherness and alterity are not exactly new, and they have a longer heritage than their current iterations and have played a more fundamental role in Western epistemology and ontology. Thus in continental philosophy, theology and the many disciplines that were to sanction the colonial project from the eighteenth century onwards, the other has been a consistent although immanental trope. In this connection, one does not need to reference the ontological and existential questions of Heidegger and Sartre respectively, the nature of the psyche in Lacanian psychoanalysis, the divine alterity of the Judeo-Christian God, or the implicit racial difference of the subject races under Western colonialism, in order to remind us of the prior incarnations of otherness.

However, what seems to be notable in earlier traditional applications of otherness was the way they both functioned alongside and reacted to empiricism and positivism. As noted earlier this modernist tension did indeed give rise to the anxiety that positivism stymies the way observers comprehend the other because it disguises and obscures the 'particularity of one's own understanding as a researcher'. Consequently in the humanities and the social sciences, comparative or comparativist studies popularly came to be suggested as ways of accommodating difference without reducing the other to the observer self. More specifically such actions were applications of *Verstehen*, which in its variations from Dilthey to Weber was a hermeneutical method in contextualizing the other. Shields presents *Verstehen* as an ongoing theoretical project, which although cannot be simplistically reduced to 'empathetic understanding' or a 'romantic' attempt to understand the other from his or her point of view,[57] no variation of *Verstehen* has been capable of dislodging the deeply embedded structures of Eurocentrism and modernity. In effect, *Verstehen*'s ethical commitment revolves more around the need of improving disciplinary practices than the recovery of the other, and its application can in no way come from an 'authentic, unalienated imagination of another person or group'.[58] Paradoxically, *Verstehen* as a way of speaking about the other continues to revalidate the Western self.

Therefore, what makes the current academic and intellectual fascination with otherness and alterity notable is the emergence of irony and the incommensurable: that solutions to the modernist tension between hermeneutical and positivist approaches both displace and reinforce a radically self-altering modernity, while critical practices in recovering the other becomes the ethical basis of inquiry rather than the means to improved research methodology. There are a few characteristics through which current concerns about alterity have come to be expressed. The first is the implicit absence of relativism. Rather than resorting to unhelpful assertions that every community or individual is always an 'other' to someone else, the idea of alterity is also intricately tied to marginality and subalternality. This leads to the establishment of the archetypal dominant model of the self, the white, male, bourgeois subject, in the face of the countless throng of the oppressed others. Not unexpectedly the second characteristic then is that these specific notions of self and other enable the language of social justice, drawing one's attention to the way positivist work is unaware of its complicity with the dominant self and to the occlusion, suppression and invalidation of alternatives. Finally, knowledge can no longer be thought of as a priori, given or prediscursive, but needs to be framed as mulitplicitous and contentious.

In operational terms, this issue of otherness has much to do with what Edward Said sees as the 'crisis in representation', in which accuracy was no longer possible but a battle involving 'consciousness of linguistic forms and conventions' and 'the pressures of such transpersonal, transhuman, and transcultural forces as class, the unconscious, gender, race, and structure'.[59] Abstracting from this in terms of his more famous work, it is possible to see how *Orientalism* is emblematic of this crisis, since the representation of Oriental thought, culture and people are directed by the necessities of the Western imperial discourse. Yet on this notion of 'representation', various (mis)readings of Said's claims about Orientalism have emerged, leading to uni-dimensional conceptions of otherness. These readings go like this: in order to support and justify imperial power and logic, the Western self needed to fabricate an inaccurate and erroneous representation of the Oriental other and the Oriental is generally stereotyped as inferior, barbaric, primitive, dangerous, and this list potentially goes on. While this account provides a basic synopsis of Said's thesis, it glosses over the more complex and ambivalent reasoning that underpins Said's oeuvre. In this connection the application (once again) of Western empiricism and positivism stymies more productive understandings of otherness, which I have addressed elsewhere as disjunctive.[60] Basically, the tendency to think of the alterity problem as the Western validation of self and the vilification and belittling of the other is only part of the 'ambivalent economy of desire', linking alterity to more finely ingrained operations of the psyche. In this sense, both 'self' and 'other' are not delineated from each other's production.[61] In other words, the Western imperial discourse is able to bolster its own position not simply because it can requisition the intellectual's wherewithal in affirming the other's inferiority, but that it can at different times and places vacillatingly equate the other as self, depict the other in a positive light, sustain a fantasy of attraction and exoticism for the other, while still inherently retaining a separate but co-functioning vision of the other as threatening, repulsive and licentious. It is these tensions in alterity that have continued to sustain postmodern or feminist critiques or exercises in colonial discourse analysis by allowing, for instance, Said's idea of the Orientalist discourse, to be seen as enduringly complex.

As I have attempted to intimate here, the alterity enterprise is expansive, and what was at one time the preserve of continental philosophers and theologians is now a fundamental concern of a wide array of scholars in the humanities and social sciences. Nonetheless, the depth of alterity problem seems to be relatively confined to one level of axial politics, namely, the dynamics of interactions between the Western metropolitan core and *its* periphery, and the frame of reference remains the 'West'. This raises the question about the politics of alterity at the periphery. What happens when we invert the direction of the gaze, in this case, the way the periphery perceives or looks back at the metropole? What happens in these configurations of 'self' and 'other' when certain groups of people look at other groups of people within the same periphery? And are these questions about identity politics even universally applicable or are they modes of interrogation more peculiar to the Western post-Enlightenment present? And on what basis do we accept the other as representing a viable community, if the basis of recognizing communities are structured within Western ontological modalities?

These questions are significant because they represent certain modes of inquiry in the politics of alterity that have been mentioned so far. They represent extremely dense patterns of interactions that involve hierarchy, eliding and fluid subjectivities, mimicry and the colonization of the mind. For instance, women's status as a marginalized group within patriarchy is an especially well-trodden fact, but yet women *qua* white women may also disavow their marginality in their collaboration with white men to subjugate the colonized other. Singapore's inheritance of a rational capitalist modernity also complicates the politics of alterity at the periphery. As the other in the British colonial narrative of Southeast Asia, ruling elites in Singapore have in the 1950s and 1960s employed the language of nationalism and anti-colonialism, thus identifying themselves with many similar parties in the same region. Yet even around the same time, the inherited Western epistemologies meant that elites Singapore could also redeploy Western Orientalist discourse unproblematically in coming to terms with the rest of the region, while also employing the same as

Singaporeans saw themselves as becoming economically superior in the decades that followed. And even as certain modes of representing otherness might have come to be repudiated as 'politically incorrect' in current discourse, the lag with which Singaporean discourse encounters in attempting to move out of a Victorian frame of reference ironically leads to persistent hyper-Orientalisms not (or no longer) seen in the West.[62] Furthermore, to what forms of communities should distinctions of self and other gravitate? Since the sovereign state has had tremendous influence in the way political organization is shaped, it seems natural to speak about the British or American self in opposition, perhaps, to the Chinese or Japanese other, just as the latter could be rescaled as the Japanese self and the Korean other. But recognizing the contingent nature of national communities and possibilities of many other sub-state and trans-state communities, the politics of alterity at the periphery could also give rise to a whole array of different self-other dynamics. For instance, the Hindutva movement geographically imagines and locates India as the home to Hindus worldwide, and in many of its confrontations with the Islamic other in the provincial state of Uttar Pradesh, it has had to mobilize a transnational movement of diasporic Hindu Indians. In this way the self-other dialectic was activated on terms that exceeded the sovereign state.

Nonetheless, this second angle on the politics of alterity is not necessarily distinct and separate from the first, in that they both exist in a state of mutuality and tension. If, in the first angle, the concern for the other is in reference to a preconceived Western self and how these relationships have been constantly reconfigured, the second is more finely attuned to the lived experience of otherness. In this context, the ambivalence associated with alterity is no better articulated than by examining how 'native' intellectuals like Frantz Fanon, Octavio Manoni and Ashis Nandy have attempted to come to terms with their otherness. Undoubtedly they rely heavily on the Western language and logic of psychoanalysis in symptomatically framing the anxieties and traumas that have come to occupy the colonial subject's psychical space. Yet, at the same time the colonial subject is also positioned as a very different entity that can never be fully assimilated into the Western self and constantly vacillating between a Western-imposed identity and an otherness that is ceaselessly in negotiation with an elusive self. In this regard, Fanon's discussion of Jean Veneuse, a displaced Antillean in France and Nandy's narrative of Aurobindo Ackroyd Ghose bear many similarities. Both Veneuse and Ghose were subjects of ethnic and cultural displacement. For Veneuse, whose entire growing years and adult life were spent in France, his identity became fraught with the inability to reconcile his own sense as the 'other' while constantly being recreated by French society as 'really one of us'.[63] Likewise, Ghose, although brought up in India, was subjected to intense Anglicization by parents who sought to eradicate all forms of Indian-ness from him. While the narrative in both cases takes us to different aspects of their lives, the ambivalence that circulates around both can be discerned. Nandy presents Ghose's adult life as a reaction to his upbringing, thus instead of continuing to embrace Anglicization, he revolts against it, adopting certain revolutionary politics that was to link him to early Indian nationalism.[64] As for Fanon, Veneuse more precisely becomes epigrammatic of the potential tensions emerging from the (sexual) desire of the black man for the white woman. Borrowing the professional language of psychiatry, Fanon describes him as an 'abandonment-neurotic' in which his love for a white woman – despite overtures of her reciprocity – collapses in order to avoid the anxiety of abandonment. Fanon thus quotes Germaine Guex, '"I am the The Other" is an expression I have heard time and again in the language of the abandonment-neurotic. To be "The Other" is to feel that one is always in a shaky position, to be always on guard, ready to be rejected and . . . unconsciously doing everything needed to bring out exactly this catastrophe'.[65]

In dealing with this second angle of alterity, the word that comes to mind is 'schizophrenia', in that for the subaltern, the certainty of a dominant identity/ subjectivity is constantly threatened by any number of competing subjectivities ceaselessly playing out differentials of self and other. For this present volume of Asian otherness, this provides some helpful insights. Particularly, Eurocentrism is inescapable and the volume does not pretend that it is. But to think about these notions of alterity at the periphery opens up possibilities of reframing the 'decolonization question'. Borrowing from Kuan-Hsing Chen (who also references Fanon, Manoni and Nandy, among others), these notions of otherness 'would then . . . deconstruct, decentre, deform, debunk, disarticulate the colonial cultural imaginary produced in the historical process, and to reconstruct, rearticulate, reconnect a more democratic kind of imaginative lines of flight'.[66] The following implications are mobilized. First, how do we contend with the fluidity of otherness in Asia? How do we understand the multiplicity of axes and the different forms of community around which different groupings of 'selves' and 'others' could be organized? Second, how do we introduce the notion of power especially when in Asia there is no shortage of disparity in this aspect? Conversely, at what point and under what conditions does the 'other' become equated with the 'self' in more than a tokenistic way? Finally, what kinds of mutually constitutive relationships could there be between the politics of producing Asian knowledge and alterity/otherness?

Toward alterities in Asia

As I mentioned at the beginning of this introductory essay, the topical interests of the volume potentially raises far more questions than a volume of this size and scope is capable of and prepared to address. In this sense, the essays in the volume are much more modest. They neither claim to have ready answers to the complexities surrounding Asian alterities, nor do they assert that there is a singularly unique characteristic or quality about alterity in this part of the world. In effect, the authors also adopt varying approaches and positions toward otherness and identity; some agreeing, while others sceptical, that the subaltern identity could be recovered, that intercultural contact could be equalitarian or at least outside Western patriarchal models of power and conquest, and that certain qualities of Asian-ness could direct relations between different communities in ways outside the paradigmatic orientalist mode. However, what the chapters in this volume do is to convey 'alterity' in Asia as multifarious and not reducible to any single position that is commonly expected by the Western/modern rhetorical need for a coherent and singular 'thesis'. In this volume, geographers, political scientists, cultural historians and literary critics ask questions relating to different objects of knowledge; for example, how post-war Korea sought to identify itself with other parts of Asia, how the Chinese and Indian search for culturally nuanced forms of nonalignment could function under more dominating structures of modern international diplomacy, whether or not Thais and Filipinos could recognize each other's difference non-hierarchically, and if the new wave of Asian horror cinema is capable of reconciling inter-Asian otherness. Thus, on the one hand, these questions could have a centrifugal effect, directing readers' attention to these knowledge objects rather than the core issue of Asian alterities. But on the other hand it is because of this slippery quality of alterity that calls for this particular approach. As I argued earlier, alterity is disjunctive and a volume that adopts a centripetal approach would be less productive and returns us to a fantasy of an (post) exoticized notion of Asian Otherness that is different from 'Western' conceptions. In this way, the chapters were all intended to illustrate what I raised as 'axial politics'.

The three chapters to follow assess different historical and geographical axes through which Asia (or parts of) has come to be represented. Kim Ye-rim's chapter examines how, for Cold War Japan and South Korea, the imagination of Asia as a region was notably different, in spite of the assimilation of both countries into the American led strategy of Containment in Northeast Asia. As the US sought to 'reconstruct' Japan, Kim argues, it retreated rapidly from its wartime stance of creating a 'Greater East Asian Co-Prosperity Sphere' to one that sought to distance itself from and to 'forget' Asia. As an erstwhile colony of Japan, Korea's attitudes and perceptions of Asia were by far more ambivalent, reflecting its colonial circumstances, anti-colonialist reactions, economic needs, and its incorporation into the American Cold War ideology. What materialized in this regard was an imagination of Asia that was located not just between the Japanese colonial legacy and its American-inspired Cold War present, but also outside of these contexts. The author re-narrates the historical trajectory of South Korea's Asianism and demonstrates an underlying 'Pacific Fantasy' that in itself had colonial roots motivated by Japanese Asian regionalism, but was also ironically fuelled by the expressions of Asian nationalism and anti-imperialism that were to emerge after Japan's defeat at the end of the Second World War. This fantasy was to vacillate and as it became more embedded into the Cold War; it perceived an Asia that was divided along ideological lines, culminating with the Korean War. Notwithstanding such ideological divisions, the author asserts that South Korea's image of Asia became reconsolidated in the cultural sense, identifying with communities that straddled across the ideological divide. While this chapter does not deal explicitly with abstractions like 'self' and 'otherness', it has implications for the volume. In particular the chapter demonstrates that the construction of South Korea's Asian discourse is not reducible to its ideological dominance by Japan or the US. But rather, across different historical epochs, its imaginations of Asia were both ambivalently influenced by and also a reaction against the prevailing thought about the region.

Sally Percival Wood's chapter (Chapter 3) continues to focus on the Cold War Asia of the 1950s and, in particular, the implicit politics of alterity surrounding attempts by the superpowers to co-opt Asia into its universal strategic view of the world on the one hand, and measures taken by various Asian nations to assert nonalignment on the other. While dominant historical narratives depicted both China and India as gravitating towards the Soviet Union during this time, the Asian–African Conference in Bandung in 1955 underscored alternative diplomatic assertions, collectively framed under Jawaharlal Nehru's policy of *Panchsheel* or 'the five principles of peaceful coexistence', which China signed up to in November 1954. Specifically, the chapter explores Asia's assertion of its diplomatic voice at the Bandung Conference, positing Nehru and Zhou Enlai as the 'oriental statesmen' who envisioned a diplomatic role for Asia through the idea of *Panchsheel*. To do so it first examines the influence and commitment of India and China to the Afro-Asian solidarity movement as it evolved. Relative to the conceptualization of a world divided into imperial regions, the chapter questions the historicity of geopolitical definitions, asking precisely what 'Asia', or 'the Orient' meant in international relations of the 1950s. Were these inordinately geopolitical terminologies, which together with 'the Middle East', to be understood as constructs of Western imperial hegemony? And to what extent did these categories retain such imperial tropes in a post-war world reorganized around the avowed egalitarianism of the United Nations? The naming of the Asian–African Conference itself presented some challenges, not only in terms of the composition of nations at the conference but in terms of its implied solidarity within the confines of geopolitical zones defined by the West. Second, the chapter interrogates *Panchsheel*, which became the central premise of India's foreign policy in agreement with China, and more broadly with their Asian neighbours in Burma, Ceylon and Indonesia, as a distinctive Asian strategy for peace in the Cold War. However, the prospect of an Asian solution to 'peace' threatened to destabilize the prevailing knowledge-power paradigm that had politically subjugated and culturally obfuscated the Asian 'other' since the beginning of Europe's systematic invasions of Asia. The chapter examines the extent to which an alternative spatial category – the Anglosphere (collectively the US and Soviet Union and inheritors of the imperial legacy) – relied on those historical templates to diplomatically emasculate Asia at a time when Asians could alternatively be seen as asserting solutions to problems created by their former colonial rulers via their newly won claims to sovereignty. So in a sense, while *Panchsheel* was fundamentally underpinned by Western concepts of sovereignty, its clause of peaceful coexistence as a tenet of nonalignment estranged India and China from the Anglosphere in the Cold War world of the 1950s.

The following chapter raises questions similar to the previous two and adopts an approach that historicizes the knowledge and imagination of Asia while locating them as a product of shifting sociocultural forces coming from within and without. In particular David Walker's chapter focuses on Australia and contextualizes its ongoing Asian question – whether or not it was and continues to be part of the region – as associated with a longer historical trajectory; one that wove in shifting ideas of what race, identity and belonging meant to Australians against a similarly unstable Asian backdrop. Tracing Australia's Asian discourse back to the early nineteenth century, the author demonstrates how White Australians' displacement from Britain raised searching questions about European racial health in the midst of a changing Asian other that shifted from the climate and physical environment to the potentially invasive hordes coming namely from China and Japan. At the turn of the twentieth century, the invasion narrative paralleled other intellectual activities that were to institutionalize Asia and its corollary, the Pacific, as a field of studies. Such positions were to undergo vacillating tendencies of both distancing and embracing Asia as an element intrinsic to Australian culture, and these were particularly nuanced in the prime ministerial transitions from Keating to Howard, and finally to Rudd. Such developments echoed more internally ambivalent attitudes towards Asia; and just as the anxieties about Asia fuelled contempt against Asians in some quarters, others openly called for moderation and increased understanding and the forging of closer ties with the region. As Walker shows in detail, these themes were to constantly resurface as Australians became confronted by regular historical episodes in which perceptions of their identity and national future came to be contested and intertwined with that of Asia.

In Chapters 2, 3 and 4 the discussion centres on historically constituted notions of otherness. Although the Asian as 'other' is not explicitly teased out, the discussion provides an important basis on which later discussion in the volume can draw on. In particular, this has to do with the fact that the Asian 'other' is not necessarily the other of the Western Orientalist imagination, but one that is both a product of as well as a reaction against it. Each of the chapters that follow reiterate, reframe and operationalize these themes in many ways. In Chapter 5 Leong Yew raises the 'Orientalism' problem in the context of how Asian countries – particularly those with a significant colonial history and thereby most subjected to Westernization and modernization – construct and represent other parts of Asia. In this chapter, Singapore and its representation of Southeast Asia is used as an important example of how Orientalism could both inform how Singaporeans think about the region but also how their specific circumstances induced by an ambivalent nationalism could also fundamentally alter Orientalism itself. First, Singapore's adoption of modernity/Westernization and capitalism has led to Orientalism as the very means by which it frames and understands Southeast Asia. Moreover its inordinate military, economic and intellectual preponderance in the region places Singapore in a pseudo-imperial position in which its regional interests and power are now tied firmly to the production of knowledge in Southeast Asia. This ability to assume a colonizing view of the region is what Yew labels as 'franchised Orientalism'. Yet in its processes of mimicking its former colonial overlords, Singapore's regional discourse is at once also forced to contend with nationalism, which casts a disjunctive shadow over how and why the region needs to be imagined in certain ways. Hence, the chapter examines two sets of texts, recent mass-marketed political thrillers by Douglas Chua and the literary works of Edwin Thumboo, as a way of elucidating how distorted views of the Southeast Asian other emanate from nationalist anxieties. And as a consequence such forms of franchised Orientalism re-work stereotyped views of Asia by originating both from an adopted Western self as well as from an identity that is fraught more with uncertainty and ambivalence.

If Chapter 5 attempts to rework Orientalism, then Chapter 6 takes Orientalism's apparent inversion, Occidentalism, and repositions it in the light of recent Southeast Asian – particularly Malaysian and Singaporean – literature. Such fiction typically features cross-cultural conflicts attending to the imagined Asian self, and how in turn they give rise to the imagined Western other. What particularly informs this chapter is the contradiction surrounding Asian authors' attempts at communicating Asian-ness vis-à-vis a (Western) literary market with a profound appetite for 'boutique multiculturalism' and the 'postcolonial exotic'. Both of which suggest that Asian authors generally inflate and accentuate the Asian stereotype in order to pander to this new globalized market driven particularly by its desire to consume difference, even if this difference appears to be more culturally 'sensitive'. In Tamara Wagner's examination of writings by Malaysian and Singaporean novelists like Fiona Cheong, Josephine Chia, Catherine Lim and Suchen Christine Lim, this tendency to pander to new literary tastes is not so clear-cut. In her analysis, the author locates such work within an exoticism that occurs at two levels: the authors are not merely 'Asian' women but also members of minority groups within their home countries. As such texts can be seen to be more than just a form of self-exoticization or neo-Orientalism, since in doing so they draw readers' attention to the violence of their 'double victimization'.

Subsequently, the following two chapters rationalize or anticipate and propose scenarios in which Asian otherness should and could be reworked as having vital self-constitutive capabilities. By doing so, the familiar power relations attending to the imagination of the Asian other either by the 'West' or 'Asians' themselves are called into question or suspended in favour of a non-hegemonic, non-subsuming but parallel ways of relating to the multiplicitous and intersecting nature of Asian identities. In Chapter 7, Karina Bolasco contributes to this argument by reconsidering generally Southeast Asian and specifically Filipino consumption of books by Asians and about Asia. This consumption is at once heavily entrenched in past colonialisms, their legacies and their persisting structures: they impose a set of literature they consider canonical, enact an Americanized form of global culture, and continue to exert a powerful hold on how books authored by Asians are published, marketed and distributed. Considering the regional consciousness of Philippine education and the increasing prominence of Asian authors in the global literary market, there should be ways by which one could circumvent or consciously respond to these imperial structures. Bolasco acknowledges such a response in what she sees as 'second period of resistance, or rehabilitation' but then stresses that there is still a considerable amount of uncertainty surrounding it. Indeed, colonial texts have also incited the emergence of nationalist texts, produced by 'native' anti-colonial intellectuals and now by a lot of diasporic Asian writers residing in the West. However, this resistance is also obfuscated by other problems, recalling for instance the 'boutique multiculturalism' mentioned in the previous chapter, but also logistically the problem of translation, as Asian literature will still need to be translated into English before it can be consumed elsewhere in Asia, the presence of American and British publishing houses, and a latent anxiety of the role of women's intellectualism.

If Chapter 7 expresses a yearning for greater and more substantive intercultural contact and transformation within Asia, then Chapter 8 helps to suggest how this could be done. The chapter seeks to establish a space in which the notion of otherness in the Asian context need not necessarily be subsumed within an intractable hierarchical structure in which the construction of alterity simply serves as a way of privileging self over the other. Through his reading of Derrida, Antonio Contreras intimates that 'language' and 'difference' are inseparable. On the one hand, because the dichotomous nature of language provides social meaning to difference, it gives rise to a system in which certain categories come to be privileged over their antinomies. While on the other hand, the 'undecidable', unfixed and unstable aspect of language allows social meaning to be in a constant state of 'deferral', which consequently allows the other or the marginalized to resist and challenge openly established hierarchical structures. Within this ironic structure of 'difference', Contreras introduces the notion of the 'parallel other', which recognizes the existence of the alterity but in a way that refuses to impose a hierarchy or subsume the other into the self. In this way, the case of the Philippines perceiving Thailand as the 'parallel other' provides a useful application of Derrida, emphasizing particularly the means by which institutional, cultural and political similarities between the two provide a system by which different phenomena could in the Philippines be uncovered through the act of establishing a non-hierarchical differentiation with Thailand.

In the final two chapters of the volume, the authors examine different configurations or outcomes of Asian alterity, particularly how otherness could be appreciated when set in communities in scales other than the national self or how the recovery of Asian other may not be as positive as in the previous chapter. Chapter 9's rationale is articulated thus. In this volume, the self-other delineation has in many instances been aligned with national communities. Although the authors in no way claim that alterity in Asia should solely be constituted along national lines, their objects of analysis may have led them to focus on alterity in that manner. What other forms of alterity should be broached? In many parts of Asia, the project of (Westphalian) nationalism oftentimes obscures the more problematic processes of the forced inclusion of ethnic minorities. Examining such communities more closely, one finds broader instances of self-description and assertions, and minority groups do not always share the same ideas of national identity as the dominant ethnic group or the nationalist bourgeoisie, as Partha Chatterjee calls them.[67] In border areas, for instance, members of the same ethnic group residing on both sides may identify with each other more than with their respective sovereign states. What do such communities tell us about alterity in Asia? In this chapter, Ian Baird attempts to shed some light on this by examining the processes of alterity within Cambodia as ethnic Khmers confront their minority 'Others' through the construction of indigeneity. This chapter provides various perspectives. First, it recognizes that the global discourse of indigeneity has now come to be marked by new forms of ethical sensibilities – that the indigenous have the potential of becoming victims and should have unique rights and recognition within various national and international contexts. Second, the notion of the indigenous is much more complex in Asia than in former Western settler colonies, owing to the various national politics and the more eccentric patterns of intra-regional migration. Third, the chapter shows how Cambodia is an example of this complexity, particularly noting that the discourse of indigeneity is a more recent evolution of the dominant Khmer's interaction with the Highland minorities. Thus going back to the thirteenth century, consciousness of the 'Highland Other' was already fairly well developed, and it required the politics of the 1990s such as the internal struggles for power, the techniques of constitutionalism (especially the institutionalizing of land law) and the activities of non-governmental organizations for the Highland Other to be now reclassified as the 'indigenous Other'. What is fascinating in this process then is that through the discourse of indigeneity in Cambodia, the politics of identity is highly mediated, creating new channels for the Khmers to identify its internal Others, while also creating the basis of self-identification among the indigenous.

Both Chapters 7 and 8 present a more positive way in which the Asian other could be deployed within the region, stressing that by creating an environment of mutual learning and relegating neighbouring communities as the 'parallel other' might help redirect inter-Asian relationships. However, the volume concludes with a different and more negative perspective on this question. In this final chapter, as in the penultimate, the emphasis is not so much on identities predicated along the lines of national communities; rather they reflect more on the transnational communities that might be tenuously forged through some 'shared' cultural event, which the author uses here is Asian cinema. Theoretically, what informs the chapter is the idea of global capitalism that both regulates and restricts expressions of postcolonial identities. In this way, attempts by Asians to 'recover' and 'understand' their others are dogged both by an innate desire to do so on socially just terms and the persistent commoditization of that process. In operationalizing the argument, SelvaRaj broaches the topic of the Asian horror cinema, which despite its increasing prolificacy and appeal to inter-Asian audiences has not incited much scholarly attention, while at the same time cannot be seen as a mere extension of a formulation emanating from Hollywood. Through a postcolonial reading of otherness, the Asian horror cinema becomes an ideal venue to witness the double encoding of the spectral other and the Asian other. In an analysis of the successful *Ringu* and the failed *Return to Pontianak*, the author examines how both texts represent a gesture to empathetically recover the Other. However, the films, and by inference Asian cinematic texts, do not allow for a dialogic exchange between the diegetic self and the other. Thus stripped of an opportunity for a sustained synthesis, the postcolonial Asian subject produces the obstacle for reconciliation of his or her other.

Notes

1 *Pirates of the Caribbean: At World's End*, dir. Gore Verbinski (Burbank, CA: Walt Disney Pictures, 2007).
2 Leong Yew, *The Disjunctive Empire of International Relations* (Aldershot and Burlington: Ashgate, 2003), 60–75.
3 Fredric Jameson, *Postmodernism, or, the Cultural Logic of Late Capitalism* (Durham: Duke University Press, 1991).
4 Ziauddin Sardar, *Postmodernism and the Other: The New Imperialism of Western Culture* (London: Pluto Press, 1998).

5 Graham Huggan, *The Postcolonial Exotic: Marketing the Margins* (London and New York: Routledge, 2001).
6 Sardar, 13.
7 See Richard Rorty, *Contingency, Irony, and Solidarity* (Cambridge and New York: Cambridge University Press, 1989).
8 Harry D. Harootunian and Masao Miyoshi, 'Introduction: The "Afterlife" of Area Studies', in *Learning Places: The Afterlives of Area Studies*, ed. Masao Miyoshi and Harry D. Harootunian (Durham: Duke University Press, 2002), 14.
9 Boon Chan, 'Ahoy There Singapore!', *The Straits Times*, 28 March 2007, Life section.
10 Chan.
11 Huggan, 12.
12 Dipesh Chakrabarty, *Provincializing Europe: Postcolonial Thought and Historical Difference* (Princeton: Princeton University Press, 2000).
13 By Spivak's admission this is not an entirely new book. The chapters in the book have previously appeared elsewhere, but they are in this title revised and repositioned to produce a narrative responding to a more contemporary issue.
14 Gayatri Chakravorty Spivak, *Other Asias* (Malden: Blackwell, 2007).
15 I placed scare-quotes around the word, critical, because this is an overused and often abused term in academic discourse. In a generic sense, anything could be 'critical' if it engages a more profound and probing way of thinking about knowledge, thus each of Habermas' three interests, technical, practical, and emancipatory, could be seen as being critical. The particular nuance that is being employed here is in some sense connected with the notions, 'critical consciousness' or 'critical social theory'. Neither of these two is reducible to each other but they mark a current phase of (Western) academic thought, namely how consciousness about the bases of knowledge, the type of truth they sustain, their foundations and the ethical implications of these are open for contestation and reconsideration.
16 See for example Bryan S. Turner, *Marx and the End of Orientalism* (London; Boston: Allen & Unwin, 1978); Abdul Latif Tibawi, *English-Speaking Orientalists: A Critique of Their Approach to Islam and Arab Nationalism* (London: Luzac, 1964); Abdul Latif Tibawi, *Arabic and Islamic Themes: Historical, Educational and Literary Studies* (London: Luzac, 1976); Syed Hussein Alatas, *The Myth of the Lazy Native* (London: Frank Cass, 1977); and Anouar Abdel-Malek, 'Orientalism in Crisis', *Diogènes* 11, no. 44 (1963): 103–40.
17 Edward W. Said, *Orientalism: Western Conceptions of the Orient* (New York: Pantheon, 1978).
18 Mari Yoshihara, *Embracing the East: White Women and American Orientalism* (New York: Oxford University Press, 2003), 6.
19 Christina Klein, *Cold War Orientalism: Asia in the Middlebrow Imagination, 1945–1961* (Berkeley: University of California Press, 2003).
20 Ford Foundation, *1996 Ford Foundation Annual Report* (New York: Ford Foundation, 1996), 93.
21 Ford Foundation, 130.
22 'Project for Critical Asian Studies', Simpson Center for the Humanities, http://depts. washington.edu/critasia/home.html (accessed 26 March 2010).
23 Harootunian and Miyoshi.
24 K.M. Pannikar, *Asia and Western Dominance: A Survey of the Vasco Da Gama Epoch of Asian History 1498–1945* (London: George Allen & Unwin, 1953).
25 Donald K. Emmerson, '"Southeast Asia": What's in a Name?', *Journal of Southeast Asian Studies* 15, no. 1 (1984): 1–21.
26 See also Heather Sutherland, 'Contingent Devices', in *Locating Southeast Asia: Geographies of Knowledge and Politics of Space*, ed. Paul H Kratoska, Remco Raben and Henk Nordholt Schulte (Singapore: Singapore University Press, 2005), 20–59.

27 For example, see Felix Greene, *The Enemy: What Every American Should Know About Imperialism* (New York: Vintage Books, 1971).

28 Editors and Directors, BCAS, 'Introducing Critical Asian Studies', *Critical Asian Studies* 33, no. 1 (2001): 3.

29 Cited in Carlo Bonura and Laurie J. Sears, 'Introduction: Knowledges That Travel in Southeast Asian Studies', in *Knowing Southeast Asian Subjects*, ed. Laurie J. Sears (Seattle: University of Washington Press, 2007), 6–7.

30 Jim George, *Discourses of Global Politics: A Critical (Re)Introduction to International Relations* (Boulder: Lynne Rienner, 1994), 77–8.

31 See Arjun Appadurai, 'Disjuncture and Difference in the Global Cultural Economy', *Public Culture* 2, no. 2 (1990): 1–24.

32 Jameson.

33 Arif Dirlik, *The Postcolonial Aura: Third World Criticism in the Age of Global Capitalism* (Boulder: Westview Press, 1997).

34 Chakrarbarty.

35 All chapters in the volume were written by US-based scholars, with the exception of Ariel Heryanto. His chapter was previously published elsewhere but reproduced here.

36 Arif Dirlik, 'Asia Pacific Studies in an Age of Global Modernity', *Inter-Asia Cultural Studies* 6, no. 2 (2005): 164.

37 Thongchai Winichakul, 'Writing at the Interstices: Southeast Asian Historians and Postnational Histories', in *New Terrains in Southeast Asian History*, ed. Abu Talib Ahmad and Tan Liok Ee (Athens, OH: Ohio University Press; Singapore: Singapore University Press, 2003), 18.

38 Thongchai, 'Writing at the Interstices', 24.

39 Dirlik, 'Asia Pacific Studies', 164–5.

40 Kuan-Hsing Chen and Chua Beng Huat, 'Introduction: The Inter-Asia Cultural Studies: Movements Project', in *Inter-Asia Cultural Studies Reader*, ed. Kuan-Hsing Chen and Chua Beng Huat (London and New York: Routledge, 2007), 1.

41 Kuan-Hsing Chen, 'The Decolonizing Question', in *Trajectories: Inter-Asia Cultural Studies*, ed. Kuan-Hsing Chen (London and New York: Routledge, 1998), 29.

42 Dirlik, 'Asia Pacific Studies', 167.

43 Initially SEASREP was made up of a handful of universities in Indonesia, Philippines, Malaysia and Thailand, but has since gradually sought increased relationships with other parts of Southeast Asia. See Maria Serena I. Diokno, 'Ten Years and More of Seasrep', SEASREP Foundation, http://www.seasrepfoundation.org/about.html (accessed 26 Mach 2010).

44 See Kuan-Hsing Chen, ed., *Trajectories: Inter-Asia Cultural Studies* (London and New York: Routledge, 1998); C. J.W.-L Wee, ed., *Local Cultures and the 'New Asia': The State, Culture, and Capitalism in Southeast Asia* (Singapore: Institute of Southeast Asian Studies, 2002); Abu Talib Ahmad and Tan Liok Ee, ed., *New Terrains in Southeast Asian History* (Athens, OH: Ohio University Press; Singapore: Singapore University Press, 2003); Srilata Ravi, Mario Rutten and Beng-Lan Goh, ed., *Asia in Europe, Europe in Asia* (Leiden: International Institute for Asian Studies; Singapore: Institute of Southeast Asian Studies, 2004); Paul H. Kratoska, Remco Raben and Henk Nordholt Schulte, ed., *Locating Southeast Asia: Geographies of Knowledge and Politics of Space* (Singapore: Singapore University Press; Athens, OH: Ohio University Press, 2005); Kuan-Hsing Chen and Chua Beng Huat, ed., *Inter-Asia Cultural Studies Reader* (London and New York: Routledge, 2007); Laurie J. Sears, ed., *Knowing Southeast Asian Subjects* (Seattle: University of Washington Press, 2007); Wang Hui, 'The Politics of Imagining Asia: A Genealogical Analysis', trans. Matthew A. Hale, *Inter-Asia Cultural Studies* 8, no. 1 (2007): 1–33.

45 Allen Chun and A.B. Shamsul, 'Other "Routes": The Critical Challenge for Asian Academia', *Inter-Asia Cultural Studies* 2, no. 2 (2001): 167–76.

46 Chun and Shamsul, 168.

47 Sun Ge, 'Globalization and Cultural Difference: Thoughts on the Situation of Trans-Cultural Knowledge', trans. Allen Chun, *Inter-Asia Cultural Studies* 2, no. 2 (2001): 266.
48 Stefan Tanaka, *Japan's Orient: Rendering Pasts Into History* (Berkeley: University of California Press, 1993).
49 See Sun Ge's two articles in 'How Does Asia Mean? (Part I)', trans. Hui Shiu-Lun and Lau Kinchi, *Inter-Asia Cultural Studies* 1, no. 1 (2000): 13–47; and 'How Does Asia Mean? (Part II)', trans. Hui Shiu-Lun and Lau Kinchi, *Inter-Asia Cultural Studies* 1, no. 2 (2000): 319–41. As an imperial power in its own right, China's interests in Southeast Asia did necessitate the production of knowledge of the region that has not been sufficiently recounted, and cannot be seen as occupying the same set of dynamics as Western imperial-inspired knowledge. Wang Gungwu, for instance, gives a brief account of this in 'Two Perspectives of Southeast Asian Studies: Singapore and China', in *Locating Southeast Asia: Geographies of Knowledge and Politics of Space*, ed. Paul H. Kratoska, Remco Raben and Henk Nordholt Schulte (Singapore: Singapore University Press; Athens, OH: Ohio University Press, 2005), 60–81.
50 Thongchai Winichakul, *Siam Mapped: A History of the Geo-Body of a Nation* (Honolulu: University of Hawaii Press, 1994).
51 Thongchai, 'Writing at the Interstices'; Thongchai, *Siam Mapped*.
52 Dilip Parameshwar Gaonkar, 'On Alternative Modernities', in *Alternative Modernities*, ed. Dilip Parameshwar Gaonkar (Durham, NC: Duke University Press, 2001), 1.
53 Gaonkar, 15.
54 S.N. Eisenstadt, 'Multiple Modernities', *Daedalus* 129, no. 1 (2000): 1–28.
55 William S.W. Lim, *Asian Alterity: With Special Reference to Architecture and Urbanism through the Lens of Cultural Studies* (Singapore: World Scientific: 2008), 56–62.
56 Dirlik, *The Postcolonial Aura*, 68–9.
57 Rob Shields, 'Meeting Or Mis-Meeting? The Dialogical Challenge to Verstehen', *British Journal of Sociology* 47, no. 2 (1996): 277.
58 Shields, 281.
59 Edward W. Said, 'Representing the Colonized: Anthropology's Interlocutors', *Critical Inquiry* 15, no. 2 (1989): 205–6.
60 I have used the term 'disjuncture' in numerous places in this chapter. While it immediately brings to mind the term used in Arjun Appadurai's much referenced essay, I have in mind the formulation I adopted in *The Disjunctive Empire of International Relations*. Here I make a distinction between 'delineated' and 'disjunctive' approaches, both of which traverse the modern, Western and also postcolonial subject's worldviews, and they are cohabitative states of mind. 'Delineations' function on the basis of boundaries and logocentricity, and they form the basis of reason and logic. 'Disjunctures' are messier as they represent the various psychical inabilities to fully live out Modernity's expectations of the rational and sovereign subject. To think in terms of disjuncture is thus not only to herald the impossibility of Modernity but also to invite critiques of the dominant paradigms and subjectivities to be constituted by fragments and hybridity, rather than certainty and coherence [Yew, 17–20].
61 Yew, 60–75.
62 In a presentation on Asian modernity, Dipesh Chakrabarty reminds one of his conception of the '"not yet" version of history' ['"Asia" and the Twentieth Century: What is "Asian Modernity"?', in *We Asians: Between Past and Future: A Millennium Regional Conference*, ed. Kwok Kian-Woon, Indira Arumugam, Karen Chia and Lee Chee Keng (Singapore: Singapore Heritage Society, 2000), 23] in which inheritors of the colonial tradition (namely postcolonial subjects) are victims of deferral; that the history of the progress of the postcolonial subject is made to match the teleology of Western history. So at any given moment, regardless of the 'progress' made, the postcolonial subject will always remain structured into a phase that lags behind that of the West.

63 Frantz Fanon, *Black Skin, White Masks*, trans. Charles Lam Markmann (New York: Grove Weidenfeld, 1967), 68.
64 Ashis Nandy, *The Intimate Enemy: Loss and Recovery of Self Under Colonialism* (Delhi: Oxford University Press, 1983), 92–3.
65 Fanon, 76.
66 Chen, 'The Decolonizing Question', 29.
67 Partha Chatterjee, *Nationalist Thought in the Colonial World: A Derivative Discourse?* (Minneapolis: University of Minnesota Press, 1986).

2 The transformation of Asian regionalism and the construction of anticommunist identity

The discourse of 'Asia' in early Cold War South Korea

Kim Ye-rim

How was Asia[1] imagined in South Korea and Japan during the Cold War and what were the actual conditions and ideological frameworks by which this imagination was constituted? I pose this question about the past while thinking about the present South Korean society that is conjuring forth Asia as an economic, political and cultural unit more enthusiastically than ever before. The development of the entertainment industry including film, drama and popular music, and the opening of the labour market have popularized and generalized the imagining of the Asian region. Through such developments, the average Korean can imagine 'Asia' as a geopolitical, cultural or ideological unit, although their nationalistic perspective remains strong. Generally speaking, when South Korean society refers to Asia as one regional unit, a kind of collective psychology is at work. This collective psychology is deeply rooted in the national obsession with 'victory' over other nations in the region, resulting from Korea's historical experience of the 1910–45 colonization by Japan and delayed modernization. For a long time, that colonization has meant the frustration of the nation itself, and such self-awareness has intensified not only the desire for the rebirth of nation but also the competitive spirit with others in Asia.

Of course, we can pay attention to reflective discourse on Asia, which tries to approach past and present relations between Asian countries to create a fundamentally future-oriented blueprint for peaceful coexistence based on mutual understanding. Some critical theorists and scholars in East Asia have introduced the term 'post-Asia'[2] to indicate an alternative conception of 'Asia' than the one that stems from Japanese Imperialism and the Cold War order. 'Asia' is currently an important topic of debate in Korean intellectual discourse. Serious critical analyses can reveal the superficiality of government-inspired 'Asianism' rooted in the demands of the free market or national development. Such analyses also have the potential to suggest alternative approaches to Asian regionalism.[3] However, the image of a post-Cold War Asia called post-East Asia[4] is not so clear or distinct. Although both actual activities in support of the Asian economic bloc and diverse cultural exchanges are increasing in globalized Asia, contemporary conflicts and the dark shadow of past colonization of the Cold War remain unresolved.

We have entered a stage in which critical reflection and analyses of Asian regionalism are urgently needed. To this effect, it is very important to trace the historical formation and transformation of Korean perceptions of Asian regionalism. Because it is only when we reveal the ideological basis and desire concealed within the regionalist imaginary–geography that a new map of regional imagination could be made. What imaginary–geography was constructed between the colonial period and the period of globalization in the history of modern South Korea's reinvention of 'Asia'? Focusing on the case of South Korea, this article analyses the context in which 'Asia' was imagined in the Cold War period. The main object of this analysis is the ideological situation; the structure of political–cultural imagination in South Korea in the decade immediately following liberation in 1945. In 1945, Korea was liberated from Japan. A government was established three years later. The Korean War began in 1950, followed by an armistice in 1953. This chapter mainly deals with the South Korean situation in comparison with that of Japan. This is because South Korea and Japan are closely related in terms of their subsumption under US influence, even if their actual political positions and values in US Asian policy were very different.

To discuss how 'Asia' was imagined in South Korea and Japan during the Cold War also requires one to trace the structure of self-identification of these two countries that were incorporated into the US-led anticommunist bloc. After the collapse of the colonial world order and during the ascendance of Cold War hegemony, South Korea and Japan entered the phase of nation-(re)building. In this process, what happened in the field of regional imagination? What was the inter-relationship between regional and national imagination? So far, South Korean scholars have primarily dealt with this issue by reducing it to a question of the Rhee Syng-man regime's diplomatic policy.[5] With regard to the imaginary geography of 'Asia', the focus has just been on the 'Asia' discourse of the colonial period. Alternatively, I think that the scope of discussion on the discourse of Asia needs to be expanded in two ways.

First, it must be noted that the 'Asia' discourse cannot be explained sufficiently through one political leader's acts. A large amount of material from this period shows that the 'Asia' discourse was widely shared and supported by the power elites and intellectuals, including scholars and journalists. Thus, the structure of the imaginations of those who were allowed to possess information, knowledge, and perspective on the nation, region and the world should be examined in a more complex manner. It is neither proper nor sufficient to reduce the question of 'Asia' to a narrow meaning of politics – as a mere technique of diplomacy. From this point of view, I regard South Korea's 'Asia' discourse of this period as an ideological layer of the Cold War system.

Second, we have to reconsider the scope of the research. Because contemporary South Korean scholars have mainly paid attention to the Asianism of the colonial period,[6] the Asian regionalism that emerged after Korea's liberation from Japan has not been discussed. As a result, no one seems to have questioned how this Asianism, based on a previous colonial/imperialist mapping, was transformed and reconstructed in a different historical phase. Japanese Imperialism played an important role in South Korea's mapping of Asia before 1945. However, after 1945, it was within a postcolonial Cold War system that a new Asian regionalism was formed. To trace the historical continuity or discontinuity in the field of regional imagination, we must closely evaluate the 'Asia' discourse of the Cold War period as a historical product.

This chapter examines the collective psychology of South Korean intellectuals of the Cold War period. It is possible to approach the structure of Asian regionalism and self-identification by (re)reading official policies, government slogans and articles written by intellectuals. Examining these articles together, one is able to recognize that not only policymakers but also intellectuals tried to promote a form of 'Asian' regionalism during this period. South Korean intellectuals expressed a great deal of interest in the political situation of the countries in Northeast and Southeast Asia. Many articles, reports and comments on current issues in these regions were published in various newspapers and magazines at the time. It is notable that there was no large gap between the opinions of intellectuals, such as writers, educators and scholars, and that of the power elite, especially on the task of 'building an anticommunist Asia'. There is no 'conflict' but only 'amplification'. Anticommunist homogenization of the 'Asia' discourse implies that proponents of regionalism had internalized the logic of the Cold War.

The main texts examined in this research are the monthly magazines *Sincheonji* (New world) and *Sasanggye* (Circle of thought). The former was published from 1946 to 1954 and the latter from 1953 to 1970. *Sincheonji* is a prominent publication with which we can picture the scene of ideological confusion between left and right-wing factions and their psychological complexity with regard to the US in the period of nation-building. In addition, *Sasanggye* is very significant because it records South Korea's move towards a pro-US stance and the sweeping transformations on all fronts after the Korean War. With an analysis of these two publications, which show the ideological position of intellectuals after the liberation of South Korea, we can grasp the mechanism of anticommunist regionalism as well as the process of nation-building in the Cold War order. Beside these magazines, other magazines and newspapers are surveyed and used as supplementary references.

Imagining 'Asia': 1945–50

The technology of dis/covering Asia

After the end of the Second World War, Japan and South Korea adopted different conceptions and constructions of Asia. Ideologically, post-war Japan adopted a different approach toward Asian regionalism, and the internalization of the Cold War ideology played a major role in its self-identification. The kernel of these topics can be summarized as follows: how did Japan 'forget' Asia or Asian regionalism after its defeat in 1945? During the Age of Imperialism, Japan acted as an 'Asian hero' that would realize the cultural and political 'co-prosperity' of Asia by defeating the West. But after its own defeat, Japan had to abandon its dreams of empire as soon as possible and reposition itself as a singular and self-contained nation state. This was the only precondition for Japan's re-entry into post-war international society. Japan's situation at that time was to embrace the technology of 'forgetting'. Critical Japanese scholars analysed the mechanism of 'forgetting' and the technology of 'self-effacement' of post-war Japan in various ways. For example, Oguma Eiji's *Minshu to Aikoku* (Democracy and patriotism), Michiba Chikanobu's *Senryo to Heiwa* (Occupation and peace), Marukawa Tetsushi's *Regionalism* (sic.) and *Reisenbunkaron* (The Cold War culture theory), Sato Takumi's 'Sengo Seron no Seiritsu' (The establishment of postwar public opinion), and Ogusi Junji's 'Sengo no Daishu Bunka' (The popular culture of postwar Japan) all concentrate on the problem of 'forgetting' and 'self-effacement'.[7] They discuss Japan's fabrication of memory after the defeat. To analyse this they critically approach the binary recognition system such as pre-war/post-war, the theory of a homogeneous nation-state, nationalistic aspects of the ideology of moral culture, the 'Japan culture theory', and the structure of 'nostalgia' as a consummate form of memory/forgetting.

However, because South Korea's political and ideological context was different, the method of questioning needs to be changed as follows: After liberation, how or why did South Korea 'remember' Asia? I have two aims in changing the mode of questioning in the case of South Korea. First, I intend to explore the complicated field of international forces of the Cold War period in which South Korea re-discovered Asia. Furthermore, I will inquire whether something like introspection or ethics existed in South Korea's Asian regionalism in this period. If Japan's strategy of memory erasure meant 'forgetting' Asia, then Korea's strategy of discovery would conversely imply 'remembering' Asia.

It is the differing relationships with the US that led South Korea and Japan to adopt different attitudes toward Asia. Compared with a US-occupied – and hence protected – Japan, South Korea lay beyond US international interest. Therefore, South Korea had to determine its course of action not only 'between' Japan and the US but also 'outside' of them. The fact that South Korea was located in so obviously an uneven and insecure position within the triangle of international forces dispersed its gaze. This was the reason why South Korea had to imagine 'Asia', although it was also tightly bound to US influence. In the 1960s – the age of economic development in South Korea – the Southeast Asian region, in particular, became more important as a foreign market. This meant that at this time, the frame of Asian regionalism was changed from a political and ideological one to an economic and practical one. Needless to say, South Korea's desire, fear and national interest were constructed and intensified in the Cold War system through the formation of a Southeast Asian market.

From solidarity to division: transformation of the Pacific fantasy

Immediately following the liberation in 1945, South Korean intellectuals expressed passionate feelings of solidarity towards newly independent nations as well as nations struggling for liberation. Poet Park In-hwan highly admired Indonesia as a hero 'fighting against imperialism',[8] and emphasized the fact that Indonesia was 'a colony like us'.[9] In addition he wrote a poem celebrating the struggle in Vietnam as follows:

The nation of Angkor Wat
People's arm
The sound of firearms for resistance
all of you falling asleep in Asia,
listen to this sound
If you open your eyes
the fragrance of the south
soak into our mind.[10]

Works that share Park In-hwan's perspective on Asia are rare but they deserve attention because South Korea's imagination of Asia is vividly embodied in literature. We can find many materials showing that intellectuals in South Korea had a deep interest in newly liberated nations in the Asian region and regarded them as companions with whom to build a new world.

In this way, other postcolonial nations were imagined as partners who shared the historical trauma of colonization. Their past struggles and present victories were extolled enthusiastically. With the end of the age of Japanese imperialism, many intellectuals in South Korea began to construct a new symbolic map based on morality of nation. On this map of Asia, Japan, often represented as 'a nest of snakes',[11] was located far away from South Korea while China and other nations in the Southeast Asian region, agencies of anticolonial struggle, were located very closely. Therefore, how can we evaluate South Korea's self-imagination and that of the Asian region in this period?

While Korea (Chosun) was a colony of Japan, it passionately advocated an Asian community in the name of 'the Greater East Asia'. Of course, this idea was an imitation and repetition of Japan's. In particular, at the end of 1930s the Chosun intellectuals generally accepted Japan's 'Greater East Asia Co-Prosperity Sphere' project with loud acclamation. Both the left and right believed in the fantasy of 'one Asia' and the final victory of the Eastern world over the West. Chosun intellectuals made various assertions supporting Japan's Asia project and, for them, the 'Greater East Asia Co-Prosperity Sphere' was not just a political project but also a cultural and ideological one. At that time, Chosun intellectuals, following the imperial ideology, thought that Japan would win the 'final world war', namely, a war between Japan and the US. There was strong faith that Western civilization would collapse and the East could initiate a new age of history. It is interesting to note that the left-wing could not free itself from the fantasy of the end of capitalism and coming of great changes in world history. Their anti-capitalist views made them accept the empire's project.[12]

However, as soon as Japanese imperialism collapsed, the imitated fantasy of 'Greater Asia' propagated by Chosun intellectuals disappeared. But in order to understand the situation of South Korea after this failure, we need to pay attention to the fact that South Korea completely forgot its own support for Japan's

Asia plan. South Korea's new post-colonial imagination of Asia evolved based on the complete omission of colonial Asianism. I think of this as a form of collective and voluntary omission. The South Korean intellectuals then began to re-imagine the map of Asia under these new circumstances and as if no prior forms of Asian regional consciousness existed in Korea.

From 1948–9 developments in China, notably its emergence as a communist state, brought about a decisive change in South Korea's map of Asia. Solidarity with the small and weak peoples resisting imperialism became more complicated and less firm with the emergence of 'red' China. The issue was with whom South Korea should forge an alliance. The Chinese Revolution, the transformation of the US–Asia policy and the revival of Japan all intensified this dilemma. As the Cold War progressed, South Korea's anxiety intensified, which finally led to the discovery of 'the Pacific', the name of a new Asian solidarity based on strong anticommunism.

Of course this was not first time South Korea discovered 'the Pacific' as a unified imaginary-geography. Let us briefly examine the prehistory of this discovery. Chosun intellectuals wrote songs celebrating the occupation of Singapore by Japan in 1942. One went like this:

> Wake up, billions of people in Asia . . .
> Let's sing a song together, you, people on hundreds and thousands of the
>   islands on the Pacific
> The young man in the desert and the daughter of the equator, too
> At the place where the bomb of justice explodes
> The sun of a new world will rise.[13]

Such was the intellectuals' support for and agreement with Japan's idea of the 'Greater Asia'. To them, Japan's occupation of Southeast Asia meant the liberation from Western imperialism and the building of one Pacific region. This is the reason why the Pacific fantasy was so widely accepted. The quoted song, entitled 'Victory of the Pacific', is just one example among various works showing Chosun's passionate support for Japan's imperialistic expansion in the South, with the Pacific being an oceanic metaphor for an aggressive perspective toward this region.[14]

However, Chosun's Pacific fantasy, which was constructed in the late 1930s, re-emerged within the Cold War world-system. We can examine the symbolic meaning of the Pacific at this time through publications such as *Taepyeongyang* (The Pacific, 1946), *Sintaepyeongyang* (The new Pacific, 1947) and *Amiriga* (America, 1947). With clear titles and images related to the Pacific, these materials tell us at least two things. First, the Pacific was a geographical metaphor for a bright new age. Second, it was an imaginary–geography of political solidarity, which could never be imagined without the US. But in this phase, the Pacific has a somewhat vague and loose meaning as a symbol of peace or a region where Koreans have lived for a long time. But the political imagination concerning the Pacific began to strengthen increasingly.

Figure 2.1 Korean Sub-imperialism in Southeast Asia
Note: In this image, a giant-sized Korean is shown visiting an unspecified location in Southeast Asia.
        Although it depicts some amount of cordiality, the discrepancy in height could culturally be read
        as a subtle assertion of Korean dominance hidden behind overt gestures of friendship.
Source: *Silhwa* (Nonfiction), 1939.

As the Pacific fantasy strengthened and became more clearly defined, South
Korea's attitude towards its regional neighbours also changed. The solidified Pacific
fantasy now followed the US position fundamentally and absolutely. South Korea
stopped expressing amity toward the countries of Southeast Asia because they were

Figure 2.2 America and the Pacific fantasy in Korean publications
Note: The magazines *Amiriga* (America, 1946) and *Taepyeongyang* (The Pacific, 1946) show the
    Korea–America relationship and South Korea's Pacific fantasy.

exposed to the danger of communism. It also reinforced South Korea's wariness of
Japan, demanding that the US guarantee its security. The key point of the Pacific
fantasy was to establish anticommunist association in Asia. The proponents of the
Pacific project regarded Asia as an economic, cultural and political inferior that
was susceptible to the 'communist virus'. But at the same time they considered
some Asian countries as strong agencies that could resolve the problems and contradictions of Asia itself, resulting from its inferiority, and eventually attain peace
in the region. It was perfect unity among anticommunist nations in Asia that was
needed for this difficult task.

In 1949 the Pacific Pact was proposed by Rhee Syng-man (South Korea), Quirino
(Philippines) and Chiang Kai-shek (Taiwan). Of course, Korean intellectuals also
expressed their approval. The slogan of the Pacific Pact can be summed up as 'building Asia by Asian people'.[15] There were two intentions behind this slogan. On the
one hand, they would aid the independence struggle against European imperialism
in Southeast Asia, and on the other hand, they would protect the region from the
communist threat. These intentions also underscored a particular Pacific fantasy,
namely the idea that the nations that experienced 'true liberation and freedom
with the help of the American occupying forces' should rescue/surveil Southeast
Asian countries, which were suffering from not only the exposure to 'red' China
but also the struggle against the 'ambition of Western imperialism'.[16] In spite of
these visions, the Pacific Pact could not be realized because the US had already
selected Japan as a partner and did not need to promote an alternative plan with
these nations.[17] Although the Pacific Pact did not materialize, the anticommunist
Asian alliance model has exerted continuous influence on the self-identification
of South Korea since then.

Imagining Asia after the Korean War (1950)

The international Cold War map and the location of South Korea

It has been a general phenomenon since 1945 for intellectuals in South Korea to consider the history of Asia as a 'terrible history of self loss'[18] mixed with serious confusion, contradiction and inferiority. South Korea has always defined itself as 'Asian' while Japan has used the dual frame of Asian/non-Asian.[19] To South Korea, being 'Asian' meant political, cultural and economic inferiority. But Japan was able to circumvent this problem by perceiving itself as both Asian and non-Asian, according to the historical phase and also depending on its desire. In addition, as the logic of the 'Greater East Asia Co-Prosperity Sphere' shows, Japan even changed the meaning and value of 'the Asian'. South Korea, however, did not utilize such flexible identity-politics. It has always conceived itself as a part of Asia or the Asian, which had rigidly been defined as backward.

In 1945, the direction of US policy toward Japan shifted from 'democratization' to 'reconstruction', and Japan focused steadily on national development. But under the US military administration, South Koreans saw themselves as being colonized once again. Many intellectuals shared this kind of consciousness and directly criticized the policy of the US military administration authorities. In addition, various opinions concerning problems such as the destruction of colonial remnants, the arousal of patriotism, and cultural reconstruction were initiated. Popular morality of the period reproached those who adhered to 'American culture', saying 'stupid intellectuals who only drank coffee or milk couldn't undertake the task of nation-building'.[20] Around 1950, policies to promote 'national morals', which affected the everyday lives of ordinary people, began to be established. Nation-building policies and nationalistic discipline were gradually expanded and intensified throughout the 1950s as part of the need/desire for 'national reconstruction'.

What kind of transformation occurred in the structure of South Korean self-identification after the Korean War? Starting with this war, South Korean intellectuals located the imaginary position of their country at the centre of the Cold War map. Similar to Rhee Syng-man, they were discontented with the fact that they could not defeat the 'red enemy' because of the US-led truce with North Korea. Of course, they were full of pride derived from the experience of their 'heroic' struggle against the communist force. A belligerent hostility to communism and a dogmatic self-conceit overlapped each other. In such a spiritual, psychological atmosphere, South Korea donned a more active and aggressive self-image in this period. First of all, the war experience stimulated this change. South Korean intellectuals regarded their home country as both a symbol of justice and a scapegoat in the Cold War system.

With this type of consciousness, most intellectuals began to conjure with international relations, historical tasks and even the significance or value of their country in the Cold War order. With a delusive self-image and worldview, many intellectuals began to take up universalistic concepts such as 'world-building', 'the problems of the world', 'rescue of all mankind' and 'world peace'. These were actually very familiar and essential ideological-terms to South Korean anticommunist intellectuals in the 1950s. Grand concepts like 'world history' or 'humankind' appeared most frequently in discussions that dealt with the significance of the Korean War. In such an exaggerated frame, the ideologues of South Korea remarked passionately on the responsibility and mission that had been newly imposed upon them after the anticommunist war. It is not difficult to find sentiments such as, 'the reality of South Korea, which is the spearhead of the world, is the reality of the world'[21] or 'particularly, the Korean War gave us the opportunity to be a subject who should create world history. We became an active agency in reforming the world, whether we wanted to or not'.[22] Assertions like the one below further show the typical logic of the mentality:

> We were compelled to make sacrifices not only in our lives but also with regard to our national fortune. This is a fatal sacrifice, which resulted in total abandonment, destruction and loss. The U.S. is trying hard to win the war. But our sacrifice is not just a serious one; it is an infinite, endless one. The war that occurred in this country belongs to both of us. But at the same time, it is a war of the whole chaotic world that all humankind is undertaking together. South Korea was selected as a place of resolution for the problems of the world. We became the spearhead of world peace.[23]

They emphasized that South Korea held the key to peace in the new world. The political plan concerning the Pacific vigorously evolved in the name of world peace, pretending to carry universalistic or humanistic value. The assertion that 'the pivot of history has distinctly moved into the Pacific region since the Korean War occurred in 1950'[24] gained favour and was linked to the recognition that only when the Asian region was safe would the West be safe, too. Needless to say, Asia or the Pacific map in the 1950s documented the anxiety about potential enemies, namely, industrialized Japan, or politically ambiguous neutral states. In 1954, the Pacific project was revived and as a result the Asian People's Anti-Communist League (APACL) was organized. Its motto was that anticommunist Asian nations would unite and overcome Asian backwardness. Of course, the so-called solidarity of Asia also maintained that as long as 'Red countries' existed in Asia, 'the disruption of Asia is inevitable'.[25]

'The East' and its cultural–historical identity

It can be said that it was after the Korean War that the Asia which was initially imagined as a political unit began to be re-characterized in cultural terms. With the emergence of the political map of Asia in 1953, interest in the history and culture of 'the East' also intensified. As the cultural historical rewriting and redefining of this region evolved in intellectual discourse, the terms 'the East' or 'the Eastern society' became circumscribed, referring only to the East Asian region. Of course, backwardness and inferiority in all aspects continued to be regarded as the main characteristics of the East. Many intellectuals in South Korea pointed out as follows: first, Eastern society has not been a prominent power because of the invasion of

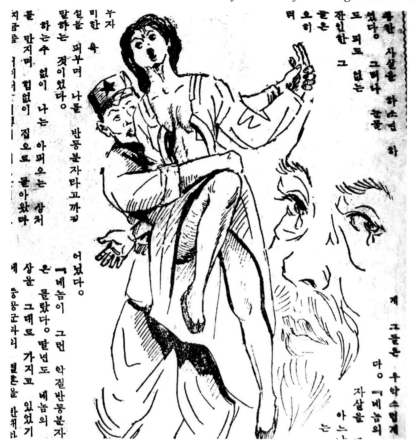

Figure 2.3 Popular yellow anti-communism
Notes: This illustration depicts a Korean woman being assaulted by a communist Chinese
       soldier.
Source: *Ibuk Silhwa* (The nonfiction of North Korea), 1956.

foreign powers; second, Eastern society has been marked by feudalistic stagnation; and third, in the process of accumulating tragic experiences, Eastern people
have internalized a defeatist historical view. For example, the economic critic Pae
Seong-lyong described the inadequacy of Eastern political thought as follows:

> In western political thought, modern philosophy is considered more seriously
> than ancient philosophy. But in the East, ancient philosophy is thought to
> be more important. This is the reason that the Eastern world could not cast
> off stagnation for several thousand years . . .. Today, although Eastern socie-
> ties are carrying out democracy, they cannot accomplish the advancement to
> a new political phase. Although China, Korea and Japan are different from
> one another, none of them can escape from the evil essential to the Eastern
> society.[26]

The premise of not only the Asia discourse but also the discourse of 'the East' was economic stagnation and cultural regression. And South Korea was regarded as a typical Eastern nation that embodied both of these characteristics. Kim Deok-lyong inquired about the backwardness of South Korea as follows: 'In terms of the vicious cycle of Asia, China is more representative than other nations, but it is what has made all of Eastern societies stagnant for a long time . . .. What is the reason why we cannot achieve a modern scientific civilization like that of the West and that we cannot catch up with the stream of the world?'[27]

On the surface, the discussion of 'the East' takes the form of historical science and deals with historical facts or information. But we must pay close attention to its hidden desires. It was not until 1958 that papers on the ancient cultures of South Korea, China and Japan were edited in the form of a scholarly journal titled *Asia Yeongu* (Asian studies). And the first Oriental studies symposium was held in 1962. These facts show that Asia or 'the East' was not a scientific object of study until at least 1960. It is difficult to detect a scientific or academic discourse of 'the East' in the early 1950s. What was the intention of those who emphasized the significance of Asian studies, appearing in the form of historical science during that time? And how were these views articulated with the Cold War ideology? When we analyse the deep structural relationship between the discourse of 'the East' and the Cold War ideology, the politics of the imaginary geography of Asia is revealed.

Let me examine the context in which South Korean intellectuals discussed 'the East'. It is important to consider the possibility that the rise of Asian studies in the US influenced South Korea's own construction of the discourse of 'the East'. Since the Second World War, Asian studies began to flourish with the boom in Area Studies in the US.[28] Indeed the scope of Area Studies in the US was very broad because of the wide-ranging and global scope of the US Cold War system. While observing that Sinology is booming in academic circles across the world, one proponent of the discourse of 'the East' provided the reason why Asian studies had to be developed in South Korea. According to him, in order to understand the origin and national character of South Korea, it is indispensable to know China, which had a significant influence on South Korea for a long time. Ultimately, the intention of 'the East' discourse was to inquire about 'the present', not 'the past': 'I attempt to get acquainted with Eastern culture in order to find out the dominant tendency of the real state of affairs of South Korea. I think that both the lowliness of the nation and its social confusion are derived from the process of the development of Eastern culture'.[29]

The proponents of 'the East' discourse generally believed that China was mainly responsible for Asia's backwardness because China's feudal system dominated Asian society for a long time so development was delayed. At the same time, Japan was pointed out as the 'evil' that destroyed the history of Asia by colonizing and exploiting it. According to this discourse, China damaged Asia in the past while Japan harmed modern Asia. It was generally considered that Japan disgraced the 'history of the East' because 'it did not possess awareness of itself as an Eastern nation'.[30] The participants in 'the East' discussion insist that now the Asian world must escape from the chain of decline and attenuation repeatedly imposed by China and Japan. In the words of Pae Seong-lyong, the most problematic essence of Eastern thought was its 'fatalistic view of history'. He added that this 'unproductive and uncreative' outlook 'denied the advancement of history and development of culture'.[31]

'The East' discourse constructed in the early 1950s was fundamentally influenced by the powerful ideology of the Cold War. Its main intent and underlying assumptions can be summarized as follows: First, to inspect the common origin of the confusion and contradictions of present Asia; second, to reveal the deleterious influence of ancient Chinese culture; third, to judge the 'treason' of imperial Japan; fourth, to analyse the problems of South Korea itself by examining its unfavourable historical circumstance; and fifth, to liquidate the entangled past and launch the rebirth of Asian history. This desire to make a new Asian blueprint cannot be separated from anticommunism. Particularly, in the criticism of China, China's underdevelopment and communism became linked with each other. Most anticommunist intellectuals in South Korea believed that only when their society escaped from spiritual and material poverty would it be safe from the danger of communism or the communist 'virus', which was seen as the 'common enemy of Asia'.[32] This was the primary reason why anticommunist ideologues persisted so vigorously in claiming that not only South Korea but also Asia required the will to rebuild. As a result, the proponents of 'the East' discourse of the early 1950s had a dual motivation. First, they intended to establish the origin of Asian inferiority on the level of culture. In addition, they planned to promote the anticommunist rebirth of Asia, clarifying the selective exclusion/inclusion of particular nations. In this way, the Cold War ideology grew stronger by borrowing the cultural account of the imaginary geography of 'Asia' or 'the East'.

Conclusion

This chapter attempted to analyze South Korea's regional imagination in the Cold War era focusing on the period from 1945 to 1955. In Japan, there were conflicting opinions between the left- and the right-wing surrounding the peace treaty with other Asian countries. I did not sufficiently examine the clashes within Japanese intellectual circles, and this problem is very important in understanding their perception of US and Asia. After 1945, Japan acknowledged its defeat and criticized itself for its 'lack of morality', obeying the stronger power symbolized by MacArthur.[33] Analysing the various opinions concerning the problem of Japan's security and peace negotiation, Oguma Eiji pointed out that the proponents of the overall peace agreement expressed an interest in the Asian region. However, according to Oguma, they were anxious only about the economic damage which the severance of diplomatic relations with China would bring about.[34] Through the process of post-war reparations started in 1951, Japan could utilize the Southeast Asian region as a very useful market with the help of the US. We need to pay heed to the criticism that the reparations were actually a form of 'trade' by which Japan was able to benefit from the Cold War system.[35] In this process, Asia as the space in which the responsibility for colonization and war could be seriously assumed and reflected disappeared, and only the market or Asia as market remained.

However, South Korea could not help imagine Asia for its own self-protection in the Cold War system. During the period between liberation and the Korean War Armistice Agreement, South Korea shifted its position from the periphery to the centre of the Cold War map. In this process, particularly after the Korean War, it began to delude itself with the self-image of an 'international-nation', believing that South Korea was a symbolic kernel of the Cold War world. This compound term, 'international-nation', was proposed in the discussion on nationalism and cosmo-politanism. The proponent, Oh Jong-sik, suggested the 'international-nation' as a desirable contemporary model of the nation. The 'international-nation' refers to a nation that 'is neither confined to a particular nation-state nor dissolved into an abstract world-nation'.[36] Of course, he willingly accepted that the 'international-nation' took the form of the nation-state. His main idea was that South Korea had to change itself into an 'international-nation' to obtain peace and prosperity in international society.

Most anticommunist ideologues thought that the nation needed a region to which it could belong so as not to wander beyond bloc boundaries within the Cold War system. This is the reason behind South Korea's construction of the imaginary regional geography of 'Asia'. The 'international-nation' model shows South Korea's aware-ness of both Asia and itself in the Cold War period. In addition, it is notable that the criticism of cosmopolitanism also evolved at this time. While the significance of nationalism and internationalism were strongly emphasized, cosmopolitanism was regarded as a 'dangerous' ideology because it was thought to obscure and destabilize both the national and ideological boundary.

In the 1960s, developmentalist nationalism began to strengthen in South Korea. Developmentalist nationalism was based on the belief that the long standing anti-communism and the realistic need for development adhere closely to each other. As mentioned above, cosmopolitanism was criticized as dangerous. In the 1960s, this assertion was so intense that any imaginary–geography beyond the 'nation-alistic' scope lost its importance. National development evolved like a total war whereby all the collective value was concentrated on economic revival. Similar to the situation of the 1950s, intellectuals in the 1960s thought that cosmopolitanism was a useless ideological fabrication. They asserted that national development would be the only way to defend the nation in a stark and divisive international society. They thought that international society was harsh, so if the nation did not obtain competitiveness it would not be able to avoid self-destruction. Therefore they could not help acknowledging the significance of Japan's economic realism: while playing within the rules of the Cold War, Japan was able to create opportunities for economic development.

How and why was cosmopolitanism rejected in South Korea in the 1960s? And how and why was developmentalist nationalism internalized so deeply? The follow-ing comment helps us understand this situation: 'It is very strange. After the Second World War, all the nations in the world are passionately supporting cosmopolitan-ism beyond the nation, but, in fact, they do not give up their own nation. This is a contradiction . . .. We must recognize that all the nations which assert cosmopolit-anism actually have their root in their nation, never in other nations'.[37] Economic development or industrialization was the absolute and decisive task in which the desire of intellectuals in the Cold War period was carved. They could not consider national interest without awareness of the Cold War and vice versa. The following assertion represents the collective consciousness of the 1960s: 'It is true that the increasing population and enormous national defence expenditure for preparation against communist aggression obstruct economical development. But we have to strive for industrialization even though it is hard'.[38] In this way, developmentalist nationalism became deeply internalized and even the regionalist perspective in the style of the 1950s paled in comparison. But paradoxically, in this process South Korea discovered Southeast Asia as a market, as Japan had already done. In the 1960s, South Korea entered the Vietnam War and earned large economic profits. Like Japan, South Korea chose the Southeast Asian region as a foothold and used it as an opportunity to expand its economic power.

How else could Asia be imagined beyond the obsession with victory under-lying the economic logic of the developmental state and the Cold War mentality? Interrogating the historical imagination of Asia can be a small opportunity to con-struct an alternative regional perspective. More recently, discussions of Asianism or regionalism have opened up to some extent in South Korea. But occasionally fundamentalism, Korea-centrism and a strong nationalism remain in the field of discussion. To avoid such conservative narrowness, we have to reflect on the his-torical context of the imaginary–geography of Asia. More specifically, the 'Asia' constructed in South Korea in the Cold War period can function as a negative model for a new regional perspective in the Post-Cold War age.

Notes

1 In this chapter, 'Asia' covers Northeast and Southeast Asia.
2 Sun Ge, *Asiaraneun Sayugongkan* [Asia as a sphere of thought] (Seoul: Changjakkwabipyeongsa, 2003); Kwan-Hsing Chen, *Jekugui Nun* [The eye of the Empire] (Seoul; Changjakkwabipyeongsa, 2003); Jeong Moongil, ed., *Dongasia, Munjewa sigak* [East Asia, problem and viewpoint] (Seoul: Munhakwajiseongsa, 1995).
3 In particular, studies of cultural traffic in Asia have played a leading role in the development of this critical viewpoint. These studies have evolved considerably in recent times and enjoy active exchange among scholars from various Asian nations. For recent South Korean publications in this area, see Lee Dong-yeon, *Asia Munwha yeongureul Sangsanghagi* [Imagining Asian cultural studies] (Seoul: Greenbee, 2006); Kim So-yeong, ed., *Trans-Asia Yeongsang Munhwa* [Trans-Asia screen culture] (Seoul: hyeonsilmunwhayeongu, 2006).
4 On this concept, see Yonetani Masafumi, 'Post Dongasia, Saeroun Yeondaeui Jogeon' [Post-East Asia, the condition of new solidarity], in *Banilkwa Dongasia* [Anti-Japanism and East Asia], ed. Ukai Satoshi (Seoul: Somyeongchulpan, 2005).
5 See Choi Young-ho, 'Rhee Syng-man Jeongbuui Taepyeongyang Dongmaeng Kusanggwa Asia Minjok Bangongyeonmang kyeolseong' [Rhee Syng-man regime's ideas of Pacific Alliance and the birth of the Asian People's Anti-Communist League], *Kukjejeongchinonchong* [Korean journal of international relations] 39, no. 2 (1999): 165–82; Park Jin-hee, 'Rhee Syng-manui Daeil insikkwa Taepyeongyang Dongmang

Kusang' [Rhee Syng-man's recognition of the Japan and Pacific Pact], *Yeoksabipyeong* [Critical review of history], no. 76 (2006): 90–118; Park Tac-gyun, 'Park Chong Heeui Dongasia insikkwa Asia–Taepyeongyang Kongdong sahoe Kusang' [Park Chung-hee's East Asia and his plan for an Asian Pacific community], *Yuksabipyung* [Critical Review of History], no. 76 (2006): 119–47. For the genealogy of the Asianism of South Korea, see Gi-Wook Shin, 'Asianism in Korea's Politics of Identity', *Inter-Asia Cultural Studies* 6, no. 4 (2005): 616–30.

6 The ideology of the 'Greater East Asia Co-prosperity' of the Japanese empire and its influence have been the main theme in the field of literary and historical research. Many scholars also have great interest in the problem of postcolonialism in Korea. Representatively, see Kim Chul and Shin Hyung-Ki, *Munhaksokui Fascism* [Fascism in literature] (Seoul: Samin, 2001); Yun Hae-dong, *Sikminjiui Hoesaekjidae* [The grey zone of colony] (Seoul: Yeoksabipyeongsa, 2003); Cha Seung-ki, *Bangeundaejeok Sangsanglyeokui imgyedeul* [Critical points of anti-modern imagination] (Seoul: Pureunyeoksa, 2009).

7 Oguma Eiji, *Minshu to Aikoku* [Democracy and patriotism] (Tokyo: Shinyosha, 2003); Michiba Chikanobu, *Senryo to Heiwa* [Occupation and peace] (Tokyo: Seitosha, 2005); Marukawa Tetsushi, *Regionalism* [sic.] (Tokyo: Iwanami Shoten, 2003), and *Reisenbunkaron* [The Cold War culture theory] (Tokyo: Sofusha, 2005); Sato Takumi, 'Sengo Seron no Seiritsu' [The establishment of postwar public opinion], *Shiso* [Thought] no. 980 (2005): 72–94; Ogusi Junji, 'Sengo no Daishu Bunka' [The popular culture of postwar Japan], in *Sengo Kaikaku to gyaku Kosu* [Postwar Japan reformation and the reversal of course], ed. Yoshida Yudaka (Tokyo: Yoshikawakoubunkan, 2004), 135–59.

8 See Park In-hwan, 'Indonesia Inminege Juneun Si' [A poem for Indonesian people], *Sincheonji* [New world], February 1948, 124.

9 Park, 'Indonesia'.

10 See Park In-hwan, 'Nampung' [Wind from the South], *Sincheonji* [New world], July 1947, 13.

11 See Seol Jeong-sik, 'Manjukuk' [Manchuria], *Sincheonji* [New world], October 1948, 162–3.

12 See Kim Ye-rim, *1930 nyeondae Huban Keundaeinsikui Teulkwa Miuisik* [Modern Episteme and Aesthetic Consciousness in the Late 1930s] (Seoul: Somyeongchulpansa, 2004).

13 See Ju Yo-han, 'Seungriui Taepyeongyang' [Victory of the Pacific], *Chuchu* [Time and tide], April 1942.

14 On the 'Southeast Asian boom' in colonized South Korea, see Kwon Myeong-ah, *Yeoksajeok Fascism* [Historical fascism] (Seoul: Chaeksesang, 2005).

15 Jeong Il-hyeong, 'Taepyeongyang Dongmaengui Jeongchijeok gusang' [The political plan for the Pacific Pact], *Sincheonji* [New world], September 1949, 11.

16 Lee Seon-keun, 'Haebang Asia Onyeonsa' [The history of five years after the Liberation], *Sincheonji* [New world], February 1950, 16.

17 On the Pacific Pact, see Park, 'Rhee Syng-man's'.

18 Park Ki-jun, 'Padochineun Taepyeongyang' [The wave of the Pacific], *Sincheonji* [New world], September 1949, 182.

19 For the debate on Japan's identity and Asia in post-war Japan, see Sun, 31–106; Takeuchi Yoshimi, *Ilbonkwa Asia* [Japan and Asia], trans. Seo Kwangdeok *et al.* (Seoul, Somyeongchulpan, 2004).

20 Oh So-paek, 'I Pungjin Sesangeul Mannasuni' [In the rugged world], *Sincheonji* [New world], July 1949, 70.

21 Lee Tae-yeong, 'Hankuk Jeonjaengui Yeoksajeok Uii' [The historical significance of the Korean War], *Sasanggye* [Circle of thought], May 1953, 24.

22 Seong Chang-hwan, 'Kyeongjehakeul Gongbuhaneun hakdoege' [To the young scholars who study Economics], *Sasanggye* [Circle of thought], June 1955, 101.

23 Lee, 'Hankuk', 12.
24 Kim Gi-seok, 'Hankuk Joenjaengui Yeoksajeok Uii' [The historical significance of the Korean War], *Sincheonji* [New world], March 1953, 549.
25 Kim Yong-seong, 'Asiaui Jungnipseong' [Asian neutrality], *Hyeondaegongnon* [Modern public opinion], May 1954, 258.
26 Pae Seong-lyong, 'Dongyang Jeongchisasang keup Keu Yangsangui Yeongu' [A study on the Eastern political thought and its situation], *Sasanggye* [Circle of thought], May 1953, 70.
27 Kim Deok-lyong, 'Kuksaui gibon Seongkyeok' [The basic characteristics of national history], *Sasanggye* [Circle of thought], November 1953, 53.
28 For a discussion on the state of Oriental studies, Area Studies and Asian studies in the US after the Second World War, see Kim Kyeong-il, 'Jeonhu Mikukeseo Jiyeok Yeongu Seongnipkwa Baljeon' [The formation and development of Area studies in post-war USA], in Jiyeok yeonkuui yeoksawa iron [The history and theory of Area Studies], ed. Kim Kyeong-il (Seoul: Munhwakwahaksa, 1999), 153–204; Michiba Chikanobu, Senryo to Heiwa [Occupation and peace] (Tokyo: Seitosha 2005).
29 See Pae Seong-lyong, 'Uri Minjokseongkwa Dongyanghak' [Our national characteristics and Oriental studies], *Sasanggye* [Circle of thought], January 1954, 51–9.
30 See Kim Gi-seok, 'Ilbonui Buluiwa Dongyangui Isang' [The injustice of Japan and the idea of the East], *Sasangkye* [Circle of thought], February 1954, 10–42.
31 See Pae Seong-lyong, 'Dongyangjeok Soetoesakwan Kaeron' [Introduction to the fatalist view of history of the East], *Sasanggye* [Circle of thought], March 1954, 18–30.
32 Paek Nak-jun, 'Asiawa Segye Jeongguk' [Asia and the world political situation], Sasangkye [Circle of thought], March 1954, 13.
33 For the popular psychology of the Japanese, see Kitaha Jun, *Youjikasuru Nihonjin* [Japan and infantilism] (Tokyo: Riberuta Shuppan, 2005).
34 Oguma, 474–5.
35 Usumi Aiko, *Sengo Hoshoukara Kangaeru Nihon to Ajia* [Japan and Asia viewed from war reparations] (Tokyo: Yamakawa shuppan sha, 2006).
36 Oh Jong-sik, 'Hankukui kukjejeok wichiwa kui yeoksajeok kwaje' [The international position of Korea and its historical task], *Hyndaekongron* [Modern public opinion], May 1954, 20. See also, Kim Du-heon, 'Kukka Saenghwalui Jungyoseong' [The significance of national life], *Sincheonji* [New world], May 1950, 6–13; Park Gi-jun, 'Jeonhwangiui Cheolhak' [The philosophy of the transition period], *Sincheonji* [New world], May–June 1949, 52–6.
37 Lee Cheol-beom, 'Minjokuijiui Dankyeolmani' [Only the solidarity of the national will], *Sedae* [The generation], August 1965, 152–3.
38 Lee Jong-su, 'Hyundae Samsinkiui Yokmang' [The desire for the three modern holy things], *Sedae* [The generation], July 1967, 132.

3 Constructing an alternative regional identity

Panchsheel and India–China diplomacy at the Asian–African Conference 1955

Sally Percival Wood

Introduction

The Asian–African Conference at Bandung in 1955 – often referred to as the Bandung Conference – was the first independently staged world event by and for the leaders of these two continents. Although it is seldom referred to as a 'summit', it really was the summit, or peak moment, of the Afro-Asian solidarity movement which had evolved from various freedom movements that had been gaining momentum since the late nineteenth century. European empires had determined to 'divide and rule', thus keeping their colonies apart and locked within spheres of European influence. Independence movements had therefore remained only vaguely aware of each other with little opportunity to discuss issues of mutual concern and much less of meeting on their own soil. Although the Bandung Conference was not the first gathering of African, Arab and Asian leaders, it was significant in that it brought them together as leaders of sovereign nations, independent of Western interventions.

The Bandung Conference was also the first collective, though not necessarily unified, assertion of the foreign policies of the 29 newly independent nations present. Since India gained independence in 1947, and the People's Republic of China (PRC) was founded in 1949, their foreign policies and those of their Asian neighbours had been in transition from their colonial pasts. It was after the Geneva Conference of 1954 where the Korean and Indochinese conflicts were discussed that a more definitive stance on international affairs emerged in Asia. The PRC's Premier Zhou Enlai made his debut in international affairs at Geneva and, seizing the diplomatic initiative, visited Indian Prime Minister Jawaharlal Nehru in New Delhi on his way home in April 1954. Premier Zhou had been ignored by the American delegation at Geneva – American secretary of state John Foster Dulles famously refused to acknowledge the Chinese leader with a handshake – and he was keen to forge closer ties with Asia. More importantly, the Chinese had suffered a million casualties in the Korean War and Zhou was determined to limit further American incursions into the Asian region.

Nehru also flatly refused to engage in the superpower politics of the Cold War and had formulated a foreign policy of non-alignment. Together Premier Zhou and Prime Minister Nehru agreed on a framework of 'five principles of peaceful coexistence' – or *Panchsheel* – a distinctive Asian foreign policy. It was the first assertion of a specifically Asian approach to international relations and challenged prevailing assumptions that international affairs remained implicitly the preserve of the West. Nevertheless, it was also significant in that it essentially split Asia into two groups: the non-aligned and the aligned. In the 1950s post-colonial states were being pressured to enter into pacts and this had resulted in Western-sponsored security treaties SEATO (South East Asia Treaty Organization) and CENTO (Central Treaty Organization, originally known as the Baghdad Pact), signed in 1954 and 1955 respectively. *Panchsheel* would attempt to subvert this bipolar, Western orchestration of world affairs and assert 'peaceful coexistence' as a third way to peace.

The present chapter explores this assertion of Asian diplomacy at the Bandung Conference under the leadership of India and China. Arranged in three parts, it begins with an explication of the West's geopolitical organization of the globe that marked out vast regions for imperial containment. Geopolitical terminologies – the Near East, the Middle East and the Far East – were constructs of Western imperial hegemony, but in a post-war, decolonizing world, what was their continued purpose? An egalitarian, spherical world must surely displace these centre–periphery terminologies. The West's geopolitical differentiations meant very little to the Asian–African Conference. As the high point of Afro-Asian solidarity movements, which had systematically defied the hegemonic zoning of imperialism, the conference was oriented towards a constructive alternative. The next section of the chapter discusses the evolution of Asian, African and Arab 'pan-movements' which began the process of destabilizing the imperial master/colonial subordinate nexus. It looks at how these movements functioned outside the scope of Western geopolitical organization both to challenge and restructure the international order.

Finally the chapter examines the foreign policy of *Panchsheel* as a strategy for global reorganization that continued pan-movements' resistance to Western hegemony. This was particularly daunting in an era of new imperialism characterized by the Cold War. The chapter is admittedly ambitious in its scope. However, in understanding the motivations for constructing an alternative foreign policy identity, it is first necessary to identify the prevailing imperial containment model, and second, the historical currents moving across independence movements in their attempts to subvert the centre–periphery paradigm. These contending models for inter-state interaction not only contextualize the impetus behind *Panchsheel*; they also provide context for the deliberate and systematic misinterpretation by its critics. The chapter's concluding section demonstrates that, despite these obstructions, *Panchsheel* did succeed in the longer term.

The geopolitics of containment

The naming of the Asian–African Conference carries with it an obvious reference as to who the conference was for, yet it is also somewhat deceiving. The Secretary-General of the Conference Joint Secretariat (and of Indonesia's Ministry of Foreign Affairs), Dr Roeslan Abdulgani, suggested that the conference brought together countries of 'similar international background' as the 'necessary foundation for a regional grouping as the Charter of the United Nations envisages'.[1] Yet, most of the newly independent states at the conference would have held such 'visions of regionalism [as] suspect, not least because these could potentially serve as fronts for imperialist projects, whether colonialist or communist in orientation'.[2] The formation of regions had been central to imperial organization and they remained so in the post-colonial era of the Cold War. If regionalism were to be embraced at Bandung, it would have to fit an authentic alternative that was responsive to independent Asia's aspirations rather than the dictates of the post-imperial West.

By 1955, the globe had been geopolitically organized and reorganized several times. Of the 29 nations attending the Bandung Conference, 22 – or perhaps 27 depending upon which geopolitical categories are used – came from the vast Asia region. Those 22 countries came from East Asia (Japan and China), Southeast Asia (Indonesia, the Philippines, Thailand, North Vietnam, South Vietnam, Cambodia and Laos); South Asia (India, Ceylon, Nepal, Burma [which is sometimes considered a part of Southeast Asia], Pakistan and Afghanistan [which also falls into Central Asia on some maps]); and West Asia (Iran, Iraq, Jordan, Lebanon, Saudi Arabia, Syria and Yemen). Twentieth-century maps vary as to whether Egypt, Ethiopia, Sudan, Libya and Turkey comprise a part of West Asia or not, but if they do, there were 27 Asian nations at Bandung, narrowing the field from Africa down to just two: the Gold Coast (Ghana) and Liberia. Central Asia – comprising Kazakhstan, Kyrgyzstan, Tajikistan, Turkmenistan and Uzbekistan – had by 1955 merged into the Soviet bloc and the question of their attendance was not even raised by the Colombo Five – Burma, Ceylon, India, Indonesia and Pakistan – as they planned the conference. This implies some reasoning beyond the boundaries of geopolitics or regionalism as the stimulus for an Asia–Africa gathering. As Nehru reflected, the Bandung Conference responded to a 'psychological moment' that would 'produce a new atmosphere for peace'.[3] But a new atmosphere would call for a recalibration of Western modes of international organization.

At the beginning of the twentieth century the entire area of what we now define as East, Southeast, South, West and Central Asia was known as one sphere, 'the East' (the Orient), imagined in two straightforward halves, Near and Far. The East represented the geographical and cultural opposite of 'the West' (the Occident). This bipolar division of the world into 'East' and 'West' has its roots in the Crusades, when the monotheistic religions – Islam and Christianity – vied for territorial and temporal authority: '"Europe" [or the West] became a synonym for Christianity and the "East" a synonym for the world of Islam'.[4] After the Sino-Japanese war of 1894–5 when Japan arose as a force to be reckoned with and the vulnerability of China's Qing Dynasty was exposed, the West saw a chance for further economic expansion into the East.

This intensified interest around China and Japan saw the reconceptualization of the East as two spheres: 'the Near East' and 'the Far East'. The 'Near East' was really the region referred to earlier as West Asia and was imbued with more romantic associations among Europeans as the Fertile Crescent, the Levant, the Orient or Asia Minor. Asia Minor, or Anatolia as it was also known, centred upon Turkey which, as the heart of the Islamic Ottoman Empire, was historically Christian

Europe's rival during the Crusades. Asia Minor also took in Turkey's neighbouring countries Iran (Persia), Iraq (Mesopotamia), Syria and Greece. As West Asia this area expanded to include Lebanon, Palestine, Jordan, Saudi Arabia, Yemen and the Gulf States and, depending upon which map is consulted, might also extend north to include Bulgaria and the southern parts of the Soviet Union. For Europe, this region remained 'near' not only geographically, but also nearer to Western identity as the Western hemisphere's 'cradle of civilization'.

A fundamental shift occurred when the term 'the Middle East' entered geopolitical parlance 'as the region lying between the "Near East" (the region of the Ottoman Empire) and the "Far East" (India, China and Japan), an area of strategic significance to the imperial interests of Britain and France'.[5] It was primarily Britain and America that recast this region as 'the Middle East', although the terms Near East and Middle East remained interchangeable until the 1950s. The term 'Middle East' was first used by an American naval captain, Alfred Thayer Mahan, in his work *The Influence of Sea Power upon History* (1890) which centred upon the area around the Persian Gulf and Suez Canal as one of strategic maritime significance. The term went relatively unnoticed until it was popularized by *Times* correspondent Valentine Chirol in his series of articles entitled 'The Middle East Question' written in 1902. Chirol conferred upon the Middle East a much broader sweep than Mahan had, pushing its boundaries out to touch upon the Near and Far East in the interests of Britain's imperial objectives. Chirol's Middle East stretched from 'the approaches to India, land and sea: Persia, the Gulf, Iraq, the eastern coasts of Arabia, Afghanistan and Tibet'.[6] Hence, prior to the First World War, Britain splintered 'the East' into three geopolitical zones, 'the Near East centred on Turkey, the Middle East on India, the Far East on China,'[7] the primary objective being the formation of a protective sphere around India.

The Middle East was legitimized as a region in 1920 when the Royal Geographic Society resolved that 'henceforth the Near East should denote only the Balkans; the lands from the Bosphorus to the eastern frontiers of India would be named Middle East'.[8] The following year Secretary of State for Colonies, Winston Churchill, established a Middle Eastern Department in the Colonial Office.[9] As British military supremacy shifted from naval to air power during the Second World War, so too did the region known as the Middle East expand by creeping further into Africa to include Kenya and extending as far West as Greece and Malta. At the same time the centre of regional gravity shifted from Constantinople, which became Istanbul in 1930, to Cairo which by the time of the Bandung Conference was the focal point of Middle East leadership under General Gamal Abdel Nasser.

This shift away from the Islamic Ottoman Empire as the axis of the region to the Arab centre of Cairo introduced a further conundrum as to whether the Middle East was primarily Islamic or Arabic. British Prime Minister Clement Attlee (1945–51) attempted to be more specific when he stated that the term 'Middle East' covers the Arab world 'and certain neighbouring countries',[10] however he simply made things more ambiguous. By the time Churchill became prime minister in 1951 the term the Near East had been replaced by the Middle East and, as spokesman for the Anglosphere – the English-speaking world led by America and Britain which,

combined, assumed postwar economic, military and diplomatic dominance of inter-
state organization – he declared that 'India, Burma, and Malaya [were] the East;
China and Japan the Far East'.[11] These 'recurrent redistributions reveal several
pasts, several forms of connexion, several hierarchies of importance and several
networks of determination'[12] but precisely what the 'Middle East' meant was as
imprecise as ever. As late as 1958, America's 'State Department knew no Middle
East at all'[13] and while Secretary of State Dulles assumed an interpretation similar
to the British, President Eisenhower continued to refer to the Near East.

   Twentieth-century geopolitical pedantry saw the East both multiply and merge
until it was smudged into one vast geographical blur, prompting Britain's joint under
secretary of state for foreign affairs to ask Parliament: 'Does the government share
the view that the East begins at Dover?'[14] This comment, made in 1952, represents
the urge to form what Michel Foucault called 'architectonic unities'[15] of geopolitical coherence. After the Second World War the West's anxieties around territorial
containment were exacerbated by the East's gradual release from Western tutelage,
into a sprawling, uncontained mass. The East had swollen to the point of no longer
being synonymous with Islam, but became a vast heterogeneous area counterbal-
anced against a relatively homogenous West. The unwieldy East contained Muslims
who were no longer anchored by the Caliphate, polytheistic Hindus, Buddhists and
adherents to a range of traditional and animistic belief systems. Foucault might
have called this an 'abusive amalgam of heterogeneous elements'[16] and like those
who were horded into Europe's network of asylums the non-West was strange and
unpredictable.

   As late as the 1950s the West was still growing accustomed to the fact that,
although the newly independent nations of the East might not have sufficient economic or military agency to assert political power, their interests did not necessarily
converge with those of the West. Indeed, at the same time that Britain was con-
figuring and reconfiguring the East to suit its geopolitical interests, movements
had started among Asians, Africans and Arabs challenging the imperial hegemony
that confined them within spheres of influence and, in the process, obscured their
identities. Africa had remained rather anonymous in these geopolitical machina-
tions, except for the occasional reference to its northern region being considered
a part of West Asia, the Near East or the Middle East. Yet, Africa was at the forefront of global freedom movements. This coincided not only with the geopolitical
reconstitution of 'the East', it also coincided with the rise of 'alliance diplomacy',
which came about through intensifying imperial rivalries at the beginning of the
twentieth century.[17] The confluence of these events reveals much about the nature
of colonial solidarity movement, their testing of and modes of resistance to Western
norms in international relations.

From pan-movements to Afro-Asian solidarity

In July 1900, the first pan-movement made its international debut with the opening
of the Pan-African Congress in London. The Congress was organized by the
Pan-African Association which was founded by Henry Sylvester Williams in 1898.

Originally from Trinidad, Williams had studied law in Canada before moving to London where he was admitted to the bar in 1902.[18] It was the first meeting on an international scale that brought together non-white peoples and would mark the beginning of 'continuous and intense' political activity among Africans, Asians and Arabs in the form of conferences, manifestoes, strikes and campaigns of civil disobedience.[19] It is important to note, however, that to utilize techniques such as global conferencing, sponsorship by European sympathizers and Asians and Africans resident in the West was essential. Aside from a very small elite, colonized peoples had no agency outside of the borders of their colonies.

This first group of Pan-African delegates was drawn from South Africa, West Africa, the West Indies and the United States. It was typical of early African and Asian movements in that it was heavily supported by whites: the Pan-African Association at the time was made up of fifty 'persons of African descent and 150 Europeans'.[20] The first Pan-African meeting was, however, criticized for its elitism in that it essentially represented the interests of black people living in the West, rather than those being exploited in Africa. This sort of oversight would typify early pan-movements, which were somewhat sporadic and struggled to unify their aspirations. This was, of course, understandable given the diversity across the areas that they endeavoured to encompass and the obstacles of communication and travel across imperial borders. Nevertheless in his closing speech, the 'Address to the Nations of the World', black American activist W.E.B. Du Bois, brought together the wider interests of non-white peoples everywhere when he declared:

> [T]he modern world must remember that in this age when the ends of the world are being brought so near together the millions of black men in Africa, America and the Islands of the Sea, not to speak of the brown and yellow myriads elsewhere, are bound to have a great influence upon the world in the future, by reason of sheer numbers and physical contact.[21]

The Pan-African Association was the first international group to defy the geographical containment within which the West conceptualized the world in terms of power relations. By identifying the solidarity of peoples 'black, brown and yellow' a new, supra-territorial political consciousness was invoked beyond the geopolitical borders imposed by colonialism. This began the process of destabilizing both the territorial *and* the racial order of imperialism. As Pan-Africanism was emerging in the late nineteenth and early twentieth century, so too was Pan-Arabism in its initial stages of formation. It was the Arab language that was the unifying feature at that stage and in June 1913, a joint Arab–Syrian Congress was held in Paris. This is cited as the first meeting of the Pan-Arab movement but it was poorly attended and, like the first Pan-Africa conference, was criticized by some. In fact, so inchoate was Pan-Arabism before the First World War that it was described as 'nationalism without nationalists, a movement without participants'.[22] It was not until the 1930s that Pan-Arabism, and also Pan-Islam, became more cohesive as a reaction against Zionism although Islam was criticized as 'the lowest common denominator of Pan-Arab solidarity'.[23]

Around the same time Pan-Asianism began in China and Japan Sun Yat-sen lead the reaction against Western interference in China and spread his movement to Japan. He gave a lecture in Japan in 1924 entitled 'Greater Asianism' in which he promoted the idea of *wangdao*, 'the way of the ethical monarchs and peaceful rulership, opposed to the unethical and violent way (*badao*) of the hegemon (the way of the West)'.[24] These ideas were widely popular across China where reforms to the rigid Confucian system had begun even before the revolution had overthrown the Qing Dynasty in 1911. By 1924, however, China still struggled to unify within one cohesive political system and its attempts to modernize had brought it no closer to the unity that it craved. At that stage China really was in no position to take Pan-Asianism to the region. It was a different matter for Japan which, 'having mastered Western civilisation'[25] through its conquest of Russia, had what the militarized West would perceive as a legitimate claim to regional leadership. At the same time however, this aroused suspicions of neo-imperialism.

The Association for Greater Asia was formed in 1924[26] and Pan-Asian people's conferences were held in Nagasaki in 1926 and Shanghai in 1927. They were attended by Asians from India, Korea and Japan, but at that stage Pan-Asianism, like its African and Arab counterparts, held 'no great force of conviction behind it'.[27] In Asia's case this was largely because of Japan's 'imperial pretensions'[28] which were mistrusted by its colonized neighbours. Japan, using Western geography to define a 'maximal Asia'[29] region made further moves towards Pan-Asianism with its attempt to establish a Greater East Asian Co-Prosperity Sphere in 1940. Its motto 'Asia for the Asiatics' used during the Second World War rang rather hollow, particularly after its 'liberation' of Asian colonies during the war. Japan's brutal suppression of fellow Asians confirmed suspicions that 'Asia for the Asiatics' was 'a rallying cry for military expansion'[30] in the fulfilment of Japan's own imperial aspirations.

While the idea of a Greater Asia was being explored by China and Japan, Bengali poet and Asia's first Nobel laureate Rabindranath Tagore was travelling through Japan, China, Burma, Malaya and Indonesia seeking out the historic cultural ties of 'Greater India'. Tagore was thrilled to discover the traces of Sanskrit from Vietnam and Thailand to the islands of Bali and Java where Hindu epics the *Ramayana* and *Mahabharata* were still performed in dance and drama. What was Asian to Tagore was not so much a geographic region as it was an imagined 'unity of natural and sacred space'.[31] Kalidas Nag, a Bengali scholar of Asian civilizations, travelled with Tagore several times and wrote *Discovery of Asia* (1957), which drew together the cultural ties that had bound Asia for millennia. With Tagore's blessing Nag organized a Greater India movement, which was, to use a Foucauldian analogy, rather than a 'politics of knowledge', a 'culture of knowledge' that flowed from India across the region and remained evident in its religious and cultural traditions. Unlike a politics of knowledge, such as geopolitical containment, a culture of knowledge moved freely across the borders of the East, so was less susceptible to the inhibiting forces of the West.

Pan-Asian solidarity really became a potent force among colonial elites who were studying in imperial centres between the wars. For example, Mohammad Hatta, Indonesia's first vice president and Sutan Sjahrir, its first prime minister, both studied law and economics respectively in Netherlands in the 1920s and 1930s. Both were active members of the *Indische Vereinigung* (Indies Association) which began as a social club in 1908 but by the mid 1920s it had grown into a revolutionary organization radicalized by its name change in 1922 to *Perhimpuntan Indonesia* (Indonesian Union).[32] India's future leaders Gandhi and Nehru also studied law, Gandhi graduating in 1891 and Nehru in 1912. They were followed by V.K. Krishna Menon, who would later be Nehru's key advisor. Menon also studied law, graduating from the London School of Economics where, as Secretary-General of the India Institute, he started to string together the disparate sentiments of pan-movements. Under his leadership in 1924 it became a dynamic, radical organization that brought together the otherwise regionalized groups forming elsewhere. The India Institute attracted a following that reflected a growing Afro-Asian solidarity:

> Besides hundreds of young Indians who worked for the India Institute, there were also Indonesians like Subandro [who became Indonesia's foreign minister] . . . Africans like Jomo Kenyatta [who became Kenya's prime minister] . . . U Pe Kin of Burma, where he was several times cabinet minister, and Wickramasinghe, later one of the founders of the Lanka Lama Samaj party in Ceylon. There were many young Arabs too; for the Institute, while working mainly for India, worked for Arab national causes also.[33]

This demonstrates the peripheral nature of geography to pan-identities and anticipates later attempt to form a foreign policy that would represent the wider interests of post-colonial states. The retrieval of cultural identity as Tagore imagined it was central to the gaining of independence. This could not be found in politics alone, nor in the 'relatively recent constructions that arbitrarily project[ed] certain legacies of colonial power'.[34] Cultural and religious identities both preceded and defied Western geopolitics. What drew East, South and Southeast Asia together was Buddhism as a conduit for diplomatic interaction. This was not a new phenomenon: contacts between India and China were established two thousand years before via the spread of Buddhism into China. A 'continuous cultural interflow'[35] began as Indians and Chinese traversed the deserts of Central Asia to study and translate the Buddhist *sutras* (verses), and from about the eleventh century this developed further into a trade relationship that continued to spread further into Southeast Asia through the missionaries of India's Mauryan dynasty, which predates Christianity.[36] From the seventh through to the thirteenth century, Buddhism became anchored in Burma, Thailand, Malaysia, Brunei, Singapore, Indonesia, Cambodia, Laos and Vietnam.[37] Well before Islam had spread through the region that became the Middle East and Christianity had united the West, Buddhism was established across what geopolitically became the Far East.

Harnessing Buddhism in an effort to promote 'unity of purpose and outlook'[38] in a region that had been fractured by colonialism engendered a sense of historical continuity that was revived almost immediately after independence was achieved. Sir John Kotelawala of Ceylon claims to have tried to initiate an Asian Peace Bloc between fellow Asian Buddhist nations when he suggested a 'free Ceylon, free

Burma, free India and Thailand' coalition on a visit to Burma in 1948.[39] U Nu of Burma similarly built Buddhism into his regional relationships, with Thailand, Ceylon, India and the states of Indochina. The Sixth Buddhist Synod organized by U Nu in 1955, in particular, provided an opportunity for Burma to affirm and re-establish regional ties. This was especially important for its relationship with Thailand with whom it had engaged in centuries of disputes. Burma invited Thai President Pibul Songgram to officiate at a ceremony in connection with the Synod, which went some way towards affirming friendlier Thai-Burmese relations.[40] Similarly, Burma's relationships with Ceylon and India were drawn closer together through the exchange of sacred Buddhist artefacts and rituals. U Nu was convinced of the potential of religion to bring stability to the world, but through the co-existence and tolerance of all faiths,[41] rather than the building of blocs, such as the Pan-Buddhist movement proposed by Ceylon. It was the philosophy of Buddhism, which naturally disregarded territorial boundaries that provided inspiration for Asia's first attempts at a unified foreign policy.

Panchsheel[42] as an alternative diplomatic model

Indonesia was the first Asian nation to apply Buddhism to its state philosophy through the use of the term *Pantjasila*. On gaining independence, President Sukarno introduced *Pantjasila* as the five principles upon which the Indonesian state would rest. Indonesia is religiously complex, with Buddhism, Hinduism and Islam mingling with Javanese animism over the centuries and, in addition, the later arrival of Christianity. In 1945, an Investigating Committee for the Preparation of Indonesian Independence was established, with Sukarno and Mohammed Hatta at the forefront.[43] Both were against the dominance of Pan-Islam in the new Indonesia and saw *Pantjasila* as a means of accommodating the cultural and religious diversity across their vast archipelago. The term *Pantjasila* encouraged religious inclusiveness by evoking the five rites of Islam and the five tenets of personal conduct contained in the Buddhist *panch dharma*.[44] Its application to the state in the Preamble of the Indonesian Constitution essentially promotes the ideas of democracy and secular pluralism to include: belief in one God (religion neutral); justice and civility (citizenship); unity of Indonesia (nationalism); democracy through consensus; and social justice for all.

Nehru was impressed when he learned of Indonesia's adoption of this ancient Sanskrit term in its constitution. Speaking at a public reception for Egypt's Prime Minister Nasser and Afghanistan's Deputy Premier in the week prior to the Bandung Conference he reflected: 'When I heard this phrase in Indonesia it struck me as a happy phrase which I thought was of great importance to the world today'.[45] In Sanskrit *panch* simply means 'five', but *sheela* is a more complex term. Broadly, it is the 'habit, custom, acquired way of living or acting, tendency, character, nature, good disposition, moral conduct or integrity'.[46] Ancient Buddhist literature uses the shortened *pansil* to connote 'moral conduct' and the Buddhist practice of 'taking *seel*' means renewing the *panch dharma*. In terms of its use in international relations, *sheel* also means rock or foundation stone:

It is, probably, in the latter sense that the term *Panch Sheela* is being spelt and pronounced as *Panch-Shila* or *Panch Sila* to mean five foundational principles of foreign policy. However, these may more appropriately be understood to be the five norms or rules of conduct for guiding nations in their international intercourse.[47]

Nehru claimed that the principles of *Panchsheel* had been in practice in India for millennia and, indeed, the centrality of Buddhism to Asian cultural diplomacy was as legitimate and as enduring as Christianity was to Europe. To illustrate its historical roots as representative of India's political personality, Nehru recounts a story from a Sanskrit text about the Mauryan Emperor Chandragupta (c.321–297 BCE) and his Prime Minister Chanakya:

> Chanakya was typical of the Indian genius: peace-loving, shrewd, cunning, very scholarly, proud and selfless and reputed to be a very wise man. Now some kings and chieftains opposed Chandragupta and organized themselves into a confederation and declared war on the Kingdom. Chandragupta called Chanakya to lead the defence, and this person, who appears to have been a great statesman and a superb diplomat, succeeded in confusing and defeating the enemy front without resorting to anything like a war or even a battle. Somehow the enemy was won over. Then came the test. Chandragupta asked Chanakya's advice as to what to do next. Chanakya replied that his job was done. He had dispersed the foe and won a victory for his king. All he desired now was to be relieved of his responsibility so that he may retire to the forest and attend to his reading and writing. The King was shocked. For who would substitute Chanakya as the Chief Minister? Chanakya's reply was classic and very symptomatic of Indian thought. He told the King to get the defeated leader of the enemy confederation to serve him as his Chief Executive. That was the only way to restore peace and goodwill to the Kingdom. Now that was co-existence some 2,000 years ago. Wasn't it?[48]

Nehru believed that this philosophy was 'fundamental to Indian thought throughout the ages' from Emperor Ashok through to 'Gandhiji who organized it into a practical philosophy of action'.[49] Historically Buddhism had also influenced Asia in that states that were not politically organized around a Chinese Confucian model were likened to a Buddhist *mandala* form. The mandala formation concentrates political power at the centre and radiates outward. It is a political structure first described in the *Arthasastra*, said to be written by Chanakya (who was also known as Kautilya),[50] whereby the power at the centre pays tribute to the outlying regions and through inter-marriage and trade, interdependence and alliances are cemented. One of the most distinctive features of the mandala model is that it is not fixed within borders, nor is its power base grounded in one region over the long term. As an 'architectonic unity' it was therefore not so much a program of containment as it was one of conformity. *Panchsheel* similarly attempted to position inter-state relationships, trade and alliances within a different template that overrode territoriality yet respected sovereignty. Significantly it was a model antithetical to containment, which had proven fundamental to both imperial and Cold War geopolitics, and this would only have added to its appeal for newly independent nations determined to remain free of any such constraints.

Premier Zhou Enlai, returning from the Geneva Conference in April 1954 where the air was thick with containment strategies, stopped off at New Delhi to meet with Prime Minister Nehru. America's push for a 'united action' plan for Asia had cast a sense of gloom over Asian leaders whose only wish in their first decade of independence was to sustain peace and economically develop. Indonesian Prime Minister Ali Sastroamidjojo articulated the mood of the region when he commented: 'The joy and relief resulting from the Geneva agreements, which augured well for peace in Asia and also possibly throughout the world were reduced to nothing by [this] new development'.[51] The new development he referred to was SEATO, which was signed on 8 September 1954 by Pakistan, the Philippines and Thailand, along with the United States, Britain, France, Australia and New Zealand. It 'formally and officially'[52] split Asia into two camps: the aligned and the non-aligned.

Panchsheel was initially an agreement on 'trade and cultural intercourse between India and the "Tibet region of China"'.[53] With the advent of SEATO it was recognized as a 'third way' out of the bipolarity being imposed on Asia by the West. So when India and China reaffirmed the agreement on 28 June 1954, it was agreed that the five principles of peaceful coexistence should be taken to the wider Asia region. They were a simply articulated set of inter-state norms, including: mutual respect for each other's territorial integrity and sovereignty; non-aggression; non-interference in each other's internal affairs; equality and mutual benefit; and peaceful coexistence. By the end of 1954 Burma, North Vietnam, Cambodia and Laos had all entered into *Panchsheel* agreements, and Nepal and Indonesia would follow in 1955.

For Nehru, *Panchsheel* was not merely a foreign policy that rejected bipolarity and containment; it was the articulation of a philosophy inseparable from Indian, and more broadly Asian, political life. Although he was an avowed secularist, Nehru was committed to the Gandhian philosophy of *satyagraha*, a term that embodied non-violent resistance as the forces of the truth and of the soul.[54] It is hardly necessary to reiterate the guiding principles of Gandhi's program of action for *Hind swaraj* (home rule) through *satyagraha*, non-violent resistance. They are well known. But it is perhaps less understood that Nehru, as Gandhi's heir, carried his philosophy as a solution, not just for Asian unity, but for world peace. The recognition of Gandhian philosophy as a potential solution for global peace was demonstrated by a seminar held in New Delhi from 5 to 17 January 1953 'to consider the contribution of [the] Gandhian outlook and techniques to the solutions of tensions within and among nations'.[55] The meeting, supported by UNESCO, was attended by 'leaders of thought from both East and West',[56] who considered how a Gandhian program of action could be undertaken on an international scale to bring about peace. Leaders from ten countries attended with Nehru opening the seminar and the President of India, Dr Rajendra Prasad, addressing the concluding session. The seminar may have disappeared from historical memory but Gandhian thought, which guided Nehru's commitment to non-alignment and *Panchsheel*, survived as the philosophy that would underpin the Non-Aligned Movement (NAM) which took definitive form after the Bandung Conference.

If *Panchsheel*, for India, was a model for Asian diplomacy, deeply rooted in its philosophical traditions, for China it was a policy of much more pragmatic value. From the founding of the People's Republic of China in 1949 the new Chinese government had 'firmly, unequivocally, persistently, and successfully resisted the major interests of Western capitalism'.[57] After the Geneva Conference Zhou Enlai's resolve to limit American influence in Asia was strengthened and he therefore needed to demonstrate to his Asian neighbours that China had no hostile intentions in the region. At Geneva he was observed by French Prime Minister Pierre Mendès-France to be 'one of the most intelligent men I have ever met. He has the calibre of a world statesman, the sharpest, finest mind one could wish for'.[58] This view of Zhou Enlai was widely, if at times reluctantly, shared by all who encountered him in international forums. Having proven his ability to broker diplomatic solutions at the Geneva Conference, one of the twentieth century's toughest negotiations, Zhou now needed access to his Asian counterparts in order to diminish the powers of American persuasion in the region. Entering into *Panchsheel* with Nehru, the most popular and influential Asian statesman at the time, provided an ideal opportunity to seize the momentum of his success at Geneva. Zhou enthusiastically embraced the spirit of *Hindi–Chini bhai bhai* (India and China are brothers), and though India and China never ceased to 'proclaim their undying friendship' in the mid 1950s, India remained 'more effusive in expressing the attachment'.[59]

Once India and China had sealed the five principles of peaceful coexistence, Nehru took a new interest in Indonesia's proposal for an Asian–African Conference, an idea mooted at the Colombo Conference in April 1954, but one that had failed to stimulate much interest at the time. Nehru now saw it as a golden opportunity to promote *Panchsheel* and to introduce Premier Zhou to his Asian neighbours. At Bandung, Zhou wanted to communicate to Asia a message of respect for sovereignty, disclaiming the significance of ideological difference, and urging his fellow delegates to come to China to see for themselves that communism posed no threat.[60] It could not have been more opportune timing. America was predicting a military attack on the islands of Quemoy and Matsu by mainland China in April 1955. The attacks never transpired, and so Zhou could demonstrate to Asians in all sincerity that the Chinese communists were not a party to the scaremongering tactics promoted by America, nor did the PRC endorse Cold War bipolarity.

Conclusion: from *Panchsheel* to the Non-Aligned Movement

It is clear that *Panchsheel* was a very Indian pathway towards peace and away from containment. From Tagore's Greater India to Buddhist and Gandhian philosophy, *Panchsheel* positioned India at the centre of a foreign policy for independent Asia, in the process conferring a sense of moral continuity led by India. Assuming moral leadership did not, however, always endear Nehru to his Asian neighbours. Nehru's preaching of *Panchsheel* and his often self-righteous bearing could appear as somewhat messianic. At Bandung he had a tendency to intimidate: Abdulgani found both Nehru and Menon arrogant[61] while the Philippines' Carlos P. Romulo thought that he 'typified the affectation of cultural superiority' which had 'come to be the hallmark of Indian representatives to international conferences'.[62] It was true that *Panchsheel* and its Buddhist persuasion invoked 'a powerful myth, the myth of the Mystic East and of Spiritual India'.[63] Perpetuated in the nineteenth century, this mantle deprived India, and Asians more broadly, of a reputation for the more masculine traits valorized in the West. As the centre of some of the world's oldest belief systems, Hinduism and Buddhism in India, Confucianism and Taoism in China, overlaid with the later arrival and mingling of Islam, Zoroastrianism, Jainism, Sikhism, Christianity and Judaism, Asia did have a legitimate claim to being a centre of spirituality and philosophy. But these religions, it seemed, had no place in international affairs. Godfrey H. Jansen, author of *Afro-Asia and Non-Alignment* (1966) believed *Panchsheel* was a misguided attempt 'to drape secular and political non-alignment in the sweeping robes of moralistic religiosity'.[64] Jansen thought this damaged India's foreign policy credibility and its claims to be a secular nation. It also opened up an opportunity for the West to be quite deliberately confused about *Panchsheel* and non-alignment.

Much of the confusion around *Panchsheel* was manufactured and revolved around the interchangeable terms ascribed to it, from 'peaceful co-existence' and 'non-alignment', to 'non-involvement' and 'neutralism' which at times quite wilfully obfuscated the meaning of *Panchsheel*. Surprisingly, this obfuscation has not been interrogated by historians and has thus been repeated ever since. Examples are peppered across histories of Asia in the 1950s. For instance, Michael Leifer used non-alignment and neutralism interchangeably in *The Foreign Relations of New States* (1972)[65] and much later, Mark T. Berger's *The Battle for Asia: From Decolonization to Globalization* (2004) retained the ambiguity, stating that the Bandung Conference was (in part) a reaction against Eisenhower's caution to the nation-states of Asia that they 'should not try and remain neutral' in the Cold War.[66] The distinction between neutralism and non-alignment is important. First, the perpetuation of the error misreads the fine detail of Asian foreign policy in the 1950s and, second, it privileges the Western perspective of Asian history. Eisenhower and Dulles were wrong entangling non-alignment with neutralism, and not disentangling the terms muffles the Asian voice in the dominant historical narrative.

This confusion of non-alignment and neutralism was frustrating for Asian leaders. Indonesia's President Sukarno argued: 'We do not belong to either of the two blocs but our policy is not one of neutrality. It can never be neutral as long as tyranny exists in any part of the world'.[67] Nehru gave additional emphasis to this point when he stated emphatically that '*our policy is not one of neutralism*'.[68] He goes on to explain that, to be neutral suggests that there is a war in relation to which a state remains neutral, that is, another country or countries are either at war or have taken a belligerent stance. Non-alignment applied only in relation to entering into military alliances which Nehru believed were more likely to destabilize prospects for world peace. India's Ambassador to the United States, G.L. Mehta, was also at pains to make this point to Americans when he addressed the Chicago Council on

Foreign Relations in April 1955. He explained that neutrality was not the correct way to describe Indian foreign policy, rather non-alignment, which was 'virtually indistinguishable from American foreign policy from 1789 to 1937' and represented the 'desire of a nation which is still in the early stages of development to avoid being dragged into rivalries and conflicts' of external powers.[69] Yet, such a policy in the hands of Asians was considered 'an *effete* force in solving international conflicts',[70] and India was accused of being 'befuddled' by *Panchsheel*. That *Panchsheel* 'confused her friends abroad and laid her wide open to the attacks of her enemies'[71] was, however, more due to a wilful refusal to appreciate the clear distinction between non-alignment and neutralism. Quite simply, Cold War actors chose to be baffled in order to discredit an uncooperative policy. Dulles, for example, was known to become 'apoplectic' on the subject of neutralism,[72] quite forgetting that America had 'clung to a laissez-faire dislike of mass standing armies and avoided fixed military obligations to allies'[73] right up until the Second World War. His apoplexy reveals the exasperation that the West continued to feel towards 'the East', and it exposes what Foucault termed 'the sovereign power of the *imperial* gaze'[74] which did not lose its intensity upon decolonization.

The imperial strategy of organizing the world into spheres of geopolitical containment had been revived before the process of decolonization was even completed across Asia and Africa. On 2 April 1954, three weeks before India and China initiated *Panchsheel*, Pakistan had signed an accord with Turkey, an agreement which would become the Baghdad Pact when Iraq, Iran and Britain signed on in February 1955. Followed by SEATO, these strange coalitions bore no resemblance to the West's earlier geopolitical organization of the globe, nor did they reflect any higher aspirations such as were reflected in pan-movements or Afro-Asian solidarity. They were really alignments of fear – CENTO aimed at containing Russia, SEATO at containing China – and they infuriated Nehru who saw them as a wholly unjustified interference by the colonial powers. In an interview with black American journalist Carl T. Rowan, Nehru 'pounded his desk [and] almost shouted: "I don't think I can tell you how much we dislike it." He then stalked out of the room'.[75]

The Asian states that entered into military pacts with the West viewed *Panchsheel* with mistrust. In his opening speech at the Bandung Conference, Thailand's Prince Wan asked:

> What exactly does this mean? Does it mean 'live and let live' which is the right principle? Does it imply the practice of tolerance as is explicitly stated in the Charter of the United Nations? For the Charter says: 'to practice tolerance and live together in peace with one another as good neighbours.'[76]

Thailand's response to *Panchsheel* at Bandung was shared by its SEATO partners Pakistan and the Philippines. The three American allies had been primed by Washington with a range of support materials on American foreign policy, suggested tactics for the committee meetings and proposals for speech content in the opening sessions. High on America's agenda for Bandung was that efforts be made to 'avoid formal endorsement by [the] Conference of [the] Five Principles',[77] that is, *Panchsheel*. However it was of the 'utmost importance' America urged, that discretion be maintained so as not to create an impression that the US was 'exerting influence'.[78]

Pakistan appeared to relish the opportunity to undermine its archrival India. On instructions from America's State Department, in his opening speech Prime Minister Mohammed Ali set about 'driving a wedge'[79] through the India–China agreement on the five principles for peaceful coexistence. Ali's speech was largely about peace, but it was articulated through what he called the Seven Pillars of Peace. The word 'coexistence' was absent and, while six of the seven points generally reflected the spirit of *Panchsheel*, the major departure was in the clause: 'Right of self-defence, exercised singly or collectively'.[80] None of America's allies would use the phrase 'peaceful coexistence' in their speeches at Bandung because it was antithetical to the containment strategies of CENTO and SEATO. 'Our friends led by Mohammed Ali', American Ambassador to Indonesia Hugh Cumming reported to the State Department, 'were concerned to bury Chou–Nehru 5 principles, not much caring whether 7, 10 or 15 principles emerged'.[81] On the final day of the Bandung Conference, 25 April 1955, Mohammed Ali reported to the State Department that his speech 'among other things would shake [the] Chou–Nehru friendship' and force the five principles out of existence.[82] In the Bandung Conference Final Communiqué a 'Declaration on the promotion of world peace and co-operation' set out ten guiding principles, one of which endorsed 'respect for the right of each nation to defend itself singly or collectively'.[83] The phrase 'peaceful coexistence' was nowhere to be seen.

What found currency at Bandung was a new form of conceptual containment of post-colonial Asia and Africa, that is, the Third World. The Asian–African Conference is generally recognized as the point at which the idea of the Third World took root. It is a term coined in 1952 by French demographer Albert Sauvy who likened the decolonizing world to the Third Estate of the French Revolution and named it the Third World.[84] The First World was the United States and Europe (the West); the Second World was the Soviet sphere; and the Third World was the global underclass of decolonizing Asia and Africa, plus Latin America. What remained the same, of course, was that the West, as First World, remained the hegemon. Essentially the West's inclination towards dualism through containment – manifest in the twentieth century as communism and capitalism as the new East and West – could not accommodate a Third World that was consigned to a sort of global underclass. The recognition of a Third World did, however, temporarily solve the organizational conundrum of how to categorize that swarming heterogeneous mass now that it had released itself from imperial tutelage.

It is significant that, under pressure from the Cold War power blocs that replaced imperial power blocs, Asia and Africa once again found themselves theoretically contained within a geographical zone that mirrored their colonial pasts. It is also significant that this new formation, the Third World, represented the unity of Pan-African, Pan-Arab and Pan-Asian movements as sovereign agents in 'the World', albeit within a third tier of global relevance. This continuity is evident if one superimposes a map of the Afro-Asian Solidarity Movement over a map of the

NAM that grew after Bandung from the seeds of *Panchsheel*. The NAM dislodged *Panchsheel*, and India, as a new centre of politico-cultural dominance. However what remained was an alternative regional identity that ultimately defied Cold War containment, as pan-movements had defied the earlier geopolitics of imperialism. The NAM, like pan-movements, was imperfect but it was significant as a potent symbol of defiance against Western hegemony.

Notes

1 Roeslan Abdulgani, *Bandung Spirit: Moving on the Tide of History* (Jakarta: Badan Penerbit Prapantja, 1964), 22.
2 Amitav Acharya and See Seng Tan, 'Introduction: The Normative Relevance of the Bandung Conference for Contemporary Asian and International Order', in *Bandung Revisited: The Legacy of the 1955 Asian-African Conference for International Order*, ed. See Seng Tan and Amitav Acharya (Singapore: NUS Press, 2008), 3.
3 Indian prime minister Jawaharlal Nehru quoted on the frontispiece of *Panch Sheela – Its meaning and History: A Documentary Study* (New Delhi: Lok Sabha, 1955).
4 Thomas Scheffler, '"Fertile Crescent", "Orient", "Middle East": The Changing Mental Maps of Southwest Asia', *European Review of History* 10, no. 2 (2003): 261.
5 Fethi Mansouri and Sally Percival Wood, 'Exploring the Australia–Middle East Connection', in *Australia and the Middle East: A Front-line Relationship*, ed. Fethi Mansouri (London: I.B. Tauris, 2006), 5.
6 Roderic H. Davidson, 'Where is the Middle East?', *Foreign Affairs* 38, no. 4 (1960): 668.
7 Davidson, 668.
8 Davidson, 668.
9 Scheffler, 265.
10 Davidson, 672.
11 Davidson, 670.
12 Michel Foucault, *The Archaeology of Knowledge*, trans. A.M. Sheridan Smith (London: Tavistock Publications, 1982), 4.
13 Davidson, 666.
14 Davidson, 672.
15 Foucault, *The Archaeology*, 5. Philosopher Emmanuel Kant conceptualized 'architectonic' as the systematic, structured and unified organization of knowledge. Foucault uses the term 'architectonic unity' as the correlative of his knowledge–power relation.
16 Michel Foucault, *Madness and Civilization: A History of Insanity in the Age of Reason* (London and New York: Routledge, 2001), 41.
17 Paul Kennedy, *The Rise and Fall of the Great Powers: Economic Change and Military Conflict from 1500 to 2000* (New York: Vintage, 1989), 249.
18 Henry Sylvester Williams to Booker T. Washington, London, 27 September 1898, in *The Booker T. Washington Papers*, vol. 4, *1895–1898*, ed. Louis R. Harlan (Urbana: University of Illinois Press, 1975), 475–6.
19 G.H. Jansen, *Afro-Asia and Non-Alignment* (London: Faber & Faber, 1966), 26.
20 J.R. Hooker, 'The Pan-African Conference 1900', *Transition*, no. 46 (1974): 20.
21 W.E.B. Du Bois' speech at the Pan-African Conference 1900 quoted in Imanuel Geiss, *The Pan-African Movement: A History of Pan-Africanism in America, Europe and Africa*, trans. Ann Keep (New York: Methuen, 1974), 191.
22 Ernest Dawn cited in Efraim and Inari Karsh, 'Reflections on Arab Nationalism: Review Article', *Middle Eastern Studies* 32, no. 4 (1996): 372.
23 Karsh and Karsh, 382.

24 Prasenjit Duara, 'The Discourse of Civilization and Pan-Asianism', *Journal of World History* 12, no. 1 (2001): 115–6.

25 Duara, 107.

26 David Kimche, *The Afro-Asian Movement* (Jerusalem: Israel University Press, 1973), 7.

27 Jansen, 38.

28 Vijay Prashad, *The Darker Nations: A People's History of the Third World* (New York: New Press, 2007), 27.

29 Martin W. Lewis and Kären E. Wigen, *The Myth of Continents: A Critique of Metageography* (Berkeley: University of California Press, 1997), 72.

30 Lucien Pye, *Asian Power and Politics: The Cultural Dimensions of Authority* (Cambridge, MA: Belknap Press of Harvard University, 1985), 348.

31 Sugata Bose, *A Hundred Horizons: The Indian Ocean in the Age of Global Empire* (Cambridge, MA: Harvard University Press, 2006), 254.

32 Ali Sastroamijoyo, *Milestones on My Journey: the Memoirs of Ali Sastroamijoyo, Indonesian Patriot and Political Leader*, ed. C.L.M. Penders (St Lucia: University of Queensland Press, 1979), 43–4; and J.D. Legge, *Sukarno: A Political Biography* (London: Allen Lane, 1972), 87.

33 Jansen, 21.

34 Bose, 6.

35 Lokesh Chandra, 'The Philosophical Roots of Panchsheel: The Western Paradise and the Celestial Kingdom', in *Panchsheel and the Future*, ed. C.V. Ranganathan (Delhi: Smaskriti, 2005), 4. Chandra provides considerable detail of these cultural exchanges during the first 500 years of the millennium. See Chandra, 6–12.

36 Geng Tinzeng, 'The Historicity of Panchsheel: Mutual Respect Through the Ages', in *Panchsheel and the Future*, ed. C.V. Ranganathan (Delhi: Smaskriti, 2005), 21; and Ian C. Glover and Elizabeth H. Moore, 'Civilisations in Southeast Asia', in *Old World Civilizations: The Rise of Cities and States*, ed. Goran Burenhult (St Lucia: University of Queensland Press, 1994), 87.

37 Ninian Smart, *The World's Religions* (Cambridge: Cambridge University Press, 1992), 149.

38 Keith Callard, *Pakistan: A Political Study* (London: George Allen & Unwin, 1957), 314.

39 Sir John Kotelawala, *An Asian Prime Minister's Story* (London: George G. Harrap, 1956), 74.

40 U Nu, *Saturday's Son* (New Haven and London: Yale University Press, 1975), 270.

41 U Nu expressed these views in a speech 'Religion the Hope of the World' delivered at the YMCA annual meeting in Rangoon on 11 February 1951. See U Nu, *From Peace to Stability* (Rangoon: Government Printing and Stationery, 1951), 72–6.

42 There are several different spellings of this term. While *panch* always remains the same, *Panchsheel* variously appears as *Panch Sheel, Panch Sheela, Panchsila* et cetera. I have adopted the spelling *Panchsheel* throughout except where quoting directly from sources that differ.

43 Douglas E. Ramage, *Politics in Indonesia: Democracy, Islam and the Ideology of Tolerance* (London and New York: Routledge, 1997), 10–11.

44 These included refrain from injuring living things, stealing, sexual immorality, lying and drinking alcohol. *Panch Sheel – Its Meaning*, 2–3.

45 Quoted in *Panch Sheel – Its Meaning*, 1.

46 *Panch Sheel – Its Meaning*, 1.

47 *Panch Sheel – Its Meaning*, 1.

48 Jawaharlal Nehru, *The Mind of Mr Nehru: An Interview*, by R.K. Karanjia (London: George Allen & Unwin, 1960), 24.

49 Nehru, 23.

50 Martin Stuart-Fox, 'Political Patterns in Southeast Asia', in *Eastern Asia: An Introductory History*, ed. Colin Mackerras, 3rd ed. (Sydney: Longman, 2000), 84.

51 Sastroamijoyo, 279.
52 Jansen, 169.
53 Khagendra Chandra Pal, 'The Panch Shila and World Peace', *Modern Review* 99, no. 2 (1956): 112.
54 Yogesh Chadha, *Rediscovering Gandhi* (London: Century Books, 1997), 506.
55 Humayan Kabir, 'The Gandhian Way', *UNESCO International Social Sciences Bulletin* 5, no. 2 (1953), 397.
56 Kabir, 399.
57 Colin Mackerras, *Western Images of China* (Hong Kong: Oxford University Press, 1989), 175.
58 Han Suyin, *Eldest Son: Zhou Enlai and the Making of Modern China, 1898–1976*, (London: Jonathan Cape, 1993), 238.
59 Michael Brecher, *Nehru: A Political Biography* (London: Oxford University Press, 1959), 589.
60 Sally Percival Wood, '"Chou Gags Critics in Bandoeng" *or* How the Media Framed Premier Zhou Enlai at the Bandung Conference, 1955', *Modern Asian Studies* 44, no. 5 (forthcoming 2010).
61 Roeslan Abdulgani, *The Bandung Connection: The Asia–Africa Conference in Bandung in 1955* (Singapore: Gunung Agung, 1981), 26.
62 Carlos P. Romulo, *The Meaning of Bandung* (Chapel Hill: University of North Carolina Press, 1956), 12.
63 Jansen, 122.
64 Jansen, 120.
65 See chapter 2 of Michael Leifer, *The Foreign Relations of New States*, (Camberwell: Longman, 1972), in particular 28–40.
66 Mark T. Berger, *The Battle for Asia: From Decolonization to Globalization* (London and New York: RoutledgeCurzon, 2004), 48.
67 Kimche, 41.
68 Karanjia, 93.
69 Carl T. Rowan, *The Pitiful and the Proud* (New York: Random House, 1956), 128.
70 Priyankar Upadhyaya, 'Peace-functions of Nonaligned States: Some Reflections', *Profile of Political Studies* 1, no. 1 (1985): 97.
71 Jansen, 120.
72 Joseph Burkholder Smith, *Portrait of a Cold Warrior* (New York: Ballantine Books, 1976), 209.
73 Kennedy, 248.
74 The term Foucault uses is actually 'the sovereign power of the *empirical* gaze', yet 'empirical' and 'imperial' seem almost interchangeable when considering the West's technological and political hegemony over its colonies. See Michel Foucault, *The Birth of the Clinic: An Archaeology of Medical Perception*, trans. A.M. Sheridan Smith (New York: Vintage Books, 1994), xiii.
75 Rowan, 168.
76 Quoted in Itty Abraham, 'Bandung and State Formation in Post-colonial Asia', in *Bandung Revisited: The Legacy of the 1955 Asian-African Conference for International Order*, ed. See Seng Tan and Amitav Acharya (Singapore: NUS Press, 2008), 61.
77 Outgoing telegram from Department of State to American Embassies in Bangkok, Manila and Karachi, no.04283 dated 9 April 1955. United States National Archives RG59 Box 2669 670.901/4–155.
78 Outgoing telegram from the Department of State to the American Embassy in Karachi no.01864 dated 5 April 1955. United States National Archives RG59 Box 2669 670.901/4–155.
79 Outgoing telegram, 5 April 1955.
80 Opening speech of Pakistan in Roeslan Abdulgani, *Asia–Africa Speaks from Bandung* (Djakarta: Ministry of Foreign Affairs, Republic of Indonesia, 1955), 110.

81 Incoming telegram from Djakarta to Secretary of State, no. 2027, 25 April, 1955, box 2669 670.901/4–155, RG 59, United States National Archives.
82 Incoming telegram from Djakarta to Secretary of State, no. 2026, 25 April 1955, box 2669 670.901/4–155, RG 59, United States National Archives.
83 Section G, Clause 5, Final Communiqué in George McTurnan Kahin *The Asian–African Conference* (Ithaca, New York: Cornell University Press, 1956), 84.
84 Prashad, 6–11.

4 Naming and locating Asia

Australian dilemmas in its regional identity

David Walker

Continental ambitions

In 2005, a Singapore website (ExpatSingapore) posed the question: 'Oz – part of Asia or not?'[1] An early respondent considered this a 'challenging question', adding: 'Bet the Aussies are not too sure either'. If there is a common theme running through the responses it may well be uncertainty about the criteria one might use in determining whether Australia was 'part of Asia' or not. Was it primarily a matter of geography or was it more a question of perceptions, of how Australians saw themselves and how they wanted to be seen by others? It was also conceded that those looking at Australia from Singapore might well produce a different response from those who looked outwards from Australia.

A United States respondent thought the geographical question was both fundamental and easily resolved. Australia was a continent and therefore a separate entity. It was no more part of Asia than Asia was part of Africa. This was quickly dismissed as a 'stupid' response on the grounds that what constituted a continent was somewhat arbitrary. This correspondent expanded the original question to read: 'given the current economic and political climate . . . do Aussies feel compelled to be part of Asia. If an analogy had to be drawn, it'd be more akin to asking the Brits if they feel they are part of Europe or not.' This shifted the emphasis from geography to questions of national identification.

At the very end of the exchange a participant raised a question that had not yet been considered and which he believed required an answer before the original question could be properly addressed: 'What is "Asia"? Who defines it? Is the concept cultural, and if so, whose culture? Political? If so, whose politics? Is it ethnic? Which ethnicity? Or is the whole thing, "Asia" that is, an orientalist construction – an echo from an earlier colonial era, something defined "in opposition" to the occidental?' These questions certainly problematized the categories that informed the discussion of whether Australia could be considered part of Asia. For another participant in the discussion, the question 'What is "Asia"?', raised a host of reflections upon the medley of languages, cultures, religions and ethnicities that constituted Asia. Some of these were very mixed cultures, the product of centuries of intermingling, and others (he specified Korea, Bhutan and Japan) were rather more isolated and monocultural; yet all tended to be grouped as 'Asian'.

The idea that Australia might be thought of as 'part of Asia' has a long history. While there is a powerful geographical dimension to the question, much more is at stake than geographical borders and boundaries. Alongside geography, there is a host of often fraught questions about race, identity and international awareness. However inflexible the geography may have seemed, there was always an element of choice about whether to get closer to Asia or to remain distant. When Australians referred to themselves, as they often did before the Second World War, as 98 per cent British, they sought to distance themselves from Asia by claiming to be more British than the British themselves. Slogans about Britishness gave support to claims that Australians belonged in the old world and were part of Europe. In their turn, these questions were shaped, as the 'ExpatSingapore' discussion acknowledged, both by changing representations of Asia and by the political, economic and cultural changes transforming the region. Since 'Australia' and 'Asia' are both shifting and cognitively unstable entities, it should be apparent that a historical review of whether Australia might be considered 'part of Asia' must inevitably encounter contradictory claim and counter-claim along with a degree of uncertainty and sheer muddle.

The election of Kevin Rudd as prime minister in November 2007 and his proposal to create a new Asia Pacific Community expressed both the possibilities and con-tradictions of Australia's regional location. Rudd is the product of a post-Second World War consciousness that Australia's future would be shaped, economically, diplomatically and culturally by events in Asia. The idea that Australia was 'part of Asia' was encouraged through the 1950s by the Australian Department of External Affairs in the belief that it would harm Australia's influence and interests in the region to be characterized as a nation apart from Asia. When Kevin Rudd became a Mandarin-speaking diplomat in the 1980s it was no longer sufficient for Australia to be 'part of Asia'. The times called for a more dynamic language of active 'engage-ment with Asia' backed by a new commitment to 'Asia-literacy'. While Rudd's call for a new Asia Pacific Community might seem paradoxical for a predominantly European society, his visionary language is consistent with a longer history of ambi-tious claims about the future of the Australian nation and the expansive possibilities that flowed from Australia's special status as a continent. The logic of space and expansive territory appeared to demand visionary aspirations and new beginnings, especially so perhaps in a society with a modest history. Australia seemed destined to re-imagine and re-shape the future.

Australia's historical perspectives on Asia

The belief that Australia could be thought of as an extension of the Asian landmass found clear expression in Edward Gibbon Wakefield's *Letter from Sydney*, published in 1829. Wakefield did not set foot in Australia or New Zealand, but he saw that as no impediment to lively speculation about the role of new colonies and how best to develop them in a systematic way. He noted how common it was for people to suppose that the Australasian settlements were lonely and terribly remote outposts of empire. Taking a contrary view, Wakefield pointed to the vast populations that lay to Australia's north, not to raise the spectre of invasion and vulnerability, but to point to potential markets and the availability of a valuable source of labour. He particularly admired the Chinese, commending their industry, honesty and adaptability. With Chinese help, Wakefield believed that the Australian colonists could turn a 'wilderness' into a flourishing 'garden'.[2] This was perhaps the earliest expression of the belief that Asian ingenuity and skill when combined with Australian possibilities could shape a new future.

In the 1830s the Chinese could appear as a relatively docile population that presented no particular threat to Britain's Australasian colonies. Fifty years later there were darker musings about the rising power of the East, stimulated by the spectacular emergence of Japan from obscurity to a position of some prominence on the world stage. Whereas Wakefield had seen Eastern energies and enterprise serving European ends, by the 1880s it seemed possible that a newly assertive Asia might choose to force Australia to become part of Asia. It is hard to know what weight to give the stories of Asian invasion and conquest that emerged in Australia in the 1880s, but such narratives have been persistent enough to suggest an ongoing apprehension about hostile Asian invasion – of forced incorporation into Asia.

The complexities of Australia's position were comprehensively addressed by the Oxford-educated historian, former Victorian cabinet minister and educator, Charles H. Pearson, in *National Life and Character: A Forecast*, first published in 1894. Pearson's book belongs squarely within the visionary trope although the future he envisaged was a decidedly clouded one. Pearson was persuaded that China was a rising power and well-positioned to alter the balance of global politics. He feared that the boundaries which had once separated the races would collapse. As Pearson's new Asia grew ever closer to Australia, Europe appeared to recede and grow smaller. Pearson maintained that the rise of Asia also dictated a new role for Australia as the last continent available for the regeneration and renewal of the white races. While proximity to Asia made it more important than ever for Australia to remain white, there was in Pearson's view a measure of unease about the feasibility of this project. Pearson subscribed to the climatic orthodoxies of his day, which dictated that it was impossible for Europeans to establish permanent settlements in tropical climates. The tropics constituted a non-European zone, yet large parts of northern Australia lay within the tropics. According to this view, much of Australia was climatically Asian and therefore unsuited for the development of a robust European community.[3]

The racial health of white Australia was central to the discussion of climate and to considerations of Australia's place in the region. From the late nineteenth century it was common to regard Asia as a source of disease. The Chinese were routinely blamed for outbreaks of smallpox and leprosy. Keeping Australia white and quarantined, literally and metaphorically, from diseased Asia was regarded as a necessary condition of Australian health and racial vitality. The writer and entrepreneur Randolph Bedford urged Australians to develop their continent as racially 'clean', which meant the total exclusion of non-Europeans and a clear separation between the Australian continent and Asia. Bedford wanted Australia to be treated as a continent that had no affinities, climatic or otherwise, with the region.[4] Bedford based his expansive vision of Australian possibilities on the view that, as a sunny, continental people, Australians would inevitably have a larger imaginary range than the small-minded, fog-bound, island-dwelling English. For Dr Raphael Cilento, one of Australia's foremost authorities on tropical medicine and author of *The White Man in the Tropics*, keeping Australia separate from the nations to its north was imperative for the racial health of white Australia.[5] In 1930 Cilento wrote: 'If the health of Australia is to be conserved, she must be surrounded by healthy nations'.[6] Cilento was convinced that Australia was a healthy nation compromised by the diseased nations and races to its north.

The question of where Australia was located and what that location meant could never be a simple matter of geography and lines on the map. Dominance and subservience, conquest and enslavement, racial vitality and degeneration were all at play in attempts to define Australia's relationship with Asia. As Australia achieved nationhood on 1 January 1901 a note of anxiety intruded upon the celebrations that attended the creation of the first new nation of the twentieth century. There was certainly expansive talk of the sunlit plains and vast potential of the continent, of a land flowing with milk and honey, but there was also an uneasy sense that this was still an invitingly 'empty' continent – that it was a tempting prize for the crowded nations to Australia's north. And in that emptiness lay an uncertainty about Australia's future.

Creating white Australia

It was by far the majority view that Australia should become a 'new Britannia', displaying all the pluck, energy and confidence that had made Britain the world's pre-eminent empire builder. Australian cities were compared with their British models, while British practices and precedents shaped the political, legal and administrative institutions of the new Commonwealth. Yet, there could be no escaping the fact that all of this nation-building took place a world away from Britain in a vast continent as different as it was possible to be from the mother country in climate, landscape and geo-political setting. It was assumed that the British race would change as it adapted to these new circumstances. This was also the line adopted for over twenty years in the early twentieth century by the Australian *Official Year Book*, for which the Australian population was 'fundamentally British, and thus furnishes an example of the transplanting of a race into conditions greatly differing from those in which it had been developed'. From 1908 to 1929 this summation of the Australian population was recycled in the sub-section entitled 'Race and Nationality' of the *Year Book*'s section on 'Population'. Its assertion was that 'At present the characteristics of the Australian population . . . are only in the making' and that an Australian is, consequently, 'little other than a transplanted Briton'. The biological and social significance of this transplanting was yet to be seen, it argued, and would 'ultimately appear in the effects on the physical and moral constitution produced by the complete change of climatic and social environment'. The people of Australia would emerge changed, it said, as a consequence of these 'new conditions', which 'are likely to considerably modify both the physical characteristics and the social instincts of the constituents of the population'.[7]

Among other modifications was the possibility that over time Australians might lose a number of their British characteristics. At the same time it was thought that they might also avoid the Asianizing influences commonly attributed to tropicality. Exponents of the middle way, such as Randolph Bedford, celebrated sunny Australia as a land with a Mediterranean future. Here, warmth was not only a climatic state but a desirable emotional state as well, a new and better condition of being. In the 1890s the prolific Dr Philip Muskett wrote eloquently on the subject of climate, diet and health in Australia, pointing out the benefits of a Mediterranean way of life and a diet that substituted fish, vegetables and wine for a relentless regimen of meat, stodge, tea and beer.[8] In his celebration of the new race he saw emerging in Australia, the writer and man of letters Arthur Adams declared: 'The sun gets into your blood and this is the first white race that has had that experience since the world began. Australia is the largest-sized and the most tremendous experiment ever tried in race-building, and Australia knows it'.[9] As profoundly different as their visions of Australia were, Arthur Adams and Kevin Rudd find some common ground in their belief that Australia would help forge a new future.

In these speculations, geography was primarily a matter of climatic affinity rather than geographical proximity; sun and soil were held to be the great architects of Australia's future. Climate was destiny. As important as climate could seem in the process of making and unmaking civilizations, it was difficult to ignore the ceaseless battle for power and supremacy in shaping the world's future. Through the inter-war years there was a growing conviction that the struggle for power in the Pacific would determine Australia's future and, that being so, it seemed imperative for Australians to develop a closer knowledge of the region they inhabited. They were enjoined to look to Asia if they were to understand and influence their future. The accumulated warnings about the East and injunctions to know the Orient acted as a link, however unwelcome, to the region. Events in the East, it was argued, would inevitably resonate powerfully in Australia, requiring Australians to be constantly mindful of Asia.

It might also be argued that this enforced 'mindfulness' generated some resistance and resentment among a people who wanted to enjoy and develop an egalitarian, racially homogenous community. To be reminded that Asia was on the doorstep, allegedly watching developments in Australia, could seem distracting and intrusive; it was a reversal of the natural order, which permitted 'whites' to scrutinize 'coloured' people but not the other way round. This was just the kind of unwelcome change that Pearson had foretold. It was one thing to impose severe restrictions upon the entry of non-Europeans into Australia, but quite another to keep the idea of threatening or invasive Asia at bay. According to the Australian writer and diplomat, Walter Crocker, Asia had definitely invaded the imagination of white Australia: it was 'the very apparition indeed', he said, 'that has haunted the fancy of many an Australian and has invigorated the immigration Code of his country'.[10]

Competing understandings of the region

To suggest too sharp a distinction between 'region' as a known geography and 'region' as a psychological state is hardly adequate. Before the Second World War there was no agreed description of the region. There were frequent references to the 'East' and the 'Eastern question', but the inclusions and exclusions encompassed by these terms were extremely fluid. Charles Pearson, for example, barely acknowledged the presence of Japan or the nations that now form part of Southeast Asia. He was almost entirely focused on China as a growing power and India as a vital British possession.

By the 1920s the 'Pacific' had emerged as the preferred collective term for a shared geography. In 1917, the Australian government established a 'Pacific Branch' to focus on questions of security and defence. Japan was at the forefront of this concern. By the mid 1920s the Institute of Pacific Relations (IPR) had emerged as the first international forum to focus on the region. Australian delegates attended biennial IPR conferences from 1925. Japan and China, the United States and Canada were among the major participants but Australia and New Zealand were also strongly represented. An IPR journal began publication in 1928 with the title, *Pacific Affairs*.

From an Australian point of view the 'Pacific' had distinct advantages as a regional descriptor. It included Asian nations, but it also ranged Australia alongside the 'white' nations of the Pacific. It diminished the sense that Australia faced a hostile coloured world on its own. The weighty presence of the United States was particularly reassuring in this respect. While the 'Pacific' emerged as the dominant term, it did not displace other usages. The first systematic study of Australia's place in the region, published in 1935, is titled *Australia and the Far East*.[11] Even when the book was published there was a growing realization that Britain's 'Far East' was Australia's 'Near North'. The year before, in 1934, the Australian government acknowledged the importance of Asia to Australia's future when it sent what was termed a 'Goodwill Mission to the East' led by the attorney-general, John Latham. Latham visited Batavia, Tokyo and Shanghai, but Japan was the focus of his mission.

Down to the Second World War, China and Japan dominated Australian thinking about what constituted Asia. India can hardly be overlooked in this context, but so long as it appeared to be firmly under British rule it posed no particular threat to Australia's future and generated less attention accordingly. British India was primarily a nineteenth-century enthusiasm that reached a peak in Australia with the publication in 1893 of Alfred Deakin's *Temple and Tomb in India* and *Irrigated India*.[12] There were no invasion novels featuring Indian adversaries acting singly or in collaboration with others. A similar point could be made about the Netherlands East Indies. Despite its proximity to Australia, there were no sustained concerns about these numerous and populous islands posing a threat to Australia for it was understood that the 'natives' were firmly under Dutch control. There also remained a considerable prejudice against the supposedly indolent 'natives' of tropical climes, who were believed incapable of mounting a serious challenge to the white races. China and Japan received the most attention in Australia largely because they appeared to pose the greatest threat to Australia's security. Moreover, theories of degeneration based on climate hardly applied to countries which experienced winters more severe than Australia's.

When the Australian writer and public intellectual Donald Horne reflected upon how the world looked to an Australian schoolboy growing up in the 1930s, he recalled maps of the world showing the vast sweep of the British Empire coloured in red. So long as substantial parts of Asia were coloured red, not least India, the dominant note was British and imperial. This was a global empire that resisted specific regional identifications. Young Donald was very aware of the empire and its stories of heroic endeavour, but unaware of how Australia related to Asia. That world was largely unknown and had no place in the school curriculum.[13]

Knowing the region was not helped by confusion in the naming of it. The uncertain terminologies used to describe the region are apparent in the first Australian journal devoted to an examination both of 'Pacific affairs' and Australia's relations with Asia. The journal emerged from the growing interest among intellectuals in Asian affairs. Both Latham's Goodwill Mission and the appointment in 1935 of trade commissioners to Batavia, Tokyo and Shanghai pointed to a closer and, some believed more independent Australian approach to developments in Asia. Yet, there remained the problem of what to call such a journal. In the event, it appeared as the *Austral-Asiatic Bulletin*, an awkward title for a still awkward and poorly defined relationship and region.

One of the key figures in this publishing initiative was William Macmahon Ball, the Melbourne academic and writer. Ball would emerge as a leading advocate of closer ties with the region and urged greater knowledge of the countries and cultures of Asia. In similar vein, the first textbook that sought to locate Australia in a regional context was edited by R.M. Crawford, another Melbourne academic. Crawford's *Ourselves and the Pacific* was first published in 1941 and included, along with an historical overview of Australia and New Zealand as Pacific nations, chapters on the history of Japan and China, reinforcing the view that these two countries dominated Australian thinking about Asia. Crawford wrote: 'Today, Australians and New Zealanders have no doubt that their destiny is to be influenced by the fact that they border the same ocean as China, Japan, the United States and Russia. But our knowledge of the Pacific environment lags behind a sense of its importance to us.'[14] While New Zealand is considered vital to this account of the region, smaller Pacific nations are not; also, Russia joins China, Japan and the United States as a key regional presence.

Crawford's appeal for a greater knowledge of the Pacific was a polite rephrasing of a persistent complaint, namely that the Australian population was stubbornly insular and worryingly ignorant of the turbulent world they inhabited. These were 'lotus eaters' occupying a 'fool's paradise', complacently unaware, so critics maintained, of the dangers they faced. From the 1880s one of the purposes of the invasion novel was to awaken slumbering Australia to a keener sense of patriotism and national purpose. The popular novelist Herbert Strang wrote *The Air Scout*, his story of an attempted Chinese invasion of Australia, which he subtitled *A Story of National Defence*.[15] The story was fervently patriotic. A cartoon published in 1923 depicts Australia as an empty continent where a lanky fellow lay asleep under a tree. The crowded nations of Asia looked on, distinctly unimpressed by this show of uncaring indolence.[16] According to this view, the surrounding nations were much more aware of Australia than it was of them. The dominant theme of the invasion narrative was that these were dangerous people to antagonize, dangerously numerous, and resentful at being excluded and looked down upon by white Australia.

The examination of Australia's place in the region was an attempt to understand and overcome what critics considered Australian ignorance and insularity. It was also a project designed to define and clarify what was understood by 'Asia' and the 'Pacific'. The growing demand for more knowledge of Asia from the 1930s was frequently accompanied by a warning that a radical change of attitude towards the peoples and cultures of Asia was imperative. There were few critics of the White Australia policy in the 1930s, but there were those who warned that hostility towards coloured people would have to change. From the late 1930s there were increasing references to Australia's 'neighbours', a designation that acknowledged proximity, albeit in a rather vague way, while also creating an impression of Australian friendliness and hospitality.

Summarizing Australia's position in 1936, Macmahon Ball found a depth of Australian ignorance and apathy about Pacific affairs which was, he said, more appropriate to 'desert tribesmen' with 'a lowly state of mental growth' than to citizens of a modern democracy. It is an interesting passage explicitly designed, it would seem, to puncture the self-esteem of a comfortably British people, whose opinion of themselves was, in Ball's view, altogether too high.[17] It was a deadly insult to suggest they were no better prepared and no wiser than the Aboriginal people they had supplanted. Ball's remarks are also a reminder that in any society an understanding of the geo-political landscape is a minority interest. In the 1930s, Australia had few groups with a formal interest in international affairs. At the outbreak of the Second World War no Australian newspaper had a foreign correspondent stationed in Asia, nor did the Australian Broadcasting Commission. Political scientists accept that foreign policy issues rarely determine the outcome of Australian elections.[18]

The state of knowledge about the region on the eve of the Pacific war is nicely summarized by the publication of two books on Australia and Asia. The first, Jack Shepherd's *Australia's Interests and Policies in the Far East*, was published by the Institute of Pacific Relations in 1940. Shepherd retained the old terminology of the 'Far East' but noted how rapid change in the region had been, which made it impossible to predict with any confidence what might occur in the near future. It was one thing to know the region, but almost impossible to know what might emerge from one month to the next.[19]

Paul McGuire's *Westward the Course: the New World of Oceania* carried a similar lament. The book was written in 1941 and went to press two days after the bombing of Pearl Harbor. As is the case with Shepherd, McGuire's book is a product of the intellectual awakening to Asia in the 1930s and, like Crawford's *Ourselves and the Pacific*, was presented as an urgent reminder of the need to know more about the region. However, McGuire's use of the term 'Oceania' underlines the fluidity that still surrounded attempts to describe where Australia was located in the world. The confusion is emphasized in the publisher's note to the New York edition of the book, where the object of McGuire's inquiry is referred to as the 'southwestern

Pacific'. There is a familiar admission of ignorance followed by an injunction to know more: 'Interest has been developing slowly, and it took the Japanese attack on Honolulu to shake us into the general realization that Australia, New Zealand, the Dutch East Indies and British Malaya are in one sense very close and in every sense vital'.[20] This was a view of the region premised on European interests and the continuation of Western dominance. Nonetheless, McGuire's book is marked by a recognition that knowledge of Asia was in desperately short supply. It was equally a book about the need to understand the peoples and cultures of the region and the necessity of living on amicable terms with them. What also stands out in McGuire's account and which is of particular importance here is the conviction that in playing a larger role in Asia, Australia would not only provide leadership in the region but in doing so would discover a new and reinvigorated sense of national purpose. In discovering Asia, McGuire maintained, Australians would renew themselves.

Australia as part of Asia

If the intellectual foundations of the idea that Australia was part of Asia were laid in the 1930s, the Second World War, particularly the war in the Pacific, not only underlined and dramatized Australia's proximity to Asia; it also drew attention to Australia's distance from Europe. If Australia was inescapably a Pacific nation, it appeared necessary to consolidate ties with the United States and strengthen links to the region. One of the most trenchant critics of Australian policies and mentalities at this time was the novelist and newspaper editor, Brian Penton, author of a pugnacious book entitled *Advance Australia – Where?*, published in 1943, at the height of the war. Penton was scathing about Australia's failure through the inter-war years to recognize that its future lay in Asia, tracing this failing to a psychological dependence on Britain and a slavish attachment to English standards in all things. For Penton 'it was clear as the sun at noon that Australia, sitting on a tough spot at the bottom of the Pacific, on the fringe of Asia, had one hope for the future: to find friends close at hand among her neighbours . . .'.[21]

In the course of the war George Johnston, one of Australia's best known war correspondents, captured the mood with a racy little book entitled *Pacific Partners*,[22] which sought to connect pioneering histories and shared values of Australians and Americans. American terminology also began to influence the way the major regions of the world were described. The term 'Southeast Asia' first came into use during or right after the Second World War when the United States of America and its allies imposed directional designations upon all quadrants of the globe, which had previously had more exotic and evocative but less precise terms. In this way, the undifferentiated 'Orient' (from the United Kingdom perspective) and 'Pacific' (from the United States perspective) soon became East Asia, Southeast Asia, South Asia, Central Asia, and the Middle East (the latter being an inexact, colonial hold-over.) Hence, during the Second World War MacArthur's command was the 'South West Pacific Area', or SWPA (which did not enter the language), and Mountbatten's was the 'South East Asia Command', or SEAC (which did).[23]

Soon after the war Johnston updated and affirmed another of the familiar tropes about Asia in a book entitled, *Journey Through Tomorrow*. Asia was not so much a defined region as a destiny. It was the future, but Johnston also suggested it was a return to the past: 'There are many who believe we stand at the very beginning of another great cycle of civilisation; a cycle that some day will push the centre of gravity of civilisation back to the Orient . . . the soil from which our earliest civilisations sprang'.[24] The 'Orient' was a hard term to relinquish, and especially so when the alternative was the dry terminology of military commanders.

In Johnston's account 'Asia' was more a continent and a civilization, than a region. His focus was India, China, Tibet, Burma and Japan, with Tibet and its spiritual traditions taking centre stage. Burma is the only country in Southeast Asia to enter Johnston's story, but more for its connection with China than on account of any specifically regional logic. In 1948, *Near North: Australia and a thousand million neighbours* brought together three of the great post-war themes: proximity, population pressure and the need to cultivate a neighbourly approach to the people of Asia. In his preface H.V. Evatt, minister for External Affairs in the Labor government, noted that following the war 'it is now obvious to most Australians that we must continue to develop a policy of our own in relation to the Western Pacific and South Asiatic countries'.[25] Less obvious perhaps was the continuing uncertainty of how to name and categorize the countries deemed to be of special interest to Australia. 'Western Pacific' echoed American terminology while 'South Asiatic' has a stronger northern hemisphere logic than an Australian one.

Neighbourly rhetoric reached a highpoint in the 1950s, but the neighbours had to be chosen with some care. The People's Republic of China was considered ominously close, but it was impossible to regard a communist regime as a neighbour. Indonesia was a more suitable object of neighbourly emotion: it was close and the presence of a strong communist movement meant that it needed to be wooed and won over. The Colombo Plan, initiated in 1951, was the most ambitious attempt to win the goodwill of what Australia's minister for External Affairs in the 1950s, Richard Casey, referred to as 'free Asia'. The Colombo Plan provided an ideological overlay to the mapping of the region, targeting the nations that might be saved from communism, while avoiding those already lost, as source countries for Australia's Colombo Plan students (an indication of what the major source countries were can be gauged from the 1956 figures in Table 4.1, Australia's Colombo Plan students). There was no particular regional logic in this distribution, however.

Through the 1950s Richard Casey was Australia's foreign affairs spokesman and the Menzies government's most senior and articulate exponent of closer ties with Asia. He deplored the use of the term 'white Australia' and admonished journalists for using it, though without much effect. Casey was attached to the term 'neighbours' as a description of Australia's relationship with Asia, bringing it into almost everything he wrote on the subject, including his book, *Friends and Neighbours: Australia in the World*. While neighbourly relations with the region were important to Casey, relations with Britain and the United States were absolutely vital in maintaining democracy: 'Australia is a link in the world-wide chain of democratic

Table 4.1 Australia's Colombo Plan students, 1956, by number and place of origin

Place of origin	No. of students
Indonesia	483
India	217
Malaya	204
Pakistan	198
Burma	164
Ceylon	157
Singapore	99
Philippines	77
Thailand	71
North Borneo	54
Vietnam	45
Sarawak	41
Brunei	7
Nepal	7
Cambodia	6
Laos	1

Source: *Australia in Facts and Figures*, no. 52 (Canberra: Australian News and Information Bureau, Department of the Interior, 1956), 66.

countries that comprise the grand alliance against international communism. Our survival depends on all the links in the chain'.[26]

In explaining 'Australia's Outlook', Casey uses a phrase that leaps out at the modern reader. 'Australia', Casey writes in a quite unselfconscious way, 'is geographically a remote country'. Europe encompassed what seemed important in the world and the distance from Australia to Europe was considerable. While there were countries in the space between Australia and Europe, they were evidently not countries to which Australia could feel closely related. Casey went on to note that in a rapidly 'shrinking' world the region had drawn much closer and become more inter-related. For Casey, the Colombo Plan was an impressive example of the cooperative demands of the new post-war order and, in making this point, he named 'South and Southeast Asia' as regions of particular importance to Australia. While the shifting array of terms to describe the region would continue, by the early 1950s South and Southeast Asia had replaced the 'Pacific' as preferred terminology. That said, it was clear that the United States was understood to be Australia's senior partner in the region.

Casey went on to comment on the divide in Australia between its history as a community of British origin (no mention here of Aboriginal Australia) and its geographical location in Asia. An awareness of this paradox had been evident for some time. In 1910 the British writer, John Foster Fraser, had referred to Australia as an Asian landmass accidentally occupied by British settlers.[27] Casey's immediate predecessor as minister for External Affairs and one of the architects of the Colombo Plan, Percy Spender, was attracted to this account of Australia's position: arguing that 'No nation can escape its geography', he continued:

> Even though our cultural ties have been and will remain preponderantly with Europe, there is nothing we can do to alter our geographical position. We live side by side with the countries of South and South-East Asia, and we desire to be on good-neighbour terms with them.[28]

Casey summed it up more simply: 'we are a European community living alongside and working with Asia'.[29] But it was Macmahon Ball, writing in the 1930s, who most clearly drew attention to the natural outcome of this paradox, which led to Australia being given 'a picture of the world as seen through British eyes'.[30] He continually warned of the dangers of Australia's being too tied to British interests and policy, pointing out that 'in certain areas of the world, especially in the Pacific, Australia is likely to have special interests which are different from, even though not antagonistic to, the dominant British interests', before going on to cite Japan as a particular case in point.[31]

It was clear that 'working with Asia' implied a good deal of practical assistance in helping raise living standards. Referring to Australia's new sense of obligation, Casey wrote: 'To London and Washington the problems of Asia may still be distant problems. To Australia they are part of our immediate environmental problem – almost a metropolitan problem'. Asia had become Australia's unavoidable 'problem' and, in doing so, the region had become associated with instability, weakness and chronic disadvantage. One way or another, the region was understood to be troubled and, unless Australia stepped in, it might become much worse. While the region was an unavoidable commitment, other links and associations were more willingly embraced. Casey wrote warmly of the Commonwealth and of the English-speaking peoples:

> We sincerely believe that the survival and progress of our present civilisation depends substantially on the English-speaking peoples and that British-American relations must be intimate and confident not only between Great Britain and the United States but also between Australia and the United States. Our intimacy with America means no weakening of our ties with Britain – it is in fact one aspect of Anglo-American co-operation.[32]

The conviction that the world to Australia's north was dangerously unstable only added to the dilemma of knowing how to describe it. Writing for the *Observer* in 1958, the poet and academic James McAuley observed that 'the belt of protective powers which once safeguarded Australia has become a volcanic zone of incoherent nationalisms, which can be brought to co-operate only with difficulty, or not at all . . .'[33] This was not so much a region, in McAuley's view, an area that could be defined and comprehended, but an unpredictable tangle of primal forces. While McAuley's language is much more apocalyptic than Casey's, both named Southeast Asia as a dangerous power vacuum. For Denis Warner, then one of Australia's most experienced Asian correspondents, there was not much evidence, despite loud protestations to the contrary, that the Australian people had an interest in their Asian neighbours. 'The fact is', he declared, 'we don't know Asia and its people and we don't want to know them'.[34] As far as Warner could judge, mainstream Australia knew only that Asia was too close for comfort; otherwise, it was largely consigned to the dangerous unknown. Leaving aside whether Warner was right or wrong, his regular articles on Asian affairs in the *Observer* acknowledge that developments in Asia were of immediate importance to Australia whether the population at large recognized the point or not.

Donald Horne, the editor of the *Observer*, and a trainee diplomat in the 1940s, was instrumental in having both foreign affairs and Australia's place in Asia included as regular topics in the paper. He titled an essay, in March 1959, 'Living with Asia' and was perhaps the first to use the phrase that others would adopt, among them the Labor politician Jim Cairns, who used it for the title of a book on Asia published in 1965.[35] Horne began his striking essay by noting that the term 'Asian' had unfortunate consequences when applied to the nations to Australia's north. He maintained that the term induced 'emotional responses' and created an impression that the region was not only mired in problems, but problems beyond the reach of diplomacy. Horne dismissed the view that Asia constituted a particularly intractable and dangerous world, noting that European diplomacy had long dealt with similar problems now designated as uniquely 'Asian'. He added that the business of seeing diplomatic relations with Asian countries as normal was made harder by the 'quite widespread feeling that we are finished anyway and that it does not matter much what we do . . .'.[36]

Horne felt that Australia's foreign policy was caught somewhere between 'panic and sentimentality' with 'Asia' contributing disproportionately to the panic. While Australia's relationship with Indonesia and the West Papua dispute loomed large in Horne's discussion, the 'Asia' to which he referred was an inclusive category in which China was a central consideration. Horne's key point was not directed to an understanding of the region; he was attempting to address the manner in which accumulated and often unexamined speculation about dangerous Asia and vulnerable Australia made it appreciably harder to formulate an Australian foreign policy. He attributed the regular appeals to neighbourliness and expressions of friendliness towards Asia as rather hollow attempts to placate and soothe. For Horne, 'living with Asia' was imperative, but it was also a relationship troubled by distorted thinking that made it hard to find a measured, emotionally stable pattern of interaction.

The politics of Asian engagement

Australia's relationship with Asia has always been steeped in politics. It was the conservative United Australia Party that made the first tentative moves towards engagement in the 1930s with the Goodwill Mission followed by the appointment of trade commissioners to key Asian locations. It was the Menzies government that made the first diplomatic appointments to the region, sending John Latham to Japan, Frederic Eggleston to China and Richard Casey to Washington. This didn't stop Brian Penton, in his review of Australia's inter-war policies, accusing the conservative side of politics of being so attached to Britain that no independent Australia policy towards Asia could emerge.[37]

The Labor tradition has even fewer claims to an independent policy in the inter-war years, choosing to rest its case on the policies of H.V. Evatt, minister for External Affairs from 1941 to 1949 and those of Dr John Burton, the secretary of his department (1947–50). Evatt and Burton drew upon the arguments of geo-graphical proximity which had emerged during the 1930s and added, over the following decade, a measure of support for Asian decolonization and the resolu-tion of international disputes through the United Nations. Both Evatt and Burton made sizable claims for the leadership Australia was able to provide in determin-ing the future of the region. While Labor sought to show a friendlier face to Asia, its case was weakened by a commitment that bordered on zealotry to maintain a white Australia.

By the 1990s, the Labor government led by Paul Keating insisted that Labor was the only party with the policies and the vision to engage Asia. Keating placed a particular emphasis on Indonesia, but his comments related to Asia as a whole. In making this claim, Keating insisted that it was the Whitlam Labor government that took the historically important initiatives that redefined Australia's place in the region: it was the first government to commit to a non-discriminatory immigra-tion policy, thereby removing a long-standing source of resentment; secondly, in recognizing China, Whitlam laid the basis for an independent Australian foreign policy. Between 1983 and 1996 the Hawke and Keating Labor governments urged closer ties with the region and a deeper knowledge of Asian societies, cultures and languages. Where Bob Hawke spoke of the need for 'Asia-literacy', Paul Keating insisted on closer 'engagement' with Asia. In each case the enthusiasm for Asia was underscored by the economic benefits that Australia derived from the boom economies of Asia. Asia had been progressively redefined as a region of possibil-ities rather than a zone of entangling 'problems'. Moreover, the case for engaging Asia was closely linked to a domestic political agenda designed to modernize and internationalize Australian thinking and build a more competitive, export-oriented economy.

Just ahead of his election as prime minister in 1996, John Howard delivered a speech to Asialink, a Melbourne-based non-academic organization promoting public knowledge of Asia, in which he pointed out the Coalition's credentials in linking Australia more closely to the region: 'I am proud to address you tonight as Leader of a Party which has always been committed to developing the range and depth of Australia's relations with the countries of the Asia–Pacific region. A Party with a long and proud record not only in policy achievement but also in leading the debate within the Australian community on Asia–Pacific issues'.[38] It was an audi-ence that wanted to be reassured that engagement would remain a priority under a Howard government. Where Keating invoked a Labor tradition of engagement, Howard saw the need to make a counter-claim. Accordingly, Howard emphasized the Coalition's role in creating a stable security environment through the Anzus Treaty and the Five Power Defence Agreement. He went on to cite the Colombo Plan and the 1957 trade agreement with Japan as Coalition initiatives. Howard ended more controversially with the claim that it was a Coalition government that finally put an end to the White Australia policy. The content of these competing party political claims is less important in this context than the fact that engaging Asia was sufficiently important to both sides of politics for speeches to be made on the superior leadership the respective parties had shown on this topic. Even so, it can be noted that whereas Keating was more inclined to refer to 'Asian engagement', Howard's preferred term was 'Asia–Pacific'.

Among the many 'Asias' invoked by politicians and commentators was the rhetorical Asia – that generalized collective of races, nations, cultures and religions that had traditionally given rise to a good deal of anxiety among the settler population of white Australia. This was the Asia that appeared to look critically upon Australia, resenting the space, freedom and opportunities its citizens enjoyed and criticizing their exclusivity. Donald Horne was one of the first to suggest that it might become a sign of Australian leadership to move beyond the view of 'Asia' as constituting a series of intractable problems and disabling threats to reach a point where dealing with Asia was part of the normal business of government. Paul Keating was convinced that Labor had shown itself to be the party that had moved beyond the old anxieties to a new and easy accommodation with Asia, reflected in his close relationship with Indonesia's President Suharto. The relationship with the Malaysian prime minister Mahathir Mohammed posed some difficulties but those continued after Howard came to power. Keating maintained that the Coalition in general, and John Howard in particular, were still locked into an older and more suspicious frame of mind about dangerous Asia, which effectively precluded both closer ties with the region and a significant role in shaping regional outcomes and institutions.

Keating's taunt that John Howard was incapable of showing real leadership on Asian engagement was not forgotten, and certainly not by Howard himself. He returned to the subject on his first official visit to Vietnam for the Asia Pacific Economic Cooperation (APEC) meeting in November 2006. The prime minister was reported to have said that Australia was 'now a natural, comfortable and permanent part of Asia'. In making this claim at a press conference, Howard reminded his audience that it was once alleged that he was not equipped to deal with Asia. He now felt that simply reminding his audience of this suggestion was sufficient for it to be dismissed as false.[39] As prime minister, John Howard cultivated the 'aspirational' middle-class voter and it may afford some insight into his newly found sense of ease and familiarity with Asia that it, too, was rapidly becoming middle class: 'The most amazing transformation is occurring. The centre of gravity of the world's middle-class is shifting to this part of the world and will remain here'.[40] It was clearly a comforting thought that a middle-class Asia would have a lot in common with Australia, the world's first suburban nation with a middle-class that had provided powerful, though not uninterrupted, electoral support for the Coalition parties from the 1950s onwards.

The return of Asia-literacy

Howard might have been content to imagine that he was speaking to like-minded friends across the region, but his primary concern remained to strengthen local values rather than reinforce regional ones. This he did through urging a focus on Australian history and its narrative of a traditional Australian ethos. I have suggested elsewhere that this became the Howard government's means of neutralizing the Hawke–Keating government's emphasis on Asia-literacy and its engagement with the region.[41] For the Rudd Labor government, however, picking up the baton of Asia-literacy that had been allowed to drop by the Coalition under Howard seemed the natural move to make, given Rudd's own involvement in the genesis of the strategy, his diplomatic background and his knowledge of China. Just as it had formerly been under Hawke and Keating, the importance of a mutual ability to understand and effectively communicate between Australia and its Asian neighbours was once more elevated to a position of significance in the government's thinking on foreign relations. The return to Asia-literacy was accompanied by a domestic agenda of engagement with indigenous Australia and the formal acknowledgement of the injustices they had suffered at the hands of successive Australian governments.

Much interest was engendered, in the region as well as at home, over the extent of Kevin Rudd's personal connection with China, where he had studied and served as a diplomat; his grasp of Mandarin even gave him an unrivalled opportunity to upstage Howard at the APEC meeting in Sydney in September 2007. China was woven into Rudd's personal narrative in a way that caused some to wonder what it might mean for Australia's relations with other Asian nations, some of whom were already uncomfortable about China's dominance of the region as an emerging great power economically, politically and militarily. Asked during ABC television's *Q&A* programme, in May 2008, why he had studied Mandarin, Rudd replied: 'I was always interested in China and interested because, as a kid growing up, I thought it would have a big impact on us in the future, and it's kinda turned out that way'.[42]

Rudd's personal engagement with China led some to suggest the possibility of its over-weighting Australian foreign policy with an unhealthy closeness to China. This is to overlook the nature of the relationship under Howard, which saw a great expansion in economic inter-dependence with China, something that was touted as giving Australia an advantage in the current global economic hard times. So long as the Chinese economy continued to expand, both the previous and the current governments were happy to find virtue in the strength of the relationship.

There was no doubting the conviction behind the Rudd government's engagement with Asia, even if for some there still remained a question over which 'Asia'. From the start, however, while acknowledging the immense influence China through its size alone has on the region we inhabit, Rudd continually sought to identify the region much more broadly, arguing that 'we are at the beginning of an Asia–Pacific century'. In an address to the Asia Society just seven months after being elected Rudd indicated that Asia–Pacific relations were being placed at the forefront of government policy, as what he described as 'the third pillar of the Government's foreign policy – our policy of comprehensive engagement in the Asia–Pacific region'.[43] A key element of this fresh engagement was the government's determination to turn Australia into 'the most Asia-literate country in the collective West'.[44] Rudd has consistently argued since the 1990s that we need to build our relationships across the whole Asia–Pacific region by becoming much more educated about our neighbours and their languages and cultures. As he pointed out to his television audience during the *Q&A* programme:

> the rise of China, the rise of India, and the continuing role of Japan and our nearest neighbour Indonesia, are going to so fundamentally shape this country's future . . . in all its dimensions – security policy, strategic policy, economic policy, social policy, language, culture, the rest. Frankly, if I've got a hope it's that we become not just the most Asia-literate country in the collective West but also the most China-literate country, because it's going to be such a huge impacting factor for Australia's future.[45]

The importance of 'Asia-literacy' to the government's strategy for preparing Australia for the 'Asia–Pacific century' was also signalled by Julia Gillard, then deputy prime minister and minister for Education, only a month after the election, when raising the issue of Asian language education with State and Territory leaders at the December 2007 Council of Australian Governments (COAG) meeting. She pointed out that Australia had a lot of catching up to do in this regard:

> We're a long way behind where we need to be. Obviously, speaking the languages of our region is vital for this nation's future. The former government, the Liberal Party, ended Australia's Asian languages and studies program in Australian schools in 2002. That was the wrong decision.[46]

Some might see an irony in the Rudd 'Asia-literacy' agenda once again being brought up at COAG. This was the same venue at which 13 years previously the whole process had been originally set in motion following the presentation of a report on Asian languages and the economic future of Australia from a specially constituted COAG working party chaired by a Queensland public servant who was then little-known (nationally), Kevin Rudd.[47] While this report was not the first to recommend boosting the learning of Asian languages, it did set out a detailed, costed national programme aimed at enabling school students to graduate from Year 12 in 2006 having completed a 10-year study of an Asian language.[48] As a consequence, the programme was set in motion in September 1994 when the Keating Labor government set up the National Asian Languages and Studies in Australian Schools (NALSAS) taskforce charged with coordinating and overseeing the strategy (actual implementation being the responsibility of States and Territories) – the very taskforce that the Howard government axed in 2002, thus cutting short the projected study-time for the students who had already commenced the programme.[49]

The difference was that, whereas in 1994 the effectiveness of the programme was compromised by reluctance on the part of the Commonwealth to fully share in its funding, after 2007 Rudd was now in a position to enforce his vision. In the May 2008 Budget, the Rudd–Gillard commitment was cemented by new funding provisions setting aside $62.4 million to establish a new National Asian Languages and Studies in Schools Program (NALSSP), with Julia Gillard this time placing the programme within the context of 'global challenges such as climate change and regional security', arguing that 'Familiarity with the languages and cultures of Asian neighbours will make it easier to work with regional neighbours to positively address these challenges'.[50]

India: part of Asia?

One regional neighbour, whose national languages have not so far been part of an Asian languages programme in Australian schools,[51] had been watching the Rudd government's moves with particular interest. India, with a new aspiring and prosperous middle-class currently estimated to reach about 583 million people by 2025, has a presence in the region that cannot be ignored. It has obvious strategic concerns over Chinese expansion and views Rudd's apparent closeness to China with some suspicion. The Indian commentator B. Raman, a retired member of the Indian Cabinet secretariat, and now with the Chennai Centre for China Studies, has drawn attention to what he sees as Rudd's China-focus. Writing in April 2008 of Rudd's recent overseas tour, Raman observed that 'China, China, China, China and more of China was the recurring theme of his speeches in the countries visited by Mr. Rudd' and that 'His indifference to India was apparent . . .. Wherever he spoke, his preoccupation was with Australia's relations with the US and China. Hardly any reference to India.'[52]

India has not been as central to Australian foreign policy considerations in recent times as its size and growing economic power might suggest: there has been no Indian prime ministerial visit for 20 years and relations over this period have been troubled by what the Lowy Institute commentator Rory Medcalf characterized as 'frustrating bilateral differences, not to mention patches of sheer indifference'.[53] Yet, it might strike one as odd that some of the things India and Australia have in common have not made for a closer relationship: both countries are federalized democracies; they also have a shared heritage as part of the British imperium and have been long-standing trading partners, since the nineteenth century. And more recently, as Medcalf points out, India has emerged as a major export market for Australia,[54] and 'People of Indian origin are changing Australia's society and economy overwhelmingly for the better, as a major source of overseas students and desperately-needed skilled migrants'.[55] Through 2009 and into 2010 Australia's relationship with India has sustained serious and possibly long-lasting damage as attacks on Indian students continue in Melbourne, drawing accusations of racism in the Indian media. These episodes have re-awakened many of the ghosts from Australia's past as a white nation opposed to Asian immigration.

Some have argued that attacks on students are not all that is impeding the future progress of the relationship; there is also the unresolved question of uranium sales. According to the journalist and Asia-watcher Greg Sheridan, 'the enormous damage Australia has suffered in India as a result of the attacks is not so much with the policy class . . . but with the great Indian public'. While Rudd, on his visit to India in November 2009, was attempting to engage with that 'policy class', he had to acknowledge that the export of uranium was 'the one "unresolved" part of the energy relationship'. In Sheridan's judgement, so long as that remained the case the Rudd government's effort to raise the status of the relationship would fail.[56]

It can also be argued that Australia in the past has taken India, as a former imperial colony, too much for granted. Never regarded in the popular conscious-ness as a threat, historically, in the way other Asian countries have been, India shares some things in common with Australia, one being language, which also makes it less straightforward to fit India into the 'Asia-literacy' paradigm. The fact that Indian politicians and officials, and its educated classes, speak English so readily has led Australians to believe that we are always talking the same language. The study of Indian sub-continental languages and India's history and culture in Australian universities has been sporadic and is weaker now than in the 1960s–70s. Equally, Australian diplomatic representation in India has been minimal, especially compared to Australian representation in China. As Rory Medcalf points out:

> DFAT has not cultivated a single Hindi-speaker in a decade. . . . to consider it not to be worth schooling a single Australian diplomat in that language is a false economy, not to mention an insult to a major world civilisation.[57]

An Asia Pacific community

Rudd had been careful to include India in his public pronouncements, naming it early on as one of the other equally significant emergent powers in the region apart from China that Australia needed to engage. Reinforcing the Labor govern-ment's commitment to building Australia's relations with the countries to its north was Rudd's desire to move beyond the current regional architecture of bilateral arrangements and structures such as APEC and ASEAN, to build a new structure which would embrace India as much as other states in a broader re-defined region stretching from the Pacific to the Indian Ocean:

> We need to have a vision for an Asia Pacific Community, a vision that embraces:
>
> - A regional institution which spans the entire Asia–Pacific region – including the United States, Japan, China, India, Indonesia and the other states of the region.
> - A regional institution which is able to engage in the full spectrum of dialogue, cooperation and action on economic and political matters and future challenges related to security.[58]

While it is yet to be seen whether Rudd's proposal for a new 'regional institu-tion' will garner support at home or in the region, a number of commentators have pointed to the more intangible advantages of becoming a more Asia-literate nation: it goes to the heart of Australia's new relationship with Asia and the terms of engagement that allow the relationship to flourish politically, culturally and economically. 'My vision is for the next generation', Kevin Rudd has said, 'of Australia's businessmen and women, economists, accountants, lawyers, architects, artists, film-makers and performers to develop language skills which open their region to them'.[59] In this context, to have a leader that can communicate effectively in another language is a symbolic marker of the rejection of the old 'monolingual mindset' that has characterized the rhetoric of Australia's engagement with its near neighbours since the Second World War. Language is important, as Michael Clyne observed, because it 'is not only a means of communication but also a symbol of common ground and a way of gaining deep access to a people'.[60]

By the end of the nineteenth century a narrative had already been established for Australia's relationship with the region to its north. There was certainly anxiety at being taken over or submerged by populous Asia, but also a persistent belief that as an advanced democracy Australia might emerge to play a leadership role in the region. With the growth of Asia's influence after the Second World War there were those who argued that Australia's security and future prosperity would depend on how well we understood 'Asia'. The sense of urgency over Asian engagement and Asia-literacy grew, fuelled particularly by the growing economic strengths of our northern neighbours. By the late twentieth century it seemed more important than ever for Australia to be accepted as part of Asia. While a more powerful Asia generated some unease about the shifting balance of power in the region, it also played to a long-standing search for a leadership role for Australia in regional affairs, a presence, commensurate with her status as a free-standing continent. In this search for regional influence the way Australia has been viewed and received in the region is crucial. Kevin Rudd's ambition to create a new Asia–Pacific community encountered many barriers not least, perhaps, the ongoing suspicion that Australia has no deep affinity for the region or, worse, harbours racist hostilities to non-Europeans. As the recent and relentlessly bad press that Australia has received in India demonstrates, seeing Australia as outside Asia has by no means been consigned to the past.

Notes

1 The question was posted on 29 March 2005 and ran until 8 April 2005, on ExpatSingapore online discussion forum, http://www.expatsingapore.com/forum (accessed 10 March 2007).
2 Edward Gibbon Wakefield, *A Letter from Sydney and Other Writings* (London: J.M. Dent, 1929 [1829]), 92–9.
3 Charles H. Pearson, *National Life and Character: A Forecast* (London: Macmillan, 1894), ch. 1.
4 Randolph Bedford, 'White, Yellow and Brown', *Lone Hand*, 1 July 1911.
5 Raphael Cilento, *The White Man in the Tropics: With Especial Reference to Australia and its Dependencies* (Melbourne: H.J. Green, 1925).
6 Raphael Cilento, 'Health Conditions in the Pacific Islands', *Medical Journal of Australia*, 31 May 1930, 724–77.
7 Commonwealth Bureau of Census and Statistics, Melbourne, *Official Year Book of the Commonwealth of Australia 1901–1919*, no. 13 – 1920, prepared by G.H. Knibbs

(Melbourne: Albert J. Mullett, 1920), section IV, 90–1. After Charles Wickens took over as Commonwealth Statistician, in 1922, basically the same text was retained but in a slightly edited form, until 1929.

8 Philip E. Muskett, *The Illustrated Australian Medical Guide* (Sydney: William Brooks, n.d.).

9 Arthur H. Adams, *The Australians: A Novel* (London: Eveleigh Nash, 1920), 30.

10 W.R. Crocker, *The Japanese Population Problem: The Coming Crisis* (London: George Allen & Unwin, 1931), 30.

11 S.H. Roberts *et al.*, *Australia and the Far East: Diplomatic and Trade Relations*, ed. Ian Clunies Ross (Sydney: Angus & Robertson, 1935).

12 Alfred Deakin, *Temple and Tomb in India* (Melbourne: Melville, Mullen & Slade, 1893); Alfred Deakin, *Irrigated India: An Australian View of India and Ceylon, Their Irrigation and Agriculture* (London: W. Thacker, 1893).

13 Donald Horne, *The Education of Young Donald*, rev. ed. (Ringwood: Penguin Books, 1988 [1967]), 54–6, 61–2.

14 R.M. Crawford, 'Preface', in *Ourselves and the Pacific*, ed. R.M. Crawford (Melbourne: Melbourne University Press, 1945 [1941]), vi.

15 Herbert Strang, *The Air Scout: A Story of National Defence* (London: Oxford University Press, 1912).

16 'People or Perish', *Millions Magazine*, 15 October 1923.

17 W. Macmahon Ball, *Possible Peace* (Melbourne: Melbourne University Press, 1936), 115.

18 For an examination of international awareness in Australia from the 1930s to the 1950s, see J.D. Legge, *Australian Outlook: A History of the Australian Institute of International Affairs* (Sydney: Allen & Unwin, 1999).

19 Jack Shepherd, *Australia's Interests and Policies in the Far East* (New York: International Secretariat, Institute of Pacific Relations, 1940 [1939]), xi.

20 Publisher's note in *Westward the Course! the New World of Oceania*, by Paul McGuire (New York: William Morrow, 1942), v.

21 Brian Penton, *Advance Australia – Where?* (London and Sydney: Cassell & Company, 1943), 57.

22 George H. Johnston, *Pacific Partners* (London: Victor Gollancz, 1945).

23 According to Harry Benda, the popular acceptance of 'Southeast Asia' as a geographical entity dates from the creation of SEAC in 1943; see Harry J. Benda, 'The Structure of Southeast Asian History: Some Preliminary Observations', in *Man, State and Society in Contemporary Southeast Asia*, ed. Robert O. Tilman (New York: Praeger, 1969), 3 and n1.

24 George H. Johnston, *Journey Through Tomorrow* (Melbourne: Cheshire, 1947), author's note.

25 Robert J. Gilmore and Denis Warner, *Near North: Australia and a Thousand Million Neighbours* (Sydney: Angus & Robertson, 1948), v.

26 R.G. Casey, *Friends and Neighbours: Australia in the World* (Melbourne: Cheshire, 1954), foreword.

27 John Foster Fraser, *Australia: The Making of a Nation* (London: Cassell, 1910).

28 Percy Spender, 'Statement on Foreign Policy by the Minister for External Affairs (The Hon. P.C. Spender, K.C., M.P.) in the House of Representatives 9th March 1950', in *Politics and a Man*, by Percy Spender (Sydney: Collins, 1972), 315.

29 Casey, 8.

30 W. Macmahon Ball, 'The Australian Press and World Affairs', in *Press, Radio and World Affairs: Australia's Outlook*, ed. W. Macmahon Ball (Melbourne: Melbourne University Press, 1938), 13.

31 Ball, 'The Australian Press', 16.

32 Casey, 11.

33 J. McAuley, 'Power Vacuum to Our North', *Observer*, 5 April 1958, 109.

34 D. Warner, 'Advance Austral-Asia Fair', *Observer*, 14 June 1958, 268.

35 J.F. Cairns, *Living with Asia* (Melbourne and London: Lansdowne Press, 1965).

36 D. Horne, 'Living with Asia', *Observer*, 7 March 1959, 145.

37 See Penton, 215.

38 The Hon. John Howard, MP, 'Australia's Links with Asia: Realising Opportunities in our Region' (Fifth Asialink Lecture, The Myer Store, Melbourne, 12 April 1995), http://www.asialink.unimelb.edu.au (accessed 12 March 2007).

39 John Howard in Ho Chi Minh City, Vietnam, quoted in Graeme Dobell, 'PM Highlights Strong Asia Relationship', 21 November 2006, AM, ABC Online, http://www.abc.net.au/am/content/2006/s1793482.htm (accessed 12 March 2007).

40 Howard quoted in Dobell.

41 David Walker, 'The "Flow of Asia": Vocabularies of Engagement: A Cultural History', *Australian Journal of Political Science* 45, no. 1 (2010): 45–58.

42 Kevin Rudd interviewed in *Q&A*, television programme, Sydney: ABC Television, 22 May 2008.

43 The Hon. Kevin Rudd, MP, Prime Minister of Australia, 'It's Time to Build an Asia Pacific Community' (address to the Asia Society, AustralAsia Centre, Sydney, 4 June 2008). http://www.asiasociety.org.au/speeches/speeches_current/s55_PM_Rudd_AD2008.html (accessed 15 February 2009). The other two pillars of the government's foreign policy identified by Rudd were, first, the alliance with the United States and, second, the United Nations (that is, 'a strong rules-based international system').

44 Rudd, 'It's Time to Build an Asia Pacific Community'.

45 Rudd interviewed in *Q&A*.

46 The Hon. Julia Gillard, MP, Deputy Prime Minister, Minister for Education, Minister for Employment and Workplace Relations, Minister for Social Inclusion, quoted in Scott Bevan, 'Asian Languages in Schools', *The World Today*, ABC News (radio), 19 December 2007. http://mediacentre.dewr.gov.au/mediacentre/AllReleases/2007/December/Asianlanguagesinschools.htm (accessed 20 February 2009).

47 National Asian Languages and Cultures Working Group, *Asian languages and Australia's economic future: A Report prepared for the Council of Australian Governments on a Proposed National Asian Languages/Studies Strategy for Australian Schools* (Brisbane: Queensland Govt. Printer, 1994). Also known as the Rudd Report. Kevin Rudd was then director-general of the Office of Cabinet in the Wayne Goss Queensland Labor government.

48 National Asian Languages and Cultures Working Group, 135–70.

49 For an account of the genesis of Rudd's Asia-literacy agenda, see Deborah Henderson, 'Politics and Policy-making for Asia Literacy: The Rudd Report and a National Strategy in Australian Education', *Asian Studies Review* 32, no. 2 (2008): 171–95.

50 The Hon. Julia Gillard, MP, Deputy Prime Minister, *Budget: Education Revolution 2008–09*, statement, *Budget Papers*, 13 May 2008 (Canberra: Australian Government, 2008), 39.

51 The Rudd Report's determination of 'the four priority Asian languages' was based on an analysis of which languages apart from English were thought to be those 'in which Australia will have its most significant economic dealings over the next 20 years and beyond'; in 1994 India only appeared as a significant export market from 2012 and didn't appear on the list of significant languages. National Asian Languages and Cultures Working Group, 40–8.

52 B. Raman, 'Kevin Rudd: All the Way with China', Chennai Centre for China Studies, 24 April 2008, http://www.c3sindia.org/india/236 (accessed 12 April 2010).

53 Rory Medcalf, 'Australia's Relations with India', The Interpreter: Lowy Institute for International Policy, 21 December 2007. http://www.lowyinterpreter.org/post/2007/12/21/Australias-relations-with-India.aspx (accessed 12 April 2010).

54 In 2007 India was Australia's seventh-largest market for goods and services combined, according to an Australia–India FTA feasibility study by the Australian Department

of Foreign Affairs and Trade. 'Australia–India FTA Feasibility Study', Australian Government: Department of Foreign Affairs and Trade, http://www.dfat.gov.au/GEO/india/fta-study/index.html (accessed 7 March 2009).

55 Medcalf.
56 Greg Sheridan, 'It's a Start, but India Ties Need Attention', *Weekend Australian*, 14–15 November 2009, Commentary, 23.
57 Medcalf. He also asks, if Canberra deploys diplomats in Shanghai, Guangzhou and Hong Kong, why not also in Mumbai, Chennai or Kolkata?
58 Rudd, 'It's Time to Build an Asia Pacific Community'.
59 Kevin Rudd quoted in Kathe Kirby, 'Is Australia Asia smart?', ABC News, 18 August 2008, http://www.abc.net.au/news/stories/2008/08/18/2338257.htm (accessed 20 February 2009).
60 Michael Clyne, 'Show-offs Urgently Required', *Australian*, 14 November 2007, http://www.theaustralian.news.com.au/story/0,25197,22753216–25192,00.html (accessed 17 February 2009).

5   Singapore, Southeast Asia and the place of orientalism

Leong Yew

Introduction

Edward Said's concept of Orientalism has, by now, become a particularly familiar framework with which scholars have used to analyse, explain or characterize how area knowledge – especially of that part of the world called the Orient – has come to be constituted. Traditionally, the way individuals have understood or attempted to study geographical areas and regions has been shaped largely by positivism and empiricism, thus leading to the assumptions that objective and universal truths about these places could be uncovered and accurately represented. Orientalism's usefulness, then, lay in its ability to dismantle these assumptions by uncovering power relationships, such as between power and knowledge, between a more powerful observing subject and a weaker subordinate object. Ultimately, the Orient is not a passive, lisible object waiting to be represented, but was imaginatively created and willed out of the observer's preconceived fantasies, anxieties and stereotypes of these places.[1]

While Said undoubtedly left an important legacy, he was not alone in developing this critical position, and others like K.M. Pannikar, Anwar Abdel-Malek, Syed Hussein Alatas and Bryan Turner have drawn on the same theoretical armature either before him or in parallel.[2] Nonetheless, these perspectives that warn of the entanglements between politics and the production of area knowledge adopt two broad conventions: the constitutive nature of alterity and identity and the unidirectionality of the Orientalist gaze. First, because Orientalists – the scholars, colonial administrators and travellers who wrote about the Orient – could not be accepted as producing factual and truthful knowledge about this part of the world, what was more important were the underlying and often unconscious forces that informed what they wrote or knew about the Orient. Fundamentally, identity licensed the Orientalist project because knowledge of the Orient became predicated on the distinction between the Orientalist observer as 'self' and the Oriental as the 'other'. In this way Orientalism sought to understand the Oriental as based on difference, thus crudely the Oriental other has often been seen varyingly as barbaric, exotic, primitive, cunning, dangerous, mysterious, alluring and so on. Second, critiques of Orientalism have tended to be unidirectional. Said's own work and the many that followed[3] have broadened the scope of critique. While Said's main focus was on

Western representations of the Middle Eastern Orient, many other scholars have adapted and transmuted *Orientalism* such that other parts of the world subordinated (not just officially colonized) to the West like East Asia, South Asia, Latin America, Africa and the Pacific Islands were investigated for how they too became objects of Western knowledge and differentiation.

While these critiques of Orientalism have richly contributed to an academic field called 'cultural studies', my concern is that this West/self–Oriental/other uni-directionality and a Western-centric distillation of alterity preoccupy the majority of these works. As I mentioned in an earlier chapter of the present volume, 'axial politics' in studies about alterity in Asia should take into consideration the multiply constituted nature of knowledge relationships in the region. For instance, while many critiques of Orientalism might be interested in the way different 'Western' observers may have come to terms with the region, it is also equally vital to query how Asians may have done the same to other Asians, leading to innumerable per-mutations of different axial relationships that imbricate varying gradations of power. For example, a study of Orientalism in Japan or the Philippines would involve a fairly static politics of otherness even though the places under study are different. However, how Vietnam might conceive of China as other would be based on a set of power relations that might be very different from the way it relates to Laos. In brief, because different agents and entities in Asia conceive of relations to other parts of Asia in varying ways, what axial politics imply is the presence of hetero-Orientalisms or plurality in the way they come to terms with difference. How then can we conceptualize or make use of Orientalism in Asia? If certain nations adopt or internalize Western knowledge frameworks as a means of understanding other places in the region, do they *ipso facto* also become Orientalists themselves? What happens when the gaze is inverted, such as the case of Asians looking back at the West, thus constituting a form of Occidentalism? Does the assumption of power within the region (such as Japan and China – themselves objects of Western Orientalism) create new empowered or alternate forms of Orientalism? And does the legacy of colonialism create intellectuals who, mimicking and internalizing modernity and Western epistemologies, also become Orientalists themselves?

These questions about Orientalism internal to the Orient themselves require a considerable amount of scholarly attention. While the present chapter hopes in some ways to articulate their relevance, its scope is more modest. Particularly, this chapter is about Singapore and what is at stake in considering Singaporean Orientalism in Southeast Asia. To a large extent, the archetypal Western Orientalist seems to find his (or her) double in Singapore. Even though it was once a British colony, and therefore subjected along with the rest of the Malay world/peninsula to British Orientalism,[4] it continued to embrace the same mental frameworks in order to come to terms with the region post independence. As Singapore embarked on industrialization in the 1960s and 1970s, seeking developmental assistance and investment from first world countries, it also institutionalized Western epistemolo-gies and modern rationalities. So implicitly the Orientalism that was structured into Western cultural production and modes of learning was reproduced at the national level. Typically, Singaporean consumption of Hollywood or adoption of research centres like the (initially) Western scholar-led Institute of Southeast Asian Studies led to the acceptance of Orientalist ways of knowing and thinking about the region. In addition, Singapore's phenomenal economic growth and increasing clout further fuelled its sense of exceptionalism and superiority, and in this way Orientalism provided Singaporeans a way of distinguishing themselves from their 'others' and for explaining the backwardness and developmental slowness of Southeast Asia, particularly prior to the 1990s.

While there may be much evidence to support the claim that Singaporeans are Orientalists, there are also instances in which the Saidian conception of this term does not apply neatly. Political and economic clout aside, Singapore's sense of power does not translate into a systematic form of imperial discourse, something that is crucial to the Saidian formulation. More importantly, however, there are also ambiguities that disclaim any regional consciousness in contradictingly allowing Singaporeans to display more empathetic forms of identification. In an essay by Shirley Geok-lin Lim, there is doubt that there is any systematic regional representation in Singapore's cultural production. In effect, Lim stresses that the twin discourses of globalism and localism in Singapore feature much more prominently in imaginative fiction, hence the politics, social commentary and settings/characterizations featured in these works have much more to do with either Singapore itself or its relations with other global centres outside the region.[5] Although Lim immediately restricts her essay to English language writings and to 'imaginative literature', she implicitly conflates this with the larger Singaporean cultural production throughout her text. This denial of a regional consciousness, however, seems to run against C.J.W.-L. Wee's analysis of Singapore's pop icon, Dick Lee, where regional consciousness appears to be of paramount importance. Indeed, Wee suggests that Lee's songs, musical theatre and other compositions, do parallel the state's own understandings of Northeast and Southeast Asia, and in particular, its own sense of purpose and destiny in it.[6] For example, although Dick Lee sometimes appears to oppose the state mentality, he inordinately (and perhaps subconsciously) reinforces it, since his attempts to locate his newly found Asian identity in his hybridized blends of Western and Oriental musical forms very closely interoperate with the Singapore state's own relocation in Southeast Asia during the era of the Asian values debate in the 1990s.

At the same time too, Singaporeans who continue to be subjected to how modes of Orientalist representations by the US[7] still rely on an implicit subalternality to counter what is perceived to be overbearing encroachments of the West. For example, in Michael Hill's critique of Asian values in Singapore, the pontifications of a fairly monolithic Asian culture that is unique and different from that of the West is noted as 'reverse Orientalism',[8] implying that the substance of this Asian culture was the basis of the Western stereotype of Asia in the first place. Hence, what Singapore assumes to be an original and authentic culture is a Western creation, which it has ironically used in its Occidentalist critique of the West. Similarly Ang and Stratton's discussion of Singaporean nationalist identity also invoke the mantle of Orientalism, arguing that Singapore's attempt to culturally position itself within the 'East' and the 'West', reiterates how these binary poles are configured in the

Western imagination. Both articles attempt to expand the current thinking about Orientalism by suggesting that Singapore's involvement here is more ambivalent, thus 'unsettling and reinforcing' imperial discourse.[9]

Can we then speak of a Singaporean discourse on Southeast Asia and is Orientalism an adequate explanation for how this discourse functions? The purpose of this chapter is not so much to address these two issues in turn but to critique the place of Orientalism in Singapore's cultural production, in terms of the ambiguous nature of regional representations. At first glance, Singapore's official discourse of modernity derives very much from its colonial antecedent, and as such Orientalism is manifestly integrated into its grand perceptions of identity and difference. Yet, the nature of its nationalism contains traces of postcolonial ambivalence, which do resist and transform Orientalism to some degree. This chapter, therefore, attempts to investigate the function and place of Orientalism in Singapore and how it potentially conditions the way it thinks of Southeast Asia. In doing so it neither dispenses with it nor embraces it fully, suggesting instead that a form of 'franchised Orientalism' needs to be viewed in tandem with the two other aspects of Singaporean cultural production: nationalism and its inherent postcoloniality. What emerges out of this is a more dynamic picture of regional representation that at some levels comfortably adopts Western exoticism and fascination with the Southeast Asian Orient, while also refuses to be simply mimicry of the West at other levels.

The place of orientalism

Although Said's particular distillation of Orientalism is by now 32 years old, it continues to remain fairly persistent in two discourses. The first, which I shall crudely term the 'everyday discourse', is the language used by educated and culturally conscious individuals to recognize the increasing multiculturalism of various societies or demonstrate anxiety or sensitivity toward global ethnic or cultural differences. In this context Orientalism is seen casually to be a Western stereotyping of the other, at best a pejorative form of recognition about the biases and prejudices that inform Westerners about peoples inhabiting other cultural and ethnoscapes. The second discourse, which attends to the more specialized academic circle of the humanities and social sciences, appears to have more intellectual utility. It is more conscious of Said's 'worldliness'[10] and more prepared to take on the specific theoretical armature and political focus of his book. In this case, it is Said's twinning of Foucault's conception of discourse with Gramsci's hegemony in order to suggest how knowledge about the Orient is textually derived,[11] drawing on as much as feeding a herculean semiotic system that continues to sustain the imperial power and position of the West. So while the 'everyday discourse' reduces Orientalism to stereotype, the academic discourse veers towards the other extreme, that of heterogeneity, debate and complexity.[12] Said's ideas of Orientalism is taken as a starting point for others to oppose, critique, challenge and extend. On the one hand, critics have pointed out that his reliance on colonial textuality trivialize the material violence of imperialism, while others have stressed that *Orientalism* glosses over the diversity of colonial experiences and ignored instances in which Orientals have themselves resisted materially or textually against the West.[13] On the other hand, more sympathetic scholars have adapted and expanded Orientalism in such a way that subaltern geographical areas not covered, or alternative texts, genres and modalities not used by Said have been given attention as well.

These developments in the history of Orientalism-as-cultural-critique thus beg an important question. Considering the enormity of critical Orientalist discourses, where does the cardinal position of the West figure? This is important for a number of reasons. First, although Orientalism's unstated and underlying ethical purpose attempts to redress the subjection of the Oriental to Western power, the object of analysis – who is performing the representation of the Oriental – is still resolutely the 'Western subject'. Second, because of the binary positions inherent in Orientalism, both the West as the 'knowing self' and the Oriental as the 'known other' are entrenched as mutually constitutive categories. The 'West' is therefore inseparable from the 'Orient' as the object of knowledge can only achieve material reality in relation to the knowing subject. Third, for Said, the West is still tied to particular sovereign identities, such as Britain, France and the United States. But yet, the 'West' is a more slippery concept, intertwining with modernity in such a way that the cultural platform from which the subject perceives the world is constantly elided, disguised and occluded. In this sense, the 'West' is not merely a sovereign or geographical entity, but a more Manichean ethnic and cultural trope. For instance, because the West is also fused with modernity, subjects who do not identify themselves as Western nonetheless reproduce Western metadiscourse because of their openness to modern forms of technical rationality. Thus even though Said does not address this substantially, Orientals themselves either self-Orientalize or reproduce the terms by which other Orientals are represented.

Reconsidering the trajectory of the academic discourse on Orientalism, I am inclined to aver that the West continues to be reproduced as the knowing subject, and this shows little sign of mitigation. As Robert Young argues in his well-known critique of modern historicism, poststructuralism and postmodernism (which licenses Said's project) are Western forms of epistemological self-critiques:

> Today, if we pose the difficult question of the relation of poststructuralism to postmodernism, one distinction between them that might be drawn would be that whereas postmodernism seems to include the problematic of the place of Western culture in relation to non-Western cultures, poststructuralism as a category seems not to imply such a perspective. This, however, is hardly the case, for it rather involves if anything a more active critique of the Eurocentric premises of Western knowledge. The difference would be that it does not offer a *critique* by positioning itself outside 'the West', but rather uses its own alterity and duplicity in order to effect its deconstruction.[14]

Thus many of the works that either challenge *Orientalism* or extend its coverage to other representers or subaltern areas continue to be trapped in a mode of Western self-referentiality. At best, critical works that attempt to delink modernity from Western historicism or to establish 'alternative discourses' demonstrate concerns among 'non-Western' academics to identify ways by which intellectual agency could be reconfigured or structured into the production of regional knowledge. However, in order to effect these discussions, the classic axis of centre–periphery, West–East continues to be reproduced.[15]

Apart from the persistent Western-centricity of Orientalism, there is another issue that is of relevance to my argument. This is the problem of considering Southeast Asia as an 'Orientalized' region and the particular politics involved in the way Singapore has attempted to construct its own discourse in relation to this part of the world. Said, as it needs to be mentioned, did not have much to say about the Asian world situated at the Pacific Rim, let alone its smaller subdivision called Southeast Asia. Yet, Western imperial and colonial interests here paralleled that of Said's Orient; for instance, the region's colonial experience and varied colonial histories and, most importantly, the textuality of the Western experience in Southeast Asia. On this point of textuality, the region possessed no shortage of cultural material as the Western search for spices and souls to save became twinned with what the West saw, or willed into existence, in the colonial mirror. Southeast Asia became seen as a place teeming with ecological diversity, filled with exoticism, barbarity, chaos and political disorder. Southeast Asia's varied history can therefore be said to have Orientalist structure, a strategy by which complexities like varied imperial experiences and different historical eras were reduced to latent similarities. For instance, Alfred Wallace's *The Malay Archipelago* could be seen as operating on the same premise as the shipwreck novels of Dutch writer Willem Bontenkoe. And this, in turn, is linked to the ostensibly more sympathetic works of colonial reformists like Edward Douwes Dekker or the more recent manifestation of American imperial anxiety like Francis Ford Coppola's *Apocalypse Now*.[16]

Southeast Asia as a place for potentially thinking about the operations of Orientalism has therefore two possibilities. The first involves levelling critiques against the essentialism of Southeast Asia as a 'natural' region and attempts to address the Eurocentric nature of Southeast Asian studies. This possibility has, admittedly, over the last decade been quite systematically broached by both Western-based scholars who are now more conscious of Orientalism in Southeast Asian studies as well as regional 'home' scholars.[17] In a number of recent publications, attempts have been made to interpolate new objects of historicism in Southeast Asian studies, such as postnationalism or thinking differently about interstitiality and marginality,[18] conceptualize different ways through which Asia and Europe can mutually produce knowledge,[19] raise possibilities in the use of Southeast Asia even though its essentialism and ontological status has come into contestation,[20] and reconsider changing East–West power relations as also leading to new forms of knowledge about the region.[21] While there are undoubtedly many more state-of-the-field studies like these, it is crucial to note that the anxieties in how instituting more epistemologically conscious and critical forms of Southeast Asian studies have never been greater.

The second possibility for Southeast Asia and Orientalism is the way former objects of the Western Orientalist gaze could now be interrogated for the way they either participate in their own self-Orientalizing or think about or conceive of other

Orientals. It is therefore tempting to place Singapore into this equation. There is much to suggest that Singapore is unusual within the region because of its rapid modernization and industrialization, such that by the 1980s, it was fundamentally set apart from the rest of Southeast Asia. Unlike many of its neighbours who upon decolonization attempted to dismantle the linguistic and administrative structures of their colonial pasts, Singapore openly embraced them, to the extent of celebrating a Briton as its modern day founder. Nonetheless, the continued legacy of British colonialism in the form of modern bureaucratic and technical rationality, its economic and military clout, as well as its sense of exceptionalism raise the question of whether or not Singapore has its own form of Orientalism with regards to Southeast Asia or continues to adapt and reproduce Western imperial discourse.

In its earlier phase of industrialization, there were efforts directed to 'Asianize' its population,[22] a programme of ethnic management that also involved a process of deculturation, with modern technical rationality moving in to replace this cultural vacancy. Thus, this adoption of modernity provided the founding knowledge and epistemologies for how the region was to be perceived. For instance, Western writers and Western-style historiography dominated the teaching of Southeast Asian history in secondary schools, and at a higher level, the Institute of Southeast Asian Studies, which was created in 1967, relied on Western academic figures to helm its research because it wanted to dispel the problems of nationalistically charged scholarship.[23] At the state level, Western political science, history and geography informed Singapore's leaders how Southeast Asia in the 1960s and 1970s was to be seen as a zone of crisis: the emergence of nationalism, the failure of Western-style socialism and liberal democracy, the problems of political legitimacy and the developmental impediments confronting its neighbours.[24] As Singapore progressed through the 1980s, its developmental achievements and increasing economic preponderance fuelled the state's sense of exceptionalism,[25] and with the sense of increasing difference from the rest of the region, gave rise to discourses of nostalgia and exoticism of the poorer and less-developed parts of the region. In travel magazines like *Destination ASEAN* for instance, Singapore has often been represented as a progressive, dynamic and booming metropolis, while other parts of the region are expressed through Orientalist discourse: thus Southeast Asia is made up of Malaysian jungles awaiting Conradian self-revelation and discovery,[26] sex and massage parlours in Bangkok's Patpong district for the modernized and overworked executive,[27] and innumerable repositories of heritage and culture that are in contradistinction to Singapore's de-traditionalized urbanity.

While Singapore's discourse on Southeast Asia in the 1960s and 1970s appeared to mimic Western Orientalist representations in the same region, its increasing cultural identification in the following two decades with this place needs to be considered. The burgeoning Southeast Asian economies in the early to mid 1990s created ambivalent attitudes among the Singaporean elites towards the region. On the one hand, the expansion of the regional economy meant that Singapore's neighbours were, function-wise, becoming financially and industrially similar. Consequently, the threat that the region would now compete with Singapore for foreign investment and export markets meant that the nation had to differentiate itself and to reinvent itself as having moved on to a new 'higher' level of economic production and sense of purpose. This has come in the form of 'knowledge economy', as a distinction from the 'industrial economies' of the past. On the other hand, another discourse existed in tandem with this, capitalizing on identifying with the region as an attempt to authorize and monopolize the logic of the Asian economic miracle as having predominantly ethnic and cultural underpinnings. This is, in a sentence, the premise of the 'Asian values' debate, which in a complex way pitted Western accusations of authoritarianism against an 'Asian' discourse on communitarian democracy. Textually, this 'new' Orientalism found itself ensconced in many cultural developments in Singapore. For instance, the creation of the Asian Civilisations Museum claimed to showcase Asian ethnography while promoting 'the awareness and appreciation of the ancestral cultures of Singaporeans and their links to Southeast Asia and the World'.[28] Dick Lee's new Asian pop music and musical theatre like *Nagraland* claim to foster new sense of regionalism by creating hybrid musical forms.[29] And furthermore, new consumption habits toward Southeast Asian 'exotica' like Indochinese cuisine/fashion,[30] Balinese massage and home furnishings appear to indicate that Singaporeans are becoming more disposed towards a regional cultural identity.

The earlier phase in directly relying on Western references to understand Southeast Asia and the latter phase of ambivalent differentiation and identification, do not immediately suggest that Singapore's discourse on the region is incompatible with Orientalism, at least in the Siadian sense. In effect they seem to restate his distinction between manifest and latent Orientalism in which he argues that historical change and the shift from one imperial hegemon (Europe) to another (the United States) indicate manifest forms of Orientalism that, at a microscopic level, vary across time and space, but latently, the Western solipsism, condescension, biases and sense of cultural superiority remain constant at a more macroscopic setting.[31] Using this transfer of imperial hegemons as a precedent, I argue that new centres within new core–periphery formations, like Singapore, could continue to employ these latent forms of Orientalism without the Western cultural gaze being necessarily displaced from it. Thus whatever progress Singaporean leaders may have made in identifying with Southeast Asia is constantly offset by the overall sense of the island's exceptionalism, imagined place and desire to be an authority on how the region is to be understood. To this effect, whatever ambivalence there may be in Singapore's Orientalism suggests that while some inroads have been made in identifying Singapore with the region, the overall sense of the island's exceptionalism, imagined place, desire to be the authority on how the region is to be understood remains firmly intact.

At the risk of contradicting myself, I wish to introduce what I will now call, 'franchised Orientalism' as a way of thinking about the possibilities of Orientalism as 'provincialized'. By this term I am alluding to interventions by postcolonial intellectuals that historicism does not have a Western, universalist monopoly but different 'provincialisms'.[32] In this sense, Western historicism is not necessarily dismissed, but now recognized as forming a disjunctive relationship with other subaltern forms of historicism. Thinking about Orientalism as provincialized then compels one to rethink how axial politics would refigure the different core–periphery relations or the innumerable combinations of subaltern – subaltern relations. For instance, the growing interest in 'Orientalism in reverse' or 'Occidentalism' demonstrates how scholars have attempted to reposition the gaze or the place of the observing subject within an ex-colonial centre–periphery axis.[33] While Said has denied the possibilities of inverting this relationship,[34] other scholars like Wagner have also attempted to separate Occidentalism into two strands, with an emulative form in which the Western subject remains reproduced, and a revisionist one in local subjects take on an agency that disrupts and subverts the West.[35]

More specifically, there are a number of writings that provide an overture to or suggest how Orientalism could become provincialized. This has come about as subjects (who might otherwise have been Orientals in the Western gaze) attempt to come to terms with both their marginality and the presence of other 'Orientals'. For instance, Louisa Schein, who writes about the representation of Miao minority women by Han men in China, activates multiple layers of power relations like gender and ethnicity. Imperial discourse, which is central to Said's Orientalist critique is not so prominent here, but rather a form of internal Orientalism linked to the Chinese national agenda of state paternalism and national unification.[36] Jennifer Robertson looks at Japanese Orientalist discourse and examines how Japanese all-female revues multiply represented Asia in a way that supported the country's Second World War ambitions, ideals and efforts.[37] In Leshkowich and Jones' aptly entitled essay, 'What Happens when Asian Chic becomes Chic in Asia', the argument was not so much to suggest that self-Orientalism or the adoption of Western Orientalist tastes in Asians' consumption of Asian exotica is the only explanation for such occurrences. Rather, Leshkowich and Jones assert that through 'performative practices' it is possible to see subject positioning as multiply constitutive, implying that depending on the class, consciousness and social position, Asian consumers and producers either reproduce or have different degrees of ability at reworking or redeploying Orientalist tropes.[38] Collectively, these interventions into Orientalism's provinciality anticipated more recent attempts by López-Calvo to reconceptualize Orientalism outside the West/centre–Oriental/periphery axis through the pluralized notion of 'alternative Orientalisms'. Although López-Calvo emphasizes Latin America, his volume is instructive because contributors show how different axes of Orientalism, such as between Latin America and Asia, do not necessarily rehearse the power/knowledge–hegemony framework of Western Orientalism, but in effect give into the play of 'transculturation, hybridity, liminality, double consciousness, and cultural identity'.[39]

Taking a leaf out of the evolution of Orientalism in postcolonial thought, I wish to interject another possibility in which one of the provincialisms of Orientalism could be understood as a form of 'franchise'. By franchise I am referring to the common business model in the globalized commercial world in which a brand or a product is exported to places outside its national or cultural site of origin. Fast food names like McDonalds and Burger King come readily to mind because they demonstrate the disjunctive cultural processes by which a particular commodity becomes resignified under globalization, consequently retaining the cultural influence of its origins on the one hand, while also becoming subverted, reconfigured and reinvested with new interpolations of the locality that hosts it.[40] This franchised model of fast food restaurants do have very clear sites of origin, like the United States, but do not exhibit clear hierarchical relationships. This is because the franchisee exists in an ambivalent relationship of subsidiarity and local reinventiveness. The 'export' in this connection is not top down but is instead requested by the franchisee and the latter's capital. Yet, there cannot be any demand in this unless there is already a locality that has been previously moulded by the centre to desire the consumption of this product. Conversely, while the franchisee needs to conform to certain standards established by the headquarters, there is often much room for the franchisee to become absorbed by the locality, fusing local outlets to local cultural and ethnoscapes and demonstrating creative transformations of global products. For example, in Singapore the existence of a 'Rendang Burger' or a 'Prosperity Burger' demonstrates both the power of the global/American culture in changing the local and the subversive and appropriative possibilities of the local to rework the global.

In this way, franchised Orientalism suggests a particular conjunction between its original critique as a self-referencing Western discourse and its heterogeneous and provincialized alternatives. It implies that we cannot disregard the prevalence of the Western, modern rationality that in Ziauddin Sardar's view gives rise to the 'Orientalized Oriental' or 'brown Sahib'.[41] Thus Orientals in this sense continue to subsidiarily reproduce Western tropes of the Orient even as Asian informants they claim to see the Other from their own perspective. Disjunctively, there are also other layers and forms of Orientalism that emerge out of other types of axial relationships, invoking a repertory of political processes other than an imperial gaze, for example global capitalism, nationalism or anxieties unique to the franchised Orientalist's community. It is this tension I wish to explore in the case of Singapore, and in particular, the following examines the realm of national discourse and postcoloniality in its franchised Orientalism.

The national discourse

The idea of franchised Orientalism needs to be further developed in order for it to have greater bearing towards Singapore's representational strategies in Southeast Asia. First, since franchised Orientalism and imperial discourse are interconnected, it suggests that those who practice it inadvertently extend the scope and reach of Western imperialism because they have already placed so much intellectual and emotional investment in it. Furthermore, franchised Orientalism could also imply that a new form of subsidiary imperialism is being asserted, which in the case of Singapore appears nebulous. Does Singapore's role as a franchised Orientalist suggest that it contributes to the persistence of Western imperial discourse, or does it also mean that it exercises a new form of imperialism in the region, given its relative economic and military preponderance? Second, can there be views of the Southeast Asian other that are not so easily attributable to the operations of Orientalism? In examining the various cultural, social or political expressions made in Singapore about the region, the presence of differing sentiments across society and at different historical junctures intimate that these expressions are more complex than just merely reproductions of an inherited Western mentality. To what extent then can we attribute Singapore's regional views to other forces like globalization and Singaporean nationalism?

In dealing with these possible limitations of franchised Orientalism, the place and function of nationalism and the national discourse provide an effective point of contention and departure. Just as imperial discourse refers to a system through which the knowledge of empire is regulated and disciplined through an enormously large and diverse body of statements and ideas, national discourse is also constituted by a variable collection of 'texts' through which elemental beliefs about the nation – its sense of purpose, its origins, its place in the larger world and who is allowed membership – are reinforced and reproduced. Yet imperial and national discourses are not necessarily mutually exclusive. As Ben Wellings shows in his study on the formation of Britain in 1707, British nationalism was more narrowly a derivative of English imperialism *per se*, and this in turn allowed the latter to be hidden under 'Britain's' own sense as an empire.[42] Thus the very instances of national discourse such as the nation, the state and race could also be seen as providing impetus for British imperialism. This merging of imperial and national discourses raises the prospect that the ideals of nationalism that former colonial subjects inherited from their colonial masters would possess these inflections of empire as well. For instance, in many parts of the former colonial world, the creation of national museums serve an important function in putting officially sanctioned national heritage on display. This consolidation of national discourse seems appropriate but the adoption of Western museology as the method of running these institutions have also tended to replicate the imperial function that their counterparts in the colonial metropoles actively played.

In surveying Singapore's national discourse, such collusions between nationalism and imperial discourse do seem to have pride of place as well. Extending the museum analogy, the Asian Civilisations Museum (ACM) appears to also perform a vital function in Singapore's national identity in the 1990s and beyond. Yet, the museum is unable to function without Western museology as its guiding principle, and as such, areas like the Southeast Asian gallery relies on Orientalist ethnography – the exoticism, the mysticism and the tribalism – to provide it with its narrativizing logic. Nonetheless, unlike metropolitan centres where tropes of nationalism and imperialism co-function unproblematically, there is a far greater amount of ambivalence, incommensurability and disjuncture governing these relations in peripheral places like Singapore. This adoption of Western museology may appear to be a dominant logic but circulating around these are also national themes that may not always cohere with Orientalism. For instance, Ooi argues that the ACM, along with other national museums in Singapore, needs to self-Orientalize so as to pander to the tourist's preconceived Orientalist taste, while also reformulating Orientalism so that Singapore becomes positionally superior to other Southeast Asian countries.[43] While this may be one way to think of the ACM, it is also important to conceive of the museum as an attempt to self-inject an Asian culturalism that is in line with the state's management of the national ethos disciplining its own citizens. Thus the franchised Orientalism I speak of tends to be a mutated form than its Saidian predecessor, featuring a larger degree of discomfort between nationalism and inherited imperial mentalities, greater difficulty at determining the textual constitution of colonial discourse and an overall ambivalence even towards ideas like nationalism itself. For this I first turn to the novels of Singaporean writer, Douglas Chua, to demonstrate how nationalism and survivalist anxieties overshadow the traditional nuances of imperialism/colonialism in Orientalism. Nonetheless this nationalism does not stand independently on its own, and is later countered with the ambivalent postcolonial attitudes adopted by writers like Edwin Thumboo.

For many years, as Tamara Wagner intimates, Singapore's literary landscape has been dominated by the social problem genre and 'Chinese chick lit'.[44] There have been a number of more middlebrow works but it is in the 1990s that they have become increasingly popular. Chief among these are the spy thriller-science fiction-action adventure novels of Douglas Chua, who according to *The Straits Times* was labelled, 'Singapore's Jeffrey Archer'.[45] This comparison with the British author is hardly incidental as it acknowledges the mass-marketed Western literary genre in influencing Singapore's publishing scene. In his novels like *The Missing Page, Crisis in the Straits: Malaysia Invades Singapore, Ransom* and *The Missing Island*,[46] the modalities and genre have been clearly influenced by figures like Archer, Tom Clancy and Ken Follett,[47] and the resulting effects on the novels have been stark. In his first three novels, the protagonist, Alex Han, is a James Bond-like[48] super spy, complete with a patriotism, debonair attitude, invincibility, cunningness and a sexual appetite to match. Set in Singapore, the novels also feature intelligence organizations that are very much derived from the pop symbolism of institutions like the CIA, FBI and MI5. In Chua's imagined Singapore, the 'Inter-Service Intelligence' and 'Command and Investigation Service' similarly possess the cultural and institutional power that approximates with that of their Western counterparts.[49] Chua's villains are also divided between the fanatical and megalomaniacal masterminds who initiate their plans of terror and their superhuman and virtually indestructible henchmen who put the plans into action. What unifies these modalities with the worldliness of Western thrillers is the latter's tacit involvement with the politicized cultural discourses centred in Britain and the US. Hence if Western thrillers and science fiction are discursively produced through local political developments writ large (like the Cold War, terrorism, post-Cold War perils), Chua's appropriation of such genres would structurally inherit these concerns, no matter how far removed they may be from these themes.

In Chua's depiction of Southeast Asia, however, Western Orientalism seems to play a more tangential – even peripheral – part, particularly from a thematic point of view. Chua's themes are decidedly nationalistic, reflecting the interconnectedness of Singapore's exceptionalism and survivalist anxiety, the intermingling of the island state's sense of economic superiority, geographical centricity and the anxiety that its sovereignty will forever be threatened by a barrage of changing and invented threats. In virtually all novels, Singapore is presented as a dynamic, thriving, cosmopolitan and prosperous entity capable of sustaining an unwavering civic loyalty among its subjects. In comparison, other parts of the region are simplistically poor, undeveloped and backward. In *The Missing Page*, for example, Singapore in the twenty-first century has pulled itself economically and culturally away from its neighbours. Malaysians once again flock to Singapore for construction work; an earthquake completely levels Bali but partially destroys Jakarta thus converting Batam[50] into Indonesia's new tourist hub and second capital. And in *Ransom*, a new impoverished state in the South China Sea called the 'Republic of Sulu' suspiciously mirrors the nearby Philippines. These characterizations are deliberate in that they allow envy and rivalry from Singapore's neighbours to drive the novels' plots. In *The Missing Page* an historic document capable of rescinding Singapore's sovereignty is unearthed at a construction site by Malaysian workers, sparking a frantic and violent rush by opportunistic Malaysian politicians and a super-secret faction within Singapore to acquire the document. For the Malaysian antagonists, the greatest prize the document offers is the return of Singapore to Malaysia and the untold benefits this would bring to the Malaysian economy. Similarly, in *Ransom* the Sulu Republic's dire economic straits force some of its top politicians to contemplate using threats of terrorism on Singapore to extort $100 billion.[51] The anxieties of survivalism are, therefore, also clearly discernible. *The Missing Page* and its sequel, *Crisis in the Straits*, rehearse the age-old collective fear among Singaporeans that, although economically strong, Singapore's physical size will forever be overshadowed by Malaysia and that its military contingency has always been directed towards an invasion, the cessation of water supply from Johor and other acts of hostility. *Ransom* likewise subjects Singapore to terrorist threats,[52] with the poisoning of its water supply as the culmination of this danger. Finally, in *The Missing Island*, extra-terrestrial forces target their vanishing rays on Singapore, causing the entire island to disappear and be replaced by a cloud of haze-like smoke. In this novel, not only does Chua allude to Singapore's environmental fragility vis-à-vis the occasional regional smog caused by Indonesian forest fires, he constantly plays with the virtual invisibility of Singapore in the consciousness of outsiders. Here, the US president has to be constantly reminded of where (or what) Singapore is and the international media like CNN have to preface news reports on Singapore's disappearance with its erstwhile geographical location as south of the Malay Peninsula.

As far-fetched as these storylines may be, these novels do illustrate how Singapore exceptionalism and survivalist anxiety work together for the larger purpose of national discourse. For Singaporean readers the worldliness of Chua's fiction is reasonably clear. *The Missing Page* and *Crisis in the Straits* provide the artistic driving force for lessons on national history and in particular, Singapore's expulsion from the Malaysian Federation in 1965 and the too-commonly told story of its rise to success are reproduced as a form of poetic justice. *Ransom* as well seems to implicate Malaysia metonymically through a third (although obviously) Filipinized enemy, since this threat to Singapore's water supply is more often articulated through Malaysian–Singapore foreign relations. More precisely, *Ransom* was published at the same time as deadlocks between Singaporean and Malaysian authorities over the price of the sale of untreated raw water to the island state were coming to a head. Interestingly, the novel's climax could not be more apt at intertwining nationalist pride with the anxiety of living with Malaysia since Singapore's reliance on its neighbour for water constitutes one of the remaining obstacles in its achievement of 'true' independence. Here, Alex Han discovers that terrorists have resorted to the unthinkable: the poisoning of bottled water that would be distributed to the thousands of spectators gathered at the stadium for Singapore's national (independence) day celebrations. The hero arrives in time to stop the impending disaster, and a frantic highway chase ensues to stop the villain from fleeing the country. If anything, *Ransom* at this juncture virtually deals a form of poetic justice: it re-declares Singapore's sovereignty by metonymically suggesting as triumphant and resolute in solving its water problem in the face of craven attempts by its suppliers to disrupt it. The function of Chua's novels within the larger framework of Singaporean national discourse, therefore, gives rise to some implications. First, the representations of Southeast Asia appear to be secondary to the purpose of reproducing nationally motivated sentiments of exceptionalism and survivalism. Second, if representations of Southeast Asia parallel Western Orientalist images of the region or elsewhere, we cannot be certain that the former are immediately derivative of the latter. In effect, Singapore's unique historical circumstances that have given rise to these anxieties and its own cultural locus is enough to make Chua's texts Occidentalist and thereby providing a transformative or resistive impact on Orientalism itself.[53]

To a large extent Chua's works are emblematic of the broader state-led national discourse using survivalism and the constant reconstruction of the nature of external threats as a way of fostering national cohesiveness and unity. But to this point, the Singaporean 'national discourse' has been spoken as if it were unproblematic, since the assumptions that a state-led national hegemonic consensus exists because of the omnipresence of Singapore authoritarianism. As I have argued elsewhere, what constitutes the national discourse cannot be so easily surmised in the case of Singapore.[54] As with 'Third World literatures', the propensity to use mostly publicly accessible published texts as constituents of a particular discourse appears most inordinately to privilege the structure and composition of Western, liberal and literati societies.[55] Hence books, papers, music, art and so on are taken as elements that are broadly reflective of a collective cultural communion that spans all classes and segments of the national society. By analysing these forms of work, it is assumed that one *ipso facto* derives a sense of what that societal discourse is all about. However, in the case of many postcolonial societies, such texts may not so neatly be representative of the society at large, and could in effect, be more indicative of the discourse of a smaller, more privileged class of intellectuals and state administrators. In Singapore, the cultural scene at best appears more frenetic with the racial and class divisions generating different cultural affinities and alignments. Hence the upper class in a Western society may be positioned there on the basis of monetary wealth but identify themselves with the consumption of 'highbrow' cultural texts. In Singapore, such associations may not be so easily arrived at since the upper class may have other sources of cultural identification, which to the West may appear lowbrow. For instance, the consumption of nationally recognized literature such as the poetry of Edwin Thumboo or the novels of Catherine Lim may not necessarily have a place in the Singaporean upper class but be the preserve of a smaller, English-educated literati class. What this suggests is that the discourse analysis of published, public domain texts (like the sort performed by Said in *Orientalism*) may not be so applicable in this context, and that alternative textual sources may be needed.

The question here deals more specifically with 'discourse' and discourse analysis being a problematic component in understanding national frames and ideology, and that other forms of cultural expressions that are not so practically recorded could be obscured or devalued. Putting this problem aside, the 'national' element also seems to be conceptually troubling since it is never distant from the shadow of authoritarianism, hence the assumption that national discourse is also state discourse. Thus national writers like Thumboo and Arthur Yap are instantaneously labelled as state propagandists or de facto spokesmen of the state. For critics like Shirley Lim and Lily Rose Roxas-Tope, this may not be so much due to the Singaporean state itself than the way modernity has been incorporated as the pre-eminent rationalizing force for national discourse.[56] A consequence of this has been the relegation of literature (and other cultural productions) to the aesthetic sphere having little to do with the political aspects of society. In this way, English language writers have been cast as ambivalent because they can be seen as operating outside state ideology in a realm that is purely for art's sake.[57] Writers like Thumboo, however, seem more difficult to position since the nationalism of his poetry does play an important role in reproducing the national discourse, with his vacillating and changeable allegiance to the state discourse being one of its main features. In some of his poetic works for instance, Thumboo transcends the Singaporean state, often speaking for the wider national community by chastising and parodying state-led campaigns.[58] Yet in his other works like '9th of August – I', '9th of August – II', and his imaginative encounter between the Greek classical hero Ulysses and the artificially constructed tourist symbol – the merlion, his role as a state propagandist is most clearly exposed. For Roxas-Tope, this dissonance between the national 'state' and national 'community' arises much more out of the postcoloniality of Singapore, rather than the confluence of nation and state. This subsequently leads to Thumboo to become 'a fissured and fractured, imperfect and ambivalent postcolonial subject'.[59]

Both Chua and Thumboo obviously represent different segments of Singapore's literary discourse and the roles they play in buttressing nationalism are also fairly disjointed. Chua is by far more reproductive of state-interpreted nationalism as he produces texts for the more mainstream, middle class readership, while Thumboo's appeal circulates more in academic and literati circles. However, when taken together, both takes on Singaporean nationalism demonstrate how franchised Orientalism attains its transformative potential. Even though Chua and Thumboo invoke varying levels of state-complicity in their accounts of nationalism, what unifies them is the vacuity of what constitutes Singaporean nationalism and national identity itself. Thus when the crises and threats to Singapore's sovereignty are stripped away, and when the celebratory stance towards the patriotism of Chua's characters and the exceptionalism of Singaporean society and institutions are put aside, there is no substance to national identity apart from the quality of being ambivalently different from and similar to the rest of Southeast Asia. Similarly, a poem like Thumboo's 'Ulysses by the Merlion' juxtaposes two mythic characters – one classical and the other contemporary – and while the merlion becomes a metonymic double for and celebration of Singapore's swift emergence from economic and political obscurity, the nature of the Singaporean nation is reaffirmed as both mythic and constructed.

Conclusion: postcoloniality

This chapter has attempted to reconsider Singapore's conceptions and representations of Southeast Asia through the trope of Orientalism. While the case for this is fairly strong, considering the emotional, intellectual and discursive investment in adopting Western/modern frames of reference, there tend to be moments in which the simple extension or replication of Western imperial discourse does not so neatly fit. At first glance, much of Singapore's cultural productions, whether or not they directly or indirectly impinge on either various places in Southeast Asia or the region as a whole, reflect coherence with generic Western representations. Hence Singaporean travel magazines, music, film, literature and governmental speeches and papers often internalize a Western-self as the basis on how they come to terms with their other. The very malleable constructions of Southeast Asia as strife-torn, confronting crises of legitimacy, or simply exotic, nostalgic and dangerous that colour so many Western accounts of this region also become the very language that many Singaporean accounts use. Theoretically, very little work has been done to assess the extent of the colonial imagination in Singaporean Orientalism or whether or not other conditions give rise to different provincialisms of Orientalism. The term 'franchised Orientalism' was, therefore, adopted not only to suggest that the residual colonial mentality within Singapore has led to the adoption of Western Orientalism as the mechanism by which Singaporean society thinks of Southeast Asia, but that the localized histories, anxieties and experiences pertaining to post-coloniality further pluralize and transform Orientalism itself. Indeed, Singapore's provincialized Orientalism could have been addressed in numerous ways, such as the emergence of global capitalism and the commoditization of Asia, the creation of a unique discourse of crisis and national security, and the attempt by the ruling People's Action Party to sustain its hegemony. Each of these undoubtedly provide reasons and exhibit processes and mechanisms by which discourses on Southeast Asia have emerged and been sustained in Singapore. Nonetheless, this chapter examined only national discourse. This was partly due to space limitations in the volume, but mostly the idea of nationalism as a provincialized Orientalist discourse, particularly for a nation state that is not too long from the point of formal decolonization, exposes the ambivalence attending to the construction of its other. So while Singaporean nationalism is, as Chatterjee observes in an early work, a 'derivative discourse',[60] it also tends to be more illusory and slippery, highlighting particular historicisms unique to Singapore's imagined traumas and anxieties. In this sense, Southeast Asia arrives at being exotic, chaotic or backward place not just through the tropology of the Western imperial gaze, but also through alternate routes, signalling the more local needs of reifying Singaporeans' fragile sense of sovereignty and need to discipline its people through the construction of the Southeast Asian other.

Let me conclude by qualifying Singapore's franchised Orientalism and the national discourse as forms of postcoloniality and by doing so suggest how the Southeast Asian other might be perceived in terms that exceed its counterpart in the Western imperial gaze. Because of the dominance of postcolonial scholars located in the First World as well as those in/from South Asia, what has been written about postcolonialism has presented the postcolonial subject in certain specific ways. This postcolonial subject can in no way be said to be universally applicable as a standard model of subalternity and resistance, and as Ismail Talib has observed, this idea of postcoloniality is fraught with numerous contending definitions and approaches, particularly in the experiences of different Southeast Asian communities.[61] Postcolonialism, therefore, needs to be also provincialized. After all, the way postcolonial subjects in India imaginatively or concretely reactivate the past is not something that is similar to what their counterparts in Singapore might do. In effect the inability of Singapore's predominantly migrant population to lay claim to indigenousness and the particular ways in which national memory is constantly reconfigured mean that alternative modalities will have to be sought for what constitutes the postcolonial in Singapore. In a recent essay, Philip Holden suggests that there are two ways of doing this. The first is the tenuous gesture of constructing alternative memories, while the second, which echoes my call for more complex forms of axial relationships,[62] 'uses colonial memories and . . . metaphors to disturb the comfort of the present'.[63] In this way the type of discourse invoked by writers like Douglas Chua and Edwin Thumboo position national memory in a more fragmented way, inducing representations of the Southeast Asian other that are utilized in support of this process.

Although I hinted that certain forms of postcolonial criticism may not be immediately relevant to the Singaporean experience, I nonetheless wish to draw on another work by Partha Chatterjee that appears to be informed by South Asian experiences. In *The Nation and its Fragments* Chatterjee elaborates on how the postcolonial nation-state grapples with its modern form and longing for an imagined predecessor.[64] He divides 'fragments' of the nation between its material and spiritual domains. In the 'material' or outer domain Westernized and modernized modes like political institutionalism, science, technology, industry and statecraft exist, while the 'spiritual' or inner domain is where cultural identity is located. This second realm is where the precolonial or traditional is said to reside. But what connects this reading to my own perception of Singaporean postcoloniality is the fundamental condition of displacement and suspended (or contingent) essentialisms. Chatterjee does not claim that the spiritual realm needs to be authentic, but that its existence is the result of present circumstances, allowing for different national narrations to exist in parallel. Such moves to position incommensurable and parallel domains against each other are characteristics of what I have described elsewhere as 'disjuncture',[65] and they suggest that the presence of a dominant, totalizing Western discourse among postcolonial subjects together with alternative discourses that resist and subvert the former are not necessarily contradictions in terms. This disjuncture in effect inaugurates its own anti-rational, postcolonial logic. So, while Chatterjee's accounts of the spiritual realm might reference attempts of Indian intellectuals to reassert precolonial narratives, Singapore's spiritual realm can therefore be redescribed as Holden's interplay of alternative and colonial memories. As the other, Southeast Asia – its places, peoples, governments – provide much imaginative fuel, being split into different domains. Materially, Western rationality compels Singaporeans to adopt the Western Orientalist gaze and in this sense continues to culturally sustain contemporary forms of imperialism. Yet, because alternative logics and intentionality are also imbricated in Singaporean postcoloniality, the spiritual realm also gives rise to an other that is more purposefully employed to meet the needs of fragmented national subjectivities.

Notes

1 Edward W. Said, *Orientalism: Western Conceptions of the Orient* (New York: Pantheon, 1978), 5–6.
2 See K. M. Pannikar, *Asia and Western Dominance: A Survey of the Vasco Da Gama Epoch of Asian History 1498–1945* (London: George Allen & Unwin, 1953); Anouar Abdel-Malek, 'Orientalism in Crisis', *Diogenes* 11, no. 44 (1963): 103–40; Syed Hussein Alatas, *The Myth of the Lazy Native* (London: Frank Cass, 1977); Bryan S. Turner, *Marx and the End of Orientalism* (London and Boston: Allen & Unwin, 1978).
3 Carol A. Breckenridge and Peter van der Veer, ed., *Orientalism and the Postcolonial Predicament: Perspectives on South Asia* (Philadelphia: University of Pennsylvania Press, 1993); Julie F. Codell and Dianne Sachko Macleod, ed., *Orientalism Transposed: The Impact of the Colonies on British Culture* (Aldershot: Ashgate, 1998); Christina Klein, *Cold War Orientalism: Asia in the Middlebrow Imagination, 1945–1961* (Berkeley: University of California Press, 2003); Reina Lewis, *Gendering Orientalism: Race, Femininity, and Representation* (New York: Routledge, 1995); Bill Mullen, *Afro-Orientalism* (Minneapolis: University of Minnesota Press, 2004); Jane Schneider, ed., *Italy's 'Southern Question': Orientalism in One Country* (Oxford: Berg, 1998); Mari Yoshihara, *Embracing the East: White Women and American Orientalism* (New York: Oxford University Press, 2003); and Henry Yu, *Thinking Orientals: Migration, Contact, and Exoticism in Modern America* (New York: Oxford University Press, 2001).
4 In tandem with British colonial expansion in Malaya, the development of British colonial discourse could also be noted, especially in terms of Orientalism. Wallace's well-known natural history of this area [Alfred Russel Wallace, *The Malay Archipelago: The Land of the Orang-Utan and the Bird of Paradise* (London: Macmillan, 1883)], could be read in terms of how it was informed by Darwinian evolutionism and its readiness to conflate both animal/plant life with the human/social realms and subject them to a pre-formed schema of differentiation and exoticization. In the areas of anthropology and archaeology, Malaya and the surrounding region also provided Westerners with artefacts that were exported to places like Singapore, where they were to remain in institutions like the Raffles Museum or re-exported back to Europe.
5 Shirley Geok-lin Lim, 'Regionalism, English Narrative, and Singapore as Home and Global City', in *Postcolonial Urbanism: Southeast Asian Cities and Global Processes*, ed.

Ryan Bishop, John Phillips and Wei-Wei Yeo (New York and London: Routledge, 2003), 205–24.

6 C.J.W.-L. Wee, 'Staging the New Asia: Singapore's Dick Lee, Pop Music and a Counter-Modernity', *Public Culture* 8, no. 3 (1996): 489–510.

7 One does not have to look further than the representations by Western media of Singaporean society as authoritarian, richly characterized by the images of a wealthy, economically successful nation where vandals are caned, toilet users are fined for forgetting to flush, chewing gum is banned and a 'dictator' (in the words of William Safire) calls the shots.

8 Michael Hill, '"Asian Values" as Reverse Orientalism: The Case of Singapore' (Working Paper 150, Department of Sociology, National University of Singapore, Singapore, 2000).

9 Ien Ang and Jon Stratton, 'Straddling East and West: Singapore's Paradoxical Search for a National Identity', in *Asian and Pacific Inscriptions: Identities, Ethnicities, Nationalities*, ed. Suvendrini Perera (Bundoora: Meridian, 1995): 179.

10 See Edward W. Said, *The World, the Text, and the Critic* (Cambridge: Harvard University Press, 1983).

11 Said, *Orientalism*, 3, 6–7.

12 I mention Said's 'worldliness' here because acknowledging this is crucial to a fair reading of *Orientalism*. In some cases, readers who approach this work from outside postmodernism and poststructuralism are unable to appreciate the 'very assumptions of disciplinary authority' that are being challenged [Bill Ahscroft and Pal Ahluwalia, *Edward Said: The Paradox of Identity* (London and New York: Routledge, 1999), 74]. For those who do, however, *Orientalism* is often read by itself, without attempting to situate it in the context of Said's other works or his political position on public intellectualism.

13 See Aijaz Ahmad, *In Theory: Classes, Nations, Literatures* (London and New York: Verso, 1992); Dennis Porter, 'Orientalism and its Problems', in *The Politics of Theory*, ed. Francis Barker *et al.* (Colchester: University of Essex), 179–93; and Robert Young, *White Mythologies: Writing History and the West* (London: Routledge, 1990).

14 Young, *White Mythologies*, 19. See also Sankaran Krishna, 'The Importance of Being Ironic: A Postcolonial View of Critical International Relations Theory', *Alternatives* 18, no. 3 (1994): 385–417; and Ariel Heryanto, 'Can There Be Southeast Asians in Southeast Asian Studies', in *Knowing Southeast Asian Subjects*, ed. Laurie J. Sears (Seattle: University of Washington Press, 2007), 95–6.

15 See for instance, Beng-Lan Goh, 'Redrawing Centre-Periphery Relations: Theoretical Challenges in the Study of Southeast Asian Modernity', in *Asia in Europe, Europe in Asia*, ed. Srilata Ravi, Mario Rutten and Beng-Lan Goh (Leiden: International Institute for Asian Studies; Singapore: Institute of Southeast Asian Studies, 2004), 79–101; Syed Farid Alatas, 'The Meaning of Alternative Discourses: Illustrations from Southeast Asia', in *Asia in Europe, Europe in Asia*, ed. Srilata Ravi, Mario Rutten and Beng-Lan Goh (Leiden: International Institute for Asian Studies and Singapore: Institute of Southeast Asian Studies, 2004), 57–79.

16 For more works on Western texts in Southeast Asia see Clive J. Christie, 'British Literary Travellers in Southeast Asia in an Era of Colonial Retreat', *Modern Asian Studies* 28, no. 4 (1994): 673–737.

17 This concept of 'home' scholars refer to scholars who specialize in and research on topics relating to countries of their national origin, but more pointedly is identified as a site in which we may more productively question as well as inaugurate possibilities of transcending Eurocentric and modern frameworks of thinking about these countries. See Thongchai Winichakul, 'Writing at the Interstices: Southeast Asia Historians and Postnational Histories in Southeast Asia', in *New Terrains in Southeast Asian History*, ed. Abu Talib Ahmad and Tan Liok Ee (Athens: Ohio University Press; Singapore: Singapore University Press, 2003), 6–7, 18–24.

18 Abu Talib Ahmad and Tan Liok Ee, ed., *New Terrains in Southeast Asian History* (Athens: Ohio University Press; Singapore: Singapore University Press, 2003).

19 Srilata Ravi, Mario Rutten and Beng-Lan Goh, ed., *Asia in Europe, Europe in Asia* (Leiden: International Institute of Asian Studies; Singapore: Institute of Southeast Asian Studies, 2004).

20 Paul H. Kratoska, Remco Raben and Henk Schulte Nordholt, ed., *Locating Southeast Asia: Geographies of Knowledge and Politics of Space* (Singapore: Singapore University Press; Athens, OH: Ohio University Press, 2005).

21 Laurie J. Sears, ed., *Knowing Southeast Asian Subjects* (Seattle: University of Washington Press, 2007).

22 Raj K. Vasil, *Asianising Singapore: The PAP's Management of Ethnicity* (Singapore: Heinemann Asia, 1995).

23 Wang Gungwu, 'Two Perspectives of Southeast Asian Studies: Singapore and China', in *Locating Southeast Asia: Geographies of Knowledge and Politics of Space*, ed. Paul H. Kratoska, Remco Raben and Henk Schulte Nordholt (Singapore: Singapore University Press; Athens, OH: Ohio University Press, 2005), 71–2; see also Chia Siow Yue, 'Introduction', in *Institute of Southeast Asian Studies: A Commemorative History 1968–1998* (Singapore: Institute of Southeast Asian Studies, 1998), ix.

24 See for example Lee Kuan Yew, 'The Situation in South-East Asia' (speech, Royal Society of International Affairs, London, May 1962); (speech, Canterbury University, Christchurch, March 15, 1964); (speech, Civil Service Study Centre, Singapore, August 15, 1959).

25 This discourse of exceptionalism was already fairly pervasive when the British first acquired Singapore as a trading outpost, particularly in opposition to the 'closed' trading system adopted by other colonial powers in the region. For Stamford Raffles, Singapore's British founder, the island's establishment as a free port was seen as the 'Malta of the East'. Many years later, Singapore's former prime minister was known to have made many similar descriptions about the island state as the 'Venice in the Middle Ages', 'an oasis in the desert', and 'Israel in a Malay Muslim sea' [quoted in Philippe Regnier, *Singapore: City-State in South-East Asia*, trans. Christopher Hurst (Honolulu: University of Hawaii Press, 1991), 149.

26 Tan Boon Peng, 'A Jungle Journey', *Destination ASEAN*, November 1982, 11–14.

27 Marcus Brooke, 'Anything Goes is Patpong's Motto', *Destination ASEAN*, June 1982, 16–19.

28 Asian Civilisations Museum, 'About Us', Asian Civilisations Museum, http://www.acm.org.sg/the_museum/ethos_vision.asp (accessed February 8, 2010).

29 See Wee, 'Staging the New Asia'.

30 See Ashley Carruthers, 'Indochine Chic: Consuming the Vietnamese Exotic in Singapore, Tokyo and Sydney', in *Foodscapes: The Cultural Politics of Food in Asia*, ed. Lisa Law and Daisy Ng (Hong Kong: Hong Kong University Press, forthcoming).

31 Said, *Orientalism*, 206.

32 Dipesh Chakrabarty, *Provincializing Europe: Postcolonial Thought and Historical Difference* (Princeton: Princeton University Press, 2000).

33 See Sadik Jalal Al-Azm, 'Orientalism and Orientalism in Reverse', in *Orientalism: A Reader*, ed. A.L. Macfie (New York: New York University Press, 2000); and Couze Venn, *Occidentalism: Modernity and Subjectivity* (London: Sage, 2000).

34 Said, *Orientalism*, 50.

35 Tamara S. Wagner, *Occidentalism in Novels of Malaysia and Singapore, 1819–2004: Colonial and Postcolonial Financial Straits and Literary Style* (Lewiston: The Edwin Mellon Press, 2005); Tamara S. Wagner, 'Emulative versus Revisionist Occidentalism: Monetary and Other Values in Recent Singaporean Fiction', *Journal of Commonwealth Literature* 39, no. 2 (2004): 73–94. See also Chen Xiaomei, *Occidentalism: A Theory of Counter-Discourse in Post-Mao China* (New York: Oxford University Press, 1995).

36 Louisa Schein, 'Gender and Internal Orientalism in China', *Modern China* 23, no. 1 (1997): 69–98.

37 Jennifer Robertson, 'Mon Japon: The Revue Theater as a Technology of Japanese Imperialism', *American Ethnologist* 22, no. 4 (1997): 970–96.

38 Ann Marie Leshkowich and Carla Jones, 'What Happens when Asian Chic becomes Chic in Asia?', *Fashion Theory* 7, no. 3/4 (2003): 281–300.

39 Ignacio López-Calvo, 'Introduction', in *Alternative Orientalisms in Latin America and Beyond*, ed. Ignacio López-Calvo (Newcastle: Cambridge Scholars Publishing, 2007), xi.

40 See Bill Ashcroft, *Post-Colonial Transformation* (London and New York: Routledge, 2001).

41 Ziauddin Sardar, *Orientalism* (Philadelphia: Open University Press, 1999), 85–92.

42 Ben Wellings, 'Empire-Nation: National and Imperial Discourses in England', *Nations and Nationalism* 8, no. 1 (2002): 95–109.

43 Can-Seng Ooi, 'Orientalist Imaginations and Touristification of Museums: Experiences from Singapore' (Copenhagen Discussion Papers 1, Asia Research Centre, Copenhagen Business School, Copenhagen, 2005).

44 Tamara S. Wagner, 'Singapore's New Thrillers: Boldly Going Beyond the Ethnographic Map', *ARIEL: A Review of International English Literature* 37, no. 2–3 (2006): 69.

45 Quoted in Douglas Chua, *The Missing Page* (Singapore: Angsana Books, 1999), book cover.

46 Douglas Chua, *Crisis in the Straits: Malaysia Invades Singapore* (Singapore: Angsana Books, 2001); *Ransom* (Singapore: Angsana Books, 2002); and *The Missing Island* (Singapore: Times Books International, 2002).

47 Tan Gim Ean, 'Book Inspired by the Recent Malaysia–Singapore Spats', *New Straits Times*, May 26, 1999, 2.

48 Alex Han is not the only character in Singaporean fiction that mimics James Bond. In the local cinema (as well as joint productions) in the 1960s and 70s, characters like Jefri Zain and Cleopatra Wong were formed in the same mould.

49 Chua, *The Missing Page*, 55–6.

50 The local readership in Singapore would be no stranger to the knowledge that a considerable portion of Batam has been developed by Singaporean capital.

51 Owing to poor editing in the novel, the ransomed sum shifts unexplainably between $100 billion and $10 billion; but nonetheless the sum is intended to be significantly one-half of Singapore's financial reserves.

52 It is not certain whether or not *Ransom* was written in reference to the events following the September 11 terrorist attacks.

53 See Chapter 6 in this volume.

54 Leong Yew, 'Managing Plurality: The Politics of the Periphery in Early Cold War Singapore', *International Journal of Asian Studies* 7, no. 2 (forthcoming 2010).

55 See for instance the discussion in Ahmad, *In Theory*, 96–8.

56 Lily Rose Roxas-Tope, *(Un)Framing Southeast Asia: Nationalism and the Postcolonial Text in English in Singapore, Malaysia and the Philippines* (Quezon City: Office of Research Coordination, University of the Philippines, 1998).

57 Shirley Geok-lin Lim, *Writing S.E./Asia English: Against the Grain* (London: Skoob Books, 1994), 107; *Nationalism and Literature: English-Language Writing from the Philippines and Singapore* (Quezon City: New Day, 1993), 17–18.

58 Roxas-Tope, 191–2.

59 Roxas-Tope, 202.

60 Partha Chatterjee, *Nationalist Thought in the Colonial World: A Derivative Discourse?* (Minneapolis: University of Minnesota Press, 1986).

61 Ismail S. Talib, 'After the (Unwritten) "Postcolonial" in Southeast Asia: What Happens Next?', in *The Silent Word: Textual Meaning and the Unwritten*, ed. Robert J.C. Young,

Ban Kah Choon and Robbie B.H. Goh (Singapore: Singapore University Press, 1998), 59–70.

62 Philip Holden, 'Postcolonial Desire: Placing Singpore', *Postcolonial Studies* 11, no. 3 (2008): 351–4.

63 Holden, 358.

64 Partha Chatterjee, *The Nation and its Fragments: Colonial and Postcolonial Histories* (Princeton: Princeton University Press, 1993).

65 Leong Yew, *The Disjunctive Empire of International Relations* (Aldershot and Burlington: Ashgate, 2003), 16–20.

6 Boutique alterity

Southeast Asia's exotics abroad and at home

Tamara S. Wagner

Boutique alterity presents a potential dead end of, or threatening counterpart to, otherness (alterity) as an analytical concept. Its depiction in literature showcases the appropriation of critical discourses, or fields of discourses, by popular culture, while it also suggests ways of self-consciously tackling the very impasses that may undermine or typecast these discourses. Part of a current revision in approaches to alterity and specifically Asian alterity, this chapter draws on recent postcolonial and diasporic fiction set in Southeast Asia as a revealing example of both this threatening appropriation and the attendant revisionist potential. In order to develop a counter-discourse to boutique alterity, I shall begin by building on Stanley Fish's term 'boutique multiculturalism', coined in a provocative critique of the multicultural as an easily exploited consumer good: focusing on food, festivals, and food festivals, as the consumable output of neatly stratified cultural diversity, Fish speaks of 'the multiculturalism of ethnic restaurants, weekend festivals, and high profile flirtations with the other'.[1] Since Fish's 1997 article, pressing issues of self- as well as of neo-orientalization have increasingly attracted the attention of literary and cultural critics as they question the confines of what Graham Huggan pointedly terms 'the global commodification of cultural difference'[2] in his 2002 study, *The Postcolonial Exotic*. Within this commodification of difference, or otherness, terms like multiculturalism, postcoloniality, or diaspora have been in danger of being entirely reduced to 'just another buzzword'.[3] Most effectively perhaps, in her exploration of ever more divergent forms of Chinese diasporas, Ien Ang has gone further to expose any identity politics as 'strait-jackets',[4] so that the study of Asian alterity has begun to yield an important critical momentum that may crucially redirect prevalent approaches to issues of 'identity' as well as 'alterity' (or, more generally, of self and other).

This revaluation significantly includes self-consciously 'other', or revisionist, representational strategies: the literalization of difference through new narrative structures. Premised on a deliberate inversion of established ideas of otherness, occidentalist literary representation thus forms the self-conscious opposite to orientalism, which has, after all, long been taken as the other's most successful cultural appropriation. Yet, what is of most interest to note here is that this concept's fluctuation in recent discussions indicates most clearly – more than that of diaspora even – the ongoing shifts both in critical approaches and, in turn, in their appropriation and commodification as consumer goods. Newly dissecting established terminologies, therefore, constitutes a vital step in a thorough rethinking of the various foundational concepts of alterity. These include occidentalism as much as orientalism, multiculturalism or indeed any form of fashionable diversity as much as diaspora, and above all, the construction of 'identity' as much as of 'alterity' altogether. How Southeast Asia is differently 're-presented' at home and abroad, I wish to suggest, provides a particularly revealing case study as well as a continuously redeployed testing ground. Minority writing specifically (in all its frequently controversial definition), I shall show, is propelled into the popular marketplace through an exoticizing of alterity that works differently in the region and more globally, even when it concerns the same book. By bringing out the impasses of any identity discourses, the imposition of specific ethnic categories (with all their ideological baggage) on minority, diasporic, or indeed any writers, I shall further aim to show, thereby illustrates the dangers of such confining categories at large.

The attendant twofold exoticizing may act as the main selling point in already revealingly different ways, but this is always at the cost of reducing the narratives' complexities to all too expected, disconcertingly stereotyped accounts of more of the same. In part, this reduction is undoubtedly the result of intersecting strategies of marketing, consumer patterns and, unfortunately, also criticism that has at times threatened to fall into the same pattern. Boutique multiculturalism thereby all too straightforwardly extends from the literal consumption of the edible to its description or, in an additional extension, to ways of rendering anything 'exotic' consumable (and often easily digestible in the process). In other words, books are marketed very much like exotic food products. They are meant to be representative of a (minority) culture that may thus be literally incorporated: gobbled up by a continuously enlarged target group hungry for culinary and other stimulation rooted in the exoticized. Not surprisingly, this reductive and essentializing process has led writers to eschew the proffered categories and, with them, the entire package of what Ien Ang has so usefully dismissed as 'strait-jackets' manufactured by the fashionable rhetoric of identity politics in the 1990s: 'many people obviously need identity (or think they do), but identity can just as well be a strait-jacket'.[5] Not all literary or critical engagements with these confining categories, however, are necessarily successful, nor do they always resist the pull of sellable multiculturalism.

The question that then rears its head is the doubly vexed problem of self-orientalization. This problem is noticeable both in diasporic writing and in its at times intensely self-conscious rewriting within Asia. While diasporic fiction has responded to a growing demand for often self-reflexively revisionist, representations of postcolonial Southeast Asia at the international book market, local minority writers have started to engage critically both with the neo-orientalism promoted by this very project of marketing the region's specific histories and with a more general marginalization of minority communities within post-Independence nation states such as Singapore or Malaysia, formerly colonial Malaya. Since both these countries have continued to produce English-language fiction, while becoming increasingly the subject of diasporic fiction abroad, a comparison of their different exoticization can cast new light on Asian alterity's ongoing representation within and outside Asia (or 'the Orient' as equally indeterminate ideological and geopolitical constructions). In this, neither alterity as a critical concept by itself nor when viewed in conjunction with boutique alterity as its often strikingly self-reflexive counterpart offers merely an object of analysis. On the contrary, it at once demands and helps to facilitate an updated critical framework. The querying of the equally typecasting appropriation of otherness by occidentalism as much as by orientalism not only makes us think differently about minority writing (and its marketing) here and there. What popular novels do with the 'exotic' narrative potential of Asian alterities – in all their multiplicities – compels a much more encompassing reconsideration of the various straight-jackets of identity politics. A close look at the shifting representational strategies employed in Malaysian and Singaporean popular fiction, therefore, works best through a comparison of (1) locally produced novels that tackle variously imported narrative paradigms with (2) their markedly different treatment in diasporic writing overseas. Before exploring in detail these changing literary representations, however, I shall first squarely situate their complex engagement with alterity (including boutique alterity) within current discourses on the problems as well as the new potential of the exotic's marketing, whether at home or abroad.

The shifting ends of postcolonial, diaspora and alterity studies

The last decade has seen the beginnings of a much needed, large-scale overhaul of postcolonial and diaspora studies. This overhaul has primarily affected the ongoing divergence of ever new terminologies that, admittedly, differ in their usefulness. The still shifting meanings of occidentalism as the (chiefly revisionist) counterpart to orientalism illustrate the significance of this long-overdue overhaul particularly well, and this additionally makes the self-conscious evocation of occidentalist revision in Southeast Asian English-language fiction such a revealing case study. At the same time, the concept's very elusiveness prompts a detailed probing of prevalent approaches to alterity at large. In one of his last interviews, published in *Relocating Postcolonialism* in 2002, even Edward Said stressed the need to expose 'the Occident' as well as 'the Orient' as cultural constructs: 'I say even the notions of the Occident and the Orient are ideological fictions and we should try to get away from them as much as possible'.[6] In this, he revised his earlier caution, in his seminal *Orientalism*, that 'no one is likely to imagine a field symmetrical to orientalism called occidentalism'.[7] *Pace* Said's original caution, scholars did not feel the need to wait for its retraction in 2002. In his introduction to *Occidentalism: Images of the West*, James Carrier already called for the critical analysis of the 'stylised images of the West' in 'the East' and their continued production and reproduction in 'the East' and 'the West'.[8] For better or worse, both concepts have become an essential part of a vocabulary that cannot be divorced from alterity's current reconceptualizations.

The most important legacy of this initial dispute over the viability of occidentalism as a critical concept (and not just an inversion of orientalism) has been the rejection of 'the West' as a stable point of referent – a dubious concept indeed that had long been in need of a thorough questioning. As Neil Lazarus has already so provocatively pointed out in his insightful essay 'The Fetish of "the West" in Postcolonial Theory', 'the West' as unthinkingly evoked concept 'has no coherent or credible referent': as 'an ideological category masquerading as a geographic one', it is not a polity or a state, but 'something altogether more amorphous and indeterminate'.[9] Stuart Hall may similarly have suggested that 'the West' is 'no longer only in Europe, and not all of Europe is in "the West"',[10] yet this of course only adds to the concept's notorious amorphousness without actually doing away with it. In fact, this may all sound commonsensical enough, and yet occidentalism as a retaliatory strategy continues to associate 'the West' not only with specific geographical locations or imaginaries, but with people from or residing in these areas, with vaguely defined value systems, rendered homogenous from the outside, as it were. What is more, as an intrinsically retaliatory as well as revisionist strategy, occidentalism is constantly in danger of inadvertently re-establishing stereotypes in its affirmation of cultural alignments. It at once contributes to a prevailing confusion about 'the West' as an ideologically framed entity and fosters the very conflation of 'the East' or Orient that occidentalist discourses set out to disperse in the first place.

It is these impasses that a critical revaluation of occidentalist approaches to alterity needs to address before it can enter into any more detailed discussions of its self-reflexively revisionist potential. The circularity of revisionism as it revolves on the (frequently inadvertent) stereotyping of alterity is not even all that there is to the central problem of defining occidentalism. It's very meaning diverges into such diametrically opposite directions as to mark out capturing it as a discourse as increasingly impossible. Still, its very heterogeneity and proliferation may tell us surprising news both about recent developments of postcolonial and diaspora studies. Fictional functions of these theorizations, I shall then proceed to highlight, may usefully react against and rework some of their perhaps most provocative outgrowths.

The result of revisionist occidentalism at its most basic level is often nothing more than a polarized juxtaposition of occidentalist and orientalist prejudices that ends up reinforcing both by simply standing stereotypes on their heads. Nevertheless, what can help us here is precisely the resultant amorphousness as a useful indicator of shifting terminologies and hence also of the need for their careful reassessment. The very shiftiness, as it were, in their usage unearths underlying inconsistencies. Beyond mere terminological problems, especially occidentalism's recent proliferation in literary and cultural theory can additionally assist in pinpointing larger issues. At the centre of this proliferation stands the oscillation of its reference to a study of 'the West' and to a revisionist strategy. Symptomatically, the *Oxford English Dictionary* lists only one meaning of 'occidentalist' as 'one who favours or advocates Western customs, modes of thought' or 'studies the languages and institutions of Western nations'.[11] Dictionary definitions aside, it has become undeniably common to use 'occidentalist' and 'occidentalism' to describe a primarily hostile reaction to 'the West'. In *Occidentalism: A Theory of Counter-Discourse in Post-Mao China*, for example, Chen Xiaomei defines occidentalism as 'a discursive practice that, by constructing its Western Other, has allowed the Orient to participate actively and with indigenous creativity in the process of self-appropriation'.[12] By contrast, in 'Orients and Occidents: Colonial Discourse Theory and the Historiography of the British Empire', D.A. Washbrook diagnoses it as an essentialization of 'the West' that adheres by orientalist standards so closely that it fails to provide a useful counter-discourse.[13] It replicates and thereby reinforces the methods of objectification of 'Western', or European, orientalism. All that this play with established stereotypes (most commonly attempted through their straightforward inversion) can offer, Washbrook convincingly argues, is a replacement of categories in an inverted evaluation that strives to move 'the West' from the top to the bottom of what is still assumed to be a hierarchy:

> The reverse side of [Said's] 'Orientalism' is an 'Occidentalism' whereby his analysis of 'the West' follows precisely the same Enlightenment malpractices which he criticises in the latter's approaches to 'the East.' He represents European culture in ways which essentialise, objectify, demean, de-rationalise, and de-historicise it; and he re-evaluates it negatively in the light of its own standards of Reason and Freedom.[14]

Occidentalism, Washbrook further shows, is already endemic to Said's conceptualization of orientalism. The same propensities he criticized in orientalist discourses are clearly evident in his own treatment of the Occident.[15] As a result, it has become more and more vital to re-examine both the various, somewhat randomly circulating forms of occidentalism and (self-)orientalization through a different lens. This prominently includes the critical investigation of alterity's fashionable promotion: of the exploitation of otherness as a defining feature of presumably 'alternative' identities repackaged for global consumption.

Occidentalist inversions of orientalist stereotyping, in fact, is only the most overt – and hence most easily identifiable – indicator of the growing awareness of identity's (and alterity's) elusiveness as interrelated concepts. The current questioning of the usefulness of increasingly indeterminate, fluid, perhaps all too flexible and extendable meanings of diaspora is another case in point, although it is perhaps not quite as extreme as the quick coinage, at times admittedly dubious appropriation, and often prompt dismissal of occidentalism in recent theoretical developments. In an often-cited article, Stuart Hall has already stressed that 'Diaspora identities are those which are constantly producing and reproducing themselves anew, through transformation and difference'.[16] More recently, Daniel and Jonathan Boyarin have pleaded for a consequent extension of the term that is premised on a 'privileging' of dispersal and a 'dissociation of ethnicities and political hegemonies as the only social structure that even begins to make possible a maintenance of cultural identity in a world grown thoroughly and inextricably interdependent'.[17] On one level, then, diaspora's multiplicity has initiated a vital move away from simple dichotomies structured around home- and host-land.[18] But this is only one way of curtailing the elusiveness of established concepts. No wonder, then, that recent studies like Gijsbert Oonk's 2007 *Global Indian Diasporas: Exploring Trajectories of Migration and Theory*, have begun seriously to question whether such terms as diaspora (Oonk's focus of interest) really are more than 'just another buzzword'.[19] In a similar vein, in *Colonialism/Postcolonialism*, Ania Loomba addresses the central problem whether 'postcolonial' or 'ethnic' have become 'shorthand for something (fashionably) marginal'.[20] Like Fish's 'boutique multiculturalism', the fashionably marginal encapsulates the deliberate production of the exoticized 'other'.[21] The boutique minorities of Southeast Asia, I seek to show, shed a significantly different light on the shifting theorization of both identity and alterity.

Boutique minorities made for local consumption and export

In order to illustrate the revealingly divergent narrative engagements with fashionable alterity made to sell, the case study of Southeast Asia's 'exotic' minority cultures (and the writers they have produced) is premised on a comparison between, on the one hand, the presentation of boutique minority groups abroad and, on the other hand, their very different functions within the region's self-consciously multiracial societies. To write about migrants from Southeast Asia in itself demands a revision of long unquestioned approaches to diaspora and, by extension, to alterity more generally. As Shirley Geok-lin Lim and Cheng Lok Chua have pointed out in the introduction to *Tilting the Continent: Southeast Asian American Writing*, traditionally, literary criticism of fiction by Southeast Asians abroad has largely subsumed their work under the strikingly amorphous and yet oddly restrictive category of 'the ethnic community now recognized as "Asian Americans"'.[22] It is not only that the dual diaspora of ethnic Chinese coming from, or via, Southeast Asian nations already calls for a conceptual inversion of the diasporic paradigm: 'In crossing over to the United States of America, immigrants from Southeast Asia carry with them their multicultural histories'.[23] An outwardly similar subsuming to seemingly mainstream minority cultures within Asia itself describes a diametrically opposite trajectory. This is particularly pertinent in some of the most self-consciously multiracial countries such as Singapore with its majority and largely mainstream Chinese culture and, in pointed contrast, in Malaysia, in which the remaining Chinese diaspora communities now form a minority. To confuse the issue even further, despite a majority status within the nation state and a minority status within the region, abroad (and specifically in 'Western' postcolonial studies) Singapore's Chinese population has indiscriminately been lumped together with the Chinese Malaysian minority (among others) as part of the 'Chinese diaspora'. Conversely, especially within Singapore's aggressively racialized categorization of its population, the significance of Asian alterities becomes a particularly vexed and hence also particularly revealing issue.

The unique composition of the officially multiracial nation state Singapore, it has regularly been deplored, is still 'caught by, imprisoned in, a discourse inherited in a colonial history that continues to be re-produced by powerful contemporary re-constructions: re-formulated, re-vised, and definitely continuing a crucially neo-Orientalist social reality'.[24] The country's multiethnic makeup was without doubt to a large extent the direct result of colonial policies. Yet what is now often forgotten is its rootedness in pre-colonial trade routes and the less formal and systematic settlements they facilitated. On the contrary, precisely the intrinsically hybrid population engendered by these variously diasporic movements have generally been edited out of prevalent histories as well as of contemporary agendas. Only very recently, Singapore's traditional race policy – dubbed CMIO (Chinese-Malay-Indian-Others) – has been extended to include the (ironically now dwindling) Eurasian element. With an additional ironic twist, in fact, the country's traditional Eurasian communities, based on centuries of intermarriage and cultural hybridity, are thereby further placed under threat due to an essentially confused terminology that lumps together a century-old hybrid culture with more recent forms of cosmopolitan hybridity. Be this as it may, what is important to note here is that the often peculiarly, ideologically slanted perception of Singapore's ethnic make-up renders especially visible the essentialization of diasporic community formation (in all its consumable manifestations) that underpins so much boutique or consumerist multiculturalism.[25] Whether CMIEO (Chinese-Malay-Indian-Eurasian-Others) or simply CMIO, such race policies continue to abide by a neatly stratified cultural hegemony according to neat boxes. Not surprisingly, minority groups such as the Eurasians or the equally hybrid, traditionally diasporic 'Straits Chinese' or 'Peranakan' (Malay for locally born) community – a community whose origins date back to intermarriages between Chinese merchants and Malay women over the centuries – have reacted very critically to these identity politics. Their depiction in different forms of fiction, whether marketed abroad or locally, significantly seeks to explode any streamlining of ethnicity and multiethnicity.

Of course, this does not entirely prevent their absorption into a rhetoric of multicultural diversity. On the contrary, especially Peranakan culture has recently been reduced to its traditional cuisine and fashions. Local fiction reflects that in different ways, as I shall show in more detail. Nevertheless, the self-representation of minority cultures within an otherwise seemingly so neatly stratified multiracial society symptomatically questions the ways in which national and international discourses on identity politics both make and constrict minorities. How, in fact, do they direct and confine 'the minority writer' even as they seek to propel him or her into the book market? Why is writing in and about multiethnic nation states like Singapore doubly conflicted by issues of representativity, and what can this tell us about the most disturbing output of, yet also about possible solutions to, a growing demand in vaguely defined 'exotic' literature that simultaneously promotes and victimizes its authors? What happens when dwindling minority groups – like the Peranakans and Eurasians of Southeast Asia – fall into the fissures of ethnic policies and, with a particularly disconcerting irony, are elided by the very discourses on multiracialism that seek to prevent the recurrence of racial discrimination? In an exploration of the narrative and socio-political potentials as well as the problems of the 'exotic' victim's twofold exploitation, I shall contrast the first full-scale novel by Malaysian-born, Peranakan, Chinese American writer and critic Shirley Lim, *Joss & Gold* (2001), published simultaneously in Singapore and in New York,[26] with Singaporean minority fiction, i.e. fiction not by any of the main ethnic groups. The Straits Chinese, or Peranakans, in fact, have recently been subject to an internal (local) boutique multiculturalism that provides a good parallelism to the exoticizing treatment of diasporic fiction.

A particularly insightful point of comparison to Lim's novel is Josephine Chia's *Frog under Coconut Shell*, published in 2002 by Times Books International in Singapore.[27] Partly published abroad and partly in the region and sporting such telling titles as *Isn't Singapore somewhere in China, Luv?* (1993),[28] a short story collection, or Chia's growing list of heavily autobiographical novels, *My Mother-in-Law's Son* (1994),[29] *Frog Under Coconut Shell* and *Shadows Across the Sun* (2005),[30] the fiction of this Malaysian-born Peranakan writer seems at first sight primarily concerned with East–West conflicts played out in the domestic sphere. The representation of Peranakan culture, however, increasingly upstages this dichotomy. *Frog under Coconut Shell* perhaps most explicitly renders the distinctive experience of growing up Peranakan in a Southeast Asia of the recent past the novel's central theme. After declaring the Peranakan community as 'the true Singaporeans' precisely because Peranakans embody a history of intertwined cultural as well as ethnic hybridities, however, the novel then unfortunately lapses into a replication of boutique multiculturalism that reduces any idea of (cultural) fusion to the edible after all. The repeated emphasis on the newly fashionable Nyonya cuisine, named after Peranakan women (Nyonyas), confines Straits Chinese identity to an easily marketable consumer good. It is as if identity could be attained through food alone: '*Peranakans* incorporate Malay customs, language, cuisine and mode of dressing into our culture though we retain Chinese names, religion and New Year. I believe we are the true Singaporeans, a people who have absorbed and integrated with the locals, not just remaining an immigrant race'.[31] The novel symptomatically also features the publication of a cookbook, 'a book of Singaporean recipes for Western kitchens'.[32] The irony of this intertextual commentary on edible alterity, however, is never completely realized. Instead, the attempt to create a distinct minority fiction within the region becomes all too easily absorbed by a boutique multiculturalism that capitalizes precisely on the literal consumption of diversity.

A similar struggle between (at times inadvertent?) self-irony and the demands of a market intrigued exactly by the most consumerist output of minority cultures and minority writing can be seen to fissure diasporic self-presentation abroad. This fissuring expectedly receives an additional booster when writers describe the dual, or triple, diaspora of Southeast Asians abroad. The Peranakan abroad necessarily takes this yet another step further. What I wish to highlight here first, however, is that a quick look at the established patterns of minority fiction about the traditional 'locally born', or Peranakan, Chinese within Southeast Asia helps to outline some decided differences between diasporic and 'local' fiction. A retained confusion in the terminology usually employed to refer to Singapore's post-Independence writers can therein prove salutary rather than misleading. Catherine Lim and Suchen Lim were born in colonial Malaya, now Malaysia, but are both now acknowledged as the most successful, best remembered, and most frequently evoked Singaporean women writers of their generation. Both parallel the emergence of a former colony as an independent nation state with their (autobiographically inspired) heroines' childhood, identifying personal generation conflicts with postcolonial struggles and a nation's symptomatic 'identity' crisis. Externalizing a shift in the past's reconstruction in post-Independence Singapore, the intertextually represented 'History-Art project'[33] undertaken by Suwen, the heroine of Suchen Lim's *Fistful of Colours* (1993), for example, is pointedly set against her mother's sanitization of a traumatic history of victimization that metonymically expresses interlinked imperialist as well as more general patriarchal forms of suppression. At the end of the novel, Suwen symptomatically returns to Malaysia in search of her roots and new subjects for her art.[34] But if this suggests an embrace of revisionist rewriting in which women's critical art (or literary) projects upstage established imperialist and nationalist histories, *Fistful of Colours* at the same time also contains perhaps the most explicit elaboration on desire and repulsion in occidentalist conceptualizations of the 'other':

> A white nude male, white as death, with a thick fat organ dangling between his white hairy thighs. And at this point, she had turned resolutely away and stopped her mind from fantasising such nonsense. She could never go to bed with a white man, she told herself. She was too much of a Chink.[35]

Throughout the novel, Suwen ineffectually struggles against inculcated prejudices: 'We've got to face this black–white thinking all the time. East is good; West is bad. East is disciplined; the West is permissive'.[36] Despite such self-reflexivity, this appropriation of originally orientalist stereotyping as the foundational structures of occidentalist fiction tends to dominate throughout representations of otherness.

In accordance with occidentalist revisionism as a straightforward inversion of (neo-orientalist typecasting, it is the occidental, the non-Asian, who is 'the other' in the resultant fictional engagements with alterity's narrative potential. Especially in Singapore's early postcolonial writing, this stereotyping could often be very cursorily done indeed, capturing a type in order to 'write back' to orientalist fantasies of 'foreign affairs'. Thus, in Suchen Lim's own first novel, *Rice Bowl* (1984), for example, the vaguely characterized Hans Kuhn is best summed up as the 'Confused American'[37] who predictably becomes involved in both political and sexual affairs in Asia. Even more symptomatically, Catherine Lim's romances may be as different as possible from Suchen Lim's socially critical and increasingly historically aware works, but they share the same reworking of 'Western'/'Eastern' dichotomies. Without featuring any foreign 'others', Catherine Lim's first novel, *The Serpent's Tooth* (1982) shows this dichotomy of 'Western modernisation' on the one hand and 'Asian tradition' on the other incorporated into Singaporean society itself.[38] The result is a highly predictable, overtly polarized, plot premised on an emphatically realist rendering of symbolic generation gaps that encompasses a postcolonial nation state's emergence. Providing an important contrast to this social allegory, Lim's next two novels, *The Bondmaid* (1995) and *The Teardrop Story Woman* (1998), were published abroad, over ten years later.[39] In pandering to an international readership interested in the exotic past, they leave the interest in contemporary problems behind to romance the past instead. But especially *The Teardrop Story Woman* instead conforms all too predictably to a marketing of what Huggan has so pointedly termed the 'postcolonial exotic': set in colonial Malaya, it revolves around the love story between a French priest and the novel's beautiful Chinese heroine. Perhaps most interestingly among Catherine Lim's continuously expanding oeuvre is that the next novel, *Following the Wrong God Home* (2001), combines the historical thrust of the two previous novels with a rewriting of the recent past: the early eighties (the present-day, incidentally, of her first, far less successful and locally published work).[40] The typecasting of the 'other' lover – in this case an American exchange lecturer – however, is likewise markedly straightforward. An easily dismissible type, he leaves more space for the heroine's struggles with the aftermath of her adulterous affair. The very commonness of his exoticized attributes (such as his bushy beard) may well make one wonder what this (yet another) preternaturally beautiful heroine could possible see in him. Symptomatically, however, his attractiveness is simply tantamount to his otherness and specifically to the presumed 'permissiveness' ascribed to 'the West' (as it is similarly in *Fistful of Colours*).

This quick overview of what still is a largely unfamiliar territory outside the region significantly showcases both the similarities and the symptomatic divergences between diasporic and locally produced – or between neo-orientalist and self-consciously Occidentalist – representational strategies. Publishing both locally (primarily in Singapore, yet also in Malaysia) and in the United States, Shirley Lim offers a glaring case in point of the resultant struggles with shifting potentials as well as problems that cut across these divergent developments. Back in the mid 1990s, the subtitles of her autobiography, *Among the White Moon Faces* (1996), published as *An Asian–American Memoir of Homelands* in New York and as *Memoirs of a Nyonya Feminist* in Singapore,[41] already successfully repackaged her identity as an Asian American at the global book market and as a member of the Peranakan minority in the region. *Joss & Gold*, her first novel, was similarly published simultaneously by Times Books International in Asia and the Feminist Press at the City University of New York in 2001. It also appeared in the same year as *Following the Wrong God Home* and not surprisingly perhaps employs exactly the same occidentalist stereotypes in pairing a (yet again) beautiful young Chinese heroine in Malaysia with an 'exotic' male character. Like her predecessors in both colonial and postcolonial accounts of such foreign affairs, this attractive, young, 'wild',[42] and indeed self-consciously 'Western'[43] woman deserts 'such a China-type',[44] her husband, for a 'hairy and sweaty'[45] foreign lover. Repeatedly, she is herself typecast as a mimic woman: 'She was like a Western girl – bold, loud, and unconcerned about her reputation'.[46] The choice of the 'other' lover hence all too overtly literalizes her internalized split. It is a predictable development that fiction writers increasingly tackle as a confining cliché that demands to be dismantled, not just inverted. In conclusion, I shall focus in more detail on the self-consciously evoked, diametrically opposed representational strategies that shape *Joss & Gold*.

Diasporic Dead Ends and Occidentalist Desire

On a surface level, Shirley Lim's first novel cuts across established dichotomies by lashing out equally against occidentalist stereotyping of the 'Westerner' and against neo-orientalist ideas of the 'East'. It is a two-plot novel that alternates between here and there, between Southeast Asia and the 'West' concentrated in uptown New York. The Malaysian race riots of 13 May 1969, the night the heroine's daughter is conceived, act as a catalyst of conflicted language and race policies. The violent rejection by the Malays, which the riots come to symbolize, literally drives Li An into the arms of the 'West' as embodied by Chester Brookfield, an ineffectual member of the Peace Corps. Back in America, he watches a performance of Puccini's *Madama Butterfly* more than ten years later and is 'overcome by the obscenity of the pathos', which he neatly diagnoses as 'the West's degradation of Asia, the imago of what had gone wrong in Vietnam'.[47] The links he draws between the orientalist opera and his experience in the Peace Corps in 1960s Malaysia and Indonesia are, however, haphazard, fuzzy, and cannot be communicated to his closest friends in upper-class 1980s New York: 'But what did the opera have to do with tourism in Bali or Southeast Asian refugee . . .. It was a stretch, something academics invented for lack of more significant work'.[48] Such easy alignments simply are no longer sustainable. On the contrary, they threaten to subject any parallelism between personal and national, postcolonial experience – a convenient fictional strategy in postcolonial as well as diasporic writing generally – to ridicule. This is exactly the danger that Chester's confused comments pinpoint and enhance.

Despite this intriguing self-reflexivity, however, the novel to an undeniable extent plays into the pairing of stereotypes that structures earlier postcolonial and diasporic fiction after all, replicating the narrative trajectories of *Rice Bowl* as much as of *The Teardrop Story Woman*. Although Li An eventually becomes an independent woman who brings up her daughter without either absconded lover or betrayed husband, but instead with the help of a female friend acting as second parent, as a young woman she completely, embarrassingly, falls for the 'hairy and sweaty'[49] foreigner because he is different: simply 'an other'. What is disconcertingly represented as oddly akin to a rape that replicates as well as coincides with the race riots is, for Li An, a markedly ambiguous tale of cultural seduction. A Peace Corps teacher, Chester neatly conforms to the new occidental stereotype of the meddling, bumbling expatriate: 'Chester was different, she supposed, because he was American. For one thing, he didn't have an important job. He was teaching woodworking at the Petaling Jaya Vocational High School'.[50] What is more, even before the riots' reality explode her ideals of a multiethnic nation, they are exposed in a tongue-in-cheek way as essentially foreign, 'Western': '"Give us a few more years and we'll be a totally new nation. No more Malay, Chinese, Indian, but all one people." "Hey, Lee Ann," Chester said, beaming, "you almost sound like an American"'.[51]

But then again, exactly this inability to escape a confining straight-jacket made by specific ideological discourses, it forms the novel's most successful exposure of revisionism's dead ends. Multiculturalism as a founding myth in parts of Southeast Asia as well as America, like hybridity, is significantly dismantled in the novel.

The tripartite structure slices apart any easy dichotomy suggested by an outwardly two-plot ('American' and 'Asian') narrative. It moves from the cataclysm of the race riots in 1960s Malaysia to the xenophobia towards Asian immigrants in 1980s America and then to the problematics of hybridity in Singapore. The Asian, perhaps Korean, perhaps Filipino, owner of a store in New York embodies a new immigrant presence that urges Chester's friends to revise their attitudes towards the exotic East. Having replaced 'the burly Italian guy', he is 'the first alien storekeeper in their town', and although he does not, contrary to expectations, 'change the store, put in eels and dried mushrooms', he remains a silent presence, unutterably alien to Chester's wife Meryl, who 'wondered if he'd have also remained silent in his own country'.[52] Unlike most Asian American writers, Lim refrains from projecting thoughts either into other subaltern, immigrants. Chester remains the central consciousness throughout much of the novel, and it profits from this choice, successfully averting the pitfalls of many Asian American novels.

Joss & Gold may thus be seen as successfully exposing and at the same time showing new ways to avoid especially neo-orientalist as well as (retaliatory) occidentalist representational strategies. What the novel perhaps most effectively eschews is the random idealization of hybridity in diasporic writing. In 1980s Singapore, the young daughter is repeatedly identified with the children of Americans and Vietnamese, the offspring of the American War in Vietnam: 'American dirt you leave behind in Asia'.[53] With a bizarrely comical effect, the biological father's critical appraisal of his own offspring in Southeast Asia explodes the hybrid daughter's vanity as a green-eyed (and hence openly exoticized) Singaporean schoolgirl: 'She was sun-colored brown, pecan-shelled, and her hair appeared dark, Chinese, in the low-lit café. He saw that she needed braces; her large teeth crowding in a small mouth would need expensive orthodontic repair to straighten the haphazard angles'.[54] The much used stereotype that it 'is the way with Eurasians' to be beautiful is devalued as just another cliché: 'These children will always have problems, so beauty is the gift to sweeten their path'.[55] The child's choice between two absent fathers, a biological parent and her mother's Malaysian–Chinese ex-husband, who have both failed to take an interest in her for her first ten years, significantly remains unsolved.

Beyond boutique alterity?

Lim's *Joss & Gold* instead ends with the endorsement of a cultural hybridity that reasserts a literary tradition: Li An takes up her long neglected copy of *The Oxford Book of Modern Verse*, muses on the ridicule with which both the men in her life used to regard her love for English literature, and sits down to write her own poetry – in English. This completes the novel's rejection of nationalist and racial policies in the region. As Li An notices in 1960s Malaysia, the systematic erasure of the country's Chinese minority entails an imposition of a homogenous streamlining that would effectively silence her: 'Could they really do it, she wondered? What would happen if they all suddenly switched to Malay right now? How would she express herself? Like a halting six-year-old, groping for light in a darkened world? . . . But without her language she would be as handicapped as any armless and legless beggar in the street.'[56] The same applies to Singapore's 'Speak Mandarin' policies in their erasure of the vastly different traditions and communities that go with specific dialect groups. More interestingly still, despite Li An's (temporary) enthusiasm for the decisively American ideal of being one 'totally new nation' and 'all one people' comprising divergent ethnic groups, this ideology of a multiethnic identity is pointedly exposed as just yet another foreign imposition: "'Hey, Lee Ann," Chester said, beaming, "you almost sound like an American."'[57] Whatever she says or does, the Chinese woman from Malaysia has her voice taken from her. Her final turn to an English literature textbook hence only offers a very ambiguous solution.

Nevertheless, in its very ambiguity, the novel shows how recent fictionalizations of the minority writer's dilemma can be seen to co-opt the plots proffered by forms of a double victimization (sexual and political, for example) to expose the violence done to their narratives through their marketing as minority texts. Drawing on *The Oxford Book of Modern Verse* to write in English as a chosen language is at least a viable alternative to rehearsing imported ideologies: to 'sound like an American'[58] or to repeat 'something academics invented for lack of more significant work'.[59] *Joss & Gold* is thus self-reflexively structured on a dismantling of clichés that nonetheless significantly sell. How indeed may a self-critical rewriting of expected stereotypes successfully engage with the vicious circle generated for a continuously saturated market hungry for a continuously new fusion of boutique alterity? Whatever may be the narrative attractions of boutique alterity, they tend to reach all too quickly a glaring dead end, whether in diasporic or in local minority fiction, although attempts to circumvent these impasses can differ widely.

Another question raised by a comparison of the changing representations of Southeast Asia's 'exotics' in both diasporic and local fiction is what happens when marginalized, even dwindling, diasporic groups within Asia, such as that of the Peranakans, are exported abroad. Do they simply become absorbed into a general category of Asian alterity? Or does this doubling (and tripling) of the diasporic rupture the simplifications and often all too easy identifications that underpin exactly such a streamlining? Shirley Lim's *Among the White Moon Faces* may have had a double life, as it were, through its twofold marketing of Peranakan identity in the region and Asian Americanness abroad; *Joss & Gold* instead only engaged with the double diaspora of the Chinese Malaysian woman re-viewed through the lens of an American who lumps together all of Southeast Asia in his own guilt stricken musings on 'the West's degradation of Asia, the imago of what had gone wrong in Vietnam'.[60] The Peranakans are symptomatically erased in what already is a complicated (at least dual) diaspora that needs to be made understood on a more global (and yet first and foremost American) market. Lim's next novel, *Sister Swing* (2006), likewise concentrates on an East–West duality to the pointed exclusion of any additional complications.[61]

In pointed contrast, to bring the Peranakans out in internationally marketed fiction may draw more attention to the sheer diversity of diasporic (and other) identities and, more significantly still, thereby also to the perhaps inevitable confines of attempts at their categorization. And yet, it is not as if this has not been attempted before. Vyvyanne Loh's 2004 *Breaking the Tongue*, for example, is a historical novel by a diasporic Singaporean Chinese that simply denounces the Straits Chinese as colonial collaborators and mimic men to be ridiculed.[62] The imitation is notably expressed through food, as colonial Peranakans are shown to be consuming imported tea as a (rather confusingly) typified 'English' product, bought 'at Cold Storage, the European food emporium which caters mainly to the expatriate population'.[63] Packaged for the international market, the Peranakans are typified through their consumption of variously appropriated products (Assam tea sold in expatriate supermarkets in Singapore to would-be colonials) and thereby rendered easily consumable for a global readership, if misleadingly so. What this renders clear, even as it completely obscures Peranakan identities, is that boutique alterity comes out the most easily when expressed in food and food symbolism. Perhaps the 'pecan-shelled' daughter in need of braces as well as the Chinese store-keeper who does not sell eels when he takes over an Italian grocery in New York in Lim's *Joss & Gold* presents a much more important step in a dismantling of the impasses that threaten to create dead ends for any perception or representation of either self or other.

Notes

1 Stanley Fish, 'Boutique Multiculturalism, or Why Liberals are Incapable of Thinking about Hate Speech', *Critical Inquiry* 23, no. 2 (1997): 378.
2 Graham Huggan, *The Post-Colonial Exotic: Marketing the Margins* (London and New York: Routledge, 2001), vii.
3 Gijsbert Oonk, *Global Indian Diasporas: Exploring Trajectories of Migration and Theory* (Amsterdam: Amsterdam University Press, 2007), 14.
4 Ien Ang, *On Not Speaking Chinese: Living Between Asia and the West* (London and New York: Routledge, 2001), vii.
5 Ang, vii.
6 Edward W. Said, 'In Conversation with Neeladri Bhattacharya, Suvir Kaul, and Ania Loomba', in *Relocating Postcolonialism*, ed. David Theo Goldberg and Ato Quayson (Oxford: Blackwell, 2002), 1.
7 Edward W. Said, *Orientalism: Western Representations of the Orient* (New York: Pantheon, 1978), 50.
8 James G. Carrier, *Occidentalism: Images of the West* (Oxford: Clarendon, 1995), 1.
9 Neil Lazarus, 'The Fetish of "the West" in Postcolonial Theory', in *Marxism, Modernity, and Postcolonial Studies*, ed. Crystal Bartolovich and Neil Lazarus (Cambridge: Cambridge University Press, 2002), 44.
10 Stuart Hall, 'The West and the Rest: Discourse and Power', in *Modernities: An Introduction to Modern Societies*, ed. Stuart Hall *et al.* (Malden: Blackwell, 1996), 185.
11 *Oxford English Dictionary*, 2nd ed., s.v. 'occidentalist'.
12 Chen Xiaomei, *Occidentalism: A Theory of Counter-Discourse in Post-Mao China* (New York: Oxford University Press, 1995), 4–5.
13 D.A. Washbrook, 'Orients and Occidents: Colonial Discourse Theory and the Historiography of the British Empire', in *Historiography*, ed. by Robin W. Winks and Alaine Low, vol. 5 of *The Oxford History of the British Empire*, ed. Wm. Roger Louis and Alaine Low (Oxford: Oxford University Press, 1999), 606.
14 Washbrook, 606.
15 Washbrook, 606.

16 Stuart Hall, 'Cultural Identity and Diaspora', in *Identity: Community, Culture, Difference*, ed. Jonathan Rutherford (London: Lawrence and Wishart, 1990), 235.

17 Daniel Boyarin and Jonathan Boyarin, 'Diaspora: Generation and the Ground of Jewish Identity', in *Theorizing Diaspora*, ed. Jana Evans Braziel and Anita Mannur (Oxford: Blackwell, 2003), 110.

18 Kim D. Butler, 'Defining Diaspora, Refining a Discourse', *Diaspora* 10, no. 2 (2001): 192.

19 Oonk, 14.

20 Ania Loomba, *Colonialism/Postcolonialism* (London and New York: Routledge, 1998), xii.

21 In *Beyond Postcolonial Theory*, E. San Juan similarly situates postcolonialism within the framework of the structural crisis of international capitalism to disclose the ways in which practices of consumerism forge and continuously reshape the multicultural imaginary more generally. Starting out by denouncing a '[p]ostcolonial ventriloquism [that] has even ventured to deprive subalterns of speech', San Juan goes further to expose both what he terms 'the platitudes of fundamentalist postcolonialism' and 'paltry essentialisms and indulgence in the Euro-American immigrant syndrome' that he finds indiscriminately extended to other 'immigrant' and specifically Asian American writing [E. San Juan, Jr., *Beyond Postcolonial Theory* (Basingstoke: Macmillan, 1998), 8; 54; 179].

22 Shirley Geok-lin Lim and Cheng Lok Chua, 'Introduction', in *Tilting the Continent: Southeast Asian American Writing*, ed. Shirley Geok-lin Lim and Cheng Lok Chua (Minneapolis: New Rivers Press, 2000), xii.

23 Lim and Chua, xii.

24 Nirmala Srirekam PuruShotam, *Negotiating Language, Constructing Race: Disciplining Difference in Singapore* (Berlin: Mouton de Gruyter, 1998), 226.

25 The most successful and established Eurasian writer in Singapore was the recently deceased Rex Shelley, whose 'Eurasian Quartet' was published in the 1990s: *The Shrimp People* (Singapore: Times Books International, 1991), *People of the Pear Tree* (Singapore: Times Books International, 1992), *Island in the Centre* (Singapore: Times Books International, 1995), and *A River of Roses* (Singapore: Times Books International, 1998). Eurasian families metonymically represent the region's development. Peter Wicks speaks of 'Eurasian Images of Singapore': 'Shelley comes from the numerically small Eurasian community, and it is the distinctive historical experience of this minority, also known colloquially as *mesticos, serani*, or *gerago*, that richly frames his fiction' [Peter Wicks, 'Eurasian Images of Singapore in the Fiction of Rex Shelley', in *Singaporean Literature in English: A Critical Reader*, ed. Mohammad A. Quayum and Peter Wicks (Serdang: Universiti Putra Malaysia Press, 2002), 377]. Patricia Wong even maintains that *The Shrimp People* may at first sight appear like 'a litany of names, for it is certainly replete with Portuguese–Eurasian, Dutch–Eurasian, Anglo–Eurasian names. The litany forms a registry of Eurasian society, primarily the Eurasian society in Singapore, but also to a much lesser extent in the novel the parallel communities in Malacca, Seremban and Penang' [Patricia Wong, 'Rex Shelley's The Shrimp People: What Manner of Beast is it?', in *Interlogue: Studies in Singaporean Literature: Fiction*, ed. Kirpal Singh (Singapore: Ethos Books, 1998), 45]. As I have shown in detail elsewhere, C.M. Woon's recent novels, *The Devil's Advocate* (Singapore: Times Books International, 2002) and, more extensively, *The Devil to Pay* (Singapore: Marshall Cavendish, 2005) succeed in doing the same for the Straits Chinese communities [See Tamara S. Wagner, *Occidentalism in Novels of Malaysia and Singapore, 1819–2004: Colonial and Postcolonial Financial Straits* (Lewiston: Edwin Mellen Press, 2005), ch. 6]. As they similarly combine the spy or detective novel with the detailing of specific minority histories, they certainly offer more than merely a 'tale . . . woven around a small minority in Southeast Asia: mixtures of the East and West known as Eurasians [or Peranakans]', as it is put in Shelley's quartet (Shelly, *The Shrimp*, 5).

26 Shirley Geok-lin Lim, *Joss & Gold* (Singapore: Times Books International; New York: Feminist Press at the City University of New York, 2001).

27 Josephine Chia, *Frog under a Coconut Shell* (Singapore: Times Books International, 2002).

28 Josephine Chia, *Isn't Singapore somewhere in China, Luv?* (Singapore: Angsana Books, 1993).

29 Josephine Chia, *My Mother-in-Law's Son* (Singapore: Landmark Books, 1994).

30 Josephine Chia, *Shadows Across the Sun* (London and Baltimore: PublishBritannica, 2005).

31 Chia, *Frog*, 12.

32 Chia, *Frog*, 42.

33 Suchen Lim, *Fistful of Colours* (Singapore: EPB, 1993), 90.

34 Lim's next and so far most recent novel, *A Bit of Earth* (2001), leaves urban Singapore behind to tell the story of Chinese coolies in nineteenth-century Malaya. This historical novel symptomatically moves away from the two-plot exotic novel with its postmodern potential to create a realist narrative that primarily consists of a list of atrocities and triumphs over adversity.

35 Lim, *Fistful*, 140.

36 Lim, *Fistful*, 217.

37 Suchen Lim, *Rice Bowl* (Singapore: Times Books International, 1984), 132.

38 Catherine Lim, *The Serpent's Tooth* (Singapore: Times Books International, 1982).

39 Catherine Lim, *The Bondmaid* (London: Orion, 1995); *The Teardrop Story Woman* (London: Orion, 1998).

40 Catherine Lim, *Following the Wrong God Home* (London: Orion, 2001).

41 Shirley Geok-lin Lim, *Among the White Moon Faces: An Asian–American Memoir of Homelands* (New York: Feminist Press at the City University of New York, 1996); *Among the White Moon Faces: Memoirs of a Nyonya Feminist* (Singapore: Times Books International, 1996).

42 Lim, *Joss*, 9.

43 Lim, *Joss*, 15.

44 Lim, *Joss*, 9.

45 Lim, *Joss*, 38.

46 Lim, *Joss*, 15.

47 Lim, *Joss*, 235–6.

48 Lim, *Joss*, 236.

49 Lim, *Joss*, 38.

50 Lim, *Joss*, 38.

51 Lim, *Joss*, 45.

52 Lim, *Joss*, 156–7.

53 Lim, *Joss*, 220.

54 Lim, *Joss*, 257.

55 Lim, *Joss*, 220.

56 Lim, *Joss*, 69.

57 Lim, *Joss*, 45.

58 Lim, *Joss*, 45.

59 Lim, *Joss*, 236.

60 Lim, *Joss*, 236.

61 Shirley Geok-lin Lim, *Sister Swing* (Singapore: Marshall Cavendish, 2006).

62 Vyvyanne Loh, *Breaking the Tongue* (New York and London: W.W. Norton, 2004).

63 Loh, 19.

7 Misreading Asia

A survey of what Filipinos read of Asia[1]

Karina Africa Bolasco

There is no book trade taking place among countries in Southeast Asia today. We are not buying one another's books; neither are we trading translation or adaptation rights. Whatever publications developed and put out on grants or by the Association of Southeast Asian Nations – Committee on Culture and Information (ASEAN –COCI) are not sold but donated to libraries or circulated to member countries at 100 copies per country. An amazing waste of resources as, usually, nobody when asked seems to have seen or read those publications. The book trade that happens is exclusively the purchase, usually huge, by Southeast Asian bookstores, libraries and schools, of books by American and British publishers. It is never ever the other way around.

Books carry men and women's ideas across cultures, across the world. And to not be able to read books from nations in our part of the world is to be separated again and again from these neighbours even after the age of colonialism, or what Eric Hobsbawm called the age of empire, has long passed. In that age, year 1800, the Western empire physically held 35 per cent of the planet; by 1914, they had '85 percent of the earth as colonies, protectorates, dependencies, dominions, and commonwealths'.[2]

We remember distinctly how the Western empires once upon a time divided up Southeast Asia: The British had Burma, Malaysia, Singapore and northern Borneo; the Dutch had Indonesia; the Portuguese, eastern Timor; the Spaniards and Americans, the Philippines; the French, Vietnam, Cambodia and Laos; and quasi-independent Thailand survived 'on the sufferance between the colonies of rival London and Paris'.[3] Rivalry among these empires was such that they closed off their territories to other influences, thereby entrenching more deeply and irreversibly their control over these territories. It is therefore not natural nor an accident that till today, despite our nearness to one another, we are not interested in one another's literature, history, arts and ideas.

Our considered classics of world literature discussed to this day in centres and circles of learning and culture are early European writing on Africa, India and parts of the Far East, and striking in these narratives are the descriptions of the 'mysterious East' and 'notions about bringing civilization to primitive or barbaric peoples, the disturbingly familiar ideas about flogging or death or extended punishment being required when "they" misbehaved or became rebellious, because "they" mainly understood force or violence best; because "they" were not like "us," and for that reason deserved to be ruled'.[4] Consciously or not, these novelists helped the European effort to rule distant lands and peoples. Said says in *Culture and Imperialism* that 'stories are at the heart of what explorers and novelists say about strange regions of the world; they also become the method colonized people use to assert their own identity and the existence of their own history . . . nations themselves *are* narrations'.[5] The stories they tell privilege certain narratives and exclude others.

The Thomasites, American public school teachers who arrived in the Philippines in 1901 aboard the ship US transport ship *Thomas*, brought with them an English–American literature canon that until now is in our school curricula. But this, the coming of the white man to the mysterious East, also brought forth a culture of resistance. A whole generation of novelists, raised in it, reclaimed their own stories of enslavement and hardship under foreign abuse, their own memories or recol-lections of a time without the foreigners, asserted nationalist identities and roused readers to fight for self-determination – drive away the colonial masters from their lands. Our own Jose Rizal's *Noli Me Tangere* and *El Filibusterismo* inspired a revolution against the Spanish empire, the very first revolution in Southeast Asia. The great decolonization movement gathered the best and the brightest all across the so-called Third World of the 1970s, or developing world as these territories would be called thereafter, pitting the white man against an active local or native resistance intellectual or fighter, with the resistance always winning out in these grand narratives of 'enlightenment and emancipation'. To the colonial masters, these works were by 'prophets of rebellion', romantic, unrealistic and backward-looking people who opposed the modernity Europe or the West brought to their lands. They were crazy millenarians or cults of native traditions, troublemakers who valorized a pure past.

After the Second World War, the great colonial structures were dismantled and from the vast colonies emerged a hundred independent nation-states; however a sense that the Empire still continues to exert, at the present, considerable influence on the thinking and values in these ex-colonies is widely shared. Michael Doyle in his book, defines empire as 'a relationship, formal or informal, in which one state controls the effective political sovereignty of another political society. It can be achieved by force, by political collaboration, by economic, social or cultural depend-ence'.[6] Recovering geographical territory, which is what it means to decolonize, is not the finish line, so to speak. It must be followed by the period of secondary, that is ideological, resistance, when a people try to recover what is buried and sup-pressed, reconstitute a fragmented community and even truly imagine their nation, and empower it to sustain withstanding pressures of, by, or from the Empire. The famous Nigerian fictionist Chinua Achebe said, 'I would be quite satisfied if my novels . . . did no more than teach my readers that their past – with all its imperfec-tions – was not one long night of savagery from which the first Europeans acting on God's behalf delivered them.'[7]

This is where we are now, or should I say still? At a time when the all mighty United States is Americanizing world culture through Hollywood, music and fash-ion, science and technology and medicine, education (textbooks in many developing countries are bought by World Bank loans; also these countries' intellectuals acquire their master's and doctoral degrees from American universities), food via McDonald's and Coca-Cola and all the other fast food chains, sports (soccer from Europe and basketball from the USA), books and magazines. In the last four years, American outsourcing through offshore call centres, which Arundhati Roy of *God of Small Things* fame refers to as 'cultural abasement which . . . demonstrates a one-way cultural transmission, reinforcing the global spread of American culture and practices, creating pseudo-Americans in locations far removed from the United States'.[8] The playwright Rustom Bharucha questions why the young of the rest of the world have to learn in detail about the United States of America, to the extent of studying street layouts and their credit card laws for them to qualify as call centre professionals who then will have really meaningful conversations with the American public they service. This he claims is extremely lopsided because people in the USA are never ever encouraged to learn about the other nations with whom they share the planet Earth.[9] Today's fast-growing call centre industry in the Philippines and India strengthens, and even deepens, the American narrative and extends its reach – the young employees of these centres become acculturated without even having to live in the US.

We are in this second period of resistance, or rehabilitation, but as to how we will carry this out we are even of completely different minds. Ideas on cultural work are bitterly disputed. Nativists claim there is a pure past to go back to. Which is Philippine culture – all of it as it is today including the aspects from the Americans or the Spaniards or Mexicans? We have Filipinized the foreign, including their English (although the call centres, which are also changing the English curricula in universities, are forcing us to go back to American English, idiom, accent and all) and many other aspects of that pop culture we ape. Is going back to our own heritage and artistic traditions now high culture as opposed to popular culture? How do we find a basis for the widest unity possible among multi-ethnic and regional groups? These questions may now seem juvenile as we already confronted our identity crisis 20 or 30 years ago. Or so we thought.

According to Said, there are three important elements of a decolonizing cultural resistance: First, the right to see and know our community's history as a whole, coherent and integral entity. Second is acknowledging that resistance, 'far from being a mere reaction to imperialism, is an alternative way of conceiving human history'; it is founded on the removal of cultural barriers. And third, a 'more integrative view of human community and human liberation', which comes as a result of moving away from separatist nationalism.[10] I cannot stress enough, in the context of what needs to be done, the role of writing and making books and trading them. Benedict Anderson points to print capitalism's role in helping people come together and imagine a nation, imagine Asia. The search was on, so to speak, for a new way of linking fraternity, power and time meaningfully together. 'Nothing perhaps more precipitated this search, nor made it more fruitful, than print-capitalism, which made it possible for rapidly growing numbers of people to think about themselves, and to relate themselves to others, in profoundly new ways.'[11] Printing created a mass reading public.

African and Asian literatures in the secondary curriculum

What of Asia is read in schools? Unlike in the rest of ASEAN, learning about Asia is mandatory in our secondary education curricula. History in the second-year level is focused on Asian histories and civilizations and Communication Arts or English, and on African and Asian literatures. While the exposure to the literatures of Africa and Asia is laudable, the literary pieces are used mainly as springboard material to teach the four basic communication competencies: reading, writing, speaking and listening. Literature is not taught to draw pleasure from, nor to be appreciated and read critically.

Folktales, fables, stories, poems, essays, novel excerpts, one-act plays are the genres included. And due to lack of access (through translation and sales) and non-familiarity with the real literatures of Asia and Africa, the same writers are anthologized over and over again in the different textbooks.

Hardly is there anyone from the last 50 years, or what could be referred to as contemporary. Apart from problems in accessing, it could be that because books older than 50 years require no permission or copyright transfers, they are preferred over the others. Here are the writers regularly anthologized and to some extent made canonical.

- *Rabindranath Tagore*, who lived from 1861 to 1941, won the Nobel Peace Prize in 1913. A devoted friend to Gandhi, he participated from time to time in India's nationalist movement. Tagore was first and foremost a poet who had 50 volumes to his name but he also wrote dance and musical dramas, novels, short stories, travel diaries, autobiographies and all types of essays. He was knighted by the British government in 1915 but gave it up soon after in protest of British policies in India.
- *Lu Hsun* is considered one of the greatest figures in twentieth-century Chinese literature. His famous story 'Diary of a Madman' was considered China's first Western-style story. He was a Marxist and sympathetic to the communist movement. In Mao's Cultural Revolution, his name was used in political campaigns and his works, canonized by literary historians. In the post-Mao era, his works were re-read and he was considered an anti-authoritarian individualist and a voice of moral conscience.
- *Matsuo Basho*, seventeenth-century Japanese poet, is the finest haiku writer in the formative years of the genre. He turned back on his roots (he was born into a samurai family prominent among nobility), and became a wanderer, studying Zen, history and classical Chinese poetry. He lived as a destitute, all the time dependent on patronage and donations.
- *Firdausi*, one of the most eminent Persian poets, was born in AD 940. His main poem 'Book of Kings' was considered by Sir William Jones 'a glorious monument of Eastern genius and learning; which, if it should be generally understood *in its original language*, will contest the merit of *invention* with *Homer* himself'.[12]

- *Kahlil Gibran* is a Lebanese poet, philosopher and artist who is the genius of his age to millions of Arabic-speaking peoples. His fame and influence spread far beyond the Near East, compared to William Blake by Rodin. He lived in the United States in the last 20 years of his life. *The Prophet*, illustrated with his mystical drawings, continues to be a bestseller worldwide.
- *Cevdet Kudret*, poet, writer, lawyer from Istanbul (a Turk, Ohran Pamuk, just won the Nobel Prize for Literature 2006) was a Literature teacher and part of the Seven Torches Movement.
- *Wole Soyinka* is a Nigerian playwright, poet, novelist and critic. He is the first black African who was awarded the Nobel Prize for Literature in 1986. An outspoken critic of his government, Soyinka was imprisoned several times. He has combined influences from Western traditions with African myth, legends and folklore. His plays range from comedy to tragedy, from political satire to the theatres of the absurd.
- *Chinua Achebe* is a prominent Nigerian writer famous for his novels describing the effects of Western customs and values on traditional African society. Achebe's satire and his keen ear for spoken language have made him one of the most highly esteemed African writers in English. In 1990, Achebe was paralyzed from the waist down in a serious car accident.

There are textbooks and there are textbooks for this course – the good ones properly situate the Asian and African selections in decent country situationers and provide proper literary backgrounds for appreciation and discussion. If not for this subject in second-year high school, complemented by an Asian history subject, Filipinos will not have read anything by Asian writers. We would have watched Thai, Hong Kong and Chinese films in our cinemas; we would have fanatically followed Taiwanese and Korean television dramas in our homes. Our young would have sung Taiwanese F-4 songs even without understanding the lyrics. Filipino–Chinese continue to read newspapers from the mainland and we all use Asian products – from Japanese cosmetics and toothpaste to Malaysian chocolates to Thai dried fruit candies and of course, the usual Chinese reliables – from sauces to ham. But aside from Japanese anime, which literary texts from our region will we read?

Asian writers in bookstores

I recall a conversation with a university librarian many years ago. He asked why there is no Asian Books category in the National Bookstore outlets, and I said those books would fall in their proper categories as Fiction, History or Sports and that if he meant importing books from Asian publishers other than those in Singapore, it was not going to happen. Singapore then till now has been more of an outpost for American and British publishers – at that time, for academic books, the Singapore edition was the Asian edition. Apart from Periplus that actively publishes trade books on travel, cuisine, art, design and health and wellness and the Institute of Southeast Asian Studies (ISEAS), attached to the National University of Singapore, that aggressively produces academic and scholarly books on the wide range of issues which concern Southeast Asia, there are hardly English titles in significant numbers being produced in our neighbour countries in Asia. Therefore, unless books are translated to English, these would not be accessible to other countries in the region.

This gap has become more palpable as more and more literary festivals take place in Ubud, Hong Kong, Singapore, Seoul and Manila. At the end of a conference in Seoul, I became good friends with a Korean writer, Oh Soo-Yeon, and she said when we parted, 'It's a pity you can't read my novel.'

What will follow is a table (Table 7.1) that lists both Asian writers regularly carried by the National Bookstore chain and occasional new writers. Titles of their novels and quantities of importation are also indicated. The idea for this survey is to show what novels and by which Asian/Southeast Asian writers are known to and read by Filipinos. The National Bookstore chain with its close to a hundred outlets (National, Powerbooks, NBS Express) all over the country is the largest bookstore chain and therefore also the largest importer of books.

The table does not present the entire selection of Asian authors in National Bookstore. Importation quantities only of authors from the major American publishers have been extracted from the huge database. They are easier to track down by virtue of their significantly huge lists. These are Simon & Schuster, Random House (US and UK), Pan Macmillan (UK), Harper Collins, Penguin, Holtzbrinck Publishers (a group of twelve publishers in the US that includes Picador held by Verlagsgruppe Georg von Holtzbrinck based in Stuttgart, Germany) and Publishers Group West (PGW is the largest book sales and distribution company in the US, representing over a hundred client publishers). It is important to note at this point that again, even the books of Asian writers are brought and sold to Asia by the mainstream American publishers. Even the books of Periplus and ISEAS in Singapore are distributed by American groups.

Data here indicate orders placed within the three-year period of 2004–6. Some figures are aggregates of two to three repeat orders within that period. Some are special cases that warranted a grant of reprint rights.

Titles by certain authors are imported continually but at the time data came in, pre-2004 orders had just been placed and no longer are reflected here. Regular or staple authors like Tagore, Vikram Seth, Kazuo Ishiguro, Oe Kenzaburo and Michael Ondaatje may not show in this list but are continuously stocked.

Except for the Japanese novelists: Kawabata, Mishima, Murakami and Yoshimoto who are all writing in Nippongo from Japan and are translated by American publishers, and for Arundhati Roy, the first non-expat Indian and woman to win the Booker Prize, all the writers in this list can fall under Asian–American or South Asian–American categories. Their writing is of the immigrant, the diasporic, always negotiating between cultures, caught in 'competing and conflicting memories, aspirations, and motivations.'[13] These are stories or literature written by people of Asian descent in the US, as individuals and as a racialized group aware that their histories are distinctive in relation to their presence in the United States. It is literature written in English – the language that at first separated the immigrant from all the rest. He or she is reviled in that language but it is also in the same language, even if

Table 7.1 Sales of Asian-authored or Asian-themed works by the National Bookstore chain, Philippines

Author/Title	Delivery date	No. of copies sold (2004–6)
Monica Ali		
Alentejo Blue	June 2006	165
Brick Lane	May 2004	350
Arlene Chai		
The Last Time I Saw Mother	NBS Reprint	10,000
Eating Fire and Drinking Water	NBS Reprint	10,000
Anita Desai		
The Zigzag Way	July 2005	100
Kiran Desai		
The Inheritance of Loss	December 2006	500
Kahlil Gibran		
The Prophet	July 2004	6,000
Ha Jin		
The Crazed	August 2004	300
War Trash	October 2004	300
Waiting	September 2005	600
Jessica Hagedorn		
Dogeaters	July 2004	200
The Gangster of Love	July 2004	200
Dream Jungle	September 2004	100
Yasunari Kawabata		
Thousand Cranes	February 2004	50
Palm of the Hand	December 2006	20
Maxine Hong Kingston		
The Fifth Book of Peace	December 2004	50
Jhumpa Lahiri		
The Namesake	October 2004	300
Yann Martel		
Life of Pi	March 2004	1,750
Yukio Mishima		
Patriotism	June 2005	30
The Sailor Who Fell from Grace with the Sea	August 2006	200

Table 7.1 (continued)

Author/Title	Delivery date	No. of copies sold (2004–6)
Haruki Murakami		
Sputnik Sweetheart	July 2005	180
Dance Dance Dance	July 2005	180
The Elephant Vanishes	July 2005	180
A Wild Sheep Chase	July 2005	155
Hard Boiled Wonderland and the End of the World	July 2005	180
Norwegian Wood	July 2005	155
South of the Border, West of the Sun	July 2005	180
The Wind-Up Bird Chronicle		
After the Quake	July 2005	155
Kafka on the Shore	July 2005	180
Blind Willow, Sleeping Woman	January 2005	575
Birthday Stories	September 2006	120
	July 2005	205
V.S. Naipaul		
A Bend in the River	August 2005	30
A House for Mr. Biswas	August 2005	30
Guerrillas	August 2005	30
Half a Life	August 2005	30
In a Free State	August 2005	30
The Enigma of Arrival	August 2005	30
The Mimic Men	August 2005	30
The Mystic Masseur	August 2005	30
The Nightwatchman's Occurrence Book	August 2005	30
Arundhati Roy		
The God of Small Things	March 2005	3,300
Salman Rushdie		
The Satanic Verses	May 2004	180
Midnight Children	July 2005	110
Shame	July 2005	30
The Moor's Last Sigh	July 2005	25
Fury	July 2005	55
Grimus	July 2005	30
The Ground Beneath Her Feet	July 2005	30
Shalimar Clown	September 2005	355

(continued on next page)

Table 7.1 (continued)

Author/Title	Delivery date	No. of copies sold (2004–6)
Amy Tan		
The Joy Luck Club	March 2004	8,090
The Kitchen God's Wife	August 2004	1,995
The Hundred Secret Senses	March 2004	3,000
The Bonesetter's Daughter	August 2004	1,500
Saving Fish from Drowning	January 2006	1,355
Pramoedya Ananta Toer		
It's Not An All Night Fair	August 2006	30
Gail Tsukiyama		
The Samurai's Garden	February 2004	50
Night of Many Dreams	February 2004	50
The Language of Threads	February 2004	50
Annie Wang		
The People's Republic of Desire	August 2006	85
Banana Yoshimoto		
NP	June 2004	30
Asleep	August 2006	30
Goodbye Tsugumi	August 2006	30
Kitchen	June 2004	200
Hardboiled & Hard Luck	December 2005	350

Source: Internal sales data of the National Bookstore chain, Philippines.

broken, that the immigrant tells her/his story, resists, and threatens an America that violates her/his humanity. As Sumida and Wong argue, it is literature that 'often challenges any conceptions of America that exclude or alienate Asian Americans from America. It is living, dynamic, changing, conflictual and dialogic . . . it is the very process, of asking and addressing the question of what it is . . . a process [that] empowers, for it sooner or later exposes the structures that make Asian Americans into perpetual aliens or castaways whose cultures tumble nicely and helplessly in history's broad wake'.[14]

It took Wong and Sumida ten years to put together *A Resource Guide to Asian American Literature*, which was published by the Modern Language Association of America. In their introduction, they reflect on the process:

[T]hrough a difficult questioning and juggling of the following criteria (not listed in order of rank and are not applicable in all cases): aesthetic interest; commercial availability; current usage among college instructors; gender and ethnic subgroup variations; historical interest; role in the development of Asian American literature; 'track record' of responses by readers, critics, and teachers;

potential for generating intertextual linkages and encouraging comparative study; productivity in raising certain critical issues commonly debated in Asian American scholarship; and an elusive quality called 'teachability,' the reality of which can be attested to only by anecdotes.[15]

This proves that US education has recognized the need to speak to its multi-ethnic communities. They have spoken, they have published, and these voices resonate in their own countries. American publishers have effortlessly expanded their book markets.

There is so much still being said of literature in diaspora or exile, or of immigrant writing. Of how these writers having left their homelands are now then stunningly haunted by them. Of how their stories trip on image after image, or memory after memory of growing up and early life in their own countries. Suffice it to say that this literature written by Asians in the United States or Canada is refereed and judged outstanding and prize winners by Americans. The ultimate achievement for most artists here and in other Asian countries, including our novelists/fictionists, is to make it in the United States because making it there is like making it in the world or anywhere else. It is easier to make Philippine schools require the reading of books by Filipino or Filipino–American writers put out by Random House or Penguin. Even the translations, according to a Random House Asia editor, are decided on the basis of what novels sell the best for example in Japan, China or Korea where there are Random House subsidiaries, and not completely based on just sales figures. Often, they look for 'extraordinary stories of courage and perseverance, of goodness of heart and integrity of soul';[16] such as stories of extreme hardship and injustice during China's cultural revolution, the story of the nurse in Vietnam who took care of an American soldier up till after the Second World War, and other war diaries on the side of democracy and freedom as the United States defines it.

It spells all the difference too that these American publishing houses are fully equipped with the resources for simultaneous translations that are completed on time. What is truly lamentable here is that unless translated by Random House or Simon & Schuster, the rest of us in this region will not ever get to read the literatures of these other countries so close by. Again, American publishers decide which voices and stories are to be heard, and which are not to be. While on a fellowship grant in Tokyo, I realized how much more practical, and surely better as Japanese electronics have proven, textbooks on electrical engineering written by NEC staff could be for us here than all those American textbooks. How in fact we should be open to Chinese textbooks on medicine and not just limit ourselves to those from the United States. How we should bring in not just the cookbooks and travel books but even Asian books on art, architecture, interior design, health care, on Zen and yoga, origami and ikebana, Sun Tzu's *Art of War* – which have all been appropriated by so-called 'American experts' just as centuries ago Europe magnificently appropriated the Orient: German and French grammarians discovered the Sanskrit; English, German and French poets and artists retold the great Indian epics, and European and American thinkers from Goethe to Emerson found inspiration in Persian imagery and Sufi philosophy.

It is said that in a cultural exchange of non-equals, one gains and one loses. Rights distribution and related issues demonstrate this all the time – how can there be real trade if it is never two-way? Our region has always been just the big buyer, never even the small seller, of both books and rights – there is nothing they need from us, and when they do, they prefer complete control over it. *Banana Heart Summer* by Filipino fictionist Merlinda Bobis, for example, was first published by Macmillan Australia.[17] Then Anvil published it in the Philippines and she could do that because Macmillan let her keep the copyrights for her home country. When her agent sold the rights to Bantam USA, they sort of minded that Philippine rights will not be part of the world rights anymore. Bantam also bought in advance her next novel *The Solemn Lantern Maker*[18] but did not let her keep the rights for the Philippines. It could be for either of two reasons: one, that the Philippines has always been considered an extension of American market territory because its book readers continue to read in English and two, Merlinda being Filipino, is expected to sell significantly in her own country which would constitute good sales. She agonized over making that decision but only if she signed that contract would her novel get distributed worldwide.

In the year 1333, a French painter Simone Martini placed a book in the hands of the Virgin Mary in his rendition of the 'Annunciation'. The Catholic Church, unsure of women's intellectual capabilities, reacted and debated whether or not it was proper to portray the Mother of God as a book reader. It was as if book reading was witchcraft, and a person curled up in a corner, totally immersed in a book and oblivious to the world around was possessed by a power so overwhelming it must be the demon.

Alberto Manguel, author of the landmark book, *A History of Reading*, considers this act of putting in Mary's hands a red-bound book, clearly not the traditionally allowed *Book of Hours*[19] for women at that time – a subversive act of restoring to women the intellectual powers long denied them by men and by Christian iconography. 'The popular fear of what a reader might do among the pages of a book is like the ageless fear men have of what women might do in the secret places of their body and of what witches and alchemists might do in the dark behind locked doors.'[20]

Spivak, at a lecture on literature and life at the Riyadh University Center for Girls, actually proposed to women in Saudi Arabia that they 'read the world in the "proper" risky way, and act upon that lesson'.[21] And so did Azar Nafisi who wrote *Reading Lolita in Tehran*[22] to show the 'proper risky way.' Literature is, thus, a way of learning to engage with the world, and even force change in the world. So very clearly, all our roles as writers, publishers and teachers of literature are mighty important for this world.

Milan Kundera, in his essay called 'Die Weltliteratur: How We Read One Another' in *The New Yorker*, says that 'There are two basic contexts in which a work of art may be placed: either in the history of its nation . . . or else in the supranational history of the art'.[23] In Music, for instance, a musicologist will not usually bother about what language Bach spoke but because literature is tied up with language, it is always just studied in its small context of the nation. 'World literature is always presented as a juxtaposition of national literatures . . . [sic.] as a history of literatures'.[24] Kundera is not Asian but considers himself a minority and an exile in Europe. He also shows in this article how the best novelists for him are hardly appreciated in their own countries.

We cannot not read one another's literature in this our part of the world. In the stories of Asian writers, we will find a mass of experiences, ideas and insights that will affirm our own, from daily life to our encounters with the formidable forces. Language will only be incidental – look at the great writers of today: Eco, Calvino, Marquez, Kundera, we never read them in their original languages. We must gear up for good translations, for only through translations of our own choices will we in Asia be able to truly read one another's literature.

Notes

1 An earlier version of this article was delivered at 'Reading Asia, Forging Identities in Literature: Policy, Research, and Practice', Ateneo de Manila University, 1–3 February 2007.
2 Edward W. Said, *Culture and Imperialism* (New York: Alfred A. Knopf, 1994), 8.
3 Benedict Anderson, *Spectre of Comparison: Nationalism, Southeast Asia, and the World* (London and New York: Verso, 1998), 5.
4 Said, xi.
5 Said, xii–xiii.
6 Michael W. Doyle, *Empires* (Ithaca: Cornell University Press, 1986), 45.
7 Chinua Achebe, 'The Novelist as Teacher', in *Commonwealth Literature: Unity and Diversity in a Common Culture*, ed. John Press (London: Heinemann, 1965), 205.
8 Quoted Rajini Srikanth, *The World Next Door: South Asian American Literature and the Idea of America* (Philadelphia: Temple University Press, 2004), 32.
9 Cited in Srikanth, 32.
10 Said, 215–6.
11 Benedict Anderson, *Imagined Communities: Reflections on the Origin and Spread of Nationalism*, rev. ed. (London and New York: Verso, 1991), 36.
12 Sir William Jones, 'The History of the Persian Language', in *The Works of Sir William Jones*, vol. 5 (London: John Stockdale, 1807), 426.
13 Srikanth, 11.
14 Stephen H. Sumida and Sau-Ling Cynthia Wong, 'Introduction', in *A Resource Guide to Asian American Literature*, ed. Sau-Ling Cynthia Wong and Stephen H. Sumida (New York: Modern Language Association of America, 2001), 5.
15 Sumida and Wong, 2.
16 Based on an emailed interview of a Random House Acquisitions Editor
17 Merlinda Bobis, *Banana Heart Summer: A Novel* (Millers Point: Pier 9, 2005).
18 Merlinda Bobis, *The Solemn Lantern Maker: A Novel* (New York: Delta Trade Paperbacks, 2009). Delta Trade Paperbacks is a branch of Bantam Dell.
19 Developed in the eighth century by Benedict of Anane as supplement to the canonical office. Twenty years before Martini's painting, it had been the common private prayer-book for the rich. It was popular up till the fifteenth and sixteenth centuries. In many wealthier households, it was the only book.
20 Alberto Manguel, *A History of Reading* (New York: Viking, 1996), 21.
21 Gayatri Chakravorty Spivak, 'Reading the World: Literary Studies in the 80s', *College English* 43, no. 7 (1981): 671.
22 Azar Nafisi, *Reading Lolita in Tehran: A Memoir in Books* (New York: Random House, 2004).

23 Milan Kundera, 'Die Weltliteratur: How We Read One Another', trans. Linda Asher, *New Yorker*, 8 January 2007, 29.
24 Kundera, 30.

8 Inquiring into a parallel other

A Filipino gazing back at Thailand[1]

Antonio P. Contreras

While Thailand and the Philippines are both located in Southeast Asia, there is very little historical and cultural connection between them. In the contemporary Filipino consciousness, Thailand is painted as a tourist attraction, as a place for buying cheap imitation goods. In academe, there is very little academic interest in Thailand as an object of scholarly inquiries or pedagogy, except in obligatory comparative courses in Southeast Asia taught in some Universities. Thus, it is very easy to look at Thailand as a clear 'other' of the Philippines. However, as this chapter will point out, there is much parallelism in the history and political development in these two countries, making it possible to treat Thailand as a parallel 'other' of the Philippines. An analysis that would draw connections to what can be easily seen as positions of distinct otherness and difference would not only destabilize the grounds in which the categories of 'self' and 'other' are usually defined in the context of two physically and culturally distinct spaces, such as those that emerge between a Filipino 'self' and the Thai 'other', but also in the context of how such ontological positions emerge even within one country, particularly in societies like the Philippines trying to re-imagine its colonized and hybridized 'self'.

Problematizing colonized and hierarchical otherness and difference

The historical context for the production of otherness and difference, in terms of presence and alterity, is a challenging task in colonized societies, since elements of the 'other' is now an integral part of the hybridized 'self' and that there is a complex web of identity templates that make it difficult to simplify categories into linguistic dualisms. To define a 'Filipino' in the context of what is not a 'Filipino', and to further argue that the latter denotes the 'Western' presence that is privileged vis-à-vis the local Filipino alterity, are extremely difficult tasks. To search for signifiers to define 'being' a Filipino on the basis of what is 'not being one' is complicated by the historical legacies of colonial rule, where layers of alienation have become the characteristic trait of the process of 'becoming'. This is further complicated by a globalized environment, in which the process of colonization is no longer done by invading armies and friars, but by invasive symbolic forces facilitated by the information superhighway.

There is also a concept of the 'other' as a parallel alterity, one in which the other is not subordinated, but is simply a position that is different. Hence, the logic of presence and alterity does not exist as a hierarchical position of a privileged presence, and where alterity is the subordinated absence relative to such presence. This is what pervades the concept of '*iba*' (or 'other') in *Sikolohiyang Pilipino* (Filipino Psychology), where a person that is '*iba*' is not necessarily one who is subordinated, but is simply different.[2]

This non-hierarchical representation of otherness and difference stands in contrast to the idea of 'difference' which takes its linguistic roots from Derrida,[3] who refers to it as efforts by human subjects to use language, through oral and written forms, to differentiate the meanings of 'signifiers' (or symbols) in terms of the 'other'. Derrida, using Saussure,[4] considers language as a system of 'signifiers' in which social meaning is established not from the signifiers' correspondence to a world they suppose to represent but instead in terms of their inherent relations to 'difference'. As Agger pointed out using a Derridean framework, 'meaning is a product of linguistic difference rather than of language's representational correspondence to the world'.[5]

This process of constructing social meanings becomes political when language acquires the capacity to establish hierarchies and obscure otherness. Derrida argues that language is not capable of transparently conveying social meaning. In fact, language tends to simplify the complexity of human experiences, even as it effectively hides the inherent hierarchies that reside there. This is done through the effective use of dichotomies to privilege one position by defining it in terms of 'presence' of certain desirable traits, and then defines the 'other' position in the dichotomy as a subordinated 'alterity' (or difference) marked by the absence of such traits. It is in this context that otherness and difference has been defined in the context of social marginalization, where positions of 'difference', brought upon by social and political cleavages, such as class, ethnicity/race and gender, are used to define the 'other' as marginalized positions. Derrida's argument about difference and alterity posits the existence of a hierarchy that makes alterity a subordinate position.

However, the position of the 'other' is also useful in launching acts of resistance against the dominant social and political institutions, through movements associated with identity politics. This is also enabled by Derrida, through his concepts of 'defferal' and 'undecidability', in which he argued about the instability of texts to produce social meaning, and the inability of any one framework to provide stability to such texts, respectively. Through his concept of 'deferral', Derrida argues that the construction of social meaning is never final, fixed nor stable, and that there is a pervasive 'undecidability' which denies any textual vantage a privileged position relative to the establishment of social meaning. This enables political contestations and makes it possible for alternative meanings to emerge and provide challenges. For example, indigenous narratives, such as those espoused by *Sikolohiyang Pilipino*, provide for narratives in which alterities are not positioned in the context of hierarchical relationships, but as parallel constructs, or as positions from where to build affinities and a sense of similarities and community, as manifested in the concept of '*kapwa*'. Thus, the self can be imagined vis-à-vis an other that is not necessarily subordinated or marginalized, but is just treated as different.

It is within these two domains of challenge – the colonial effect, and the non-hierarchical concept of difference and otherness, that one can effectively locate the tensions, but also the opportunities, for a re-imagination of the Filipino self vis-à-vis its Asian 'others'. The Filipino self, as a product of colonial discourses and practices, is a complex terrain for the production of identities vis-à-vis an equally problematic Filipino other. The cultural constructs of what defines 'what we are not' fail to provide any reliable basis for what really constitutes 'us'. This is due to the fact that ours is an amalgamation of foreign influences, from our cuisine to our religion to our systems of governance. This leads to a situation where in what is truly indigenous is in fact even considered as the 'other' by the mainstream Westernized Filipino society. On the other hand, there exists a social psychological terrain in which one can occasionally find the non-hierarchical concept of alterity in indigenous Filipino psychology, through our definition of 'self' less on it being different from the 'other', but more through our self-identification with 'others' to which we can share close affinity, and therefore a sense of trust and community that renders the 'other' as no longer different from us. It is in this context that this chapter will re-imagine the Filipino self as it encounters a parallel Asian 'other', the Thai.

Encountering Thailand as a parallel other

Thailand is a country that is, on the surface, very much different from the Philippines. It is a constitutional monarchy, while the Philippines is a Republican state. It has never been directly colonized, while the Philippines have been under two colonial rulers. It is predominantly Buddhist while the Philippines is predominantly Roman Catholic. It is a single land mass while the Philippines is an archipelago. Linguistically, it is more homogenous; its language is tonal compared to the Philippines. There are fewer ethnic groups in Thailand compared to the Philippines.

My personal interest in Thailand started as a venture into its exotic culture and food. I began to have a liking of Thai cuisine when I was still in the United States as a graduate student. This was driven by the fact that its use of spices and coconut milk was something I was familiar with, growing up in the Bicol Region in Southeastern part of Luzon Island in the Philippines, except that its taste is more engaging and complex than the 'Bicol Express', owing to the use of other spices and herbs in Thai cuisine. Thus, my personal encounters with Thailand as an 'other' began with a sense of familiarity even as I was also engaged by its being different. Beyond food, I also relished the sensation not only of the different culinary tastes, but of the sense of empowerment when I am able to pronounce the difficult Thai names in ways which Thais themselves considered as almost like being a natural. I was so mesmerized by my first sight of the *krathongs* floating in the lagoon near the East–West Center during the November festivities held by the Thai Students

Association, a visual image which became embedded in my own construction of myself as a Filipino in my own definition of my identity. It was an experience that was both alien and welcoming.

This fascination with the Thai culture was further embedded in my sense of being during one of my official visits, now as a young professor doing research in community-based forestry, in one of the Royal Forestry projects in Northern Thailand. As our vehicle bearing the Thai Flag was travelling on a narrow mountain road, we encountered a long line of primary students on their way from school who were in various stages of youthful playfulness, but whose revelry shifted to formal reverence as they executed the *wai* in linear succession almost like falling dominoes as soon as we passed by them and they saw the emblem of authority in our Thai government vehicle. At that instant moment, I felt deprived as a colonized Filipino now living in a society whose local traditions have been replaced by Western imprints. I looked for an equivalent experience in my travels in my own country, and found the search difficult.

The Thai became an exotic other that has attracted not only my personal appetite for novel experiences, but also my academic endeavours. I was fortunate that my scholarly pursuits have brought me to Thailand on many occasions. In all these years, I have established a strong partnership with Thailand-based scholars (though not necessarily Thai nationals) and academic institutions, as well as scholars interested in Thailand, to provide me the opportunities to savour the sights, sounds, smells and tastes of Thai culture even as I go through my scholarly pursuits. This was further given impetus when I was awarded the Asia Fellowships by the Asian Scholarship Foundation, which enabled me to stay in Thailand, mostly in Chiang Mai, for a period of six months to conduct an in-depth research on the linkages between political transformation and forest governance. I conducted the research as a comparative study between Thailand and the Philippines. The experience provided me a new avenue to locate my ontological reflections about Thailand as a familiar 'other'. Indeed, my research revealed that Thailand is very much different from the Philippines. But in the same template of comparison, I also discovered the presence of significant parallelisms in the historical trajectories that shaped the development of forest governance institutions and the similar implications of what otherwise could appear as divergent modes of political transformation. A closer look at these transformations even revealed some similarities in terms of historical patterns and tipping points in the trajectories, although presented through different historical events and forms.

Thailand has no history of direct colonization, of which the Philippine has plenty. Nevertheless, the historical trajectories of both countries reveal a commonality in the general structure by which political spaces are contested in the search for freedom and are consequently opened for democratic participation by civil society forces. Both countries are children of authoritarianism, with Thailand experiencing much of its post-absolute monarchy period under military rule, and the Philippines experiencing about 14 years of Martial Law under Ferdinand Marcos. While political elites and economic elites in Thailand have their own autonomous spheres,[6] which was only broken during the period of Prime Minister Thaksin Shinawatra, the boundaries between them are porous in the case of the Philippines. However, despite this difference in the structural origins, elites in both countries were able to establish political institutions that were exclusive of ordinary people. The state in both countries emerged as a domain for elite privilege and a site for elite competition. This led to a yearning for a kind of freedom that was associated less with the State serving its contract with the people, but more as expressed through political rights based on legal entitlements and the right to self-determination. This is consistent with James Scott's argument that the concept of freedom in the Southeast Asian context is found not in association with the State, but in being freed from its power.[7]

The waves of social and democratic movements which challenged elite politics in both countries share many similarities. From working in clandestine mode during the early years, civil society forces composed of students, academics and the middle-class joined forces with workers and peasants to eventually openly challenge authoritarian forces manifested in the military-led government in Thailand and the martial law regime in the Philippines. These culminated in people-led events that led to regime change, with the People Power 'Revolution' in the Philippines ousting Ferdinand Marcos in 1986 and mass demonstrations in Thailand paving the way for a full return to civilian government in 1992 (see Table 8.1). Communist movements also emerged in both countries, albeit differing in their outcomes; with

Table 8.1 Key political events in the Philippines and Thailand

Year	Philippines	Thailand
1565	Spanish Colonization	
1782		Absolute monarchy
1896	Philippine Revolution	
1898	American Colonization	
1932		Establishment of Constitutional Monarchy
1946	Philippines gained independence from the United States	Military dominated Thai government
1972	Declaration of Martial Law	
1986	EDSA 1 people power 'revolution': President Ferdinand Marcos ousted	
1992		Full return of civilian government after massive demonstrations in Bangkok
2000	EDSA 2 people power: President Joseph Estrada ousted	
2006	Attempts to oust President Gloria Macapagal Arroyo through impeachment and coups failed	Prime Minister Thaksin Shinawatra ousted through a coup

the Thai State effectively neutralizing theirs even as forces of the left remain in the Philippines, though in a much reduced state of potency. It is also interesting to note that Islamic secessionist movements are present in the southern portions of both countries, even as more efforts for institutionalizing autonomy arrangements have been exerted in the Philippines compared to Thailand.

My engagement of Thai political institutions was done in the context of a comparative study of Forest governance, particularly in the role of civil society movements in the development of forest policy.[8] This inquiry has revealed enormous levels of similarities in the historical trajectories. Both countries have a kind of forestry science that draws its roots from a colonial discourse, even if Thailand was not directly colonized like the Philippines. Such science was deployed to lend support to the extractive activities which colonial forces enable, and which State structures and policies have formalized. The ensuing plunder of forest resources has resulted to steep ecological and social costs, which eventually led to the mobilization of social forces in civil society to provide alternative discourses for forest management and governance. These parallel patterns in terms of broad trajectories, however, had their distinct manifestation in each of the two countries, owing much to the divergent political and economic structures that precede and contain the transformation (see Table 8.2).

The development of democratic institutions in Thailand and the Philippines offer divergent trajectories, even as one can find similarities in the form in which they are manifested. One of the defining moments in the historical trajectories of both

Table 8.2 Development of forest governance institutions in the Philippines and Thailand

Year	Philippines	Thailand
1863	Establishment of Inspeccion General del Montes	
1896		Establishment of the Royal Forest Service (later to be renamed as the Royal Forest Department or RFD)
1904	Enactment of the Philippine Forestry Act	
1938		Enactment of the First Thai Law to Protect Forests
1947		Establishment of a separate Forest Industrial Organization (FIO)
1954		Passage of the Land Code which enabled farmers to own the land they cultivate
1956		Conversion of FIO into a parastatal agency under the Ministry of Agriculture and Cooperative, separate from RFD

Table 8.2 (continued)

Year	Philippines	Thailand
1970	Existence of the Philippine Council for Wood Industry Development (PCWID)	
1975	Passage of the Forestry Reform Code Implementation of the Forest Occupancy Management Program (FOM)	Implementation of the Forest Village Program which granted amnesty to residents of public forests and provided funds for forest village development
1978	Implementation of the Communal Tree Farming Program (CTF)	
1979	Implementation of the Family Approach to Reforestation Program (FAR) Issuance of Letter of Instruction (LOI) 917 which mandated all logging concessions to allocate 5 percent of their areas to wilderness reserves Issuance of Presidential Decree (PD) 1159 requiring loggers to reforest their concession areas	Implementation of the *Sit Thi Thamkin* as a community-oriented project but was seen more as a counter-insurgency measure
1982	Issuance of LOI 1260 establishing the Integrated Social Forestry Program (ISFP) Establishment of the Natural Resources Development Corporation (NRDC)	Beginning of civil society activism in forest governance
1985		Passage of the National Forest Policy
1988	Launching of a nationwide reforestation program through Department Administrative Order (DAO) 39, which included participation by civil society and local communities	
1989	Implementation of the Community Forestry Program (CFP) through DAO 123	Imposition of total logging ban Civil society forces called on government to legislate a community forestry law
1990	Implementation of the Forest Land Management Program (FLMP) through DAO 71	Implementation of the *Khor Jor Kor* Program, which required the resettlement of forest-based communities

(continued on next page)

Table 8.2 (continued)

Year	Philippines	Thailand
1992	Passage of the National Integrated Protected Areas System (NIPAS) Law through Republic Act (RA) 7586 Passage of the Local Government Code through RA 7160 Implementation of the Ancestral Domain Management Program through DAO 2	Banning of private plantations that were more than eight hectares Revision of the 1985 National Forest Policy by increasing the area of protection forests to 25% and decreasing the area of production forests to 15%
1993	Nationwide implementation of CFP was mandated through DAO 22 Launching of the Forest Land Management Program (FLMP) Institutionalization of Community Organizing as an approach in the implementation of forestry programs through DAO 62	Commercial forest plantations were again legalized
1994		Launching of a nationwide reforestation program
1995	Issuance of Executive Order (EO) 263 which adopted community-based forest management as a national policy	
1996		Drafting of a community forestry bill
1997	Passage of the Indigenous People's Rights Act (IPRA) through RA 8371	Passage of the *Wang Nam Khiew* resolution that recognized the coexistence of peoples and forests
1998		Revocation of the resolution and reversal to the old strategies for forest management

countries is the role of social institutions in the maintenance of social and political stability, albeit differently manifested. In Thailand, the Monarchy has been seen as a source of social and political consolidation. From becoming an absolute source of political power during the pre-1932 period, it became a constitutional source of stability that enabled Thai polity to navigate the otherwise tumultuous, and on many occasions, bloody political transitions. The institution of the monarchy permeates the consciousness of the Thai identity, effectively providing both the necessary restraint and impetus for political and social action and arrangements, with the former being the case in the role of the King in tempering the bloody events of 1992, and the latter manifested in the manner by which legitimacy was bestowed on the coup of 2006, which ousted Prime Minister Thaksin Shinawatra. The Thai Monarchy has been effectively embedded in Thai consciousness as well as in the operations of its social and political institutions. It became the salient force that both shapes and restrains the development of the Thai 'self'. It has become the lifeblood for Thai social capital, as it becomes a force that cements collective action particularly during times of crisis.

The Philippines does not have a Monarch to rein in its political excesses. The tempering presence of a benevolent king is a visual image that has no historical presence in post-colonial Philippines. However, the Filipino derived its sense of political restraint as well as motivation from a variety of social institutions. The institutions of religion have for many times provided that role, but have since waned. On separate occasions, religion has provided either the conservative force that quelled dissent, or the progressive force that inspired resistance. The 1986 events that led to the ouster of President Ferdinand Marcos saw how the institutionalized Church, particularly represented through the iconic presence of Jaime Cardinal Sin, became a significant player in the history of political mobilization. Nevertheless, such a display of influence was seen as more of an outcome of a confluence of events, rather than as a controlling driver for resistance. Such event is a powerful revelation of the potency not of a single institution to provide the leverage for collective action, but of a larger, perhaps amorphous, civil society that manifests enormous capacity to provide social capital. Our sense of 'monarchy' lies not in the visible institution of the king and its sometimes invisible political power, as seen in Thailand, but on the relatively invisible array of multiple 'communities' that are visibly manifested in the way Filipino political life is able to survive despite its many crises. Social capital in the Philippines is thus firmly rooted in its organic base in civil society, interpreted broadly to include institutions beyond the private domain of the household but do not exist in the official domain of the State.

It is this organic nature of social capital, one that I see not lodged in formal state institutions, but in local communities and their attendant institutional processes, which fosters resiliency, creativity and the capacity among Filipinos to bear the burdens of modern life. The Filipino sense of moving on, of '*pakikisama*', and of the image of the '*fiesta*' makes it possible for social collectives to maintain stability. The images of Filipinos celebrating like a festival the otherwise dangerous events such as the People Power mobilization along EDSA in 1986 is an imprint of people whose politics derive its logic not from the formal rituals of government but from the ordinary rituals of community. A personalistic attitude towards politics, seen in the easy association of politics with celebrity, makes the Filipino relocation of politics to a familiar terrain of social meanings, away from the exclusive halls of the State and its institutional and organizational abodes, as an effective counter-discourse to elite politics. The elevation of the celebrity politician to a significant position in Philippine political life is integral of the resistive conceptualizations of politics, where resistance is no longer driven by an overt reading of ideology as a grand narrative, but as a silent force that enables people to smile despite their sufferings. This becomes what constitutes, in the context of Pierre Bourdieu's work, our 'habitus'.[9]

The idea of an enigmatic smile in a world of suffering has always been the object both of awe and condemnation. There are those who lament that kind of smile as a symbolic form of acquiescence to domination. This makes it possible for elites to establish a kind of social and political stratification whose foundations lie on a consciousness that propel such domination through the power of silent, if not smiling, acceptance. Others, however, would see in these smiles a form of social autonomy that exists outside the confines of repression, and enable the ordinary experience of happiness as a protective shell to insulate the citizen from the corrupting effects of power politics as they are manifested in formal social and political institutions, such as the state and its associated forms of traditional politics.

My engagement of the Thai 'other' actually emanates from the parallelism of the Thai's search for and enjoyment of '*sanuk*'. Thailand is also referred to as the land of smiles. The drawing power of Thai cuisine lies in its appeal to me not only with its being different in terms of form manifested in a blend of spices and ingredients distinct from ordinary Filipino cuisine. It is engaging since it provides a structure for the search of good life, shared in communal eating, where a community actually celebrates its being one not only as a sociological entity, but as an ontological construct. Sharing a meal among Filipinos, dipping in a common sauce, eating on a common plate, drinking local wine using a common glass, are undoubtedly measures of how deep one is in community with those who are 'others'. It becomes the transformation of the 'other' from becoming a different entity into one that is familiar. It becomes a symbol for the subversion of 'otherness' as a subordinated difference. It is our version of searching for '*sanuk*' even as we celebrate the power of community, which is the repository for our social capital, our silent 'monarchy'.

Political identities in a postmodern world

The dominance of the image of the 'smile' in my engagement of the Thai as a familiar 'other' of my Filipino 'self' is not without its political implications. Politics here takes on two levels of meaning: one being in terms of how power is exercised in visible institutions of governance; the other in terms of how power is exercised as an invisible force in the formation of political identities.

The resilience of Filipinos vis-à-vis the many crises that they encounter is a silent force that has enabled them to survive. The enormous capacity of Filipinos to convert their tragedies into comic situations has produced a Filipino citizen that has subjected the grand narrative of politics to irreverence, seen in its readiness to treat politicians as capital for stand-up comedy shows, and in its talent to dish out political jokes to parody political events and personalities. To the Filipino, politics is just one spectacle, a source of amusement to a public that has accepted its limits and has searched elsewhere for political sanity. The Filipino has relocated its political logic in the domain of popular culture, as delivered through mass media, information technology and through the internet. Filipinos, while remaining as active participants in electoral exercises, with the Philippines registering one of the highest voter turn-outs, have also become active participants in the new domain of virtuality and simulation which popular media have enabled – as TV audience, cell phone users, SMS message senders and receivers, and internet gamers, chatters and bloggers. Thus, the Filipino citizen has become a postmodern inhabitant of a post-modernized community, one wherein traditional politics is no longer seen as the only venue for representation. Ideology is no longer seen as a grand narrative authored by dead white men, but as silent argument manifested in the social meanings of everyday life – in the soap operas, game shows, and internet game rooms which citizens have migrated into to find their social bearings.

It is in these silent incarnations of ideology that the 'smile' becomes a subtle symbol for many forms of citizenship. A smile, when matched with a shaking head is an expression of tolerance, a polite demeanour of a citizen seemingly disgusted with the way government has turned out, dismissive of the seriousness of the flaw but cognizant of the authority that one has to acknowledge but not necessarily accept and respect. A smile could also be a form of resistance hiding behind the façade of congeniality, a 'weapon of the weak' particularly when it becomes the external facial expression that attends feigned ignorance.

The political events that are now labelled as 'EDSA 1' and 'EDSA 2', with the former leading to the ouster of Ferdinand Marcos, and the latter with that of Joseph Estrada, are events that have been dominated by images of happiness among the crowd. Even as rage was the driving force, the festive atmosphere in both occasions were not seen as orgies leading to violence, but were more seen as a counter-narrative to the dominant construct of a mass-based mobilization. The term 'people power' to refer to non-violent, non-electoral political transitions is an offspring of the first EDSA and has since become part of the political discourse. It was later appropriated to refer to democratic mobilizations in Indonesia, Malaysia, Thailand and even in China. The presence of such a 'happy' atmosphere was manifested in the 'smiling coup' that toppled Thaksin in 2006, when people merrily posed with soldiers and their tanks, offered flowers to them, and the mood was celebratory. This was in contrast to the bloody coups in the past, even including the massive mobilization that rocked Bangkok in 1992, and again in the late 2000s when the yellow and red shirts engaged each other and the Thai state, in which the same 'smiling' rage was absent.

Traditional and the more liberal political critics have launched a guarded and qualified appreciation of the value of 'people power' and of extra-constitutional means to affect a political transition. While the 1986 EDSA event was seen in a more positive light, the second EDSA in 2001, as well as the recent coup in Thailand in 2006, were seen in a less positive light by those who value more the formal processes of constitutional democracy. There are those who argued that the events in the Philippines, and in Thailand, are dangerous developments vis-à-vis the need for constitutional restraints on people power. These criticisms deploy the argument that the best cure for ailing political systems still rest on a regime change that is brought about by the rituals of electoral exercises, rather than that of any form of extra-constitutional mobilization.

However, these criticisms fail to understand the organic roots of political life. The modes by which power is institutionalized in many societies, including that of Thailand and the Philippines, are less statist than their visible appearances try to project. The discourse of strong states is more to be seen as a public transcript that is used by the elites to justify their attempts to control the lives of the ordinary citizens, but are in fact unable to totally penetrate the hidden crevices of their everyday lives. Despite the distinct differences between Thai and Philippine political culture, the prevailing sense of community that one finds in the organic internalization of institutions that cement cohesion among the divergent forces in civil society provide citizens alternative venues for political consolidation, and for the production of political meanings and identities. In Thailand, it is the reverence to the institution of the Thai Monarchy that serves as the lifeblood for rituals of acceptance of either the status quo or of challenges to it. In the Philippines, it is the organically rooted sense of community that provides it the stability during times of crises, even as it has also propelled forces of dissent to affect political transitions. In both of these cases, it is the sense of a collective 'self' that has provided such political communities their power, a 'self' defined not in juridical notions of citizenship, but are in fact ontologically grounded in the concept of being one with 'others'. The Filipinos have a term for this: '*pakikisama*' and '*pakiki-isa*'. The Thais transcend otherness through an intermediary discourse of loyalty to the King, who serves as a symbol of unity.

The Filipino desires a happy ending for the drama of life, something which is not characteristic of most in Asia, including that of Thailand, where the virtue of detachment is dominant. Most Asian soap operas reflect this through its sad or, at best, melancholic endings, even as Filipino soaps would always have to end on a happy note. It is this predisposition that renders the Filipino a perfect audience to the drama of politics. The smiling face of the Filipino political psyche will turn into rage when there is a dramatic moment that highlights the soap operatic impact of a political event, and turn the 'bad ending' into something that could not be tolerated and must be challenged not only with a frown but with a political movement.

The act of cheating in an election may cause anger among Filipinos, but such would not be enough to mobilize such rage as a driving force towards a political transition. Attempts to unseat Gloria Macapagal Arroyo failed in the absence of a visible victim. Fernando Poe Jr. was already dead at the time that the 'Hello Garci' controversy erupted. Despite the cinematic outburst captured live on TV of the grieving widow, movie actress Susan Roces, the drama was no longer there. She was simply seen as a character lashing out, but not as a political figure around which people could rally. It could have been different had Ms. Roces declared her leadership of a political movement. Events in 1986 were, however, much different. The tragic image of a grieving widow of an assassinated politician being victimized by electoral fraud has provided the political drama its focal character, and which found its expression on EDSA 1. Similarly, in 2000, the drama of the impeachment process, which has been likewise captured on TV served as the lynchpin which translated anger into becoming a potent force for EDSA 2. In 2009, the dramatic images of the historic funeral cortege of Cory Aquino have catapulted her son Noynoy Aquino, a relatively average-performing and uncharismatic Senator, to win the 2010 Presidential elections.

One can argue that the process of democracy in the Philippines and Thailand are in better hands if left to organic structures and to civil society institutions, instead of on formal processes associated with statist political institutions. Civil society modes of institutionalization in which the positive virtues of community, either as a silent force that creates social capital, or as a consciousness inspired by a visible institution such as the Thai Monarch, are allowed to flourish. This is an appeal to a postmodern political practice, an appeal to radical pluralism, and a celebration of a community-led political culture. This would be an exciting prospect, particularly when one locates the nexus of political action not in the formal institutions of governance, but in the local institutions for the establishment of social order.

It is in this context that the Filipino political experience becomes distinctly different from the Thai experience. Thai society has been characterized by many as fully embedded in norms and rituals that are derived from a stable self-consciousness of culture. The image of the schoolchildren executing a linear succession of '*wais*' on that country road when they saw the royal emblem in a government vehicle is one of the many instances where reverence to cultural norms is evident in everyday lives. A hierarchically structured Thai society, that has put much capital on correct forms and stringent norms, is the bedrock upon which one can explain the emergence of a singularly expressed oppositional civil society identity as a logical outcome during periods of resistance. A society that lives on strict adherence to culturally defined modalities of social interaction – from the correctness of doing a '*wai*' to the elaborate details of food preparation – undoubtedly produces a form of resistance that would be as singular and rigid in form, and would be manifested as one in strict opposition to well-defined dominant structures. Thai NGOs, for example, have taken a constant suspicious demeanour on any activity from the Thai State, even as the latter have deployed antagonistic moves against the former.

In this context, the Thai 'self' becomes an embodiment of social control, whose search for freedom necessitates a discourse of resistance that may be prone to violence, if not intransigence and hostility. This is evident in the preponderance of bloody coup attempts in its history and the oppositional stance of civil society-based movements. However, the rich cultural templates found in its communities have offered a counter-ideology to an elitist and globalizing State. These provide metaphors for resistance that are more organically rooted, as expressed in indigenous worldviews and local knowledge. It is in these domains that the Thai 'self' becomes a terrain for contestations between a centrally located control nerve manifested in public policy and other official acts of the State through its institutions, and a centrally mobilized force of opposition. The 'self' thus becomes a battleground between the grand narratives of state control and of resistance.

It is, however, important to point out that Thai society is a complex array of articulations between indigenous social constructs and Western influences. Thailand may not have been directly colonized, but it was nevertheless subjected to the same forces that have colonized other societies in Southeast Asia.[10] Thus, identity formation and the construction of the Thai political 'self' are at the crossroads of the local and the global, the internal and the external. This is captured by Ganjanapan (2000) when he argued, in the context of the emergence of a discourse of resistance to State forestry, that:

Although the practices of community forestry in Northern Thailand may have some basis on local values and customs, it cannot simply be regarded as a reflection of an idealistic sense of community because it is, in most cases a creation of a new culture as a dynamic response to changing situations. Particularly, in encountering with changes in property relations, community forestry can be seen both as a production of local idioms and a construction of a new discourse with an adoption of a universal concept of rights, which allow local communities to articulate their claims to collective rights in resources. However, the reconstruction of collective rights as an anti-hegemonic ideology can be fully realized by local people not only through social struggles but also with a reinforcement of local idioms, which is possible with cultural processes of ritual.[11]

Thus, the formation of identities and discourses in Thai society becomes a process of social constructions and reconstructions, albeit done in the context of a firm grounding on a historical narrative of a well-defined national consciousness, one that is sustained by and in the end also sustains the institution of Monarchy. The volatility of politics is tempered by the unifying presence of the King, and the sense of 'moderation' that is inherent in most Southeast Asian cultures. While there is flux, there is also the unifying presence of the Thai monarchy that provides a stable anchor.

Similarly, the Filipino society has always been in constant flux. However, and unlike Thailand, we have an amorphous template upon which to draw our social cohesion. The revolutionary process at the turn of the century was interrupted, thereby leading to an incomplete process of nation building. The Filipino nation remains as a construct that is still being imagined, and such process has become increasingly made more complex at a time when the politics of identity is confronted by the political realities of a globalized world. This may have produced what some have labelled as a problematic cultural construct – a 'damaged culture' and a fractured polity. The Philippines does not have a political centre, even as its colonially constructed State apparatus would mimic those found in its Western roots. Even its discourses of resistance bear the colonial imprint, as it borrows Western metaphors of social refusal, from Marxism, to Feminism, to Western-inspired identity movements. These are empirical evidences of a Filipino identity that is socially constructed from the dialectical relationships between the 'self' and the 'other' in a fluid environment, where these dual categories are hard to imagine as purely colonial, or purely colonized.

The Filipino political identity is one that is produced in a context of fluidity and uncertain representation. Here, no single language could provide a firm grounding for the production of the Filipino political self. It is somewhat akin to what Derrida has labelled as characteristic of deferral and undecidability. There is no stable epistemological or ontological light upon which to hold the Filipino self visible for definitive construction.

In this context, and unlike the Thais, the Filipino identity is easier to see in a more postmodern lens. It is through this lens that one can understand why grand narratives of resistance have failed to produce a solidly grounded Filipino 'self'. Any great refusal would simply be not authentic to Filipino experience, for what would be required is a movement that would match the organic nature of social oppression – as manifested in everyday and ordinary lives. The Filipino political experience warrants an understanding of these everyday forms of power, for without such understanding any move to reform political practice would simply be producing a synthetic body of institutional structures and processes that would be not organically rooted.

Conclusion

Thailand, like the Philippines, is a land of good sense of humour and parody. Both provide a thriving habitat for gay beauty pageants and beauty contests for fat people, among others. Both have a natural tendency towards festivity and for the good life. Good humour becomes an embedded symbol of stability in the political psyche of both Thais and Filipinos. For the Filipino, the Thai is a familiar 'other'. The 'familiar' is seen in the important similarities in the historical trajectories, which saw the emergence of social and political institutions in both countries. I have used this view as a vantage point from which I look at the production of the Filipino political 'self'.

I have argued that the rigid norms upon which Thai identities are produced naturally leads to a strong state, and this warrants equally strong oppositional forms of resistance. Thus, even as the fabled smile is characteristically constructed as a bearer of the Thai external façade, the Thai polity can also easily erupt in bloody confrontations. However, the institution of Monarchy in Thailand, together with its natural predisposition for '*sanuk*', provides the Thai polity a potent source of political stability.

On the other hand, the Filipino self is a product of a process that is constantly becoming a more open process mediated by seemingly contradicting forces of globalization and localization. This fluidity, which for some is the root cause of its flawed systems of governance and political consolidation, could also be its source of political stability, as it is able to interrupt the grand narratives of domination not through unified forms of resistance, but by relying on the potent power of its 'silent monarchy' – the visible presence of its many forms of community, both real and virtual, and its capacity to render elite politics irrelevant, even as it is able to recuperate from its many crises.

The process of defining a modality for imagining the production of the political self vis-à-vis its difference from a familiar other has proven to be a meaningful exercise, as it forces one to engage such forms of otherness not as subordinated forms of alterity, but as templates upon which one can locate a meaning that would otherwise be dismissed as incoherent or unrecognizable. It is through the lens of the Thai experience that one can see that such parallel 'other' could indeed provide the Filipino its template for differentiation – not as an inferior form, but just as a different modality for finding social meaning. The Filipino lives in a postmodern world that is never named as such. In this context, the formation of identities could also be made relevant to the interest of the Filipino subject defining its 'self' when one is forced to look for another lens to see the promise that lies in such position of difference. This chapter attempted to show that it is possible to locate in the

Thai template a canvas upon which the Filipino political experience can be drawn and mapped.

Notes

1 This chapter is a revised version of the author's 'The Republic and the Kingdom: A Filipino Postmodern Reflection on Thailand as a Parallel Other', *Filosofia: International Journal of Philosophy* 37, no. 2 (2008): 204–24.
2 Virgilio Enriquez, *From Colonial to Liberation Psychology: The Philippine Experience* (Manila: DLSU Press, 1994).
3 Jacques Derrida, *Speech and Phenomena: And Other Essays on Husserl's Theory of Signs*, trans. David B. Allison (Evanston: Northwestern University Press, 1973); *Margins of Philosophy*, trans. Alan Bass (Chicago: Chicago University Press, 1982); *The Ear of the Other: Otobiography, Transference, Translation*, ed. Christie McDonald, trans. Peggy Kamuf (Lincoln: University of Nebraska Press, 1988).
4 Derrida, *Margins*. See also Ferdinand de Saussure, *Course in General Linguistics*, ed. Charles Bally and Albert Sechehaye, trans. Roy Harris (London: Duckworth, 1983).
5 Ben Agger, *Critical Social Theories: An Introduction* (Boulder: Westview Press, 1998), 58.
6 Pasuk Phongphaichit and Chris Baker, *Thailand: Economy and Politics* (Oxford: Oxford University Press, 1995).
7 James Scott, 'Freedom and Freehold: Space, People and State Simplification in Southeast Asia', in *Asian Freedoms: The Idea of Freedom in East and Southeast Asia*, ed. David Kelly and Anthony Reid (Cambridge: Cambridge University Press, 1998), 37–64.
8 Antonio P. Contreras, *The Kingdom and the Republic: Forest Governance and Political Transformation in Thailand and the Philippines* (Quezon City: Ateneo de Manila University Press, 2003).
9 Pierre Bourdieu, *Outline of a Theory of Practice*, trans. Richard Nice (Cambridge: Cambridge University Press, 1977).
10 Thongchai Winichakul, *Siam Mapped: A History of the Geo-Body of a Nation* (Honolulu: University of Hawaii Press, 1994).
11 Anan Ganjanapan, *Local Control of Land and Forest: Cultural Dimensions of Resources Management in Northern Thailand* (Chiang Mai: Regional Center for Social Sciences and Sustainable Development, 2000), 12.

9 The construction of 'indigenous peoples' in Cambodia[1]

Ian G. Baird

Indigenous peoples

The term 'indigenous peoples' is now in common use, and has become pervasive in both academic and popular literature and various public discourses globally. However, most people tend to apply it uncritically, frequently without thinking twice, let alone pondering its history, questioning its meaning or considering its political implications. It has become mainstream and naturalized for most. For example, the United Nations recognizes indigenous peoples, as is clear from the September 2007 adoption by the General Assembly of the 'UN Declaration on the Rights of Indigenous Peoples'.[2] One might conclude that it is easy to determine who is 'indigenous' and who is not.

The meaning of 'indigenous peoples' is, however, far from obvious or simple. Its application is complex and frequently in flux, and like so many other identities associated with nationality, religion, class, ethnicity and gender, its use has political implications and is thus often contested. Its meaning varies greatly depending on the places where it is applied, the time and context it is used, and the different peoples who employ it. Some fully endorse the concept, others acknowledge that indigenous peoples exist but deny efforts by certain groups to be classified as such, and there are many who refuse to accept the idea at all.

Even for those who recognize the concept of 'indigenous peoples', there is no consensus regarding its definition. In fact, many lobby groups working in support of indigenous peoples reject the proposition that a firm definition should even exist.[3] Instead, they insist that 'self-identification' is key,[4] thus making it possible for a wide range of groups to be classified as 'indigenous'. They also disagree with the idea that people should lose their 'indigenous rights' just because they have lost or abandoned particular practices or customs, or even languages, due to the some-times oppressive policies and practices of various dominating powers. As Margaret Fee has argued, 'For a member of a majority culture to try to deprive anyone of an indigenous identity just because of the success of this sort of program of cultural obliteration is ironic at best'.[5]

However, some believe that an international definition of indigenous peoples would be useful for better securing peoples' rights through excluding some who claim to be 'indigenous'. They argue that if anyone can be 'indigenous' the value of such a designation is diminished, especially when it comes to land and resource rights claimed by those who identify as such.[6] Gareth Griffiths has pointed out that calling everyone 'aboriginal' (first peoples) [or indigenous] suppresses the diversity of peoples in much the same way as previous colonial discourses did by lumping peoples into single categories.[7] It is, indeed, not always easy to say who should have the right to claim to be authentically 'indigenous'.

Kymlicka has pointed out that political processes often cause 'national minorities' to become identified as such due to their previously self-governing, territorially concentrated and culturally distinct societies.[8] Of course, a group's histories of incorporation – or lack of integration into states and dominant ethnic groups – is ultimately the basis for the creation of ethnic identities, including those associated with being 'indigenous' or 'aboriginal'. He believes that both national minorities and 'substate groups', such as the Tamils, Kurds, Tibetans, and so on, should have rights to language and self-government, but he questions whether 'indigenous peoples' should be given special rights in international law as compared to other minority 'substate' groups. He sees the distinction between indigenous peoples and 'substate' groups as being based primarily upon whether a people have participated in acts of nation-building processes, but does not feel that such differences justify giving the two groups different rights.[9]

The meaning of 'indigenous' has evolved considerably since it was first applied by Europeans at the end of the nineteenth century, when its use was fundamentally embedded within European colonialism. At that time the classification of people as 'indigenous' was simply a way of differentiating the colonizer from the colonized 'Other'.[10] The concept of 'indigenous' was not about empowering people – as it is often seen today – but about keeping the colonized Other in a different social space, discursively and physically separating them from dominating powers. For colonial rulers, it served their purposes to draw imaginary lines between Self and the Other, or the 'Good' and the 'Bad'. They wanted to retain the Other as such, even while transforming the 'absolute Other' to the 'domesticated Other'.[11]

Indeed, the meaning of 'indigenous' has changed, and in 1938 its meaning had already been transformed by the Pan-American Union, the predecessor of today's Organization of American States. The Union announced that, 'Indigenous populations, as descendents of the first inhabitants of the lands which today form America, and in order to offset the deficiency in their physical and intellectual development, have a preferential right to the protection of the public authorities.'[12]

This change had some parallels in French Indochinese colonialism, where at around the same time French officials increasingly recognized highlanders as the 'original' peoples, and took various steps to identify them as 'different', and to protect their lands and resources from majority lowland populations.[13] This was not just about protecting vulnerable ones, but was rather about justifying colonialism by producing a steward-role that would necessitate that the French remain in power to protect indigenous people. They needed to be saved from themselves.

Recently, the term 'indigenous' has often been used to classify marginalized and vulnerable peoples living within the boundaries of states, including those who may not be the 'first peoples' to the particular geographical spaces where they now reside. It is recognized that the displacement of these peoples has often been linked with efforts by outsiders to control them and their territories.[14]

Taking a global perspective, Christian Erni points out that the two above-mentioned concepts of indigeneity – being the original inhabitants and being marginalized and vulnerable – have dominated discourses associated with the idea of 'indigenous peoples', and over time have become important globally, being increasingly applied for political and emancipatory purposes.[15]

Andrew Gray, the former director of the International Work Group for Indigenous Affairs (IWGIA), saw the concept of colonialism as being fundamental to indigenous identities. For him, the concept of indigenous,

> refers to the quality of a people relating their identity to a particular area and distinguishing them culturally from other, 'alien' peoples who came to the territory subsequently. These indigenous peoples are 'colonized' in the sense of being disadvantaged and discriminated against. Their right to self-determination is their way of overcoming their obstacles.[16]

Gray expanded the scope of what some consider to be 'colonialism', including 'internal colonialism',[17] the domination of marginalized minority ethnic groups by other ethnic groups who occupy aspiring nation-states. The problem with the concept of 'nation-state', however, is that it essentializes the role of one particular 'nation' or 'people', thus discursively trapping or bounding groups that are expected to live under a single government, or within more than one country, even if dominated by Others. Rather than essentializing their places of origin, it is important to recognize that the categorization of peoples as being fundamentally linked only to their original geographical places can put some at a great disadvantage when those who dominate them choose to move or push them out into new spaces. Alternatively, preventing people from moving can be equally oppressive.[18]

Still, linking the concept of indigenous peoples with colonialism is useful for positioning people in the context of their relationships with Others, especially state powers, and examining these relationships have become a key part of postcolonial studies.[19] I have argued elsewhere that the ethnic Brao people of present-day north-eastern Cambodia and southern Laos have experienced various forms of colonialism over history, including during periods long preceding the arrival of Europeans to Brao areas in the nineteenth century, and continuing until the present, often under the direction of governments and their collaborators.[20]

The concept of 'indigenous' should not always be specifically associated with classification systems linked only to particular places. The place-specific circumstances of concepts of indigeneity and associated indigenous movements – even when they are variously linked to national, regional and global discourses – remain crucial. There are, in fact, frequently tensions between international, national and local frameworks for understanding identity concepts such as 'indigenous'. In this chapter, I address the relatively recent construction of the concept of indigenous peoples in Cambodia, and some of the crucial debates that are integral to the contested identity landscape that the idea of 'indigenous' is embedded in.

In essence, this chapter is about the indigenous Self and Others in the context of Cambodia.

My main argument is that the concept of indigenous peoples has only emerged and gained prominence in Cambodia in recent years, and that while it is still contested by various parties, it has gained considerable credence in identity discourses in the country. While a number of factors have converged to create the conditions for this to happen, of which the easing of Khmer nationalism is one, I argue that there are two factors that have been especially significant in the construction of indigenous peoples in Cambodia. First, the process for developing the 2001 Land Law has provided a state sanctioned recognition, the first in Cambodia, of the concept of indigenous peoples, and the special land rights conveyed to them under the law. This legislation has given people a tangible reason for wanting to identify as being indigenous, whereas there were no state-related reasons for doing so in the past. Second, I argue that non-government organizations (NGOs), both international and local, and other international organizations (IOs), such as the United Nations, have played crucial roles in constructing the concept of indigenous peoples in Cambodia, through varied efforts directed at local, national, regional and international levels. They had a strong influence on the content of the Land Law, and both before its adoption, and after, NGOs have provided key funding, networking, organizational and conceptual support to the 'indigenous movement', fundamentally influencing identity issues in Cambodia both directly and indirectly.

Rescaling the other

In the social sciences, debates in postcolonial studies often revolve around the idea of the 'national self' and the 'foreign other', especially as they relate to the legacies of the European colonial era. That includes assessing the role of 'white administration' on 'their colonies', the long-term legacies of colonialism in relation to what has emerged once the Europeans had variously withdrawn from their formal colonial administrative role, and how former colonial powers have influenced various forms of economic and social change in their former colonies and more globally.[21] A considerable literature has developed on these matters, but less has been written about the elaborate processes of Othering that occur in the context of different ethnic or cultural groups within particular countries in Asia, and the sets of discursive interplays that weave together globalized concepts, regionalisms, colonial pasts and presents, and present-day struggles and influences.

While I do not claim to be able to fully accomplish the above for Cambodia in a single chapter, I do hope to illuminate some important transformations that have occurred to the identity landscape of the country, especially in relation to ethnicity. Essentially, I am rescaling the focus on Otherness. Rather than elaborating on 'contact points' between the 'national' and the 'foreign', I am concerned with the circumstances surrounding groups often considered to be part of a single 'nation-state'.

The concept of indigenous peoples in Asia

The concept of indigenous peoples in Asia is far from clear or naturalized, especially in comparison with some other parts of the world, particularly the Americas, Australia and New Zealand, where it is often relatively easy to visibly observe who is indigenous and who is not, due to the long distance nature of large-scale European colonization, and the physical differences between the colonizers and colonized. In fact, most countries in Asia have particular conceptions of minority groups that may approximate indigenous peoples but do not necessarily match the UN concept. Many national governments in the region have adopted variations of what has become known as the 'salt water theory', which links the concept of colonialism intricately with European colonialism and colonization.[22] Illustrative of this, in some cases national governments recognize the global existence of indigenous peoples – especially in the Americas, Australia and New Zealand – but claim that all citizens within their international borders are 'aboriginal' or 'indigenous', thus essentially making the concept irrelevant for them. This is, for example, the case in Laos where all different ethnic groups (*son phao* in Lao) are classified as having equal rights. Vietnam takes the same position, as does Burma. In Indonesia, all ethnic groups also have the same rights, even if limited local autonomy has been granted in some areas, albeit for both minority and majority populations.[23]

Some governments argue that because the period of European colonialism is over in their context, with negligible European colonization having taken place in most cases, there are thus no longer any indigenous peoples in their countries. This is, for example, the position frequently put forward by the People's Republic of China. China also denies that there are any 'indigenous issues' in the country.[24] Even if some 'autonomous regions' do exist in China, and limited autonomy is recognized for particular 'national minorities', the influence of the central government on local affairs is strong.[25]

Malaysia has a different stance. They employ the concept of '*Bumiputera*', or 'sons of the earth' (a term referring to 'original inhabitants') to especially define ethnic Malays, and to justify controversial laws – including what some believe to be unnecessarily discriminatory legislation – that favour Malays as opposed to ethnic Chinese and Indians.[26] However, there are other peoples in Malaysia, typically known in peninsular Malaysia as the 'Orang Asli'[27] (forest people in Malay). They were not considered relevant in the Malaysia system, even though they better fit the UN definition of indigenous. There is a provision for Orang Asli land reserves, but these land rights can be revoked without notice or compensation. Indigenous peoples in Sabah and Sarawak, whose land and resource rights are somewhat greater, have also lost control of much of their lands to outsiders.[28]

There is also the case of Thailand, where the government does not recognize the existence of indigenous peoples, and has so far failed to grant any special land rights to upland minority populations.[29] Many highlanders who have lived within the borders of Thailand for generations have not even been granted citizen rights. The Thai term '*chao khao*', which is commonly used to refer to 'mountain people' is a fundamentally racialized and dispossessing label, one that rests on its relationship to (distance from) 'Thai'.[30]

At present, only a few countries in Asia explicitly recognize the international concept of indigenous peoples, as adopted by the countries that ratified ILO Convention 107, the predecessor of 169, which is now considered outdated because it has an assimilationist approach to indigenous peoples.[31] The Philippines is one, and particularly since 1997, when the Indigenous Peoples Rights Act was promulgated, special land rights have been provided to indigenous peoples through applying the concept of 'ancestral domain'.[32]

In recent years the Japanese government has also come to recognize Ainu people as having special indigenous rights. This was especially the case after March 1997, when the Sapporo District Court found that the local government's decision to expropriate Ainu land was illegal and that it was possible to rescind its decision under the Eminent Domain Law. Most significantly, it defined the Ainu as indigenous peoples.[33] In 2008, the Ainu were specifically recognized as 'indigenous' in the Japanese parliament.[34]

Taiwan is another case where the government has increasingly recognized its indigenous peoples and their special rights to lands. The year 1996 was a watershed period for the indigenous movement of Taiwan, as it was then that indigenous legislators were able to negotiate the establishment of a Council of Indigenous Peoples, thus giving institutional force to an emerging discourse of indigenous identity.[35] Trends toward increased recognition of indigenous rights continued during the presidency of Chen Shui-bian (Democratic Progressive Party) from 2000 to 2008, even if various problems remain.[36]

Highland minorities in Cambodia

In Cambodia, ethnically distinct peoples apart from the dominant Khmers have long been categorized as Others. For example, a Chinese visitor to Angkor court at Siem Reap in 1296–7, Chou Ta-Kuan,[37] wrote that 'savages' fed the slave markets of the country and the capital. He reported that some wealthy Khmer families had more than 100 slaves, and that only the poorest had none. These slaves were captured in the mountains, and were considered to be of a different race. According to Chou Ta-Kuan, 'So looked down on are these wretches that when, in the course of a dispute, a Cambodian is called "Chuang" [the name used for highlanders at the time] by his adversary, dark hatred strikes to the marrow of his bones'.[38] Yet these highland slaves were important for the Angkor kings, and it seems likely that their labour was important for constructing many of the great structures of Angkor. Chou Ta-Kuan also reported that there were fierce warriors that defended the highlands from intrusions by outsiders. The highlanders were far from being passive victims of slave trading. They also became involved in slave raiding and the slave trade more generally.

The fifteenth century saw the decline of the Angkor Kingdom, including the abandonment of Siem Reap as the Khmer capital in 1432, largely due to a series of defeats at the hands of the Siamese,[39] thus leading to the retraction of Khmer influence in upland areas in what is presently north-eastern Cambodia, the main part of present-day Cambodia inhabited by highland minorities today. Yet Khmer slave traders continued to prey on highland minorities, at least up the nineteenth century. The Siamese and Lao peoples who came to dominate the area in the eighteenth and nineteenth centuries did the same.[40]

Yet, Khmer–highland relations were not just about hatred and slave raiding. In particular, the Khmer interactions with Jarai highlanders were complex, and up to early nineteenth century Khmer kings exchanged tribute with Jarai 'kings'. The Khmer appear to have given the Jarai goods of considerably greater value than what they received. One explanation for this is that the Khmer were indebted to the Jarai for defending the northeastern-most part of the Khmer domain, either from Vietnamese or possibly Cham or Lao invasion. It may be that they were given large amounts of tribute in return for continuing that role. However, with the arrival of the French in 1860 King Norodom stopped these exchanges,[41] to the dislike of the Jarai who previously benefited. Another possible explanation is that the Jarai goods were considered to be as valuable, or even more valuable, as the goods that the Khmer provided because of their alleged magical powers, making them important for certain palace rituals.[42]

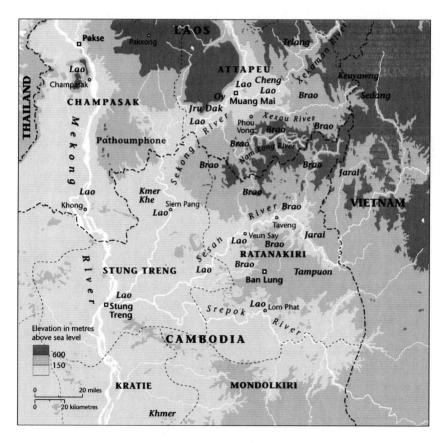

Figure 9.1 Map of some of the ethnic groups in the northeastern-most part of Cambodia and southeastern-most part of Laos (ethnic group names are in italics)
Source: Ian G. Baird.

Khmer definitions of the 'highland other'

Identities, as represented by different people, are terms of engagement. They normalize relations between different groups. The Khmer have long engaged with highlanders, and have thus used various terms to define highland Others. These discourses tell us a lot about these terms of engagement, or the 'contact point' between the Khmer and highlanders. The terms used by the Khmer have not historically been particularly respectful. In particular, they show how Khmer discourses placed the Khmer above highland Others.[43] For example, the Khmer have long used pejorative labels for identifying highland minorities, including *Samre* (a term presently meaning something like 'hillbilly')[44] to define particular peoples in the highlands[45] seen as racially different from them. Another term in frequent use by Khmers is *Phnong*[46] (probably derived from the ethnic Bunong people in present-day Mondolkiri and Kratie Provinces), which has been applied to refer, frequently in derogatory terms,[47] to all ethnic highlanders, including groups other than the Bunong.[48] Another name for highland Others that does not appear to be used much at present, but which can still be found in Khmer language dictionaries is *Srok Ai*, which refers to something from inside the country, but a little lower quality or backwards.

After Cambodia achieved independence from colonial France in 1953–4, Norodom Sihanouk embarked on a nation-building programme. As part of this effort, a new classification system was developed that resulted in the application of the terms *Khmer Loeu*, *Khmer Kraom* and *Khmer Islam*.[49] The majority Khmer population became known as the *Khmer Kandal*, or middle or central Khmer. According to one observer, the term *Khmer Loeu* was coined in order to 'create a feeling of unity between the highland tribal groups and the ruling lowland ethnic Khmer'.[50] However, Sutsakhan wrote that, 'The term [Khmer Loeu] was developed during the Sihanouk era to facilitate the integration into Khmer society of the non-Khmer hill tribes living in northeast Cambodia.'[51] Charles Meyer, an advisor to Sihanouk regarding highlander issues, was particularly suspicious of Sihanouk's motives, believing that the term was created to negate the traditional identities of the highlanders and connect them more with the 'Khmer Nation'.[52] Still, the use of *Khmer Loeu* persists today, and many highlanders are proud to be referred to as such, and also frequently refer to themselves in this way. Sihanouk also introduced *bong pa-on chun chiet* (ethnic brothers and sisters), a term with a neutral literal meaning (equality and relationship between peoples), yet very paternalistic overtones, with the Khmer seen as being the elder sibling in the relationship.

During the Khmer Rouge period, during the 1970s, all 'Khmers' were considered to be equal, with class identification being, instead, the key way of differentiating various people in the country. However, many highlanders were frequently given a higher designation than Khmers, being referred to as 'base people'. At least some of the Khmer Rouge leadership, including Pol Pot, believed that the highlanders represented a primitive form of Khmer (and Communism), relatively untouched by monarchism or capitalism. Their egalitarian natures were believed to give them the potential to become more easily adaptable to the radical socialism that the Democratic Kampuchea state desired.[53]

More recently, especially after Cambodia was liberated from Khmer Rouge rule by Vietnam in 1979, it has become common for Khmers to call highlanders *chun chiet pheak tech* (ethnic minorities), or more commonly as simply *chun chiet* (which simply means 'ethnic group'). The concept of ethnicity applied during this period was based on Stalin's conception of ethnicity.[54] It appears in article 5 of the 1981 and 1989 Cambodian constitutions. While technically even the Khmer are an ethnic group in Cambodia, in the same way as Sollor claims that 'we are all ethnic',[55] discursively the term is almost never used in common conversation to refer to the Khmer, a practice that is paralleled in other parts of the world.[56] However, it is sometimes used to describe Caucasian foreigners or other 'Outsiders'.

As pointed out by Sollor, 'it is a widespread practice to define ethnicity as otherness'.[57] Indeed, the Khmer tend to see themselves as simply Khmer and the ethnic Others as '*chun chiet*'. For them, this discourse is about boundary-constructing processes which function as cultural markers between groups.[58] Furthermore, most Khmers without a good understanding of highland minorities tend to lump all groups into a single category, considering them to be a collective Other rather than distinct peoples with significant historical, cultural and linguistic differences. Discursively, this excludes all these others from full membership within 'Khmer' society, but it also binds them together as having similar experiences in relation to the Khmer. To create this boundary, the Khmer also rely on particular stereotypes about highland minorities, in terms of language, dress, agricultural practices, religion and customs, such as assuming that many have large plugs in their ear lobes. These stereotypes are frequently reproduced by the Khmer in music videos and other cultural productions, even if, in reality, many are no longer particularly relevant as real differences. For example, many highlanders now live in the lowlands like the Khmer, or never lived in the uplands, dress like the Khmer and conduct lowland wet rice agriculture like the Khmer. Some are also Buddhists or even Christians.[59] Furthermore, while it is still common to see older highlanders in north-eastern Cambodia with large holes in their ear lobes, young highland minorities no longer make holes in their ear lobes. Still the markers remain in the minds of many Khmer, and are also reproduced and exaggerated by some highlanders themselves, thus functioning to maintain ethnic boundaries, or otherwise gain benefits associated with being different. Other cultural differences that are significant to specific highland groups, such as the types of buffalo sacrifices that are conducted by particular peoples, may be important as boundary markers between groups, like the Brao sub-groups,[60] but since they are not part of Khmer stereotypes, they are rarely evoked by highlanders when communicating about ethnic boundaries and differences with the Khmer.

Transforming the 'highland other' into the 'indigenous other' in Cambodia

The Khmer have long recognized the existence of highland peoples within the Khmer state,[61] most considering them to be different – and frequently as lowlier than them – but still as legitimate members of the Khmer state. However, the discursive transformation of the 'highland Other' to the 'indigenous Other' has been much more recent, having strongly emerged only within the last decade. This shift has been far from complete, with many Khmer people understanding indigenous to mean *chun chiet* in Khmer, without considering indigenous as referring to anything like the UN concept. The term 'indigenous peoples' is, indeed, confusing for many, including many of those who adopt such an identity. This section explains the circumstances surrounding this transformation, and the discourses and debates that have emerged in recent years.

The 1992 Cambodian constitution makes no specific reference to highland ethnic minorities, let alone indigenous peoples, instead bundling these people in with ethnic Khmer. This indicates that the concept of 'indigenous' has emerged since the adoption of the constitution.

The concept of indigenous peoples emerged, and took on real meaning, when Cambodia's Land Law was approved by the Cambodian National Assembly. This important piece of legislation is considered by many international NGO workers as having been the result of the most participatory legislative processes experienced in Cambodia to date. However, others argue that the process was participatory for NGOs but not necessarily all Cambodians, and that it resulted in NGOs essentially imposing an essentialized Western concept of indigeneity on Cambodia. In any case, the Land Law was the first legislation to make specific mention of indigenous peoples, referred to in Khmer language as *chun chiet daoem pheak tech*. From this process have emerged new identities and positionings. Crucially, this law redefined the relations between 'national minorities' and the state, creating spaces for the emergence of new identities associated with special rights. But how did this ground-breaking legislation emerge?

It is important to recognize the political circumstances in Cambodia in the late 1990s. The arguably first ever truly democratic elections occurred in Cambodia in May 1993, sponsored by the United Nations Transitional Authority in Cambodia (UNTAC), which took control of Cambodia's state administration in 1992 after the Vietnamese completed their military withdrawal from Cambodia in September 1989,[62] and the historic UN-sponsored 1991 Paris Peace agreements were signed.[63]

Although Norodom Ranariddh's *Front Uni National pour un Cambodge Indépendant, Neutre, Pacifique, et Coopératif* (commonly known as FUNCINPEC Party) won the election, the Cambodian People's Party (CPP), which controlled the government prior to the arrival of UNTAC, refused to give up full control. In the end, a compromise was brokered, which led to a power-sharing agreement that made Ranariddh 'First Prime Minister' and Hun Sen 'Second Prime Minister'. The government functioned, at least nominally, for the next few years, but the simmering conflict between the two former enemies, the two prime ministers, finally erupted into brutal violence in July 1997 when supporters of Hun Sen launched a violent *coup d'état*. Some claim that FUNCINPEC may have been planning its own *coup d'état* when the CPP struck first. In any case, several prominent FUNCINPEC politicians and military leaders were assassinated, and those who were able to escape regrouped along the border with Thailand, in areas they previously occupied during the pre-peace agreement civil war period. Fighting continued, with the already fractured Khmer Rouge – which had essentially withdrawn from the peace process soon after signing the peace agreement – supporting FUNCINPEC forces against forces loyal to the CPP. Other former Khmer Rouge soldiers fought with the CPP. Finally, in 1998, the international community successfully arranged a new political compromise that allowed for the return of FUNCINPEC to the CPP-dominated government.

It is important to consider the emergence of the concept of indigenous peoples in Cambodia in the context of the political environment that existed in Cambodia during the last few years of the 1990s. The border fighting had badly damaged the economy of Cambodia, as well as the international reputations of Hun Sen and the CPP. The country, which remained highly dependent on development aid from international donors, especially Western governments and Japan, was under increasing pressure to reform. The conflict had prevented Cambodia from joining Association of Southeast Asian Nations (ASEAN) with Burma and Laos as planned, and the Cambodian government was desperate for regional recognition so that they could join ASEAN. It was, in many ways, the 'golden age' for NGO influence in the country.[64]

In 1997 the UN Highland People's Project (HPP) started in the Ministry of Rural Development. It formed an interministerial committee made up of representatives from 12 ministries, and started an extensive consultation process regarding the development of a multisectoral Highland People's Policy. At that time the HPP referred to highlanders as *chun chiet pheak tech nev kompong reap* (upland ethnic minority groups).

In 1998, the Asian Development Bank (ADB) was developing a large agriculture development project in Cambodia, and as part of that process they imposed a conditionality on the Cambodian government to conduct a review of the 1992 Land Law. According to an NGO observer, 'It was basically a box that the ADB needed to check', and not surprisingly, the review was not regarded as being useful. Still, it provided space for international NGOs to push for pro-poor and pro-highlander land reforms. Prior to the review, Oxfam Great Britain had started the 'Land Study Project' and hired an Australian consultant, Shaun Williams, to work on this issue. He would become instrumental in advocating for the reforms that NGOs and their local collaborators were advocating. He worked with the Council of Ministers,[65] and also the Bar Association of Cambodia. Janet King from the University of San Francisco and George Cooper from Legal Aid of Cambodia were also integrally involved. NGOs/IOs initially felt that references to indigenous peoples in the Land Law should be consistent with the approved Highland People's Policy, but the government insisted that the Land Law should be approved first and the Highland People's Policy modified to conform to it. However, after the Land Law was enacted in 2001, the policy was mothballed.

Meanwhile, in Ratanakiri, northeastern Cambodia, a province with a high proportion of highlanders, the United Nations Development Programme's (UNDP) Cambodia Area Rehabilitation and Regeneration Programme (CARERE) had formed an alliance with international NGOs working on indigenous issues. CARERE decided to get more involved in supporting land reforms that would provide special rights for indigenous peoples. Although their efforts to hire a Cambodian lawyer to draft the indigenous part of the Land Law did not achieve the desired results, it did help build momentum, and CARERE's involvement was also crucial in gaining support from the provincial government, including the governor, Kep Chuktema.

Following on from the work of the NGO, the Non-Timber Forest Products (NTFP) Project with the ethnic Kreung community of Krola, O Chum District, on indigenous land-use planning, Ya Kuak, the village chief of Krola, made an impassioned plea at the closing ceremony of a workshop organized by the Cambodian human rights organization ADHOC to train workers in awareness raising on land rights for highland ethnic minorities. This ceremony was attended by senior Phnom Penh officials and Kep Chuktema. This helped gain the governor's support, and led to the provincial government's request for NGOs to help draft a sub-decree that would allow for indigenous communal land rights. Initial NGO and IO attempts to get this draft accepted by the Land Department in Phnom Penh in August–September 2008 were unsuccessful. Kep Chuktema then suggested that the way forward would be to organize a series of consultative workshops with highlanders. He asked for NGO assistance, and in November 1998 a workshop brought key officials and villagers together from the five north-eastern provinces with the largest proportions of highlanders. It was, according to the Australian Gordon Paterson, who was then the director of NTFP Project, during the preparatory discussions for the workshop that it was agreed that the appropriate term for indigenous peoples in Khmer language to be used for the title of the workshop should be *chun chiet daoem pheak tech*.[66] Adding the word *daoem*, or 'from the origin', to *chun chiet pheak tech* (ethnic minorities) created the term 'original ethnic minorities', which is commonly transliterated into English as 'indigenous peoples'. Workshop participants also adopted the term *chun chiet daeum pheak chraoen* (original ethnic majority) for ethnic Khmer, thus allowing discourses on ethnicity in Cambodia to recognize that the Khmer are also original inhabitants of the nation. The crucial difference is that they are in the majority. In many ways this discourse mirrors elements of the 'salt water theory' adopted by many other Asian governments, since both the Khmer and the highlanders were recognized to be 'original peoples' to Cambodia. However, through applying the term 'minority' instead of 'majority' for the highlanders, it created an important discursive and eventually legal difference between the two groups, even if the concept was originally presented as a simple 'minority' and 'majority', and only later came to incorporate 'special rights' for the minority. Thus, the term's meaning gradually transformed.

This was followed, in March 1999, by a National workshop that was opened by the CPP Minister of the Council of Ministers, Sok An. At the time the Cambodian government was under considerable pressure from international donors. Fortuitously, a major donor meeting in Tokyo had just taken place (the donor consultative group), in which donors had strongly suggested that the Cambodian government needed to adopt land reforms in order to retain continued donor support. This political environment was probably the main reason that Sok An announced that the Cambodian government supported adding a section into the Land Law that would recognize special land rights for indigenous peoples. He appealed for NGOs and IOs to participate in this process through supporting consultations with indigenous communities about the type of land tenure arrangements highlanders would like to see adopted. Thus, in May 1999 a coalition of Ratanakiri NGOs and CARERE helped organize consultations with 44 highland communities, all of which were in Ratanakiri Province (including people from the main indigenous groups in the province, Tampuan, Jarai, Kreung, Kavet and Brao).[67] The UNDP also engaged an ethnic Khmer indigenous peoples' consultant, Tiann Mony, to negotiate the content of a special section in the Land Law related to indigenous peoples. Oxfam Great Britain in Phnom Penh, through their land research project, was pivotal to this advocacy work, not only in relation to pushing for indigenous land rights, but more generally with regard to reforming the Land Law.

Finally, in around June 2000, a final draft of the new Land Law was complete. Some bureaucrats in the Council of Ministers threatened to cut three key articles out of the eight clauses in the indigenous community section of the draft legislation, including one that defined indigenous peoples and their communities, and another that allowed indigenous communities rights to fallow swidden lands. However, lobbying efforts, including national newspaper publicity, kept that from happening. The King, Norodom Sihanouk, stepped in and made timely statements in support of indigenous land rights. He also wrote a letter to Hun Sen in support of the unaltered legislation.[68] With all these pressures being exerted, Hun Sen ordered that the removed articles be re-included. The Council of Ministers approved the legislation in July 2000, and the new Land Law was passed by the National Assembly in August 2001. The only part of the legislation that the NGOs remained concerned about was a statement that would allow any member of an indigenous community to exit from the 'domination of the community' and its communal land system, and receive compensation from the community. This clause was of concern to some NGO workers, who felt that it could potentially lead to badly divided communities and obligations for communities without the resources to provide compensation to disaffected people. Still, one could argue that adding this provision expanded the rights of indigenous peoples for individual choice, since it provided them with new options. Since then, this issue has re-emerged in the drafting of the communal land sub-decree, with it being used to weaken indigenous land rights in the drafting of subsequent sub-decrees for implementing the indigenous section of the Land Law.

In any case, since Cambodia passed the Land Law in 2001 the process to actually develop government recognized communal land pilot villages and implementing legislation and procedures has been excruciatingly slow, and the pro-indigenous provisions of the Land Law have still not been meaningfully implemented. Neither has the sub-decree on indigenous communal land been completed as planned. Many believe that government officials and politicians are stalling the process in order to make it possible for indigenous lands to be taken. Many may fear that having two pieces of legislation agreeing with each other regarding indigenous land rights could hurt their interests. Meanwhile, cases of land grabbing, illegal land sales and the granting of large land concessions have increased dramatically, leading to what NGO Forum in Cambodia calls 'land alienation'.[69] While these land deals are illegal according to the Land Law, the Cambodian government has done little to resolve problems, and the courts have not been very sympathetic to community challenges to retain possession of their lands.[70] Still, NGOs are supporting indigenous communities in some important ongoing legal struggles, especially in Ratanakiri Province.[71]

After the Land Law – developing indigenous identities

Whatever problems have occurred in relation to realizing indigenous land rights provisions, the Land Law has become an important vehicle for raising awareness about indigeneity in Cambodia, including developing the concept of indigenous peoples, as has the 2002 Forestry Law, which also explicitly mentions 'indigenous peoples'. Even if the laws are not being implemented as intended by many NGOs, NGOs have played a crucial role in disseminating information throughout Cambodia regarding the possibilities for 'indigenous peoples' to gain special rights over their lands and resources.[72] For example, NGOs have organized meetings and workshops to raise awareness on land rights. They have also facilitated highlander participation in regional and international workshops and study trips supported by groups like IWGIA, based in Copenhagen, Denmark, and the regional indigenous support group, the Asian Indigenous People's Pact (AIPP), based in Chiang Mai, Thailand. They have in many ways shaped the meaning of indigenous peoples in Cambodia, challenging and transforming various negative stereotypes from the past.

NGOs have implemented projects, mainly linked to forestry issues and networks, in various parts of Cambodia. Through these projects, discussions about what it means to be Kui, Stieng, Bunong (and so on) began, thus helping to raise the profile of indigenous rights. Many minorities had previously been discriminated against, causing many to suppress their indigenous identities. Through different activities, people came to feel prouder about being *chun chiet*, and the discrimination they experienced also decreased as a general societal trend in many parts of Cambodia. This, in many cases, was a fundamental process, one that has often preceded the adoption of indigenous identities. Once people were more confident and more willing or able to identify as being minorities, the concept of indigeneity was easier to latch on to.

Another activity that significantly raised the profile of indigenous peoples was the nationwide indigenous peoples' land tenure consultations that were organized in the early 2000s. The German bilateral aid agency, GTZ (*Deutsche Gesellschaft fur Technische Zusammenarbeit*), was an important player at this time. These consultations represented one of the first times that many communities became aware that there were potential land rights advantages associated with being 'indigenous'.

There have also been advances in government acceptance of bilingual education for highland minorities in Cambodia, albeit mainly as a tool for integrating people into the Khmer language education system. Still, these efforts go beyond what has been allowed in many other Asian countries, and the support for bilingual education has helped raise the profile of indigenous peoples. Having written scripts for their languages is also important for raising the confidence and sense of self-worth amongst highland minorities.[73]

In addition, the UNDP has funded research regarding 'indigenous traditional legal systems and conflict resolution' in north-eastern Cambodia, and have made some efforts to lobby the Cambodian Ministry of Justice to recognize the existence and even usefulness of these systems,[74] even if there have been few tangible results so far. The participatory processes adopted for doing this research has, however, helped influence indigenous identities.

Together, these and other efforts have facilitated identity transformation processes in various parts of Cambodia. It is useful to illustrate what has happened in some highland communities – in relation to identity transformation – by providing an example from O Som Commune, Veal Veng District, Pursat Province, located in the Cardamom Mountains, south-western Cambodia. I visited this area in 2001. I had heard that there might be ethnic minorities living in the area, but despite considerable efforts, I was not able to find anyone in the commune who admitted to being a highland minority. I was informed by local leaders that there were a few people in the commune with ethnic 'Por' ('Pear') ancestry, but that virtually all of the population were ethnic Khmer, even if their dialect of Khmer is somewhat different from the mainstream.

I have not returned to O Som since, but I have heard from others, including Jeremy Ironside and Stefan Ehrentraut,[75] that after some key people from O Som attended a few indigenous workshops, the majority of the population of the commune, assumedly including many who denied being ethnic minorities in 2001, are now claiming to be 'indigenous' (*Khmer daoem*) people,[76] a group that differentiates from the 'Por' found elsewhere. The Land Law may have influenced this transition, but it is probably true that the people also started differentiating themselves from the majority because they felt there was political space to do so. They sensed that Khmer nationalism had waned enough for them to (re)exert their 'Otherness'.

The people from O Som are apparently not the only ones who have undergone identity transformations. In various parts of the country, including in the northern province of Kompong Thom, people are increasingly identifying as *Khmer daoem*.[77] One NGO observer, who asked to remain anonymous, commented, 'Indigenous people are coming out of the woodwork in Cambodia'. Yet, the idea of *Khmer daoem* has not only been influenced by discourses coming out of the indigenous movement, but also existed prior to it as well.[78]

These developments have alarmed some Cambodian government officials who were not expecting that the Land Law would help propel these new identities. Indicative of this, Prime Minister Hun Sen allegedly stated that people should stop self-identifying as *Khmer daoem*. In addition, to counter the concept of continual indigenous rights, Stalinist evolutionary and assimilative notions of ethnicity have been evoked by some government officials and politicians who claim that while there may now be a considerable number of 'indigenous minorities' in Cambodia,[79] this may not be the case in the future, if people evolve and become more assimilated into mainstream culture. This assimilative process is expected to take place as the minorities learn more Khmer language, adopt more Khmer customs, increasingly develop lowland agriculture, and generally advance materially.[80] It is expected that the 'indigenous Other' can develop to become part of the 'Khmer Self'.[81]

There is also the question of how particular ethnic groups fit into the present ethnic classification system in Cambodia. For example, what about the Cham? They do not originate in Cambodia but rather from present-day Vietnam, even though they have lived in Cambodia for generations. What about the ethnic Chinese who have largely integrated into Khmer mainstream society? What about long-established but less integrated Chinese communities? How should ethnically Vietnamese people living in Cambodia for generations be classified? Presumably, they are called *chun chiet pheak tech* (without including the *daoem*), since Vietnam exists, even if many of these ethnic Vietnamese have long resided in Cambodia. However, many Khmer I have met prefer to call the Vietnamese the 'ethnic majority', since the Vietnamese are associated with Vietnam. What about the Lao who have lived in parts of north-eastern Cambodia for generations, especially Stung Treng and Ratanakiri Provinces, but also Battambong and elsewhere? They have been living in these areas since they were parts of Siam and Laos in the nineteenth century.[82] The people of the Lao village of Phluk, in Sesan District, Stung Treng Province, refer to themselves as *Lao daoem*, even though they apparently applied this term without having been influenced by discourses associated with the indigenous movement in Cambodia. Still, the *Khmer Kraom* in Vietnam have identified themselves as indigenous peoples at the UN,[83] so does that mean that ethnic Lao people in north-eastern Cambodia could do the same? What about the long-standing Lao in Prey Veng Province in southern Cambodia? What about the well established ethnic Thais in Koh Kong Province? The answers to these questions remain uncertain, and continue to be debated. NGOs are playing an important role in defining who is indigenous and who is not. One long-time observer noted that if the NGOs decided that the Lao minority in Cambodia should be defined as 'indigenous', he was fairly sure that other minority groups would accept such a definition.

It must, however, be remembered that while supporting indigenous identities and rights to land and resources can be useful, it can also lead to unintended consequences, including negative impacts, both for indigenous peoples and those groups that are seen as threats to them. As Tania Li has reminded us, indigenous rights discourses can even contribute to brutal violence and the loss of life, including the type of 'ethnic cleansing' that was subjected against Madurese settlers in Borneo, Indonesia, at the hands of 'Dayak' warriors in 1997 and 2001, who were upset about losing their lands to Madurese settlers. The Dayak were at least partially inspired by NGO discourses regarding indigenous rights to lands and resources.[84] Of course, it is unlikely that NGOs promoted the genocidal killings that occurred, but NGOs and other actors cannot always predict, let alone control, the consequences of processes of indigenization.

Conclusions

It is difficult to know how indigenous identities will develop in Cambodia, as the concept is still in its infancy. It has the potential to transform and mutate in various ways, depending on all kinds of factors, including the nature of efforts by NGOs and other civil society groups, but also crucially, future responses by different levels of government. In fact, terms like 'indigenous' are terms of engagement, and their emergence in Cambodia reflect changes in 'contact points' between Khmer and highland Others, but also the influence that discourses promoted by NGOs are having.

The concept of indigenous peoples that has emerged in Cambodia is, indeed, closely linked to indigenous land rights movements. It is a globalized term that opens up links between people and NGOs, much more than the terms highlanders use to describe themselves, like Brao, Bunong, Kui, etc. NGOs, such as the nationally active Indigenous Communities Support Organization (ICSO),[85] the Cambodian Indigenous Youth Association (CIYA), the Ratanakiri-based 'Highlanders Association' (*Samakhom Khmer Loeu* in Khmer), and the Preah Vihear and Kompong Thom-based Organization to Promote Kui Culture (OPKC) have emerged with international support, as have programmes such as the Indigenous Youth Development Program (IYDP) and the Indigenous Rights Active Members (IRAM) network, which is not really an NGO, but has been described as an indigenous peoples network. All are supporting indigenous communities struggling to retain their land rights in the face of serious challenges.[86] However, international support can be fickle, with assistance for indigenous peoples often declining when people are seen to be 'modernizing'.

It is the rhetorical and ultimately tangible (or at least perceived) benefits associated to being identified as 'indigenous' that have been particularly significant for local people. Before the Land Law there were seemingly few benefits associated with identifying as being 'indigenous'. But the Land Law made what was previously seen as a disadvantage into an identity with associated political and livelihood benefits. Thus, the identity shifts that have occurred, and will continue to emerge, have not just been an accident or a by-product of a global movement, although that is certainly part of what is happening in Cambodia. Even though this process is fundamentally linked to international NGO advocacy efforts in Cambodia, it is also connected to other processes that have occurred between NGOs and government, local people and the state, and NGOs and the state more generally. Of course, it has sparked varied debates and discussions within communities themselves. These debates have also become intertwined with other events and NGO activities, which have introduced and reinforced particular discourses and new stereotypes. We cannot expect the results to be either uniform or stable. Identity changes are always occurring, and we all hold multiple identities, of which we choose to use different ones depending on particular circumstances. Thus, it should be of little surprise that those who choose to evoke embodied indigenous performances at certain times may also choose to identify in other ways, including as ethnic Khmers. This is especially possible in countries such as Cambodia, where mere physical characteristics are rarely sufficient for determining ethnic heritage, as is frequently the case for indigenous/non-indigenous relations in the Americas, or in Australia or New Zealand, where people perceive the indigenous Other when they first see racial and colour differences.[87] In Cambodia, and much of Asia more generally, the conditions surrounding indigenous identification, and identities generally, are thus frequently complex, going well beyond evoking racially-based stereotypes.

Furthermore, in a similar way as described for 'black' people in Britain by Stuart Hall,[88] we should not be surprised when indigenous peoples in Cambodia choose to go beyond generalized categorizations in order to apply unique identities associated with ethnic groups, sub-groups, villages or even individuals, as means for separating themselves from other so-called indigenous peoples when it serves particular purposes. We can even expect new identities and terms of engagement to gain force in the future.

As Terry Goldie[89] has pointed out, in line with ideas developed by Michel Foucault related to 'subjugated knowledges',[90] the idea of indigenous is a semiotic pawn that can only move according to rules established by Others, but at the same time, I strongly believe that it would be incorrect, indeed foolish, to suggest that indigenous peoples themselves have no human agency, and thus have nothing to do with the processes that relate so intricately to them and how they are identified, both by themselves and by Others.

Notes

1 I am indebted to Gordon Paterson for useful information about the development of the 2001 Land Law. Thanks also to Stefan Ehrentraut, Mathieu Guérin, Jeremy Ironside, Hjorleifur Jonsson, Gordon Paterson, Alberto Pérez-Pereiro, Scott Simon, Peter Swift and Leong Yew for commenting on earlier versions of this chapter or otherwise assisting me in its preparation. Needless to say, any deficiencies that remain are my responsibility. Thanks also to Eric Leinberger from the Geography Department of the University of British Columbia for helping to prepare the map.

2 Christian Erni, ed., *The Concept of Indigenous Peoples in Asia: A Resource Book*, IWGIA Document No. 123 (Copenhagen: International Work Group for Indigenous Affairs; Chiang Mai: Asia Indigenous Peoples Pact Foundation, 2008).

3 See J.R. Bowen, 'Should We Have a Universal Concept of "Indigenous Peoples' Right"?', (paper presented at the 2000 Symposium 'Development and the Nation State', Washington University, St Louis, 2000).

4 Erni, *The Concept*; Erica-Irene A. Daes, 'Standard-Setting Activities: Concerning the Rights of Indigenous people', Working Paper, Fourteenth Session, Sub-commission on Prevention of Discrimination and Protection of Minorities, Commission on Human Rights, 10 June (New York: United Nations Economic and Social Council, 1996).

5 Margaret Fee, 'Who can Write as Other?', in *The Post-Colonial Studies Reader*, ed. Bill Ashcroft, Gareth Griffiths and Helen Tiffin (London and New York: Routledge, 1995), 242.

6 Benedict Kingsbury, '"Indigenous peoples" in International Law: A Constructivist Approach to the Asian Controversy', *American Journal of International Law* 92, no. 3 (1998): 414–57; Jeff J. Corntassel, 'Who is Indigenous? "Peoplehood" and Ethnonationalist Approaches to Rearticulating Indigenous Identity', *Nationalism and Ethnic Politics* 9, no. 1 (2003): 75–100.

7 Gareth Griffiths, 'The Myth of Authenticity', in *The Post-Colonial Studies Reader*, ed. Bill Ashcroft, Gareth Griffiths and Helen Tiffin (London and New York: Routledge, 1995).

8 Will Kymlicka, *Multicultural Citizenship: A Liberal Theory of Minority Rights* (Oxford: Oxford University Press, 1995); Will Kymlicka, *Politics in the Vernacular: Nationalism, Multiculturalism and Citizenship* (Oxford: Oxford University Press, 2001).

9 Kymlicka, *Politics*.

10 Daes.

11 Terry Goldie, 'The Representation of the Indigene', in *The Post-Colonial Studies Reader*, ed. Bill Ashcroft, Gareth Griffiths and Helen Tiffin (London and New York: Routledge, 1995).

12 Daes, para. 15.

13 Oscar Salemink, *The Ethnography of Vietnam's Central Highlanders: A Historical Contextualization, 1850–1990* (London: RoutledgeCurzon, 2003).

14 Daes.

15 Erni, *The Concept*.

16 Andrew Gray, 'The Indigenous Movement in Asia', in *Indigenous Peoples of Asia*, ed. R.H. Barnes, Andrew Gray and Benedict Kingsbury (Ann Arbor: Association for Asian Studies, 1995), 37.

17 See Michael Hechter, *Internal Colonialism: The Celtic Fringe in British National Development* (Vancouver: UBC Press, 2007 [1975]); Grant Evans, 'Internal Colonialism in the Central Highlands of Vietnam', *Sojourn* 7, no. 2 (1992): 274–304.

18 See Ian G. Baird, 'Colonialism, Indigeneity and the Brao', in *The Concept of Indigenous Peoples in Asia: A Resource Book*, ed. Christian Erni (Copenhagen: International Work Group for Indigenous Affairs; Chiang Mai: Asia Indigenous Peoples Pact Foundation, 2008).

19 See, for example, Bill Ashcroft, Gareth Griffiths and Helen Tiffin, ed., *The Post-Colonial Studies Reader* (London and New York: Routledge, 1995).

20 Ian G. Baird, 'Various Forms of Colonialism: The Social and Spatial Reorganization of the Brao in Southern Laos and Northeastern Cambodia' (PhD Diss., University of British Columbia, 2008); Baird, 'Colonialism'.

21 See Ashcroft, Griffiths and Tiffin.

22 Erni, *The Concept*.

23 International Work Group for International Affairs (IWGIA), *The Indigenous World 2001–2002* (Copenhagen: IWGIA, 2002).

24 Erni, *The Concept*; International Work Group for International Affairs (IWGIA), *The Indigenous World 2005* (Copenhagen: IWGIA, 2005).

25 IWGIA *The Indigenous World 2001–2002*; IWGIA, *The Indigenous World 2005*.

26 IWGIA, *The Indigenous World 2005*.

27 Even though they often identify in various other ways.

28 IWGIA *The Indigenous World 2001–2002*; IWGIA, *The Indigenous World 2005*.

29 IWGIA, *The Indigenous World 2005*.

30 Hjorleifur Jonsson, 'French Natural in the Vietnamese Highlands: Nostalgia and Erasure in Montagnard identity', in *Of Vietnam: Identities in Dialogue*, ed. Jane Bradley Winston and Leakthina Chau-Pech Ollier (New York: Palgrave, 2001).

31 However, this concept more closely matches the aspirations of most Asian government officials.

32 Raymond L. Bryant, 'Politicized Moral Geographies: Debating Biodiversity Conservation and Ancestral Domain in the Philippines', *Political Geography* 19 (2003): 673–95; Christian Erni, 'From Opportunism to Resource Management: Adaptation and the Emergence of Environmental Conservation Among Indigenous Swidden Cultivators on Mindoro Island, Philippines', *Conservation and Society* 4, no. 1 (2006): 102–31.

33 Kaori Tahara, 'Nibutani Dam Case', *Indigenous Law Bulletin* 70 (1999), http://www.austlii.edu.au/au/journals/ILB/1999/70.html#fnB15 (accessed 23 January 2009).

34 International Work Group for International Affairs (IWGIA), *The Indigenous World 2009* (Copenhagen, IWGIA, 2009).

35 S. Simon, 'Taiwan studies and Taiwanese indigenous peoples' (paper presented at the UCSB International Conference on Taiwan Studies, Santa Barbara, 26–7 October 2007).

36 IWGIA, *The Indigenous World 2001–2002*; IWGIA, *The Indigenous World 2005*.

37 Chou Ta-Kuan, *The Customs of Cambodia*, trans. J. Gilman d'Arcy Paul (Bangkok: Siam Society, 1987).

38 Chou, section 9.
39 David P. Chandler, *The Tragedy of Cambodian History: Politics, War, and Revolution since 1945* (New Haven: Yale University Press, 1991); G. Coedès, *The Indianized States of Southeast Asia*, ed. Walter F. Vella, trans. Sue Brown Cowing (Honolulu: East–West Center Press, 1968).
40 Baird 'Various Forms'.
41 Bernard Bourotte, 'Essai d'Histoire des Populations Montagnards du Sud-Indochinois jusqu' à 1945', *Bulletin la Société des Étude Indochinoises* 30, no. 1 (1955): 1–116.
42 Mathieu Guérin, personal communication with author, 2009.
43 cf. Hjorleifur Jonsson, *Mien Relations: Mountain People and State Control in Thailand* (Ithaca: Cornell University Press, 2002).
44 It should, however, be noted that some groups in Cambodia now proudly insist on being called '*Samre*'. To some people the original meaning of the term has been fundamentally transformed. This is, in fact, a common occurrence (see, in relation to the Montagnard example from Vietnam, Jonsson, 'French Natural').
45 *Khmer Loeu* (Washington, DC: Library of Congress, 2004).
46 Joanna White, 'The Highland People of Cambodia: The Indigenous Highlanders of the Northeast: An Uncertain Future', in *Interdisciplinary Research on Ethnic Groups in Cambodia* (Phnom Penh: Center for Advanced Study, 1996).
47 *Khmer Loeu.*
48 However, the term is presently also used by Khmer and even Bunong people to particularly refer to ethnic Bunong people.
49 Jan Ovesen and Ing-Britt Trankell, 'Foreigners and Honorary Khmers: Ethnic Minorities in Cambodia', in *Civilizing the Margins: Southeast Asian Government Policies for the Development of Minorities*, ed. Christopher R. Duncan (Ithaca and London: Cornell University Press, 2004); William Collins, 'The Chams of Cambodia', in *Interdisciplinary Research on Ethnic Groups in Cambodia* (Phnom Penh: Center for Advanced Study, 1996). The *Khmer Loeu* were the Austroasiatic and Austronesian-language speakers, *Khmer Kraom* referred to ethnic Khmer people living in the present-day south of Vietnam, *Khmer Islam* referred to ethnic Cham people living in Cambodia, and *Khmer Kraom* referred to the Khmer people living in present-day southern Vietnam (Ovesen and Trankell; Collins).
50 Guérin, personal communication.
51 Sak Sutsakhan, *The Khmer Republic at War and the Final Collapse* (Christiansburg: Dalley Book Service, 1978), 63.
52 C. Meyer, 'Les Nouvelles Provinces: Ratanakiri – Mondolkiri', *Revue Monde en Développement* 28 (1979): 682–90.
53 Sara Colm, *The Highland Minorities and the Khmer Rouge in Northeastern Cambodia 1968–1979* (Phnom Penh: Document Center of Cambodia, 1996); Chandler.
54 Mathieu Guérin, 'Des Casques Blancs sur le Plateau des Herbes: Les Pacification des Aborigènes des Hautes Terres du Sud-Indochinois (1858–1940)' (PhD Diss., Université de Paris, 2003).
55 Werner Sollors, 'Who is ethnic?', in *The Post-Colonial Studies Reader*, ed. Bill Ashcroft, Gareth Griffiths and Helen Tiffin (London and New York: Routledge, 1995).
56 Sollors.
57 Sollors, 219.
58 See Fredrik Barth, ed., *Ethnic Groups and Boundaries: The Social Organization of Culture Difference* (Boston: Little, Brown, 1969).
59 See Ian G. Baird, 'Identities and space: The Geographies of Religious Change Amongst the Brao in Northeastern Cambodia', *Anthropos Redaktion* 104, no. 2 (2009): 457–68.
60 Baird, 'Various Forms'.
61 In fact, because one ethnic group overwhelmingly dominates the country, many Khmer consider 'Cambodian' to mean 'Khmer'.

62 Seki Tomoda, 'Detaching from Cambodia', in *Vietnam Joins the World*, ed. James W. Morley and Masashi Nishihara (Armonk and London: M.E. Sharpe, 1997).

63 United Nations, 'Completed Peace Keeping Operations, United Nations Transitional Authority in Cambodia [UNTAC], February 1992–September 1993', http://www.un.org/Depts/dpko/dpko/co_mission/untac.htm (accessed 5 December 2007).

64 Now, in contrast, since Hun Sen and the CPP have consolidated political power, and are less dependent on Western donors, largely due to the increased role of China as a donor, NGOs are finding that the government often ignores their lobbying efforts.

65 Land issues are now under the jurisdiction of the Ministry of Land Management, Urban Planning and Construction.

66 Later, in some drafts of the Land Law, these people were also referred to as *chun chiet antaokream*, or 'national internally displaced by conflict'. This term may be based on some Khmer stereotypes about highland minorities being continually 'displaced', since they do swidden agriculture and are thus perceived to be people without a fixed place, since they are constantly moving their agricultural fields and residences.

67 In fact, the Brao ethnic group in Ratanakiri is generally considered to be divided into five subgroups, which including the Kreung, Kavet, Umba (frequently called simply the Brao in Ratanakiri), Lun and Brao Tanap (Baird, 'Various Forms').

68 Four highlander representatives, including Ya Kuak from Krola Village, later made a special trip to Phnom Penh to personally meet the King and thank him for supporting communal land rights.

69 NGO Forum on Cambodia, *Land Alienation from Indigenous Minority Communities, Ratanakiri Province, Cambodia* (Phnom Penh: NGO Forum on Cambodia, 2006).

70 IWGIA, *The Indigenous World 2009*; NGO Forum on Cambodia; Baird, 'Various Forms'.

71 Baird, 'Various Forms'.

72 Many indigenous activists argue, in fact, that these 'special rights' act to actually provide indigenous peoples with equal rights in the face of dominant groups.

73 Baird, 'Various Forms'.

74 M. Backstrom *et al.*, 'A Case Study of Indigenous Traditional Legal Systems and Conflict Resolution in Ratanakiri and Mondolkiri Provinces, Cambodia', Phnom Penh: United Nations Development Programme, 2006.

75 Jeremy Ironside and Stefan Ehrentraut, personal communication with author, 2008.

76 'Chong' is understood to presently mean something like 'hillbilly'. Locals claim the term has long existed, and that it defines them as being different from the majority and 'indigenous', even if they speak only Khmer. Jeremy Ironside [personal communication] believes that these people were originally 'Por', but that they dropped that identity after losing their language long ago, probably partially due to intermarriage with Khmer.

77 Peter Swift, personal communication with author, 2008.

78 see Marie Alexandrine Martin, *Les Khmer Daeum: Khmer de l'Origine. Société Montagnarde et Exploitation de la Forêt, de l'Écologie à l'Histoire* (Paris: Presses de l'École Francaise d'Extrême Orient, 1997).

79 It is unclear exactly how many highland minorities are in Cambodia, but IWGIA [*The Indigenous World 2009*] estimates that there are approximately 190,000 people, or 1.4 per cent of the population, included in 17 ethnic groups. However, official statistics cannot be taken as fact for various reasons.

80 Swift.

81 This concept is even evident in the Land Law, where the process of indigenous people being assimilated into Khmer society is referred to a process of 'evolution'.

82 Much of north-eastern Cambodia was ceded by the French from French Laos to French Cambodia in 1904 (Baird 'Various Forms').

83 See United Nations Commission on Human Rights, 'Khmer Khrom: WS on the Case of the Khmer Khrom', Unrepresented Nations and Peoples Organization, http://www.unpo.org/content/view/3980/120/ (accessed 7 April 2010). One observer noted that when

indigenous people from Cambodia attended the Permanent Forum on Indigenous Peoples at the UN, and found that the Khmer Kraom were calling themselves 'indigenous', some wondered if they themselves were actually 'indigenous' or not. It caused some questioning of the concept outside of what NGOs had told them.

84 Tania Murray Li, 'Ethnic Cleansing, Recursive Knowledge and the Dilemmas of Sedentarism', *International Social Science Journal* 54, no. 173 (2002): 361–71; Ovesen and Trankell; Collins.
85 ICSO is actually a Khmer NGO working to support indigenous communities.
86 See IWGIA, *The Indigenous World 2009*; Baird, 'Various Forms'; NGO Forum on Cambodia.
87 Goldie.
88 Stuart Hall, 'New Ethnicities', in *The Post-Colonial Studies Reader*, ed. Bill Ashcroft, Gareth Griffiths and Helen Tiffin (London and New York: Routledge, 1995).
89 Goldie.
90 Michel Foucault, *Power/Knowledge: Selected Interviews and Other Writings, 1972–1977*, ed. Colin Gordon, trans. Colin Gordon *et al.* (New York: Pantheon, 1980).

10 Asian hauntings

Horror cinema, global capitalism and the reconciliation of alterity?

Christopher SelvaRaj

Introduction

> To learn to live, we must learn how to talk 'with' ghosts.[1]

In contemporary global capitalism, a tension that destabilizes the signifier 'Asia(n)' is the very 'impossibility of the thing [signified]'.[2] The appearance of Asia as a regional bloc is then, at best, the outcome of a formative process that has suppressed and disciplined 'internal contradictions . . . for the sake of commensurability and compatibility within the global distribution of cultural power'.[3] With this in mind, the emergence of Asian cinema, though a contentious term in itself, must be recognized as an important representational medium that explores and gives expression to the issues that undergird constructions of regionalism.[4] In this regard, this chapter takes as its specific focus of analysis the genre of Asian horror cinema. It maintains that Asian horror films must be seen as a body of interconnected texts through which the semiotics of Asia's 'cultural, political and economic self-definition'[5] is produced and circulated. Accordingly, a central question drives this chapter: what do Asian horror films reveal about Asian identities?

To begin investigating the relationship between the semiotics of Asian horror films and regional identity formation, this chapter first insists that Asian horror cinema must be situated as embedded within the flows and networks of international capitalism. By adopting this position, this chapter departs from a conceptualization of Asian horror cinema as a simple 'culturally-rooted aesthetic formulation'[6] and moves to locate it explicitly as very much a consequence of global processes involved in the production of alterity. Next, this chapter works to explicate the changing historical logic that has shaped, and continues to inform, these global processes of Othering. This section begins by emphasizing that any attempt to probe identity formation in the context of contemporary Asia must first be sensitive to the dynamics of the colonial Self–Other dyad and its production of alterity. Subsequently, this section considers the continuities and discontinuities in the dynamics of this Self–Other dyad that work to mould postcolonial Asian identities in global capitalism.

Following this, I suggest that a particular diegetic logic structures the representations of the encounters between the protagonists and the spectral entity in Asian horror cinema. As such, these relationships are worth sustained examination in themselves. Along this same vein, I stress that this chapter is not so much interested in the substantive content of each encounter as it is in trying to uncover the underlying principles that work to shape the cinematic representations of these confrontations. My focus on *form* rather than content allows this chapter's analysis to move beyond the confines of particular local or 'national' contexts and, in doing so, hopefully make a more theoretically oriented contribution to critical Asian studies. Hence, it will be my principal contention in this chapter that the form of the encoded encounter with, and attempted recovery of, spectral alterity in Asian horror films can be read as a *reflection* of Asia's own attempt to mediate its positioning as a site of postcolonial alterity within the imaginary of global capitalism.

To substantiate this assertion, this chapter draws on two especially intriguing horror films: *Ringu (The Ring)*, which emerged in the specific context of the Japanese horror industry, and *Return to Pontianak*, a film from Singapore. The narratives of both these films clearly suggest the possibility of sympathetic connection within the encounter between protagonist and spectral Other. However, both films also present the diegetic attempts at reconciliation with the spectral Other as futile endeavours. With no real dialogic exchange or meaningful interaction, the protagonists in each film are frustrated in their respective efforts at bridging the communicative divide with spectral alterity. These representations might be analysed at the level of the national in that the films' portrayal of the relationship between protagonist and spectral Other mirrors the contemporary predicament of Japan and Singapore in relation to the West. Specifically, both nations remain persistently marked by difference in global capitalism. However, in this chapter, I am more concerned with engaging a broader argument: that is, the representations of the failure to recover spectral alterity in Asian horror films reflect Asia's own inability to go beyond its position as a site of postcolonial alterity in global capitalism. Finally, after suggesting avenues that further work can take to refine and build on its contentions, the chapter concludes with the somewhat pessimistic observation that constructions of postcolonial Asian identities look to remain very much haunted by the disciplinary imaginings of a global capitalism that will continue to embed them in firm relations of inequality. The task at hand, for now, seems to be for postcolonial Asia to begin to learn to critically *engage* and *negotiate* identities premised on alterity.

Asian horror cinema as alterity

> Beyond the vengeful spirits, the chills and the scary music, Asian horror hides a weighty message.[7]

> 'Asia' has become a market, and 'Asianness' has become a commodity circulating globally through late capitalism.[8]

It is important, right at the outset, to offer a more precise understanding of the too often carelessly used notion of Asian horror cinema.[9] Can the term in fact capture a sufficiently discreet object of analysis? Or, is Asian horror cinema basically the product of a global culture industry?[10] In this chapter, I propose that it is the latter.

Though the literature that gives serious consideration to these issues is surprisingly sparse, a considerable number of scholars have attempted to theorize Asian horror cinema by beginning with what they assert to be a set of 'specific narrative conventions and iconographic elements'.[11] A brief consideration of one of the most 'exceedingly flexible and persistently revisited trope[s]'[12] identified in Asian horror cinema is useful at this point, so as to better understand this process of conceptualization. In his consideration of the *onryou* (avenging spirit) motif that runs through the *kaidan* (ghost) stories that, in turn, form the bulk of contemporary Asian horror films, Jay McRoy contends that '[a] careful consideration of the focus of, and the motivations behind these spirits' wrath offer valuable insights into the historical, political and economic logics informing [their] [particular] contemporary social and cultural forces'.[13] The obvious question here is why the *onryou* motif should be at all helpful to a conceptualization of Asian horror cinema when one might and, in all probability, will find examples of this trope in most horror films. However, it is important to note McRoy's emphasis that it is not the avenging spirit *per se* that should be the focus of analysis but rather the varying – but always, particular – set of impulses that compel each spirit and its actions. Such a focus, then, certainly avoids the pitfalls of attributing any simplistically essentialist characteristic to Asian horror cinema. Instead, it allows for the slightly broader contention that Asian horror cinema is a medium constituted by a constellation of distinctive social circumstances that inform its filmic narratives; in other words, Asian horror cinema consists of works of fiction that 'resonate with elements in a particular culture'.[14]

While no doubt appealing, the problem with claims that begin by insisting that some sort of cultural specificity must underlie a conceptualization of Asian horror cinema is this: these declarations demonstrate a conspicuous tendency to neglect the consideration that Asian horror cinema is often intensely engaged with larger international marketing and financial networks even as it attempts to pursue its own commercial success. In the vein, the configurations of asymmetrical power relations that Asian horror cinema must confront, and negotiate, within global capitalism are also understated, if not ignored. Take for example Ken Gelder, who not only observes that horror cinema, specifically, the ghost story, 'has flourished in *other* regional formations *outside* of Euro-American hegemony' but who also continues to locate horror cinema as an '*appropriate* medium through which to chart contemporary anxieties and reactivate old traumas'.[15] These remarks surely warrant further investigation, especially so when one considers the propensity of global capitalism to perpetuate a Euro-American dominance. Accordingly, a critical reading of Gelder's statement must position these 'other regional formations' as very much the consequence of global processes that produce alterity and are inextricably complicit in the reinforcement of Euro-American hegemony.

The ghost story as represented *through the medium of the horror cinema* to express anxieties and fears is not a neutral event. Instead, even as cultures struggle to adapt the cinematic medium to encompass their experiences, the cinematic medium imposes constraints with regards to how these experiences may be narrated and, in doing so, limits the potentials and possibilities of self-expression. The crucial point for us here, then, is that rather than attempt to theorize Asian horror cinema as somehow culturally insulated from Euro-American hegemony, it is more astute to locate Asian horror cinema as irrevocably enmeshed in larger structuring processes that produce alterity and form the basis of a shared cultural identity.

Therefore, although horror films have rightly been acknowledged to function as important modes of critical discourse engaging constantly transforming cultures and interrogating identities at vital crossroads through the 'incursion of super-natural forces in the realm of the ordinary',[16] it is also important to realize that the expressions of the fears and aspirations horror cinema reflects are often linked to the confrontations between cultural identities and the larger external influences that configure the former for entry into global capitalism.[17] Ultimately, the task in circumscribing a space for Asian horror cinema cannot afford to be one that seeks recourse to simple essentialisms nor, for that matter, one that, on the other hand, concedes the term to the rubbish heap of empty signifiers. Instead, with a cognizance that Asia cannot – and, as Aijaz Ahmad retorts to Frederic Jameson, must not – be 'constructed as an internally coherent object of theoretical knowl-edge',[18] my assertion is that any valuable analysis of Asian horror cinema must begin by recognizing it as an example of an *alterity effect* produced by the logic of the 'global distribution of cultural power'[19]. Correspondingly, Asian horror cin-ema's narratives of the encounter with and attempted recovery of spectral alterity must be seen as a repository of cultural representations that mediate and, in some cases, attempt to transgress this logic. However, I demonstrate that these cinematic representations often do little more than merely reflect and reproduce this logic.

Alterity in Asian horror cinema

> . . . the Other is never simply given, never just found or encountered, but made.[20]

The philosophical concepts of Self and Other have consistently formed the crux of larger questions regarding alterity, similarity and identity formation. In this section, I will integrate a series of theoretical perspectives on the relationship between the Self and its Other. Specifically, my explication in this chapter is informed first by the historical phenomena of colonial identity formation and subsequently by the con-temporary predicament of postcolonial identity recovery. Next, I further refract the postcolonial Self–Other relationship through the lens of global capitalism. I show that global capitalism restricts the development of transgressive symbolic identities by maintaining historically unequal power relations that limit the possibilities of cultural production. In doing so, I provide a conceptual framework within which to critically analyse the encounter with and attempted recovery of spectral alterity in Asian horror cinema. Hence, the following questions orient this section. Who is the Other? What is its relationship to the Self? Who is the colonial Other? Who is the postcolonial Other? What is the relationship between the postcolonial Other and the Asian horror cinema? What is the relationship between Asian horror cinema and the production of the Asian Other?

Elizabeth Grosz notes that the fundamental problem with thought premised on dichotomous terminology is that one term, in this case, the Self, 'can allow itself no independent, autonomous other'.[21] Moreover, rather than view the relationship between the two terms as constituting a neutral binary, it is vital to be sensitive to the fact that the binary is hierarchic: one term is consistently and necessarily privileged, and always at the expense of the other. Therefore, only the privileged term – the Self – may act independently; the other term may not do so. Furthermore, in order to affirm the authenticity of its consciousness, the Self must establish a clear boundary that unambiguously demarcates it from what it conceives it is not.[22] Beyond this boundary, then, is the realm of the Other.

This dyad between the Self and its Other formed an important plinth on which European colonial expansion and imperial conquest was built on. The modern European Self accomplished, in different geographical settings and in various guises, extensive and methodical enterprises of domination that were, in many instances, carefully tailored to subjugating and civilizing alterity. Still, what was first necessary was to circumscribe what was *not* modern or European and, in doing so, imagine the Other. With this in mind, Edward Said has most usefully outlined the discursive process – a regime of truths in the Nietzschean sense – by which the European idea of the Orient

> kept intact the separateness of the Orient, its eccentricity, its backwardness, its silent indifference, its feminine penetrability, its supine malleability [such that] every [European] writer on the Orient . . . saw the Orient as a locale requiring Western attention, reconstruction, even redemption . . . in a framework constructed out of biological determinism and moral-political admonishment.[23]

Three important points must be mentioned at this juncture. First, Said's work, that is focused on the Anglo–French–American attempts to experience the Arab world and understand Islam through the assembled category of the Orient, highlights the fact that the Orient is a systematically *produced* entity and that it did not correspond to any geographic place.[24] Second, Said alerts us that the construction of the Orient and the Oriental were not neutral events – he emphasizes that 'the nexus of knowledge and power creating "the Oriental" in a sense [obliterated] him as a human being'[25] while 'the Orient was a word which . . . accrued to it a wide field of meanings, associations, and connotations [that] did not necessarily refer to [a] real Orient but to the field surrounding the word'.[26] Third, Said's work shows convincingly that the purpose of constructing the Orient was as much a collective exercise in imagining the West as it was an exercise in defining the non-West. Accordingly, the category of the Orient became established primarily to constitute everything the West was not.

Through these processes of fixing the Orient under the sign of its backward and degenerate Other, the West attempted, besides, to ideologically fix itself under the sign of the modern, the progressive and the civilized. In this way, a reified frontier was continuously drawn and redrawn between the West and its Other, reinforcing an artificial sense of mutually exclusive and opposing identities. In this vein, Abdul JanMohamed, through his own work on colonialist texts, alerts us to what he terms the 'profound conflict of the Manichean allegory' in colonialist literature that led to 'a transformation of [presumed and imaginary] racial difference into [a] moral and even metaphysical difference . . . [that came] to dominate every facet of imperialist mentality'.[27] He goes on to elaborate:

> The dominant model of . . . relations in all colonial societies is the Manichean opposition between the putative superiority of the European and the supposed inferiority of the native. [T]he Manichean allegory – a field of diverse yet interchangeable [essentialist] oppositions between white and black, good and evil, superiority and inferiority, civilization and savagery, intelligence and emotion, rationality and sensuality, Self and Other, subject and object . . .. Instead of being and exploration of the racial Other, such [a model] merely affirms its own ethnocentric assumptions . . . it simply codifies and preserves the structures of its own mentality.[28]

Here, JanMohamed reinforces Said's earlier point that the study of the Orient as Other was crucial for the construction of European identity, more so than for any actual accumulation of knowledge about a particular geographic location or its inhabitants. However, JanMohamed also extends our thinking on the Self–Other relationship. Drawing on Lacanian theory, JanMohamed divides colonialist texts into *imaginary* and *symbolic* texts. On the one hand, imaginary texts 'fetishized a nondialectical, fixed opposition' between the European Self and the native Other.[29] Thus, 'instead of seeing the native as a bridge toward syncretic possibility . . . [these texts] use[d] [the native] as a mirror that reflect[ed] the colonialist's self image'.[30] On the other hand, symbolic texts 'tend[ed] to be more open to a modifying dialectic between Self and Other [. . .] [and] attempt[ed] to find syncretic solutions to the Manichean opposition between the colonizer and the colonized'.[31] Even so, JanMohamed also alerts us to the presence of symbolic texts that demonstrate a realization that 'syncretism is impossible within the power relations of colonial society because such a context often trap[ped] the writer in the libidinal economy of the imaginary'.[32]

The key point to extract here is simply that the dichotomy between the Self and Other, initially imagined as incommensurable, begins to show tentative signs of being figuratively displaced in favour of a depiction of difference that can be bridged.[33] Yet, at this point, we would do well to consider the work of Homi Bhabha because it reveals precisely the power of libidinal economy of the colonial imaginary in resisting the possibility of symbolic reconciliation with the native Other. In his work on the ambivalence of colonial authority and representation, Bhabha proposes that '[w]ithin the conflictual economy of colonial discourse . . . mimicry represents an *ironic* compromise. [C]olonial mimicry is the desire for a reformed recognizable Other, *as a subject of a difference that is almost the same, but not quite*'.[34] The indigenous native previously conceptualized as an irrecoverable Other to the colonial Self seemingly no longer holds. Instead, the native, through colonial tutelage, comes to be seen as the product of a 'flawed colonial mimesis'[35]. Drawing on the specific historical example of colonial India, Bhabha provides the example, via Lord Macaulay, of a class of persons 'Indian in blood and color, but English in tastes, in opinions, in morals and in intellect' in which 'to be Anglicized is *emphatically* not to be English' – this Indian native is seen as almost identical to the English colonialist, but never completely so.[36] Representations of colonial mimicry are then, paradoxically, testament to both the increasing acceptance on the part of the Self that the Other might be redeemed – in the case of the colonial power, through the civilizing process – as well as the simultaneous stubborn refusal to acknowledge the possibility that the Other can eventually be reconciled with the Self.[37]

Thus far, a common thread runs through the constructions of alterity in colonial discourse(s). Regardless of whether the Other is assembled as irreducibly different or almost the same, the imperial gaze(s) that produces these forms of alterity always explicitly 'prevent[s] a reversal of the location of the Other on the same terms'.[38] As such, the colonial Other always remains a dominated and passive presence whose partial gaze might unsettle but can never authorize or construct – the colonial Other does not have the potential to look *back*.[39]

The historical transition to postcoloniality has, if anything, brought with it the rhetoric of a renewed search for identity and a discernible shift toward more sustained attempts toward the recovery of, as well as the reconciliation with, the Other.[40] However, as Aijaz Ahmad insists, a compressed and interconnected world still entangled in a global struggle between capital and labour prevents, for example, postcolonial Asia from simply embarking on a counter-process of Othering the neocolonial West.[41] In other words, still informed by the continuing legacies of imperialism and mired in persistent international relations of inequality, it is Asia that continues to be marked by difference – as a postcolonial Other – in contemporary global capitalism. Similarly, these relations compel Asia to accept and articulate a distinct identity oriented around an (self) exoticization congruent with the global capitalist imaginary.[42] As such, Asia's endeavours at regional self-definition and representation often necessarily find themselves at the confluence of layers of tension and contradiction as the region negotiates its position as site of postcolonial alterity through a 'peculiar [demonstration] of double-consciousness, [a] sense of always looking at one's self through the eyes of others'.[43]

Asian horror cinema, in this historical setting, becomes particularly interesting when read as an example of a potentially *symbolic* postcolonial text that attempts to offer transgressive alternatives that disrupt the self–other dyad writ large in the imaginary of global capitalism that has, in turn, worked to embed Asia as a site of alterity. Specifically, I suggest that this is best represented by the dynamics of the encounters between Asian horror cinema's protagonists and the spectral Others they confront. Although the spectral Other is constituted as a locus of eerie and potentially destructive difference, there is a clear effort by the protagonists to bridge this alterity by attempting projects of sympathetic understanding. In doing so, Asian horror cinema seeks to construct a representational form that might work through spectral alterity. However, by continually representing the project of recovery as a failed pursuit, Asian horror cinema leaves us with the conclusion that attempts to reconcile alterity must ultimately fall short of the mark.

The revenge of alterity: *Ringu*

Ringu[44] tells the story of Reiko, an investigative television reporter, who is determined to get to the bottom of an urban legend involving a cursed videotape, following her own niece's mysterious death after allegedly watching its contents.[45] According to this legend, all who view the contents of the tape immediately receive a telephone call dooming them, in exactly one week, to a certain death. The search for answers leads Reiko and her ex-husband Ryuji to learn about Sadako, the daughter of the psychic Shizuko, who possessed the ability to kill by sheer force of will. Following her mother's suicide, a scientist who was romantically involved with Shizuko and, presumably, Sadako's father, pushes Sadako down a well, where her body has remained sealed ever since. Sadako's monstrous rage and desire for revenge now 'manifest [themselves] from beyond the grave through the conduits of technology, spreading her viral curse to anyone who watched the videotape'[46]. The exact origins of the videotape and questions with regards to how the videotape is able to function as the medium of Sadako's rage are left unexplained in the film. All that is revealed is that the videotape mysteriously appeared at the site of the well, 40 years after her death.

Ringu is widely regarded as having unleashed the latest global wave of Asian horror and has been analysed in terms of the anxieties of Westernization, the ambivalence of motherhood and the reconstruction of the family.[47] However, thus far, no attention has been paid to the specific dynamics of the encounters between characters in the film and Sadako. As I have suggested previously, a sustained consideration of the encounters between film protagonists and spectral alterity is an especially vital aspect of Asian horror cinema because it points to the presence of a deeper logic that inevitably disciplines the possibilities of representing this relationship. With this in mind, my analysis of *Ringu* is oriented around two specific processes that take place during the course of the film's narrative. The first is the construction of Sadako as frighteningly different, but yet as an entity that Reiko eventually comes to sympathetically identify with. Second, it investigates Reiko's attempt to appease Sadako's vengeance.

The initial evidence *Ringu* offers us with regards to Sadako's terrifying nature is indirect. Viewers are shown a flashback of the discovery of Reiko's niece's body with a contorted expression of horror etched on her face and are then told that the cause of death was the fact that her heart had stopped beating from the sheer fright. We next learn that similar expressions of horror were on the faces of all the other victims; it appears that encounters with Sadako can only result in death. When we eventually get our first fleeting glimpse of Sadako – the spectre is reflected on the television screen in the cabin where Reiko herself watches the cursed videotape for the first time – we are presented with a startling sight. A female form dressed in white stands motionless behind Reiko. More petrifying is the long unkempt hair that prevents us from seeing the figure's face – Sadako is represented as unknowable. The telephone call that soon comes further cements Sadako's alterity as Reiko can only make out screeching and inhuman sounds. How then does *Ringu* depict Reiko's gradual identification with Sadako despite this construction of a seemingly unbridgeable and monstrous difference?

To begin to understand this, we must revisit a particular episode in the filmic narrative of *Ringu* that 'piece[s] together the tragic history'[48] of Sadako. As Reiko and Ryuji gather information connected to the cursed videotape, there is a strange flashback sequence during which the two find themselves transported to the past as spectators of a public psychic demonstration event involving Sadako's mother Shizuko. In this event, they witness Shizuko's apparent telepathic abilities under intense scrutiny and suspicion by an audience of academics, scientists and journalists. Eventually, there emerges a collective disbelief in Shizuko's uncannily accurate abilities that quickly and palpably gives way to fear as she is decried as a fraud. Traumatized by this attack on her mother Sadako, who at this point is located offstage, wills through her silent gaze one particularly vehement critic dead and is immediately chastised by her mother. At this point, as pandemonium breaks out and accusations of murder are angrily hurled at Shizuko, Sadako runs toward Reiko and suddenly grabs her arm, revealing fingers with their nails torn out from them.[49] This first contact between Reiko and Sadako seems to mark the beginning of an apparent bond between them.

The rest of the narrative is intertwined with Reiko's increasingly sympathetic identification with Sadako; she begins to see the spectre as a child who was feared and despised rather than loved. As such, she comes to believe that the only way to assuage Sadako's rage and lift the curse of the videotape is to recover the spectre's corporeal remains and, in doing so, give her the affection she was starved of.[50] Eventually, Reiko sees herself as a surrogate maternal figure for Sadako. This culminates in an intensely emotional scene in which Reiko descends into the well where Sadako's body was sealed calling for the ghost that emerges as a weeping skeleton. As Reiko cradles Sadako's remains in her arms, Ryuji, who has accompanied Reiko to the site, exclaims from the top of the well that it had already been one week since Reiko watched the cursed videotape. The fact she is still alive must mean that the curse has been lifted.

It would seem to all at this point that Reiko has successfully understood the plight of Sadako, the spectral Other in the film, and taken measures to resolve the situation. Conversely, the remainder of the film depicts otherwise. As the police remove Sadako's remains from the well, Reiko wonders aloud how Sadako's father could have killed her. In response to this, Ryuji makes a strange offhand comment that Sadako's real father might not have been human.[51] Following this, in perhaps the most terrifying scene, Sadako crawls out of the television set in Ryuji's home to claim his life and in doing so assures us that her vengeance is far from over. Eric White elaborates:

> The . . . revelation of [Sadako's] tragic end has in no way assuaged this vengeful tormented spirit or prevented the continued propagation of its curse upon humankind. The curse could never have been lifted by *restoring Sadako symbolically to the human community* by means of a proper burial because *she herself was not 'human' to begin with*, and her ultimate motivation was never therefore humanly intelligible . . . Sadako is the supernatural offspring of a human being and a sea monster.[52]

Sadako's emergence to kill Ryuji must thus 'dramatically alter our understanding of the nature of the tale told in *Ringu*'[53]. Far from being a representation of the successful recovery of the spectral Other, *Ringu* displays the explicit impossibility of any real communicative understanding between Reiko and Sadako and confirms the spectral Other's 'irrecuperable otherness'[54].

Towards the end of the film, Reiko comes to the realization that she managed to avoid – she was not spared – Sadako's vengeance only because she had *copied* the cursed videotape and given it to Ryuji. As van Heeren has noted, drawing on post-Reformasi Indonesian horror film, there is always only 'a certain discursive space or practice *allotted* for the supernatural in which to operate'[55] In the case of *Ringu*, it is the medium of the videotape that structures the form Sadako's vengeance can take. This is important for our consideration of the logic that shapes the encounter between protagonist and spectral Other in Asian horror cinema. Even as Sadako's vengeance is constrained and limited by its allotted confinement to the videotape, the spectre is simultaneously made complicit with the very means of her digital captivity, perhaps an allusion to her physical captivity in the well, to perpetuate her wrath. Accordingly, the film's conclusion that the spectral Other is ultimately unfathomable and that its vengeance can never be resolved but must be deferred via some sort of perpetual *self-referential* process – the copying and dissemination of the videotape – affirms not only that the difference between protagonist and spectral Other cannot be reconciled. Additionally, it suggests that the spectral Other is, in fact, dependent on its filmic role as a locus of alterity to sustain its diegetic identity.

Sadako's rage from beyond the grave and her return for revenge must be read as an attempt by Asian horror cinema to deal with the prospects for the re-emergence of identity. As Huggan observes, ghosts are 'often the carriers of an occluded history [and] [function] as agents for the reconstruction of historical memory'.[56] However, what the representation of Sadako's return demonstrates, in my opinion more pertinently, are the problems and limitations of constructing a representational form that will allow the once silenced to speak. In this way, the representation of Sadako's plight mirrors Asia's struggle to define itself within the hegemonic discourse of global capitalism that positions the West as the global Self. Conversely, Asia must remain constructed as remote and unknowable: the 'dangerous Other of popular culture'.[57] Additionally, and reminiscent of Sadako's predicament, Asia's position in global capitalism seems often inextricably 'bound to its acceptance of its role as [O]ther, perpetrated by the external forces of [O]rientalism and an internal complicit position that sustains it'.[58]

Displaced alterity: *Return to Pontianak*

Return to Pontianak[59] tells the story of Charity Yamaguchi, an adopted Asian–American woman who has been having vivid, recurring dreams of a figure she becomes convinced is her biological mother. Compelled by these visions, Charity arranges to take a trip to the village in Borneo where she was born to seek out her mother and make peace with her. She learns that the village is located in the jungles on an island off the town of Pontianak. As Charity, her friends Raymond, Uzi and Luc as well as a local guide named Eye make – and eventually lose – their way through the jungles in search of the village, they encounter an old man as well as a mysterious woman who appears to be under his charge, and who exudes a profoundly unsettling presence. The group soon starts to notice the woman following them even as they continue to make their way through the jungles looking for a way off the island. Before long, Charity's friends begin to meet their deaths under strange circumstances and she begins to sense that something is hunting them. An encounter with the woman towards the end of the film finally exposes her monstrous nature and leaves Charity stranded on the island as the sole survivor. The film finally offers the conclusion that the woman is a Pontianak, 'a woman who dies in childbirth, or is the victim of a husband's abuse and who is subsequently held in thrall by a sorcerer'.[60]

Return to Pontianak has been the subject of less analysis and review as compared to *Ringu*. Ostensible reasons for this include its unexceptional appraisals from film critics and its intermittent art house releases in selected theatres.[61] The puzzling narrative sequences and the film's attempt to construct a Pontianak legend that is inconsistent and, at times, simply bewildering may also work to dissuade serious study. In probably the only other scholarly work on the film, Harvey reads the film as a potentially transgressive representation of what she terms 'spectral tropicality' where the repressed return as 'horrific beings and uncanny spaces' and, in doing so, unsettle and challenge the taken for granted sociocultural setting.[62] On the contrary, I point out instead that the encounters between Charity, her friends and the horrific Pontianak warrant sustained attention and examination in their own right because they exhibit clear symptoms of the disciplinary logic that *restricts* Asian horror cinema's transgressive potential. The presence of horrific beings and uncanny spaces, while indeed representations of contestation and disruption, ultimately fail to effect any substantive transformations within the diegetic narrative. In this context there are two key features of the film. First, it draws attention to the construction of Pontianak (the town) and the tropical jungles of Asia as a site of alterity, but simultaneously as a site that is still accessible and potentially recoverable. Second, it investigates the frustrating and uncertain portrayal of the relationship between Charity and the spectral Other within this assembled space of alterity.

Return to Pontianak situates its protagonists' confrontations with the spectral Other in a space that is deliberately mapped as extraneous. In contrast to *Ringu*, where encounters with the spectral Other may take place in modern, urban settings, *Return to Pontianak* immediately displaces these encounters onto the jungles of Borneo. Charity must thus travel from the United States of America, established as an apex of modernity, and together with her friends Luc, Raymond and Uzi (of unspecified nationalities) as well as a local guide enter the jungles of modern day – but, not modern – Asia where the spectral Other is to be found. This again resonates with van Heeren's earlier observation with regards to the allocation of space to the supernatural within which to operate. Subsequently, the group's realization that their modern gadgets are useless 'in the middle of nowhere' and 'the place where people's ancestors' graves are' further indicates an attempt to reinforce a reified barrier that separates the jungles of Asia from the modern world. However, despite casting Asia as a site of alterity, the film suggests that Charity is still connected to it in some way: even when she is physically outside its boundaries she can still be called to it through her dreams.

Nevertheless, most of the other protagonists demonstrate time and again their clear inability to connect with their unfamiliar surroundings as they complain repeatedly about everything from the excessive heat to the mosquitoes. The island jungle is presented as threatening, dirty and full of evil spirits; even Charity is unnerved by what she senses is a presence in the jungle watching them. After learning that the village they seek no longer exists – an inhabitant of the island tells them that it had burned down some time back – the group begins looking for a way out of the jungle. Instead they come across a strange, isolated hut and its occupants. This scene is particularly important because the group meets for the first time a mysterious woman, who will eventually be revealed as the film's spectral Other. This scene also seems to suggest some sort of bond between Charity and the peculiar woman, as the woman seems fascinated with Charity while completely ignoring the other members of the group. The exact reasons for this affinity are never made clear. However, before this encounter can develop any further, the old man seizes the woman and begins to scold her. He drags her into the hut and begins to cane her. The woman screams in pain from the beatings but the group does not intervene and instead hastily departs from the premises of the hut – they do not hear the woman's screams become monstrous.

Following the encounter at the hut, the group begins to notice the woman is constantly in their vicinity, though always some distance away. However, she does not respond to their queries and does not exhibit any interest in communicating with them. The frequent glances and fleeting moments of eye contact between Charity and the woman also do not mature into any sort of sustained interaction. As the narrative progresses and as more members of the group are killed off, Charity begins to have a series of disjointed flashbacks that involve the occupants of the hut. The flashbacks reveal the old man to be a *bomoh* – an occult practitioner – who is responsible for beheading Raymond and driving Luc into a mad frenzy during which he kills Uzi. At this point, the identity of the woman remains unclear and it seems as if the woman's appearance to the group is some sort of cryptic warning regarding the doom that awaits them at the hands of the *bomoh*. However, this reading is put to rest by the next, and final, encounter with the woman. As Charity and Eye chase a possessed Luc through the jungle, they stumble across an uncovered grave with the bodies of two babies inside. Charity is struck by an unexpected flashback that involves the mother of the now deceased infants being attacked. The mother in this flashback bears a striking resemblance to the woman in Charity's dreams, who she had presumed to be her own biological mother. Unfortunately, this connection is also never resolved. Following this flashback, Charity and Eye find Luc's body, with the woman standing in the foliage some distance away from him. Moments later, the woman attacks Eye, revealing her true grotesque form.

The film's (in)conclusion is the most important segment for this chapter's analysis for two reasons. First, it provides a frustrating finale to the disorganized narrative sequences that characterizes the film. Second, it provides substantial weight for this chapter's earlier assertion with regards to a disciplinary logic that works to limit Asian horror cinema's transgressive potential. The film ends with a scene that shows Charity collapsed in a clearing, exhausted and laughing, on the verge of a complete nervous breakdown after having escaped – she believes she is finally safe – from the spectral Other after it attacked Eye. As the camera moves away from her, we see a reverse angle shot of the woman standing some distance away, out of Charity's sight. The backs of her legs are bruised and bloody with wounds. The film then fades to black. The attempt to understanding the spectral Other is thus left unresolved, paradoxically, in my opinion, at the precise moment the plight of the Other might be articulated. Is Charity the final victim? Will Charity be spared? Will some form of communication finally occur between Charity and the spectral Other? This abrupt ending opens itself to a plethora of alternative endings. Nonetheless, what the film's (in)conclusion does leave us with is the fact that instead of making peace with the spectral Other, Charity remains indefinitely trapped in the space of alterity with no prospect of escape.

Return to Pontianak has been described for various reasons as a film that has been made 'with an eye towards internationalism'.[63] Indeed, by positioning Asia as a realm that 'remains separate from the "West" in an unbridgeable cultural gulf',[64] the film demonstrates its complicity with the imaginary of global capitalism. Moreover, by depicting Asia as a site of alterity where only chaos, confusion and death await its cosmopolitan group of protagonists, *Return to Pontianak* actively precludes the possibility of the 'construction of a new position[s] of knowledge [that might be achieved] though a careful negotiation between Self and Other'.[65] Finally, in its representation of the failure to recover spectral alterity, the film ultimately reflects the global logic that continues to intertwine Asia's identity with its entrenched position as a site of postcolonial alterity.

Conclusion: the reconciliation of alterity?

> [T]alking with ghosts does not only mean being in conversation with them. It also means to use them instrumentally and, in turn, whether one knows it or not, to be used by them.[66]

This chapter has argued that Asian horror films serve as an important repository of representations that attempt to tackle the tensions in contemporary Asian identity formation. Rooting Asian horror cinema as firmly embedded in the relations of global capitalism, this chapter suggested that the encoded encounter with, and the attempted recovery of, spectral alterity in Asian horror films can be read as reflections of a symbolic search for a regional identity, even as Asia continues to be positioned as a site of postcolonial alterity within the imaginary of global capitalism. Through an analysis of two important films from the genre of Asian horror – *Ringu* and *Return to Pontianak* – this chapter then demonstrated that although both films depict apparent efforts to provide opportunities to bridge the relationship between protagonists and spectral alterity, both films, in the end, portray these attempts at reconciliation with the spectral Other as failed endeavours. Further, both films position the spectral Other's diegetic identity as dependent on its alterity. This then mirrors Asia's own predicament within the hegemonic imaginary of global capitalism that compels it to repeatedly cast itself as a site of alterity even as it strives to achieve a distinct identity.

However, this chapter does not profess to offer any sort of conclusive diagnosis with regards to the relationship between Asian horror films and Asian regional identity. Far from it, this chapter's proposition that the diegetic logic that structures the production and representation of alterity in Asian horror films reflects the logic of global capitalism in its own production and representation of alterity leaves much room to be further refined. The relationships between these logics might be further explicated in two main ways by future work. The first would be to apply its tenets to a whole range of other films within the Asian horror genre. This will allow us to determine the extent to which this method of analysis is relevant for Asian film studies. The second way would be to abstract similar diegetic logics from horror films in a myriad of alternative contexts. We would then be able to see how and why certain characteristics of this logic change with milieu as well as which aspects remain invariant. Further, it might also be particularly intriguing to do comparative analyses on Asian horror films that have been appropriated by Hollywood. What is the relationship between the logic that structures the representation of alterity in these remakes and Hollywood's position as a key site of cultural production in global capitalism?

By way of conclusion, it would be disingenuous to conclude that this chapter is somehow suggesting that only a symbolic reconciliation with alterity will allow the Other to articulate some form of authentic identity. Similarly, in the case of Asia, I remain distrustful about perspectives that attempt to liberate Asia from its position of alterity, or theoretical stances that claim to shift Asia to the centre. Instead, it is my assertion that Asia must be concerned to critically engage and negotiate its haunting by the disciplinary imaginary of global capitalism. Working *with* alterity, rather than working to overcome alterity, to carve out identity seems the most viable route to accomplish this.

Notes

1   Jodey Castricano, *Cryptomimesis: The Gothic and Jacques Derrida's Ghost Writing* (London and Ithaca: McGill–Queen's University Press, 2001), 134.
2   Leo Ching, 'Globalizing the Regional, Regionalizing the Global: Mass Culture and Asianism in the Age of Late Capital', *Public Culture* 12, no. 1 (2000): 235.
3   Ching, 235.
4   See Wimal Dissanayake, 'Cultural Identity and Asian Cinema: An Introduction', in *Cinema and Cultural Identity: Reflections on Films From Japan, India, and China*, ed. Wimal Dissanayake (Lanham and London: University Press of America, 1988), 1–13.
5   Anne Tereska Ciecko, 'Theorizing Asian Cinema', in *Contemporary Asian Cinema: Popular Culture in a Global Frame*, ed. Anne Tereska Ciecko (Oxford and New York: Berg, 2006), 19.
6   Ciecko, 26.
7   Ting Ting Yang, 'Things that Go Bump in the Night: How Freaky Flicks are Expressing our Asianness', *Asian Geographic* 4, (2008): 38–40.

8   Ching, 257.
9   This chapter is not as much concerned with defining the notion of 'horror', identifying the boundaries of 'horror' as a genre, or embarking on an inquiry into the overall appeal of the genre. For some works on these aspects see Pam Cook and Mieke Bernink, *The Cinema Book*, 2nd ed. (London: British Film Institute Publishing, 1999), 194–204; Andrew Tudor, *Monsters and Mad Scientists: A Cultural History of the Horror Movie* (Oxford and New York: Blackwell, 1997); Philip Brophy, 'Horrality – The Textuality of Contemporary Horror Films', in *The Horror Reader*, ed. Ken Gelder (London and New York: Routledge, 2000), 276–84; Elizabeth Cowie, 'The Lived Nightmare: Trauma, Anxiety, and the Ethical Aesthetics of Horror', in *Dark Thoughts: Philosophic Reflections on Cinematic Horror*, ed. Steven J. Schneider and Daniel Shaw (Lanham: Scarecrow Press, 2003), 25–46.
10 Kenneth Paul Tan, *Cinema and Television in Singapore: Resistance in One Dimension* (Leiden and Boston: Brill, 2008), xi.
11 Ciecko, 25.
12 Jay McRoy, *Nightmare Japan: Contemporary Japanese Horror Cinema* (Amsterdam and New York: Rodopi, 2008), 11.
13 McRoy, 11.
14 Kendall R. Phillips, *Projected Fears: Horror Films and American Culture* (Westport: Praeger Publishers, 2005), 6; see also Andrew Tudor, 'Why Horror? The Peculiar Pleasures of a Popular Genre', *Cultural Studies* 11, no. 3 (1997): 443.
15 Ken Gelder, 'Introduction to Part Eleven', in *The Horror Reader*, ed. Ken Gelder (London and New York: Routledge, 2000), 350; emphases mine.
16 McRoy, 6.
17 For examples of this with reference to the Euro-American context, see Lane Roth, 'Film, Society, and Ideas: Nosferatu and Horror of Dracula', in *Planks of Reason: Essays on the Horror Film*, ed. Barry Keith Grant and Christopher Sharrett (Lanham: Scarecrow Press, 2004), 255–64; Phillips; Carol J. Clover, *Men, Women, and Chain Saws: Gender in the Modern Horror Film* (Princeton: Princeton University Press, 1992); Tudor, *Monsters*.
18 Aijaz Ahmad, 'Jameson's Rhetoric of Otherness and the "National Allegory"', in *The Post-Colonial Studies Reader*, ed. Bill Ashcroft, Gareth Griffiths and Helen Tiffin, 2nd ed. (London and New York: Routledge, 2006), 84; see also Fredric Jameson, 'Third-World Literature in the Era of Multinational Capitalism', in *The Jameson Reader*, ed. Michael Hardt and Kathi Weeks (Oxford and Malden: Blackwell, 2000), 315–39.
19 Ching, 235.
20 Quoted in Elizabeth Hallam and Brian V. Street, 'Introduction: Cultural Encounters – Representing "Otherness"', in *Cultural Encounters: Representing 'Otherness'*, ed. Elizabeth Hallam and Brian V. Street (London and New York: Routledge, 2000), 1.
21 Elizabeth Grosz, *Volatile Bodies: Towards A Corporeal Feminism* (St Leonards: Allen & Unwin, 1994), 211.
22 Grosz, 211.
23 Edward W. Said, *Orientalism: Western Conceptions of the Orient* (New York: Pantheon, 1978), 206–7.
24 Said, 322. See also Bill Ashcroft and Pal Ahluwalia, *Edward Said: The Paradox of Identity* (London and New York: Routledge, 1999), 57.
25 Said, 27.
26 Said, 203.
27 Abdul R. JanMohamed, 'The Economy of Manichean Allegory: The Function of Racial Difference in Colonialist Literature', *Critical Inquiry* 12, (1986): 79–80.
28 JanMohamed, 82–4.
29 JanMohamed, 84. With this distinction in mind, many of the colonialist texts that formed the basis of Said's analysis would fall ostensibly under this category.
30 JanMohamed, 84.
31 JanMohamed, 85.

32 JanMohamed, 85.

33 Hallam and Street, 5.

34 Homi K. Bhabha, 'Of Mimicry and Man: The Ambivalence of Colonial Discourse', in *Tensions of Empire: Colonial Cultures in a Bourgeois World*, ed. Frederick Cooper and Ann Laura Stoler (Berkeley: University of California Press, 1997), 153, original emphasis. See also Homi K. Bhabha, 'Signs Taken for Wonders', in *The Post-Colonial Studies Reader*, ed. Bill Ashcroft, Gareth Griffiths and Helen Tiffin, 2nd ed. (London and New York: Routledge, 2006), 38–43; and Gwendolyn Audrey Foster, *Captive Bodies: Postcolonial Subjectivity in Cinema* (Albany: State University of New York Press, 1999).

35 Bhabha, 'Of Mimicry', 154.

36 Bhabha, 'Of Mimicry', 154; original emphasis.

37 For a related work that traces the shifting colonial representations of the Malay from 'savage' and 'oriental' to 'medieval', see Daniel P.S. Goh, 'Imperialism and "Medieval" Natives: The Malay Image in Anglo-American Travelogues and Colonialism in Malaya and the Philippines', *International Journal of Cultural Studies* 10, no. 3 (2007): 323–41.

38 Leong Yew, *The Disjunctive Empire of International Relations* (Aldershot and Burlington: Ashgate, 2003), 60.

39 Bhabha, 'Of Mimicry', 156. For a useful work that discusses the spaces for the 'oppositional gaze' in the context of the previously marginalized black female spectators of film see bell hooks, 'The Oppositional Gaze: Black Female Spectators', in *Feminist Postcolonial Theory: A Reader*, ed. Reina Lewis and Sara Mills (Edinburgh: Edinburgh University Press, 2003).

40 Yew, 149–56.

41 Ahmad, 86.

42 Graham Huggan, 'The Postcolonial Exotic', in *The Post-Colonial Studies Reader*, ed. Bill Ashcroft, Gareth Griffiths and Helen Tiffin, 2nd ed. (London and New York: Routledge, 2006).

43 W.E.B. Du Bois quoted in E. Ann Kaplan, *Looking for the Other: Feminism, Film and the Imperial Gaze* (New York and London: Routledge, 1997), 7.

44 *Ringu*, dir. Hideo Nakata (Los Angeles: Fine Line Features, 1998).

45 For a more detailed synopsis of *Ringu*'s plot, see Ruth Goldberg, 'Demons in the Family: Tracking the Japanese "Uncanny Mother Film" from *A Page of Madness* to *Ringu*', in *Planks of Reason: Essays on the Horror Film*, ed. Barry Keith Grant and Christopher Sharrett (Lanham: The Scarecrow Press, 2004), 377–81; and Eric White, 'Case Study: Nakata Hideo's *Ringu* and *Ringu 2*', in *Japanese Horror Cinema*, ed. Jay McRoy (Edinburgh: Edinburgh University Press, 2005), 38–41.

46 Goldberg, 378.

47 See Goldberg; McRoy; Ramie Tateishi, 'The Japanese Horror Film Series: *Ring* and *Eko Eko Azarak*', in *Fear Without Frontiers: Horror Cinema Across the Globe*, ed. Steven Jay Schneider (London: FAB Press, 2003), respectively.

48 White, 39.

49 It is eventually revealed that Sadako's nails were torn out as she struggled unsuccessfully to claw herself out of the well.

50 Of course, Reiko's purpose here is not completely altruistic. It is also, in large part, to save both her son's as well as her own life after they are exposed to the contents of the cursed videotape.

51 Prior to Ryuji's comment, the film had already on many instances alluded to the fact that Shizuko and Sadako were 'non-human'. For a more detailed exegesis on this point, see White, 40.

52 White, 40, emphases mine.

53 White, 40.

54 White, 41.

55 Katinka van Heeren, 'Return of the Kyai: Representations of Horror, Commerce, and Censorship in Post-Suharto Indonesian Film and Television', *Inter-Asia Cultural Studies* 8, no. 2 (2007): 216, emphasis mine.

56 Graham Huggan, 'Ghost Stories, Bone Flutes, Cannibal Countermemory', in *The Horror Reader*, ed. Ken Gelder (London and New York: Routledge, 2000), 354.

57 Gary Needham, 'Japanese Cinema and Orientalism', in *Asian Cinemas: A Reader and Guide*, ed. Dimitris Eleftheriotis and Gary Needham (Edinburgh: Edinburgh University Press, 2006), 11.

58 Needham, 10.

59 *Return to Pontianak*, dir. Djinn (Singapore: Shaw Organisation, 2001); released in the US as *Voodoo Nightmare: Return to Pontianak*, DVD, dir. Djinn (Venice, CA: Pathfinder Pictures, 2001).

60 This is the definition that the film offers on its final title card.

61 'Return to Pontianak', Moria: The Science Fiction, Horror and Fantasy Movie Review Site, http://www.moria.co.nz (accessed 1 March 2010).

62 Sophia Siddique Harvey, 'Mapping Spectral Tropicality in *The Maid* and *Return to Pontianak*', *Singapore Journal of Tropical Geography* 29, no. 1 (2008): 31.

63 'Return to Pontianak'.

64 Needham, 10.

65 Mitsuhiro Yoshimoto, 'The Difficulty of Being Radical: The Discipline of Film Studies and the Post-Colonial World Order', in *Asian Cinemas: A Reader and Guide*, ed. Dimitris Eleftheriotis and Gary Needham (Edinburgh: Edinburgh University Press, 2006), 28.

66 Castricano, 134.

Bibliography

Abdel-Malek, Anouar. 'Orientalism in Crisis'. *Diogenes* 11, no. 44 (1963): 103–40.

Abdulgani, Roeslan. *Asia–Africa Speaks from Bandung*. Djakarta: Ministry of Foreign Affairs, Republic of Indonesia, 1955.

——. *The Bandung Connection: The Asia–Africa Conference in Bandung in 1955.* Singapore: Gunung Agung, 1981.

——. *Bandung Spirit: Moving on the Tide of History.* Jakarta: Badan Penerbit Prapantja, 1964.

Abraham, Itty. 'Bandung and State Formation in Post-Colonial Asia'. In *Bandung Revisited: The Legacy of the 1955 Asian–African Conference for International Order*, edited by See Seng Tan and Amitav Acharya, 48–67. Singapore: NUS Press, 2008.

Acharya, Amitav and See Seng Tan. 'Introduction: The Normative Relevance of the Bandung Conference for Contemporary Asian and International Order'. In *Bandung Revisited: The Legacy of the 1955 Asian–African Conference for International Order*, edited by See Seng Tan and Amitav Acharya, 1–16. Singapore: NUS Press, 2008.

Achebe, Chinua. 'The Novelist as Teacher'. In *Commonwealth Literature: Unity and Diversity in a Common Culture*, edited by John Press, 201–5. London: Heinemann, 1965.

Adams, Arthur H. *The Australians: A Novel*. London, Eveleigh Nash, 1920.

Agger, Ben. *Critical Social Theories: An Introduction*. Boulder: Westview Press, 1998.

Ahmad, Abu Talib and Tan Liok Ee, ed. *New Terrains in Southeast Asian History*. Athens, OH: Ohio University Press; Singapore: Singapore University Press, 2003.

Ahmad, Aijaz. *In Theory: Classes, Nations, Literatures*. London and New York: Verso, 1992.

——. 'Jameson's Rhetoric of Otherness and the "National Allegory"'. In *The Post-Colonial Studies Reader*, edited by Bill Ashcroft, Gareth Griffiths and Helen Tiffin, 2nd ed., 84–8. London and New York: Routledge, 2006.

Alatas, Syed Farid. 'The Meaning of Alternative Discourses: Illustrations from Southeast Asia'. In *Asia in Europe, Europe in Asia*, edited by Srilata Ravi, Mario Rutten and Beng-Lan Goh, 57–79. Leiden: International Institute for Asian Studies; Singapore: Institute of Southeast Asian Studies, 2004.

Alatas, Syed Hussein. *The Myth of the Lazy Native*. London: Frank Cass, 1977.

Al-Azm, Sadik Jalal. 'Orientalism and Orientalism in Reverse'. In *Orientalism: A Reader*, edited by A.L. Macfie, 217–38. New York: New York University Press, 2000.

Anderson, Benedict. *Imagined Communities: Reflections on the Origin and Spread of Nationalism*. Rev. ed. London and New York: Verso, 1991.

——. *Spectre of Comparison: Nationalism, Southeast Asia, and the World.* London and New York: Verso, 1998.

Ang, Ien. *On Not Speaking Chinese: Living Between Asia and the West.* London and New York, Routledge, 2001.

Ang, Ien and Jon Stratton. 'Straddling East and West: Singapore's Paradoxical Search for a National Identity'. In *Asian and Pacific Inscriptions: Identities, Ethnicities, Nationalities,* edited by Suvendrini Perera, 179–92. Bundoora: Meridian, 1995.

Appadurai, Arjun. 'Disjuncture and Difference in the Global Cultural Economy'. *Public Culture* 2, no. 2 (1990): 1–24.

Ashcroft, Bill. *Post-Colonial Transformation.* London and New York: Routledge, 2001.

Ashcroft, Bill and Pal Ahluwalia. *Edward Said: The Paradox of Identity.* London and New York: Routledge, 1999.

Ashcroft, Bill, Gareth Griffiths and Helen Tiffin, ed. *The Post-Colonial Studies Reader.* London and New York: Routledge, 1995.

Australia in Facts and Figures, no. 52. Canberra: Australian News and Information Bureau, Department of the Interior, 1956.

Backstrom, M., J. Ironside, G. Paterson, J. Padwe and I.G. Baird. 'A Case Study of Indigenous Traditional Legal Systems and Conflict Resolution in Ratanakiri and Mondolkiri Provinces, Cambodia'. Phnom Penh: United Nations Development Programme, 2006.

Baird, Ian G. 'Colonialism, Indigeneity and the Brao'. In *The Concept of Indigenous Peoples in Asia: A Resource Book,* edited by Christian Erni. Copenhagen: International Work Group for Indigenous Affairs; Chiang Mai: Asia Indigenous Peoples Pact Foundation, 2008.

——. 'Identities and Space: The Geographies of Religious Change Amongst the Brao in Northeastern Cambodia'. *Anthropos Redaktion* 104, no. 2 (2009): 457–68.

——. 'Various Forms of Colonialism: The Social and Spatial Reorganization of the Brao in Southern Laos and Northeastern Cambodia'. PhD Diss., University of British Columbia, 2008.

Ball, W. Macmahon. *Possible Peace.* Melbourne: Melbourne University Press, 1936.

——. 'The Australian Press and World Affairs'. In *Press, Radio and World Affairs: Australia's Outlook,* edited by W. Macmahon Ball. Melbourne: Melbourne University Press, 1938.

Barth, Fredrik, ed., *Ethnic Groups and Boundaries: The Social Organization of Culture Difference.* Boston: Little, Brown, 1969.

Bedford, Randolph. 'White, Yellow and Brown'. *Lone Hand,* 1 July 1911.

Benda, Harry J. 'The Structure of Southeast Asian History: Some Preliminary Observations'. In *Man, State and Society in Contemporary Southeast Asia,* edited by Robert O. Tilman, 23–54. New York: Praeger, 1969.

Berger, Mark T. *The Battle for Asia: From Decolonization to Globalization.* London and New York: RoutledgeCurzon, 2004.

Bevan, Scott. 'Asian Languages in Schools'. *The World Today.* ABC News (radio), 19 December 2007. http://mediacentre.dewr.gov.au/mediacentre/AllReleases/2007/December/ Asianlanguagesinschools.htm (accessed 20 February 2009).

Bhabha, Homi K. 'Signs Taken for Wonders'. In *The Post-Colonial Studies Reader,* edited by Bill Ashcroft, Gareth Griffiths and Helen Tiffin, 2nd ed., 38–43. London and New York: Routledge, 2006.

——. 'Of Mimicry and Man: The Ambivalence of Colonial Discourse'. In *Tensions of Empire: Colonial Cultures in a Bourgeois World,* edited by Frederick Cooper and Ann Laura Stoler, 152–60. Berkeley: University of California Press, 1997.

Bobis, Merlinda. *The Solemn Lantern Maker: A Novel.* New York: Delta Trade Paperbacks, 2009.

——. *Banana Heart Summer: A Novel.* Millers Point: Pier 9, 2005.

Bonura, Carlo and Laurie J. Sears. 'Introduction: Knowledges That Travel in Southeast Asian Studies'. In *Knowing Southeast Asian Subjects*, edited by Laurie J. Sears, 3–32. Seattle: University of Washington Press, 2007.

Bose, Sugata. *A Hundred Horizons: The Indian Ocean in the Age of Global Empire.* Cambridge, MA: Harvard University Press, 2006.

Bourdieu, Pierre. *Outline of a Theory of Practice*, translated by Richard Nice. Cambridge: Cambridge University Press, 1977.

Bourotte, Bernard. 'Essai d'Histoire des Populations Montagnards du Sud-Indochinois jusqu' à 1945'. *Bulletin la Société des Étude Indochinoises* 30, no. 1 (1955): 1–116.

Bowen, J.R. 'Should We Have a Universal Concept of "Indigenous Peoples' Right"?' Paper presented at the 2000 Symposium 'Development and the Nation State', Washington University, St Louis, 2000.

Boyarin, Daniel and Jonathan Boyarin. 'Diaspora: Generation and the Ground of Jewish Identity'. In *Theorizing Diaspora*, edited by Jana Evans Braziel and Anita Mannur, 85–118. Oxford: Blackwell, 2003.

Brecher, Michael. *Nehru: A Political Biography*. London: Oxford University Press, 1959.

Breckenridge, Carol A. and Peter van der Veer, ed. *Orientalism and the Postcolonial Predicament: Perspectives on South Asia*. Philadelphia: University of Pennsylvania Press, 1993.

Brooke, Marcus. 'Anything Goes is Patpong's Motto'. *Destination ASEAN*, June 1982.

Brophy, Philip. 'Horrality – The Textuality of Contemporary Horror Films'. In *The Horror Reader*, edited by Ken Gelder, 276–84. London and New York: Routledge, 2000.

Bryant, Raymond L. 'Politicized Moral Geographies: Debating Biodiversity Conservation and Ancestral Domain in the Philippines'. *Political Geography* 19 (2003): 673–95.

Butler, Kim D. 'Defining Diaspora, Refining a Discourse'. *Diaspora* 10, no. 2 (2001): 189–219.

Cairns, J. F. *Living with Asia*. Melbourne and London: Lansdowne Press, 1965.

Callard, Keith. *Pakistan: A Political Study*. London: George Allen & Unwin, 1957.

Carrier, James G. *Occidentalism: Images of the West*. Oxford: Clarendon, 1995.

Carruthers, Ashley. 'Indochine Chic: Consuming the Vietnamese Exotic in Singapore, Tokyo and Sydney'. In *Foodscapes: The Cultural Politics of Food in Asia*, edited by Lisa Law and Daisy Ng. Hong Kong: Hong Kong University Press, forthcoming.

Casey, R.G. *Friends and Neighbours: Australia in the World.* Melbourne: Cheshire, 1954.

Castricano, Jodey. *Cryptomimesis: The Gothic and Jacques Derrida's Ghost Writing.* London and Ithaca: McGill–Queen's University Press, 2001.

Cha Seung-ki. *Bangeundaejeok Sangsanglyeokui imgyedeul* [Critical points of anti-modern imagination]. Seoul: Pureunyeoksa, 2009.

Chadha, Yogesh. *Rediscovering Gandhi*. London: Century Books, 1997.

Chakrabarty, Dipesh. *Provincializing Europe: Postcolonial Thought and Historical Difference*. Princeton: Princeton University Press, 2000.

——. '"Asia" and the Twentieth Century: What is "Asian Modernity"?'. In *We Asians: Between Past and Future: A Millennium Regional Conference*, edited by Kwok Kian-Woon, Indira Arumugam, Karen Chia and Lee Chee Keng, 15–32. Singapore: Singapore Heritage Society, 2000.

Chan, Boon. 'Ahoy There Singapore!'. *Straits Times*, 28 March 2007, Life section.

Chandler, David P. *The Tragedy of Cambodian History: Politics, War, and Revolution since 1945*. New Haven: Yale University Press, 1991.

Chandra, Lokesh. 'The Philosophical Roots of Panchsheel: The Western Paradise and the Celestial Kingdom'. In *Panchsheel and the Future*, edited by C.V. Ranganathan, 3–13. Delhi: Smaskriti, 2005.

Chandra Pal, Khagendra.'The Panch Shila and World Peace'. *Modern Review* 99, no. 2 (1956): 111–7.

Chatterjee, Partha. *The Nation and its Fragments: Colonial and Postcolonial Histories.* Princeton: Princeton University Press, 1993.

——. *Nationalist Thought in the Colonial World: A Derivative Discourse?* Minneapolis: University of Minnesota Press, 1986.

Chen, Kuan-Hsing. 'The Decolonizing Question'. In *Trajectories: Inter-Asia Cultural Studies*, edited by Kuan-Hsing Chen, 1–53. London and New York: Routledge, 1998.

——. *Jekugui Nun* [The eye of the Empire]. Seoul: Changjakkwabipyeongsa, 2003.

——. ed. *Trajectories: Inter-Asia Cultural Studies.* London and New York: Routledge, 1998.

Chen, Kuan-Hsing and Chua Beng Huat, ed. *Inter-Asia Cultural Studies Reader.* London and New York: Routledge, 2007.

——. 'Introduction: The Inter-Asia Cultural Studies: Movements Project'. In *Inter-Asia Cultural Studies Reader*, edited by Kuan-Hsing Chen and Chua Beng Huat, 1–5. London and New York: Routledge, 2007.

Chen, Xiaomei. *Occidentalism: A Theory of Counter-Discourse in Post-Mao China.* New York: Oxford University Press, 1995.

Chia, Josephine. *Frog under a Coconut Shell.* Singapore: Times Books International, 2002.

——. *Isn't Singapore Somewhere in China, Luv?* Singapore: Angsana Books, 1993.

——. *My Mother-in-Law's Son.* Singapore: Landmark Books, 1994.

——. *Shadows Across the Sun*, London and Baltimore: PublishBritannica, 2005.

Chia Siow Yue. 'Introduction'. In *Institute of Southeast Asian Studies: A Commemorative History 1968–1998*, ix–xiii. Singapore: Institute of Southeast Asian Studies, 1998.

Ching, Leo. 'Globalizing the Regional, Regionalizing the Global: Mass Culture and Asianism in the Age of Late Capital'. *Public Culture* 12, no. 1 (2000): 233–57.

Choi Young-ho. 'Rhee Syng-man Jeongbuui Taepyeongyang Dongmaeng Kusanggwa Asia Minjok Bangongyeonmang kyeolseong' [Rhee Syng-man regime's ideas of Pacific Alliance and the birth of the Asian People's Anti-Communist League]. *Kukjejeongchinonchong* [Korean journal of international relations] 39, no. 2 (1999): 165–82.

Chou Ta-Kuan. *The Customs of Cambodia.* Translated by J. Gilman d'Arcy Paul. Bangkok: Siam Society, 1987.

Christie, Clive J. 'British Literary Travellers in Southeast Asia in an Era of Colonial Retreat'. *Modern Asian Studies* 28, no. 4 (1994): 673–737.

Chua, Douglas. *Crisis in the Straits: Malaysia Invades Singapore.* Singapore: Angsana Books, 2001.

——. *The Missing Island.* Singapore: Times Books International, 2002.

——. *The Missing Page.* Singapore: Angsana Books, 1999.

——. *Ransom.* Singapore: Angsana Books, 2002.

Chun, Allen and A.B. Shamsul. 'Other "Routes": The Critical Challenge for Asian Academia'. *Inter-Asia Cultural Studies* 2, no. 2 (2001): 167–76.

Ciecko, Anne Tereska. 'Theorizing Asian Cinema'. In *Contemporary Asian Cinema: Popular Culture in a Global Frame*, edited by Anne Tereska Ciecko, 13–31. Oxford and New York: Berg, 2006.

Cilento, Raphael. 'Health Conditions in the Pacific Islands'. *Medical Journal of Australia*, 31 May 1930, 724–77.

——. *The White Man in the Tropics: With Especial Reference to Australia and its Dependencies.* Melbourne: H.J. Green, 1925.

Clover, Carol J. *Men, Women, and Chain Saws: Gender in the Modern Horror Film.* Princeton: Princeton University Press, 1992.

Clyne, Michael. 'Show-offs Urgently Required'. *Australian*, 14 November 2007. http://www. theaustralian.news.com.au/story/0,25197,22753216–25192,00.html (accessed 17 February 2009).

Codell, Julie F. and Dianne Sachko Macleod, ed. *Orientalism Transposed: The Impact of the Colonies on British Culture*. Aldershot: Ashgate, 1998.

Coedès, G. *The Indianized States of Southeast Asia.* Edited by Walter F. Vella. Translated by Sue Brown Cowing (Honolulu: East–West Center Press, 1968

Collins, William. 'The Chams of Cambodia'. In *Interdisciplinary Research on Ethnic Groups in Cambodia.* Phnom Penh: Center for Advanced Study, 1996.

Colm, Sara. *The Highland Minorities and the Khmer Rouge in Northeastern Cambodia 1968–1979.* Phnom Penh: Document Center of Cambodia, 1996.

Commonwealth Bureau of Census and Statistics, Melbourne. *Official Year Book of the Commonwealth of Australia 1901–1919*, No.13 – 1920, prepared by G.H. Knibbs. Melbourne: Albert J. Mullett, 1920.

Contreras, Antonio P. *The Kingdom and the Republic: Forest Governance and Political Transformation in Thailand and the Philippines.* Quezon City: Ateneo de Manila University Press, 2003.

Cook, Pam and Mieke Bernink. *The Cinema Book.* 2nd ed. London: British Film Institute Publishing, 1999.

Corntassel, Jeff J. 'Who is Indigenous? "Peoplehood' and Ethnonationalist Approaches to Rearticulating Indigenous Identity'. *Nationalism and Ethnic Politics* 9, no. 1 (2003): 75–100.

Cowie, Elizabeth. 'The Lived Nightmare: Trauma, Anxiety, and the Ethical Aesthetics of Horror'. In *Dark Thoughts: Philosophic Reflections on Cinematic Horror*, edited by Steven J. Schneider and Daniel Shaw, 25–46. Lanham: Scarecrow Press, 2003.

Crawford, R.M. 'Preface'. In *Ourselves and the Pacific*, edited by R.M. Crawford. Melbourne: Melbourne University Press, 1945 [1941].

Crocker, W.R. *The Japanese Population Problem: The Coming Crisis*. London: George Allen & Unwin, 1931.

Daes, Erica-Irene A. 'Standard-setting Activities: Concerning the Rights of Indigenous People'. Working Paper, Fourteenth Session, Sub-commission on Prevention of Discrimination and Protection of Minorities, Commission on Human Rights, 10 June. New York: United Nations Economic and Social Council, 1996.

Davidson, Roderic H. 'Where is the Middle East?'. *Foreign Affairs* 38, no. 4 (1960): 665–75.

Deakin, Alfred. *Irrigated India: An Australian View of India and Ceylon, Their Irrigation and Agriculture.* London: W. Thacker, 1893.

——. *Temple and Tomb in India.* Melbourne: Melville, Mullen & Slade, 1893.

Derrida, Jacques. *The Ear of the Other: Otobiography, Transference, Translation*, edited by Christie McDonald, translated by Peggy Kamuf. Lincoln: University of Nebraska Press, 1988.

——. *Margins of Philosophy*, translated by Alan Bass. Chicago: Chicago University Press, 1982.

——. *Speech and Phenomena: And Other Essays on Husserl's Theory of Signs*, translated by David B. Allison. Evanston: Northwestern University Press, 1973.

Diokno, Maria Serena I. 'Ten Years and More of Seasrep'. SEASREP Foundation. http:// www.seasrepfoundation.org/about.html (accessed 26 Mach 2010).

Dirlik, Arif. 'Asia Pacific Studies in an Age of Global Modernity'. *Inter-Asia Cultural Studies* 6, no. 2 (2005): 158–70.

——. *The Postcolonial Aura: Third World Criticism in the Age of Global Capitalism.* Boulder: Westview Press, 1997.

Dissanayake, Wimal. 'Cultural Identity and Asian Cinema: An Introduction'. In *Cinema and Cultural Identity: Reflections on Films From Japan, India, and China*, edited by Wimal Dissanayake, 1–13. Lanham and London: University Press of America, 1988.

Dobell, Graeme. 'PM Highlights Strong Asia Relationship', 21 November 2006. AM, ABC Online. http://www.abc.net.au/am/content/2006/s1793482.htm (accessed 12 March 2007).

Doyle, Michael W. *Empires*. Ithaca: Cornell University Press, 1986.

Duara, Prasenjit. 'The Discourse of Civilization and Pan-Asianism'. *Journal of World History* 12, no. 1 (2001): 99–130.

Editors and Directors. BCAS. 'Introducing Critical Asian Studies'. *Critical Asian Studies* 33, no. 1 (2001): 3–4.

Eisenstadt, S.N. 'Multiple Modernities'. *Daedalus* 129, no. 1 (2000): 1–28.

Emmerson, Donald K. '"Southeast Asia": What's in a Name?'. *Journal of Southeast Asian Studies* 15, no. 1 (1984): 1–21.

Enriquez, Virgilio. *From Colonial to Liberation Psychology: The Philippine Experience*. Manila: DLSU Press, 1994.

Erni, Christian, ed. *The Concept of Indigenous Peoples in Asia: A Resource Book*. IWGIA Document No. 123. Copenhagen: International Work Group for Indigenous Affairs; Chiang Mai: Asia Indigenous Peoples Pact Foundation, 2008.

——. 'From Opportunism to Resource Management: Adaptation and the Emergence of Environmental Conservation Among Indigenous Swidden Cultivators on Mindoro Island, Philippines'. *Conservation and Society* 4, no. 1 (2006): 102–31.

Evans, Grant. 'Internal Colonialism in the Central Highlands of Vietnam'. *Sojourn* 7, no. 2 (1992): 274–304.

Fanon, Frantz. *Black Skin, White Masks*, translated by Charles Lam Markmann. New York: Grove Weidenfeld, 1967.

Fee, Margaret. 'Who can Write as Other?' In *The Post-Colonial Studies Reader*, edited by Bill Ashcroft, Gareth Griffiths and Helen Tiffin. London and New York: Routledge, 1995.

Fish, Stanley. 'Boutique Multiculturalism, or Why Liberals are Incapable of Thinking about Hate Speech'. *Critical Inquiry* 23, no. 2 (1997): 378–95.

Ford Foundation. *1996 Ford Foundation Annual Report*. New York: Ford Foundation, 1996.

Foster, Gwendolyn Audrey. *Captive Bodies: Postcolonial Subjectivity in Cinema*. Albany: State University of New York Press, 1999.

Foucault, Michel. *The Archaeology of Knowledge*, translated by A.M. Sheridan Smith. London: Tavistock Publications, 1982.

——. *The Birth of the Clinic: An Archaeology of Medical Perception*, translated by A.M. Sheridan Smith. New York: Vintage Books, 1994.

——. *Madness and Civilization: A History of Insanity in the Age of Reason*. London and New York: Routledge, 2001.

——. *Power/Knowledge: Selected Interviews and Other Writings, 1972–1977*, edited by Colin Gordon, translated by Colin Gordon, Leo Marshall, John Mepham and Kate Soper. New York: Pantheon, 1980.

Fraser, John Foster. *Australia: The Making of a Nation*. London: Cassell, 1910.

Ganjanapan, Anan. *Local Control of Land and Forest: Cultural Dimensions of Resources Management in Northern Thailand*. Chiang Mai: Regional Center for Social Sciences and Sustainable Development, 2000.

Gaonkar, Dilip Parameshwar. 'On Alternative Modernities'. In *Alternative Modernities*, edited by Dilip Parameshwar Gaonkar, 1–23. Durham, NC: Duke University Press, 2001.

Geiss, Imanuel. *The Pan-African Movement: A History of Pan-Africanism in America, Europe and Africa*, translated by Ann Keep. New York: Methuen, 1974.

Gelder, Ken. 'Introduction to Part Eleven'. In *The Horror Reader*, edited by Ken Gelder, 349–51. London and New York: Routledge, 2000.

Geng Tinzeng. 'The Historicity of Panchsheel: Mutual Respect Through the Ages'. In *Panchsheel and the Future*, edited by C.V. Ranganathan, 20–32. Delhi: Smaskriti, 2005.

George, Jim. *Discourses of Global Politics: A Critical (Re)Introduction to International Relations*. Boulder: Lynne Rienner, 1994.

Gillard, Julia. *Budget: Education Revolution 2008–09*. Statement, *Budget Papers*, 13 May 2008. Canberra: Australian Government, 2008.

Gilmore, Robert J. and Denis Warner. *Near North: Australia and a Thousand Million Neighbours*. Sydney: Angus & Robertson, 1948.

Glover, Ian C. and Elizabeth H. Moore. 'Civilisations in Southeast Asia'. In *Old World Civilizations: The Rise of Cities and States*, edited by Goran Burenhult, 61–78. St Lucia: University of Queensland Press, 1994.

Goh, Beng-Lan. 'Redrawing Centre-Periphery Relations: Theoretical Challenges in the Study of Southeast Asian Modernity'. In *Asia in Europe, Europe in Asia*, edited by Srilata Ravi, Mario Rutten and Beng-Lan Goh, 79–101. Leiden: International Institute for Asian Studies; Singapore: Institute of Southeast Asian Studies, 2004.

Goh, Daniel P.S. 'Imperialism and "Medieval" Natives: The Malay Image in Anglo-American Travelogues and Colonialism in Malaya and the Philippines'. *International Journal of Cultural Studies* 10, no. 3 (2007): 323–41.

Goldberg, Ruth. 'Demons in the Family: Tracking the Japanese "Uncanny Mother Film" from *A Page of Madness* to *Ringu*.' In *Planks of Reason: Essays on the Horror Film*, edited by Barry Keith Grant and Christopher Sharrett, 377–85. Lanham: Scarecrow Press, 2004.

Goldie, Terry. 'The Representation of the Indigene'. In *The Post-Colonial Studies Reader*, edited by Bill Ashcroft, Gareth Griffiths and Helen Tiffin. London and New York: Routledge, 1995.

Gray, Andrew. 'The Indigenous Movement in Asia'. In *Indigenous Peoples of Asia*, edited by R.H. Barnes, Andrew Gray and Benedict Kingsbury. Ann Arbor: Association for Asian Studies, 1995.

Greene, Felix. *The Enemy: What Every American Should Know About Imperialism*. New York: Vintage Books, 1971.

Griffiths, Gareth. 'The Myth of Authenticity'. In *The Post-Colonial Studies Reader*, edited by Bill Ashcroft, Gareth Griffiths and Helen Tiffin (London and New York: Routledge, 1995).

Grosz, Elizabeth. *Volatile Bodies: Towards A Corporeal Feminism*. St Leonards: Allen & Unwin, 1994.

Guérin, Mathieu. 'Des Casques Blancs sur le Plateau des Herbes: Les Pacification des Aborigènes des Hautes Terres du Sud-Indochinois (1858–1940)'. PhD Diss., Université de Paris, 2003.

Hall, Stuart. 'Cultural Identity and Diaspora'. In *Identity: Community, Culture, Difference*, edited by Jonathan Rutherford, 222–37. London: Lawrence & Wishart, 1990.

——. 'New ethnicities'. In *The Post-Colonial Studies Reader*, edited by Bill Ashcroft, Gareth Griffiths and Helen Tiffin. London and New York: Routledge, 1995.

——. 'The West and the Rest: Discourse and Power'. In *Modernities: An Introduction to Modern Societies*, edited by Stuart Hall, David Held, Don Hubert and Kenneth Thompson, 184–227. Malden: Blackwell, 1996.

Hallam, Elizabeth and Brian V. Street. 'Introduction: Cultural Encounters – Representing "Otherness"'. In *Cultural Encounters: Representing 'Otherness'*, edited by Elizabeth Hallam and Brian V. Street, 1–10. London and New York: Routledge, 2000.

Han Suyin. *Eldest Son: Zhou Enlai and the Making of Modern China, 1898–1976.* London: Jonathan Cape, 1993.

Harootunian, Harry D. and Masao Miyoshi. 'Introduction: The "Afterlife" of Area Studies'. In *Learning Places: The Afterlives of Area Studies*, edited by Masao Miyoshi and Harry D. Harootunian, 1–18. Durham: Duke University Press, 2002.

Harvey, Sophia Siddique. 'Mapping Spectral Tropicality in *The Maid* and *Return to Pontianak*'. *Singapore Journal of Tropical Geography* 29, no. 1 (2008): 24–33.

Hechter, Michael. *Internal Colonialism: The Celtic Fringe in British National Development.* Vancouver: UBC Press, 2007 [1975].

van Heeren, Katinka. 'Return of the Kyai: Representations of Horror, Commerce, and Censorship in Post-Suharto Indonesian Film and Television'. *Inter-Asia Cultural Studies* 8, no. 2 (2007): 211–26.

Henderson, Deborah. 'Politics and Policy-making for Asia Literacy: The Rudd Report and a National Strategy in Australian Education'. *Asian Studies Review* 32, no. 2 (2008): 171–95.

Heryanto, Ariel. 'Can There Be Southeast Asians in Southeast Asian Studies. In *Knowing Southeast Asian Subjects*, edited by Laurie J. Sears, 75–108. Seattle: University of Washington Press, 2007.

Hill, Michael. '"Asian Values" as Reverse Orientalism: The Case of Singapore'. Working Paper 150, Department of Sociology, National University of Singapore, Singapore, 2000.

Holden, Philip. 'Postcolonial Desire: Placing Singapore'. *Postcolonial Studies* 11, no. 3 (2008): 345–61.

Hooker, J.R. 'The Pan-African Conference 1900'. *Transition* no. 46 (1974): 20–4.

hooks, bell. 'The Oppositional Gaze: Black Female Spectators'. In *Feminist Postcolonial Theory: A Reader*, edited by Reina Lewis and Sara Mills, 207–21. Edinburgh: Edinburgh University Press, 2003.

Horne, Donald. 'Living with Asia'. *Observer*, 7 March 1959.

Horne, Donald. *The Education of Young Donald.* Rev. ed. Ringwood: Penguin Books, 1988 [1967].

Howard, John. 'Australia's Links with Asia: Realising Opportunities in our Region'. Fifth Asialink Lecture, Myer Store, Melbourne, 12 April 1995. http://www.asialink.unimelb. edu.au (accessed 12 March 2007).

Huggan, Graham. *The Postcolonial Exotic: Marketing the Margins.* London and New York: Routledge, 2001.

——. 'The Postcolonial Exotic'. In *The Post-Colonial Studies Reader*, edited by Bill Ashcroft, Gareth Griffiths and Helen Tiffin, 2nd ed., 421–4. London and New York: Routledge, 2006.

——. 'Ghost Stories, Bone Flutes, Cannibal Countermemory'. In *The Horror Reader*, edited by Ken Gelder, 352–63. London and New York: Routledge, 2000.

International Work Group for International Affairs (IWGIA). *The Indigenous World 2001–2002.* Copenhagen: IWGIA, 2002.

——. *The Indigenous World 2005.* Copenhagen: IWGIA, 2005.

——. *The Indigenous World 2009.* Copenhagen: IWGIA, 2009.

Jameson, Fredric. *Postmodernism, or, the Cultural Logic of Late Capitalism.* Durham: Duke University Press, 1991.

——. 'Third-World Literature in the Era of Multinational Capitalism'. In *The Jameson Reader*, edited by Michael Hardt and Kathi Weeks, 315–39. Oxford and Malden: Blackwell, 2000.

JanMohamed, Abdul R. 'The Economy of Manichean Allegory: The Function of Racial Difference in Colonialist Literature'. *Critical Inquiry* 12 (1986): 59–87.

Jansen, G.H. *Afro-Asia and Non-Alignment*. London: Faber & Faber, 1966.

Jeong Moongil, ed. *Dongasia, Munjewa sigak* [East Asia, problem and viewpoint]. Seoul: Munhakwajiseongsa, 1995.

Jeong Il-hyeong. 'Taepyeongyang Dongmaengui Jeongchijeok gusang' [The political plan for the Pacific Pact]. *Sincheonji* [New world], September 1949.

Johnston, George H. *Journey Through Tomorrow*. Melbourne: Cheshire, 1947.

——. *Pacific Partners*. London: Victor Gollancz, 1945.

Jones, Sir William. *The Works of Sir William Jones*, vol. 5. London: John Stockdale, 1807.

Jonsson, Hjorleifur. 'French Natural in the Vietnamese Highlands: Nostalgia and Erasure in Montagnard Identity'. In *Of Vietnam: Identities in Dialogue*, edited by Jane Bradley Winston and Leakthina Chau-Pech Ollier. New York: Palgrave, 2001.

——. *Mien Relations: Mountain People and State Control in Thailand*. Ithaca: Cornell University Press, 2002.

Ju Yo-han. 'Seungriui Taepyeongyang' [Victory of the Pacific]. *Chuchu* [Time and tide], April 1942.

Kabir, Humayan. 'The Gandhian Way'. *UNESCO International Social Sciences Bulletin* 5, no. 2 (1953): 397–416.

Kahin, George McTurnan. *The Asian–African Conference*. Ithaca: Cornell University Press, 1956.

Kaplan, E. Ann. *Looking for the Other: Feminism, Film and the Imperial Gaze*. New York and London: Routledge, 1997.

Karsh, Efraim and Inari Karsh. 'Reflections on Arab Nationalism: Review Article'. *Middle Eastern Studies* 32, no. 4 (1996): 367–92.

Kennedy, Paul. *The Rise and Fall of the Great Powers: Economic Change and Military Conflict from 1500 to 2000*. New York: Vintage, 1989.

Khmer Loeu. Washington, DC: Library of Congress, 2004.

Kim Chul and Shin Hyung-Ki. *Munhaksokui Fascism* [Fascism in literature]. Seoul: Samin, 2001.

Kim Deok-lyong. 'Kuksaui gibon Seongkyeok' [The basic characteristics of national history]. *Sasanggye* [Circle of thought], November 1953.

Kim Du-heon. 'Kukka Saenghwalui Jungyoseong' [The significance of national life]. *Sincheonji* [New world], May 1950.

Kim Gi-seok. 'Hankuk Joenjaengui Yeoksajeok Uii' [The historical significance of the Korean War]. *Sincheonji* [New world], March 1953.

——. 'Ilbonui Buluiwa Dongyangui Isang' [The injustice of Japan and the idea of the East]. *Sasangkye* [Circle of thought], February 1954.

Kim Kyeong-il. 'Jeonhu Mikukeseo Jiyeok Yeongu Seongnipkwa Baljeon' [The formation and development of Area Studies in post-war USA]. In *Jiyeok yeonkuui yeoksawa iron* [The history and theory of Area Studies], edited by Kim Kyeong-il, 153–204. Seoul: Munhwakwahaksa, 1999.

Kim So-yeong, ed. *Trans-Asia Yeongsang Munhwa* [Trans-Asia screen culture]. Seoul: Hyeonsilmunwhayeongu, 2006.

Kim Ye-rim. *1930 nyeondae Huban Keundaeinsikui Teulkwa Miuisik* [Modern episteme and aesthetic consciousness in the late 1930s]. Seoul: Somyeongchulpansa, 2004.

Kim Yong-seong. 'Asiaui Jungnipseong' [Asian neutrality]. *Hyeondaegongnon* [Modern public opinion], May 1954.

Kimche, David. *The Afro-Asian Movement*. Jerusalem: Israel University Press, 1973.

Kingsbury, Benedict. '"Indigenous peoples" in International Law: A Constructivist Approach to the Asian Controversy'. *American Journal of International Law* 92, no. 3 (1998): 414–57.

Kirby, Kathe. 'Is Australia Asia smart?'. ABC News, 18 August 2008. http://www.abc.net.au/news/stories/2008/08/18/2338257.htm (accessed 20 February 2009).

Kitaha Jun. *Youjikasuru Nihonjin* [Japan and infantilism]. Tokyo: Riberuta Shuppan, 2005.

Klein, Christina. *Cold War Orientalism: Asia in the Middlebrow Imagination, 1945–1961*. Berkeley: University of California Press, 2003.

Kotelawala, Sir John. *An Asian Prime Minister's Story.* London: George G. Harrap, 1956.

Kratoska, Paul H., Remco Raben and Henk Schulte Nordholt, ed. *Locating Southeast Asia: Geographies of Knowledge and Politics of Space.* Singapore: Singapore University Press; Athens, OH: Ohio University Press, 2005.

Krishna, Sankaran. 'The Importance of Being Ironic: A Postcolonial View of Critical International Relations Theory'. *Alternatives* 18, no. 3 (1994): 385–417.

Kundera, Milan. 'Die Weltliteratur: How We Read One Another', translated by Linda Asher. *New Yorker*, 8 January 2007.

Kwon Myeong-ah. *Yeoksajeok Fascism* [Historical fascism]. Seoul: Chaeksesang, 2005.

Kymlicka, Will. *Multicultural Citizenship: A Liberal Theory of Minority Rights.* Oxford: Oxford University Press, 1995.

——. *Politics in the Vernacular: Nationalism, Multiculturalism and Citizenship.* Oxford: Oxford University Press, 2001.

Lazarus, Neil. 'The Fetish of "the West" in Postcolonial Theory'. In *Marxism, Modernity, and Postcolonial Studies*, edited by Crystal Bartolovich and Neil Lazarus, 43–64. Cambridge: Cambridge University Press, 2002.

Lee Cheol-beom. 'Minjokuijiui Dankyeolmani' [Only the solidarity of the national will]. *Sedae* [The generation], August 1965.

Lee Dong-yeon. *Asia Munwha yeongureul Sangsanghagi* [Imagining Asian cultural studies]. Seoul: Greenbee, 2006.

Lee Jong-su. 'Hyundae Samsinkiui Yokmang' [The desire for the three modern holy things]. *Sedae* [The generation], July 1967.

Lee Kuan Yew. 'The Situation in South-East Asia'. Speech, Royal Society of International Affairs, London, May 1962.

——. Speech, Canterbury University, Christchurch, March 15, 1964.

——. Speech, Civil Service Study Centre, Singapore, August 15, 1959.

Lee Seon-keun. 'Haebang Asia Onyeonsa' [The history of five years after the Liberation]. *Sincheonji* [New world], February 1950.

Lee Tae-yeong. 'Hankuk Jeonjaengui Yeoksajeok Uii' [The historical significance of the Korean War]. *Sasanggye* [Circle of thought], May 1953.

Legge, J.D. *Australian Outlook: A History of the Australian Institute of International Affairs.* Sydney: Allen & Unwin, 1999.

——. *Sukarno: A Political Biography.* London: Allen Lane, 1972.

Leifer, Michael. *The Foreign Relations of New States.* Camberwell: Longman, 1972.

Leshkowich, Ann Marie and Carla Jones. 'What Happens when Asian Chic becomes Chic in Asia?'. *Fashion Theory* 7, no. 3/4 (2003): 281–300.

Lewis Martin, W. and Kären E. Wigen. *The Myth of Continents: A Critique of Metageography.* Berkeley: University of California Press, 1997.

Lewis, Reina. *Gendering Orientalism: Race, Femininity, and Representation.* New York: Routledge, 1995.

Li, Tania Murray. 'Ethnic Cleansing, Recursive Knowledge and the Dilemmas of Sedentarism'. *International Social Science Journal* 54, no. 173 (2002): 361–71.

Lim, Catherine. *The Bondmaid*. London: Orion, 1995.
——. *Following the Wrong God Home*. London: Orion, 2001.
——. *The Serpent's Tooth*. Singapore: Times Books International, 1982.
——. *The Teardrop Story* Woman. London: Orion, 1998.
Lim, Shirley Geok-lin. *Among the White Moon Faces: An Asian-American Memoir of Homelands*. New York: Feminist Press at the City University of New York, 1996.
——. *Among the White Moon Faces: Memoirs of a Nyonya Feminist*. Singapore: Times Books International, 1996.
——. *Joss & Gold*. Singapore: Times Books International; New York: Feminist Press at the City University of New York, 2001.
——. *Nationalism and Literature: English-Language Writing from the Philippines and Singapore*. Quezon City: New Day, 1993.
——. 'Regionalism, English Narrative, and Singapore as Home and Global City'. In *Postcolonial Urbanism: Southeast Asian Cities and Global Processes*, edited by Ryan Bishop, John Phillips and Wei-Wei Yeo, 205–24. New York and London: Routledge, 2003.
——. *Sister Swing*. Singapore: Marshall Cavendish, 2006.
——. *Writing S.E./Asia English: Against the Grain*. London: Skoob Books, 1994.
Lim, Shirley Geok-lin and Cheng Lok Chua. 'Introduction'. In *Tilting the Continent: Southeast Asian American Writing*, edited by Shirley Geok-lin Lim and Cheng Lok Chua, xi–xx. Minneapolis: New Rivers Press, 2000.
Lim, Suchen. *Fistful of Colours*. Singapore: EPB, 1993.
——. *Rice Bowl*. Singapore: Times Books International, 1984.
Lim, William S.W. *Asian Alterity: With Special Reference to Architecture and Urbanism through the Lens of Cultural Studies*. Singapore: World Scientific: 2008.
Loh, Vyvyanne. *Breaking the Tongue*. New York and London: W.W. Norton, 2004.
Loomba, Ania. *Colonialism/Postcolonialism*. London and New York: Routledge, 1998.
López-Calvo, Ignacio. 'Introduction'. In *Alternative Orientalisms in Latin America and Beyond*, edited by Ignacio López-Calvo, iix–xiv. Newcastle: Cambridge Scholars Publishing, 2007.
McAuley, J. 'Power Vacuum to Our North'. *Observer*, 5 April 1958.
McGuire, Paul. *Westward the Course! the New World of Oceania*. New York, William Morrow, 1942.
Mackerras, Colin. *Western Images of China*. Hong Kong: Oxford University Press, 1989.
McRoy, Jay. *Nightmare Japan: Contemporary Japanese Horror Cinema*. Amsterdam and New York: Rodopi, 2008.
Manguel, Alberto. *A History of Reading*. New York: Viking, 1996.
Mansouri, Fethi and Sally Percival Wood. 'Exploring the Australia–Middle East Connection'. In *Australia and the Middle East: A Front-line Relationship*, edited by Fethi Mansouri, 1–18. London: I.B. Tauris, 2006.
Martin, Marie Alexandrine. *Les Khmer Daeum: Khmer de l'Origine. Société Montagnarde et Exploitation de la Forêt, de l'Écologie à l'Histoire*. Paris: Presses de l'École Francaise d'Extrême Orient, 1997.
Marukawa Tetsushi. *Regionalism* [sic.]. Tokyo: Iwanami Shoten, 2003.
——. *Reisenbunkaron* [The Cold War culture theory]. Tokyo: Sofusha, 2005.
Medcalf, Rory. 'Australia's Relations with India'. The Interpreter: Lowy Institute for International Policy, 21 December 2007. http://www.lowyinterpreter.org/post/2007/12/21/Australias-relations-with-India.aspx (accessed 12 April 2010).
Meyer, C. 'Les Nouvelles Provinces: Ratanakiri – Mondolkiri'. *Revue Monde en Développement* 28 (1979): 682–90.
Michiba Chikanobu. *Senryo to Heiwa* [Occupation and peace]. Tokyo: Seitosha 2005.

Mullen, Bill. *Afro-Orientalism*. Minneapolis: University of Minnesota Press, 2004.

Muskett, Philip E. *The Illustrated Australian Medical Guide*. Sydney: William Brooks, n.d.

Nafisi, Azar. *Reading Lolita in Tehran: A Memoir in Books*. New York: Random House, 2004.

Nandy, Ashis. *The Intimate Enemy: Loss and Recovery of Self Under Colonialism*. Delhi: Oxford University Press, 1983.

National Asian Languages and Cultures Working Group. *Asian Languages and Australia's Economic Future: A Report Prepared for the Council of Australian Governments on a Proposed National Asian Languages/Studies Strategy for Australian Schools*. Brisbane: Queensland Govt. Printer, 1994.

Needham, Gary. 'Japanese Cinema and Orientalism'. In *Asian Cinemas: A Reader and Guide*, edited by Dimitris Eleftheriotis and Gary Needham, 8–16. Edinburgh: Edinburgh University Press, 2006.

Nehru, Jawaharlal. *The Mind of Mr Nehru: An Interview*, by R.K. Karanjia. London: George Allen & Unwin, 1960.

NGO Forum on Cambodia. *Land Alienation from Indigenous Minority Communities, Ratanakiri Province, Cambodia*. Phnom Penh: NGO Forum on Cambodia, 2006.

U Nu. *From Peace to Stability*. Rangoon: Government Printing and Stationery, 1951.

——. *Saturday's Son*. New Haven and London: Yale University Press, 1975.

Oguma Eiji. *Minshu to Aikoku* [Democracy and patriotism]. Tokyo: Shinyosha, 2003.

Ogusi Junji. 'Sengo no Daishu Bunka' [The popular culture of postwar Japan]. In *Sengo Kaikaku to gyaku Kosu* [Postwar Japan reformation and the reversal of course], edited by Yoshida Yudaka, 135–59. Tokyo: Yoshikawakoubunkan, 2004.

Oh Jong-sik. 'Hankukui kukjejeok wichiwa kui yeoksajeok kwaje' [The international position of Korea and its historical task]. *Hyndaekongron* [Modern public opinion], May 1954.

Oh So-paek. 'I Pungjin Sesangeul Mannasuni' [In the rugged world]. *Sincheonji* [New world], July 1949.

Ooi, Can-Seng. 'Orientalist Imaginations and Touristification of Museums: Experiences from Singapore'. Copenhagen Discussion Papers 1, Asia Research Centre, Copenhagen Business School, Copenhagen, 2005.

Oonk, Gijsbert. *Global Indian Diasporas: Exploring Trajectories of Migration and Theory*. Amsterdam: Amsterdam University Press, 2007.

Ovesen, Jan and Ing-Britt Trankell. 'Foreigners and Honorary Khmers: Ethnic Minorities in Cambodia'. In *Civilizing the Margins: Southeast Asian Government Policies for the Development of Minorities*, edited by Christopher R. Duncan. Ithaca and London: Cornell University Press, 2004.

Pae Seong-lyong. 'Dongyang Jeongchisasang keup Keu Yangsangui Yeongu' [A study on the Eastern political thought and its situation]. *Sasanggye* [Circle of thought], May 1953.

——. 'Dongyangjeok Soetoesakwan Kaeron' [Introduction to the fatalist view of history of the East]. *Sasanggye* [Circle of thought], March 1954, 18–30.

——. 'Uri Minjokseongkwa Dongyanghak' [Our national characteristics and Oriental studies]. *Sasanggye* [Circle of thought], January 1954.

Paek Nak-jun. 'Asiawa Segye Jeongguk' [Asia and the world political situation]. *Sasangkye* [Circle of thought], March 1954.

Panch Sheela – Its Meaning and History: A Documentary Study. New Delhi: Lok Sabha, 1955.

Pannikar, K.M. *Asia and Western Dominance: A Survey of the Vasco Da Gama Epoch of Asian History 1498–1945*. London: George Allen & Unwin, 1953.

Park Gi-jun. 'Jeonhwangiui Cheolhak' [The philosophy of the transition period]. *Sincheonji* [New world], May–June 1949.

Park In-hwan. 'Indonesia Inminege Juneun Si' [A poem for Indonesian people]. *Sincheonji* [New world], February 1948.

———. 'Nampung' [Wind from the South]. *Sincheonji* [New world], July 1947.

Park Jin-hee. 'Rhee Syng-manui Daeil insikkwa Taepyeongyang Dongmang Kusang' [Rhee Syng-man's recognition of the Japan and Pacific Pact]. *Yeoksabipyeong* [Critical review of history] no. 76 (2006): 90–118.

Park Ki-jun. 'Padochineun Taepyeongyang' [The wave of the Pacific]. *Sincheonji* [New world], September 1949.

Park Tae-gyun. 'Park Chong Heeui Dongasia insikkwa Asia–Taepyeongyang Kongdong sahoe Kusang' [Park Chung-hee's East Asia and his plan for an Asian Pacific community]. *Yuksabipyung* [Critical review of history] no. 76 (2006): 119–47.

Pearson, Charles H. *National Life and Character: A Forecast.* London: Macmillan, 1894.

Penton, Brian. *Advance Australia – Where?* London and Sydney: Cassell, 1943.

'People or Perish'. *Millions Magazine*, 15 October 1923.

Percival Wood, Sally. '"Chou Gags Critics in Bandoeng" *or* How the Media Framed Premier Zhou Enlai at the Bandung Conference, 1955'. *Modern Asian Studies* 44, no. 5 (forthcoming 2010).

Phillips, Kendall R. *Projected Fears: Horror Films and American Culture.* Westport: Praeger Publishers, 2005.

Phongphaichit, Pasuk and Chris Baker. *Thailand: Economy and Politics.* Oxford: Oxford University Press, 1995.

Pirates of the Caribbean: At World's End, directed by Gore Verbinski. Burbank, CA: Walt Disney Pictures, 2007.

Porter, Dennis. 'Orientalism and its Problems'. In *The Politics of Theory*, edited by Francis Barker, Peter Hulme, Margaret Iversen and Diana Loxley, 179–93. Colchester: University of Essex.

Prashad, Vijay. *The Darker Nations: A People's History of the Third World.* New York: New Press, 2007.

'Project for Critical Asian Studies'. Simpson Center for the Humanities. http://depts.washington.edu/critasia/home.html (accessed 26 March 2010).

PuruShotam, Nirmala Srirekam. *Negotiating Language, Constructing Race: Disciplining Difference in Singapore.* Berlin: Mouton de Gruyter, 1998.

Pye, Lucien. *Asian Power and Politics: The Cultural Dimensions of Authority.* Cambridge, MA: Belknap Press of Harvard University, 1985.

Ramage, Douglas E. *Politics in Indonesia: Democracy, Islam and the Ideology of Tolerance.* London and New York: Routledge, 1997.

Raman, B. 'Kevin Rudd: All the Way with China'. Chennai Centre for China Studies, 24 April 2008. http://www.c3sindia.org/india/236 (accessed 12 April 2010).

Ravi, Srilata, Mario Rutten and Beng-Lan Goh, ed. *Asia in Europe, Europe in Asia.* Leiden: International Institute of Asian Studies; Singapore: Institute of Southeast Asian Studies, 2004.

Regnier, Philippe. *Singapore: City-State in South-East Asia*, translated by Christopher Hurst. Honolulu: University of Hawaii Press, 1991.

Return to Pontianak, directed by Djinn. Singapore: Shaw Organisation, 2001.

'Return to Pontianak'. Moria: The Science Fiction, Horror and Fantasy Movie Review Site. http://www.moria.co.nz (accessed 1 March 2010).

Ringu, directed by Hideo Nakata. Los Angeles: Fine Line Features, 1998.

Roberts, S.H. *et al. Australia and the Far East: Diplomatic and Trade Relations*, edited by Ian Clunies Ross. Sydney: Angus & Robertson, 1935.

Robertson, Jennifer. 'Mon Japon: The Revue Theater as a Technology of Japanese Imperialism'. *American Ethnologist* 22, no. 4 (1997): 970–96.

Romulo, Carlos P. *The Meaning of Bandung*. Chapel Hill: University of North Carolina Press, 1956.

Rorty, Richard. *Contingency, Irony, and Solidarity*. Cambridge and New York: Cambridge University Press, 1989.

Roth, Lane. 'Film, Society, and Ideas: Nosferatu and Horror of Dracula'. In *Planks of Reason: Essays on the Horror Film*, edited by Barry Keith Grant and Christopher Sharrett, 255–64. Lanham: Scarecrow Press, 2004.

Rowan, Carl T. *The Pitiful and the Proud*. New York: Random House, 1956.

Roxas-Tope, Lily Rose. *(Un)Framing Southeast Asia: Nationalism and the Postcolonial Text in English in Singapore, Malaysia and the Philippines*. Quezon City: Office of Research Coordination, University of the Philippines, 1998.

Rudd, Kevin. 'It's Time to Build an Asia Pacific Community'. Address to the Asia Society, AustralAsia Centre, Sydney, 4 June 2008. http://www.asiasociety.org.au/speeches/speeches_current/s55_PM_Rudd_AD2008.html (accessed 15 February 2009).

Said, Edward W. *Culture and Imperialism*. New York: Alfred A. Knopf, 1994.

——. 'In Conversation with Neeladri Bhattacharya, Suvir Kaul, and Ania Loomba'. In *Relocating Postcolonialism*, edited by David Theo Goldberg and Ato Quayson, 1–14. Oxford: Blackwell, 2002.

——. *Orientalism: Western Conceptions of the Orient*. New York: Pantheon, 1978.

——. 'Representing the Colonized: Anthropology's Interlocutors'. *Critical Inquiry* 15, no. 2 (1989): 205–25.

——. *The World, the Text, and the Critic*. Cambridge, MA: Harvard University Press, 1983.

Salemink, Oscar. *The Ethnography of Vietnam's Central Highlanders: A Historical Contextualization, 1850–1990*. London: RoutledgeCurzon, 2003.

San Juan, E., Jr. *Beyond Postcolonial Theory*. Basingstoke: Macmillan, 1998.

Sardar, Ziauddin. *Orientalism*. Philadelphia: Open University Press, 1999.

——. *Postmodernism and the Other: The New Imperialism of Western Culture*. London: Pluto Press, 1998.

Sastroamijoyo, Ali. *Milestones on My Journey: The Memoirs of Ali Sastroamijoyo, Indonesian Patriot and Political Leader*, edited by C.L.M. Penders. St Lucia: University of Queensland Press, 1979.

Sato Takumi. 'Sengo Seron no Seiritsu' [The establishment of postwar public opinion]. *Shiso* [Thought] no. 980 (2005): 72–94.

de Saussure, Ferdinand. *Course in General Linguistics*, edited by Charles Bally and Albert Sechehaye, translated by Roy Harris. London: Duckworth, 1983.

Scheffler, Thomas. '"Fertile Crescent", "Orient", "Middle East": The Changing Mental Maps of Southwest Asia'. *European Review of History* 10, no. 2 (2003): 253–72.

Schein, Louisa. 'Gender and Internal Orientalism in China'. *Modern China* 23, no. 1 (1997): 69–98.

Schneider, Jane, ed. *Italy's 'Southern Question': Orientalism in One Country*. Oxford: Berg, 1998.

Scott, James. 'Freedom and Freehold: Space, People and State Simplification in Southeast Asia'. In *Asian Freedoms: The Idea of Freedom in East and Southeast Asia*, edited by David Kelly and Anthony Reid, 37–64. Cambridge: Cambridge University Press, 1998.

Sears, Laurie J., ed. *Knowing Southeast Asian Subjects*. Seattle: University of Washington Press, 2007.

Seol Jeong-sik. 'Manjukuk' [Manchuria]. *Sincheonji* [New world], October 1948.

Seong Chang-hwan. 'Kyeongjehakeul Gongbuhaneun hakdoege' [To the young scholars who study Economics]. *Sasanggye* [Circle of thought], June 1955.

Shelley, Rex. *Island in the Centre.* Singapore: Times Books International, 1995.

———. *People of the Pear Tree.* Singapore: Times Books International, 1992.

———. *A River of Roses.* Singapore: Times Books International, 1998.

———. *The Shrimp People.* Singapore: Times Books International, 1991.

Shepherd, Jack. *Australia's Interests and Policies in the Far East.* New York: International Secretariat, Institute of Pacific Relations, 1940 [1939].

Sheridan, Greg. 'It's a Start, but India Ties Need Attention'. *Weekend Australian,* 14–15 November 2009, Commentary.

Shields, Rob. 'Meeting Or Mis-Meeting? The Dialogical Challenge to Verstehen'. *British Journal of Sociology* 47, no. 2 (1996): 275–94.

Shin, Gi-wook. 'Asianism in Korea's Politics of Identity'. *Inter-Asia Cultural Studies* 6, no. 4 (2005): 616–30.

Simon, S. 'Taiwan Studies and Taiwanese Indigenous Peoples'. Paper presented at the UCSB International Conference on Taiwan Studies, Santa Barbara, 26–7 October 2007.

Smart, Ninian. *The World's Religions.* Cambridge: Cambridge University Press, 1992.

Smith, Joseph Burkholder. *Portrait of a Cold Warrior.* New York: Ballantine Books, 1976.

Sollors, Werner. 'Who is Ethnic?'. In *The Post-Colonial Studies Reader*, edited by Bill Ashcroft, Gareth Griffiths and Helen Tiffin. London and New York: Routledge, 1995.

Spender, Percy. *Politics and a Man.* Sydney: Collins, 1972.

Spivak, Gayatri Chakravorty. *Other Asias.* Malden: Blackwell, 2007.

———. 'Reading the World: Literary Studies in the 80s'. *College English* 43, no. 7 (1981): 671–9.

Srikanth, Rajini. *The World Next Door: South Asian American Literature and the Idea of America.* Philadelphia: Temple University Press, 2004.

Strang, Herbert. *The Air Scout: A Story of National Defence.* London: Oxford University Press, 1912.

Stuart-Fox, Martin. 'Political Patterns in Southeast Asia'. In *Eastern Asia: An Introductory History*, edited by Colin Mackerras, 3rd ed., 83–92. Sydney: Longman, 2000.

Sumida, Stephen H. and Sau-Ling Cynthia Wong. 'Introduction'. In *A Resource Guide to Asian American Literature*, edited by Sau-Ling Cynthia Wong and Stephen H. Sumida, 1–9. New York: Modern Language Association of America, 2001.

Sun Ge. *Asiaraneun Sayugongkan* [Asia as a sphere of thought]. Seoul: Changjakkwabipyeongsa, 2003.

———. 'Globalization and Cultural Difference: Thoughts on the Situation of Trans-Cultural Knowledge', translated by Allen Chun. *Inter-Asia Cultural Studies* 2, no. 2 (2001): 261–75.

———. 'How Does Asia Mean? (Part I)', translated by Hui Shiu-Lun and Lau Kinchi. *Inter-Asia Cultural Studies* 1, no. 1 (2000): 13–47.

———. 'How Does Asia Mean? (Part II)', translated by Hui Shiu-Lun and Lau Kinchi. *Inter-Asia Cultural Studies* 1, no. 2 (2000): 319–41.

Sutherland, Heather. 'Contingent Devices'. In *Locating Southeast Asia: Geographies of Knowledge and Politics of Space*, edited by Paul H. Kratoska, Remco Raben and Henk Nordholt Schulte, 20–59. Singapore: Singapore University Press, 2005.

Sutsakhan, Sak. *The Khmer Republic at War and the Final Collapse.* Christiansburg: Dalley Book Service, 1978.

Tahara, Kaori. 'Nibutani Dam Case'. *Indigenous Law Bulletin* 70 (1999). http://www.austlii. edu.au/au/journals/ILB/1999/70.html#fnB15 (accessed 23 January 2009).

Takeuchi Yoshimi. *Ilbonkwa Asia* [Japan and Asia], translated by Seo Kwangdeok *et al.* Seoul: Somyeongchulpan, 2004.

Talib, Ismail S. 'After the (Unwritten) "Postcolonial" in Southeast Asia: What Happens Next?'. In *The Silent Word: Textual Meaning and the Unwritten*, edited by Robert J.C. Young, Ban Kah Choon and Robbie B.H. Goh, 59–70. Singapore: Singapore University Press, 1998.

Tan Boon Peng. 'A Jungle Journey'. *Destination ASEAN*, November 1982.

Tan Gim Ean. 'Book Inspired by the Recent Malaysia–Singapore Spats', *New Straits Times*, May 26, 1999, 2.

Tan, Kenneth Paul. *Cinema and Television in Singapore: Resistance in One Dimension.* Leiden and Boston: Brill, 2008.

Tanaka, Stefan. *Japan's Orient: Rendering Pasts into History.* Berkeley: University of California Press, 1993.

Tateishi, Ramie. 'The Japanese Horror Film Series: *Ring* and *Eko Eko Azarak*'. In *Fear Without Frontiers: Horror Cinema Across the Globe*, edited by Steven Jay Schneider, 295–304. London: FAB Press, 2003.

Tibawi, Abdul Latif. *Arabic and Islamic Themes: Historical, Educational and Literary Studies.* London: Luzac, 1976.

——. *English-Speaking Orientalists: A Critique of Their Approach to Islam and Arab Nationalism.* London: Luzac, 1964.

Tomoda, Seki. 'Detaching from Cambodia'. In *Vietnam Joins the World*, edited by James W. Morley and Masashi Nishihara. Armonk and London: M.E. Sharpe, 1997.

Tudor, Andrew. *Monsters and Mad Scientists: A Cultural History of the Horror Movie.* Oxford and New York: Blackwell, 1997.

——. 'Why Horror? The Peculiar Pleasures of a Popular Genre'. *Cultural Studies* 11, no. 3 (1997): 443–63.

Turner, Bryan S. *Marx and the End of Orientalism.* London and Boston: Allen & Unwin, 1978.

United Nations. 'Completed Peace Keeping Operations, United Nations Transitional Authority in Cambodia [UNTAC], February 1992–September 1993'. http://www.un.org/Depts/dpko/dpko/co_mission/untac.htm (accessed 5 December 2007).

United Nations Commission on Human Rights. 'Khmer Krom: WS on the Case of the Khmer Krom'. Unrepresented Nations and Peoples Organization. http://www.unpo.org/content/view/3980/120/ (accessed 7 April 2010).

Upadhyaya, Priyankar. 'Peace-functions of Nonaligned States: Some Reflections'. *Profile of Political Studies* 1, no. 1 (1985): 97–105.

Usumi Aiko. *Sengo Hoshoukara Kangaeru Nihon to Ajia* [Japan and Asia viewed from war reparations]. Tokyo: Yamakawa shuppan sha, 2006.

Vasil, Raj K. *Asianising Singapore: The PAP's Management of Ethnicity.* Singapore: Heinemann Asia, 1995.

Venn, Couze. *Occidentalism: Modernity and Subjectivity.* London: Sage, 2000.

Wagner, Tamara S. 'Emulative versus Revisionist Occidentalism: Monetary and Other Values in Recent Singaporean Fiction'. *Journal of Commonwealth Literature* 39, no. 2 (2004): 73–94.

——. *Occidentalism in Novels of Malaysia and Singapore, 1819–2004: Colonial and Postcolonial Financial Straits.* Lewiston: Edwin Mellen Press, 2005.

——. 'Singapore's New Thrillers: Boldly Going Beyond the Ethnographic Map'. *ARIEL: A Review of International English Literature* 37, no. 2–3 (2006): 69–89.

Wakefield, Edward Gibbon. *A Letter from Sydney and Other Writings.* London: J.M. Dent, 1929 [1829].

Walker, David. 'The "Flow of Asia": Vocabularies of Engagement: A Cultural History'. *Australian Journal of Political Science* 45, no. 1 (2010): 45–58.

Wallace, Alfred Russel. *The Malay Archipelago: The Land of the Orang-Utan and the Bird of Paradise*. London: Macmillan, 1883.

Wang Gungwu. 'Two Perspectives of Southeast Asian Studies: Singapore and China'. In *Locating Southeast Asia: Geographies of Knowledge and Politics of Space*, edited by Paul H. Kratoska, Remco Raben and Henk Schulte Nordholt, 60–81. Singapore: Singapore University Press, 2005.

Wang Hui, 'The Politics of Imagining Asia: A Genealogical Analysis', translated by Matthew A. Hale. *Inter-Asia Cultural Studies* 8, no. 1 (2007): 1–33.

Warner, D. 'Advance Austral-Asia Fair'. *Observer*, 14 June 1958.

Washbrook, D.A. 'Orients and Occidents: Colonial Discourse Theory and the Historiography of the British Empire'. In *Historiography*, edited by Robin W. Winks and Alaine Low, vol. 5 *The Oxford History of the British Empire*, edited by Wm. Roger Louis and Alaine Low, 596–611. Oxford: Oxford University Press, 1999.

Wee, C. J.W.-L, ed. *Local Cultures and the 'New Asia': The State, Culture, and Capitalism in Southeast Asia*. Singapore: Institute of Southeast Asian Studies, 2002.

——. 'Staging the New Asia: Singapore's Dick Lee, Pop Music and a Counter-Modernity'. *Public Culture* 8, no. 3 (1996): 489–510.

Wellings, Ben. 'Empire–Nation: National and Imperial Discourses in England'. *Nations and Nationalism* 8, no. 1 (2002): 95–109.

White, Eric. 'Case Study: Nakata Hideo's *Ringu* and *Ringu 2*'. In *Japanese Horror Cinema*, edited by Jay McRoy, 38–50. Edinburgh: Edinburgh University Press, 2005.

White, Joanna. 'The Highland People of Cambodia: The Indigenous Highlanders of the Northeast: An Uncertain Future'. In *Interdisciplinary Research on Ethnic Groups in Cambodia*. Phnom Penh: Center for Advanced Study, 1996.

Wicks, Peter. 'Eurasian Images of Singapore in the Fiction of Rex Shelley'. In *Singaporean Literature in English: A Critical Reader*, edited by Mohammad A. Quayum and Peter Wicks, 377–83. Serdang: Universiti Putra Malaysia Press, 2002.

Williams, Henry Sylvester. Henry Sylvester Williams to Booker T. Washington, London, 27 September 1898. In *The Booker T. Washington Papers*, vol. 4, *1895–1898*, edited by Louis R. Harlan, 475–6. Urbana: University of Illinois Press, 1975.

Winichakul, Thongchai. *Siam Mapped: A History of the Geo-Body of a Nation*. Honolulu: University of Hawaii Press, 1994.

——. 'Writing at the Interstices: Southeast Asia Historians and Postnational Histories in Southeast Asia'. In *New Terrains in Southeast Asian History*, edited by Abu Talib Ahmad and Tan Liok Ee, 3–29. Athens, OH: Ohio University Press; Singapore: Singapore University Press, 2003.

Wong, Patricia. 'Rex Shelley's *The Shrimp People*: What Manner of Beast is it?'. In *Interlogue: Studies in Singaporean Literature: Fiction*, edited by Kirpal Singh, 45–54. Singapore: Ethos Books, 1998.

Woon, C.M. *The Devil to Pay*. Singapore: Marshall Cavendish, 2005.

——. *The Devil's Advocate*. Singapore: Times Books International, 2002.

Yang, Ting Ting. 'Things that Go Bump in the Night: How Freaky Flicks are Expressing our Asianness'. *Asian Geographic* 4, 2008.

Yew, Leong. *The Disjunctive Empire of International Relations*. Aldershot and Burlington: Ashgate, 2003.

——. 'Managing Plurality: The Politics of the Periphery in Early Cold War Singapore'. *International Journal of Asian Studies* 7, no. 2 (forthcoming 2010).

Yonetani Masafumi. 'Post Dongasia, Saeroun Yeondaeui Jogeon' [Post-East Asia, the condition of new solidarity]. In *Banilkwa Dongasia* [Anti-Japanism and East Asia], edited by Ukai Satoshi. Seoul: Somyeongchulpan, 2005.

Yoshihara, Mari. *Embracing the East: White Women and American Orientalism.* New York: Oxford University Press, 2003.

Yoshimoto, Mitsuhiro. 'The Difficulty of Being Radical: The Discipline of Film Studies and the Post-Colonial World Order'. In *Asian Cinemas: A Reader and Guide*, edited by Dimitris Eleftheriotis and Gary Needham, 27–40. Edinburgh: Edinburgh University Press, 2006.

Young, Robert. *White Mythologies: Writing History and the West.* London and New York: Routledge, 1990.

Yu, Henry. *Thinking Orientals: Migration, Contact, and Exoticism in Modern America.* New York: Oxford University Press, 2001.

Yun Hae-don. *Sikminjiui Hoesaekjidae* [The grey zone of colony]. Seoul: Yeoksabipyeongsa, 2003.

Index

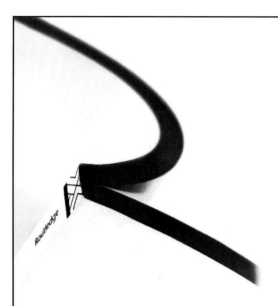

New eBook Library Collection